BROADWAY
BOOGIE WOOGIE

DAMON RUNYON AND THE MAKING
OF NEW YORK CITY CULTURE

DANIEL R. SCHWARZ

palgrave
macmillan

For my wife,
Marcia Jacobson,

my sons,
Dave and Jeff Schwarz,

and my parents,
Joseph and Florence Schwarz

BROADWAY BOOGIE WOOGIE: DAMON RUNYON
AND THE MAKING OF NEW YORK CITY CULTURE
Copyright © Daniel R. Schwarz, 2003.

First published 2003 by
PALGRAVE MACMILLAN™
175 Fifth Avenue, New York, N.Y. 10010 and
Houndmills, Basingstoke, Hampshire, England RG21 6XS.
Companies and representatives throughout the world.

PALGRAVE MACMILLAN is the global academic imprint of the
PALGRAVE MACMILLAN division of St. Martin's Press, LLC and of
Palgrave Macmillan Ltd. Macmillan® is a registered trademark in the United
States, United Kingdom and other countries. Palgrave is a registered
trademark in the European Union and other countries.

ISBN 0–312–23948–3 hardback

Library of Congress Cataloging-in-Publication Data
Schwarz, Daniel R.
   Broadway boogie woogie : Damon Runyon and the making of New York
City culture / by Daniel R. Schwarz.
      p.   cm.
   Includes bibliographical references and index.
   ISBN 0-312-23948-3
   1. Runyon, Damon, 1880–1946—criticism and interpretation.
2. Runyon, Damon, 1880–1946—contributions in journalism.   3. Broadway
(New York, N.Y.)—In literature.   4. New York (N.Y.)—In literature.
5. New York (N.Y.)—History.   6. Criminals in literature.   7. Crime in
literature.   I. Title.

PS3535.U52 Z75   2003
813'.52—dc21   2002074885

Design by Letra Libre, Inc.

First edition: April 2003
10 9 8 7 6 5 4 3 2 1

Printed in the United States of America

Contents

ALSO BY DANIEL R. SCHWARZ

Rereading Conrad (2001)

Imagining the Holocaust (1999)

Reconfiguring Modernism: Explorations in the Relationship between Modern Art and Modern Literature (1997)

Narrative and Representation in the Poetry of Wallace Stevens (1993)

The Case for a Humanistic Poetics (1991)

The Transformation of the English Novel, 1890–1930 (1989, revised ed. 1995)

Reading Joyce's *Ulysses* (1987)

The Humanistic Heritage: Critical Theories of the English Novel from James to Hillis Miller (1986)

Conrad: The Later Fiction (1982)

Conrad: Allmayer's Folly through *Under Western Eyes* (1980)

Disraeli's Fiction (1979)

EDITOR

The Secret Sharer (Bedford Case Studies in Contemporary Criticism) (1997)

The Dead (Bedford Case Studies in Contemporary Criticism) (1994)

Narrative and Culture (1994)

ACKNOWLEDGEMENTS

My work benefits from my wonderful Cornell students whom I have had the pleasure of teaching these past thirty-five years and to whom I owe a collective debt of gratitude.

I wish especially to thank Laurie Brown and Sheila Marikar for helping with indexing and proofreading. I wish also to express my gratitude to Gillian Klempner, Diana Lind, Amy Stutius, and Gregory Halfond who made important contributions at various crucial stages of this project. Over the years Robin Doxtater and Vickey Brevetti have been immeasurable aids in my professional life. So, too, has Marie Powers of the Cornell Olin Library. I have enjoyed once again working with St. Martin's/Palgrave's splendid editors and staff including my insightful and nurturing editor Kristi Long, Meredith Howard, Paige Casey, Roee Raz, and the most able production editor Alan Bradshaw—all orchestrated by Garrett Kiely.

My greatest debt is to Marcia Jacobson—my perceptive, supportive, generous, and loving wife who is my best friend and my best reader.

Abbreviations for Runyon References

DRO	*Damon Runyon Omnibus*
IOT	*In Our Town*
MGAD	*More Guys and Dolls*
MOM	*My Old Man*
MWE	*My Wife Ethel*
PFM	*Poems for Men*
RFTL	*Runyon from First to Last*
	(1954 edition published by Constable in England).
RFAL	*Runyon First and Last*
	(1945 version with forward by Clark Kinnaird)
ROB	*Runyon on Broadway*
ST	*Short Takes*
TT	*Trials and Other Tribulations*

INTRODUCTION

WHO WAS DAMON RUNYON?

WHY WRITE ABOUT RUNYON?

When I was ten years old, I remember hearing hilarious laughter from my father while he was reading downstairs in the living room. When I went down to ask him what he was reading, he answered, "Damon Runyon." It was a scene that occurred every few years when he would take all of Damon Runyon's books out of the library. My father rarely laughed out loud, and at ninety is no more a person noted for fits of hilarity than he was fifty years ago. When I reread Runyon's stories a generation later, my young sons heard me laughing out loud.

Now my sons are adults and I await grandchildren with which to share my enthusiasm. But today I still read Damon Runyon with the same response, a link to my father and a link to the New York of the Depression my father knew and grew up in, a world where, as Runyon put it, one did the "best one could." Indeed, on the streets of Manhattan, my father, who came from a most modest family whose economic circumstances were, like so many others, undermined by the Depression, sold the very magazines in which Runyon's New York stories appeared. My father used Runyonesque expressions like "What is eating you?" and spoke of a dishonest person as someone who would steal anything unless it was "nailed down." And this is hardly suprising, since many of our common phrases either originate with Runyon or were made popular by him.

While the venues of the stories vary to include sites of various racetracks in Florida, Maryland, and upstate New York and concomitant machinations at those sites, the point of view and style remain that of Runyon's New York narrator, and it is thus appropriate to think of all the stories as Broadway stories. While some may patronize Runyon's stories as "dated" and "mechanical," I reread them with great pleasure and find them hilarious, high-spirited, sophisticated, and insightful.[1] One purpose of this book is to explain why and to share my enthusiasm.

Runyon has in his fiction the ability to transform the ordinary into the extraordinary by means of humorous plot reversals and verbal play. But most important, his stories give us a complex reading of the diverse contexts that defined the image of New York City culture for Americans and Europeans—and indeed for New Yorkers themselves. Moreover, he was not merely a mirror of the world he observed but a creative force in shaping that world. When we look back at the major cultural forces shaping the history of the first half of the twentieth century, and in particular our image of New York City, Damon Runyon looms large. As New York City (and Runyonesque) columnist Jimmy Breslin reminds us, Runyon "gave off a reflection of more than three decades of the city of New York, and it has almost become the official record of the times. He practically invented at least two entire decades of his times, and had everybody believing that his street, Broadway, actually existed."[2]

At a time when the city in general and New York City in particular has become a central focus of cultural studies, it is appropriate to revisit Runyon, who was one of its leading chroniclers. My interest in Runyon derives in part from my sense that the cultural history of New York, and especially that of Broadway and Times Square, is written in the tales and columns of this most influential of journalists and short story writers. Runyon understood that his New York was as much a state of mind as an actual site in time and space. He not only helped to invent the double image of New York as a romantic, exciting, and glamorous place with an unwholesome dark and dangerous edge but also strongly suggested that this weird doubleness exists nowhere else.[3]

Now that we understand that the doings of great men and politics are only part of the way we know a culture, what better project than to examine the significance of the work of a writer who was read by millions of Americans every morning and whose stories were eagerly anticipated in popular magazines from 1929 until his death in 1946? Runyon's importance derives from his contributions to our image of New York and to the locutions he has contributed to American English. His writings took the form of columns, poems, anecdotes, and stories for mass consumption, including those that fed our voyeuristic interest in celebrity and criminal culture. Runyon heard and vividly rendered the voices of diverse ethnic and socioeconomic groups. He was in touch with the feelings of those who may not have had a university education and who were not privy to highbrow culture. Making America laugh, smile, and cry in good times and bad was Runyon's forte. Indeed, he reminds us that individual emotions, including the right to laugh at political bungling and social problems, may be one thing that distinguishes democracies from dictatorships and totalitarian regimes.

Runyon was above all a keen observer who, like Ralph Waldo Emerson, understood that we live in an ocular age. Inheriting a nineteenth-century passion for remarkable sights and transcendent experience, Runyon was more interested in content than form. Oscillating between a macrocosmic and microcosmic perspective, he eagerly shared his double optics with his audience. While enjoying the small physical deformities that differentiate one person from another—a large male chest, fatness, a large nose—he was also captivated by the sublimity of New York. While the pragmatic Runyon would hardly subscribe to a cult of personal poverty, he would have understood, notwithstanding Emerson's transcendentalism, the latter's view of the cultural observer in "The American Scholar": "The Office of the Scholar is to cheer, to raise, and to guide men by showing them facts amidst appearances"[4] Runyon was not merely an observer of urban life; he was also a player who interacted with the Broadway figures—criminals, gamblers, chorus girls, journalists—he described. With his penchant for buying huge quantities of clothing and dressing like a peacock in color-coordinated outfits—from his socks to his typewriter!—he was something of a Broadway character himself. As a newspaperman for one of the "blats"—raucaus tabloids—his trade was observing.[5] As a fiction writer attuned to the taste of his audience for tales of this fast paced subculture with its own manners and mores, Runyon knew that his business was selling fiction. More and more, as a media star he was a performer who enjoyed the attention bestowed upon him. His streetwise narrator has the voice of an on-the-scene reporter who has the inside scoop on what is really going on.

Runyon wrote for popular magazines like *Collier's, Cosmopolitan,* and, very occasionally, *The Saturday Evening Post,* which also reached a large audience. He showed how underclasses lived quite differently from the wealthy and how life was hardscrabble for many New Yorkers. Broadway welcomed ethnic diversity more than other sections, and the road to prosperity for Lower East Side Jews and others often went through Times Square. It was the quintessence of the melting pot, and Runyon reveled in its variety.

Reflecting his skepticism about elitist theoretical Marxists and other highbrow intellectuals, Runyon himself wrote a kind of popular art that was sympathetic and accessible to the common man. He identified with the outsiders and have-nots, the people who live by their wits during hard times; as he characteristically writes of Nicely-Nicely in "Lonely Heart" (1937): "What he does for a livelihood is the best he can, which is an occupation that is greatly overcrowded at all times along Broadway" (ROB 482). Often without means or credit or steady jobs, Runyon's characters live from hand to mouth and, at times, from bet to bet and from scam to scam.

Damon Runyon gave his readers a unique sense of New York in the 1930s and 1940s. He heard the city talking—its sounds, its conflicts, its history, its culture—and told the country about that city. We can hardly exaggerate Runyon's popularity and importance in shaping American popular culture during the first half of the twentieth century. His newspaper columns appeared widely across the United States; his short stories found an immense readership in major popular magazines; two of his short story collections sold over a million copies; he was widely published in England by Lord Beaverbrook in the *London Evening Standard,* and he was translated into several languages. Nor should we forget that at least sixteen of his stories were turned into films that shaped how America saw itself and in particular its major city.[6]

Runyon, like the composer Aaron Copeland, the poet Robert Frost, and the painter Edward Hopper, gave accessible, intuitive, and direct home-grown expression to aspects of American individualism in the face of socioeconomic challenges between the wars. Writing of the photographer Garry Winograd, Vicki Goldberg notes: "He catches the erratic pulse, the jazzy rhythms, the crazy energy of the 1960s in a way that seems haphazard, in a style that often appears entirely undisciplined, in images that barely hold together. All of which might be said of the decade itself. Perhaps he was practicing a kind of visual onomatopoeia."[7] If we change the operant phrase to "oral onomatopoeia," the same can be said of Runyon's rendering of the 1920s and 1930s. For Runyon, New York was a display akin to the elaborate department store Christmas displays that reign annually during the holiday season. And it was the merging of technology, commerce, and architecture in Times Square, seemingly ablaze with light in an unprecedented visual environment, that not only stimulated his imagination but also gave rise to the current Christmas megadisplay installations. A great listener, his auditory imagination caught the syncopation and texture of speech as if speech were musical notes. Thus his prose needs to be read aloud to be appreciated for its phonic sophistication—its pace, its play of sound, its heavy and frequent stresses, its rough growly texture, its invented names dependent on consonance clusters, and its kinesis mirroring the turbulence of the modern city.

New York captured the imagination of the world in part because of Runyon and his fellow columnists such as Walter Winchell. If Chicago was the city where skyscrapers were invented, it was, as Jonathan Mandell reminds us, "New York that saw both the business opportunities in more office space to rent out and the marketing value of having a unique immediately identifiable and awe-inspiring skyline."[8] As the mercantile center of the country—with Wall Street its center—throughout the nineteenth century, New York was self-consciously aware of its image and importance. As Mandell notes, "Watercolors and prints going back as far as the eighteenth century, but especially those of the nineteenth, offer sweeping views of the New York Harbour and bird's-eye views of the broad streets, particularly Broadway, taken from skyscraper-high vantage points situated either in imaginary heavens or man-made ones."[9] As much as anyone, Runyon defined the image we hold of New York as a commercial and entertainment capital of American culture, but he did so in such a way that its success is inextricably related to its aggressive, cynical, and materialistic darker side.

Given his frontier heritage, it is not surprising that Runyon drew upon another area that captured the imagination of both the nation and the world, namely, the American West, with its possibility defined by images of immense space, uncultivated land, and unformed if not inchoate communities. His sportswriting—the field in which he first made his mark—drew upon a sense of hyperbole, derived from the western tall tale tradition, with a visceral and amazed enthusiasm for exceptional athletic prowess.

Runyon's first New York job was as a sportswriter for the *New York American,* William Randolph Hearst's flagship newspaper. In 1911 when Runyon was hired, the paper bragged about its place as the leader in New York circulation and advertising. After reaching great prominence in that field and achieving a wide readership Runyon became a daily columnist, but he continued as an occasional sportswriter throughout his career. He always enjoyed sportswriting even when his beat expanded to include the Pershing expedition to Mexico—General John Pershing remained a great hero to him—and when he became a war correspondent in World War I. It was Runyon who gave Jack Dempsey the nickname the "Manassa Mauler." When he described Red Grange, the spectacular running back of the 1920s, we see how he uses his vast store of sports and entertainment knowledge to define the context which we need to understand Grange: "'He is three or four men and a horse rolled into one. He is Jack Dempsey, Babe Ruth, Al Jolson, Paavo Nurmi, and Man o'War.'"[10] Runyon not only expects his readers to recognize at least most of the references to dominant figures on the sports page, but also to enjoy turning a football player into a mythic creature, mostly human but part superhorse.

"Runyonesque" has become an adjective with multiple meanings in our culture. In the same issue of the *New York Times* in which Ira Berkow referred to Runyon's description of Red Grange, Roger Lowenstein called the father of Sandy Weill "a Runyonesque character who married three times," by which he meant a larger than life, aggressive New York figure with a distinct flare for attention.[11]

BIOGRAPHY

Given his future, how ironic and prophetic it was that Alfred Damon Runyan was born in Manhattan, Kansas, on October 4, 1880. To be sure, he spent much of his early years in Pueblo, Colorado. His mother died in Runyon's infancy, and he was raised by his father, an itinerant, hard-drinking newspaperman. Runyon's formal education ended in the sixth grade, and at the age of fifteen he was hired as a reporter by the *Pueblo Evening Press*. A typo changed his name from Runyan to Runyon, and he decided he liked Runyon. In 1911 a publisher of a volume of his poems entitled *Tents of Trouble* truncated his name to "Damon Runyon" without the Alfred. At this time, the sports editor of the *Rocky Mountain News* for which he was writing changed his byline to "Damon Runyon."

In 1898 Runyon enlisted in the 13th Minnesota Volunteers; he was sent to the Philippines during the Spanish Civil War but did not see action, although he did some reporting for *Manila Freedom* and *Soldier's Letter*. Living a rough and tumble life while writing for a succession of newspapers, Runyon himself was a hard drinker until he moved to New York in 1910. He gave up alcohol, although until 1913 he had a few relapses; after 1913 he was a teetotaler the rest of his life. In 1911 he invited his Denver sweetheart and the society editor of *Rocky Mountain News,* Ellen Egan—who had been reluctant to marry him during his Colorado drinking days—to come East and marry him, but the marriage soon foundered. Hired as a sportswriter in 1911, he was assigned a daily column in 1914 entitled "The Mornin's Mornin'." By 1916 he was a well-known journalist and was covering sports only when he has not covering something else for Hearst, such as the upheaval in Mexico and General Pershing's pursuit of Pancho Villa.

In New York Runyon spent virtually all of his nights roaming the streets of the Broadway area. Gathering information, he made the rounds of various Broadway haunts—restaurants, speakeasies, and cabarets—but especially the Broadway delicatessen, Lindy's, which was located first below 50th at 1626 Broadway and then on the corner of Broadway and 51st. What the historian David Kennedy wrote about the typical American who moved to the city in the 1920s was applicable to Runyon some years earlier when he moved to New York from Colorado: "In the streets he encountered the abundant and exotic offspring of all those immigrants who had arrived when he was a baby. Together they entered the new era when their country was transiting, bumpily, without blueprints or forethought, from an agricultural to an industrial economy, from values of simple rural frugality to values of flamboyant urban consumerism, and, however much the idea was resisted, from provincial isolationism to inevitable international involvement."[12] With the kind of tough irony that Runyon would have invoked to describe others, the Runyon biographer Edwin P. Hoyt describes his subject in the 1920s: "Damon was short, slim, trim, precise, dudish. . . . Damon never had much to say, and his companions became used to the raised eyebrow and chill stare that antagonized so many others."[13]

Runyon's night journeys were at once descents into a fascinating urban inferno that he willingly embraced and into his own unconscious need to live a life on the edge. Runyon loved conversation and except when writing did not like being alone. After giving up alcohol, he became addicted to cigarettes and coffee, supposedly drinking forty to fifty cups a day; he often listened more than talked during his night journeys. Perhaps compensating for not drinking, perhaps a function of loneliness or fear of rejection, he was a great eater, and he not only loved describing food in his stories but often ate two or three dinners a night. Much of his emotional life and that of his characters depended on male bonding. According to William Taylor, "Homoerotic bonding was at the very heart of Runyon's fiction as, one suspects, of his life."[14]

In the 1930s he enjoyed becoming a star and celebrity and, when he moved to Hollywood for more than two years in 1940, held court there as he did in New York. Runyon made a lot of money and was a big spender. He needed to be thought a winner; he bet $2 on every horse in a race and was coy about the horse on which he put the real money. Runyon was not only obsessed with horses but was an inveterate sports gambler. While he owned horses and managed boxers, he had little success in either of those endeavors.

With Ellen, Runyon had two children of his own, Damon, Jr., and Mary. After 1924 Damon was rarely home and often chased other women. While he wrote enthusiastically about marriage in his columns, Runyon and Ellen had their own rooms and beds for several years before they split. According to Taylor, "He shamelessly neglected his first wife and his children by her."[15] His wife became an alcoholic and died in 1931. As Neal Gabler observes: "[H]owever cruel and steel-hearted he was to his family, his darkling vision of life gave him a certain cachet on Broadway, where cynicism and misanthropy were the respected attitudes and where his bragging that he wrote for money, not sentiment, only enhanced his status as journalistic royalty: a newspaperman's newspaperman."[16]

In 1932 he married a younger woman, a former showgirl, Patrice del Grande, with whom he lived quite ostentatiously until their 1946 divorce. In those years in Hollywood he developed from screenwriter to successful film producer. Making enormous sums of money for a writer, when in New York he lived lavishly in the Parc Vendome on West 57th street. He also purchased a handsome property on Florida's Hibiscus Island, an island near Miami across Biscayne Bay from his friend Al Capone's Palm Island estate. He put up an expensive villa on that property. By the mid thirties Runyon divided his time between Hibiscus Island and Beverly Hills. Yet, as Hoyt writes, "He was by nature a gypsy, with no more regard for possessions than for money, and although he spoke constantly and reverently about money, no lover of money ever wasted it the way Damon did."[17]

From 1912 to 1928 Runyon submitted short stories and articles that were rejected, and he bore a particular grudge against *Cosmopolitan*—given that it was a publication of Hearst, his newspaper employer—for rejecting his work. In those years Runyon spent most of his energies on journalism. In his columns he combined anti-intellectualism and antagonism to the privileged with down home folk wisdom and cynicism. But he rarely forgot his sense of humor.

Between 1929 and the late 1930s he wrote approximately eighty Broadway stories; most of them were completed by 1935. He provided entertainment; his name on the cover of large-circulation magazines like *The Saturday Evening Post, Liberty,* and *Collier's* could sell tens of thousands of additional copies. In the years between 1932 and 1940 he was paid what was then the huge sum of $5,000 a story for thirty-four stories in *Collier's,* twelve in *Cosmopolitan,* and two in *The Saturday Evening Post.* While he had written a few western stories before leaving Denver in 1910, nothing he had done in the past anticipated the success of these New York stories in magazines and, in their reprinted forms, in books.

Runyon responded to the infinite variety of human life—the uniqueness of each person, his obsessions, frustrations, needs—and was first and foremost a reporter sharing what he saw or felt or imagined. His stories are an extension of the more inventive aspects of his journalism, for at times in his columns he either developed and embroidered characterizations based on the people he had met or invented characters out of whole cloth. And the columns inform his fiction. A principal character of "The Three Wise Guys" (1933) is a safecracker known as "The Dutchman," who owes much to a safecracker called "The Dutchman" in a column of that name (ST 210–13); the safecracker in "Butch Minds the Baby" (1930) may also derive from the same column.

Beginning about 1930, when Runyon began publishing stories, he became an intense movie buff. He saw about ten films a week, often double features. I suspect that his stories' visual and kinetic qualities owe much to film. His 5,000-word stories begin with crisp dialogue, fade out, move to another venue, change scenes rapidly, and alternate between closeups and longer views. New York City is often a pulsating character in the background. Had an hour television series been an alternative media in the 1930s and 1940s, one can imagine the sounds and images of *NYPD Blue* as backdrop. Isn't the fast-talking, cynical, yet sentimental Andy Sipowicz a Runyonesque character?

Many of Runyon's stories became films; *Guys and Dolls,* drawing upon a number of stories, most notably "The Idyll of Sarah Brown," became and still is a musical hit of immense proportions and was made into a successful film with Marlon Brando and Frank Sinatra. The 1933 film adaptation of "Madame La Gimp" as Frank Capra's *Lady for a Day* began a second lucrative career, which included adaptations of his stories, film consulting, and fees to develop scripts, including some that never made it to the screen. "Little Miss

Marker" (1934) became a film hit for Shirley Temple; so did a 1942 film, *The Big Street,* a rendition of "Little Pinks." His story "The Old Doll's House" became the film *Midnight Alibi;* "Princess O'Hara" became a film of that name.

In June 1937 the *American,* the Hearst newspaper in which his work appeared in New York, folded and was merged with *The Journal;* the man who called himself on occasion Professor Runyon began to write for Hearst's tabloid, the *Daily Mirror,* where he remained until he was shifted to the *Journal-American* in 1944. At his death in 1946, his columns were syndicated in over 100 newspapers with a readership of 10 million.

After having his larynx removed in 1944 due to cancer, he could not speak and depended for communication upon written notes. In the early 1940s he and Patrice increasingly went their own ways. In 1946 she divorced Damon and married a younger man. Damon gave her a great deal of what remained of his earnings in return for paying his income taxes and for financial support for the institutional care required by his emotionally ill daughter, Mary. During his illness he retreated to the enclave of his New York friends. He died of cancer on December 6, 1946. Damon spent much of his life estranged from Damon, Jr. and Mary. In the last years of his illness, he sought to repair the damage; he reconciled with Damon, Jr. and left half his estate to his children and a grandchild, the son of Mary and Dick McCann, a sportswriter. Runyon had earned a fortune, but when he died most of the money was gone. He typed a cynical yet poignant note to his son, who had asked him to get a close friend to help his mentally ill sister: "No one is close to me. Remember that."[18] A man who used to boast "I know everyone," Runyon died a lonely bachelor.

As Neal Gabler wrote, Runyon and the equally prominent columnist Walter Winchell were brought together by mutual needs: "Both desperately lonely, needing to fight the terror of their isolation and loving the stimulation of the city, one unable to speak, the other unable to stop talking."[19] "Around with Winchell" is a poignant Runyon column about his inability to speak and Winchell's love of talking: "I made the ideal companion in as much as I am unable to articulate and he did not have to listen to my replies" (ST 217). In his final months Runyon felt great warmth for his friend, a man whose idea of fun was picking up police calls and getting to the crime scene first. He admired Winchell for being his counterpart in amassing experience, kind of Runyon's Runyon: "I know of no man who is more entertaining than Walter when he is in the mood, nor one who has greater store of experience on which to draw" (ST 219). This, we realize, is what Runyon would have wanted to have said about him. He and Winchell developed a deep homosocial bond, with Runyon wiring Winchell at one point in his last weeks: "I am getting lonesome for you."[20] Walter had written on Runyon's pad: "I'll make sure you're never forgotten."[21]

Born only fifteen years after the Civil War, Runyon embraced American Manifest Destiny and had a belief in American democracy that took the form of recognition of the humanity of individuals. Yet his attitudes included aspects of elitism, racism, and sexism. Runyon was influenced by aspects of the nineteenth century, including a kind of puritanical attitude to sex; like many forms of Puritanism, Runyon's was not unmixed with eroticism, and his own behavior often strayed from the sexual scruples expressed in his columns. At times his cultural morality clashed with his cynicism about human motives and his fascination with the demimonde. Runyon could be priggish, condescending, and impatient, even while writing innovative and bold columns. As a sportswriter he fostered Americans' love of winners, yet as a gambler he could identify with the pain of losers. While he could be fascinated by the new, he did not seem to have much interest in the kind of innovative high modernism promoted by Alfred Stieglitz and his circle in the Little Galleries of the Photo-Secessionist Group. Yet he would surely have reveled in the way Stieglitz's pictorial and dramatic photography highlighted the city as subject.

As a former alcoholic, Runyon lived the American dream of starting over. Contradicting F. Scott Fitzgerald's dictum that there are "no second acts in American lives," Runyon's self-transformation is part of the American pattern of second acts.[22] As Michiko Kakutani writes, "The notion of second chances, new beginnings is, of course, nothing new. It's one of the founding principles of America—the western Eden, and new frontier that was supposed to offer immigrants a chance to start over, tabula rasa, like Fitzgerald's Jay Gatsby, who set about inventing a new self commensurate with his own capacity of wonder."[23] Well after he was an established figure, Runyon was not beyond reinventing himself; thus in 1934 he subtracted four years from his age in his *Who's Who in America* entry. In the same entry he stopped making claims for the pedigree of his second wife—changing her name from "Patricia del Grande of Caliditas, Spain" to simply "Patricia Amati"—and dropped the political affiliation "Democratic" for his entry because he had become more conservative politically.

Underneath Runyon's hard-bitten cynicism can be found, on occasion, a cautious optimism. Many of his stories deal with transforming second chances and efforts to transcend severely damaging and reckless past behavior. Others deal with self-delusion, misplaced optimism, and hypocrisy of those who claim they are making a new start. Variations on starting over is a frequent theme in his stories, from "The Idyll of Sarah Brown" and "It Comes Up Mud" to "Madam La Gimp" and "A Very Honorable Guy." Within the fiction, sometimes this new beginning has the force of inevitability, while sometimes it seems forced and tacked on. Furthermore, the transforming second chance is almost always tempered by a sense of mortality and a poignant awareness that no one makes it all the way back to a mint condition. Runyon's New York stories often contain versions of American conquest, but here it is not the settling and domesticating of the West—a subject of his early fiction and one to which he periodically returned—but urban territory under siege. Neighborhoods are divided among rival bootleggers, horse races are fixed, ransoms are exchanged for human conquest in the form of kidnapping, and wealthy men (and less frequently wealthy women)—who will provide jewels, furs, and fancily furnished apartments—are wooed and won. Rendering the violence and trickery of the victors, the anguish of the losers, and the reversals that turn conquerors into victims and vice versa, Runyon's stories often borrow the language used to describe the conquest of the frontier, the defining and settling of space, and the division of territory among imperialistic if illegal businesses.

Before moving east, Runyon had a wide variety of newspaper experience, working on everything from sports to business and even, in Denver, politics. Some of his stories and poems began to appear in national magazines. We can see them as testing grounds for his later Broadway stories. Let us look briefly at three 1907 stories. In "The Defense of Strikerville" (*McClure's,* February 1907) we see the beginnings of his lifelong attraction to those who are society's outcasts: old soldiers take the side of the strikers they were sent to suppress. "The Defense of Strikerville" is basically told by Private Hanks, one of the strikebreakers who sides with the strikers; he is introduced somewhat awkwardly by a nameless narrator. As if Runyon were searching for ways to attain the immediacy of the present—and anticipating the characteristic present tense technique of his New York stories—Hanks moves into the present tense for a time, but returns to the past. In "Fats Fallon" (*Lipponcott's,* October 1907) and "Two Men Named Collins" (*Reader,* September 1907), Runyon anticipates his Broadway stories by using a self-dramatizing first person narrator who is often verbally aggressive but presents a tale of male camaraderie in which violence plays a backseat to male bonding.

In the case of "Two Men Named Collins," the paranoid narrator begins with puzzling present tense non sequiturs reminiscent of the sociopathic behavior of Edgar Allan Poe's self-deluded narrator in "The Tell Tale Heart": "I know some things all right if I could only think of them. These guys say I'm crazy—crazy in the head ..." (RFTL 40). This is a story about two men whose names and characters are inextricably intertwined; it may reflect Runyon's fear that no matter what he achieves, a shadow of his dissolute Pueblo past will expose him as a drunken Runyan, his original name and identity. But the story soon moves to the past. Charles Collins, the narrator, has killed another man named Charles Collins when the latter, a deserter, had tried to escape an army prison. The narrator had hated the other man because of his belief that the latter—called "Pretty" while he is called "Crummy"—had once been held in higher regard by officers and members of his army company. Pretty had class advantages that Crummy lacked. Upon learning that his victim's wealthy parents were told a bogus story about how a prisoner shot Pretty Collins with his own gun, Crummy is furious. With the express purpose of exposing Pretty as a coward and a deserter, Crummy Collins—the man who shot Pretty Collins—barges in on Pretty's father and mother while they are taking their son's body home. But in a Runyonesque turn Crummy cannot expose Pretty to the latter's parents and hands them his own certificate of merit, which had his name and outfit engraved on it. He had not sent it home to be framed for the parlor because "I didn't have no people or parlor either." Perhaps this early story of a double in which both characters have a dark subversive side—one a cowardly deserter, the other seeking personal vengeance in the guise of doing his duty—reveals not only Runyon's fascination with the criminal mind but his fear that—like Crummy Collins—that he will always be regarded as an outsider.

JOURNALISM

Because Runyon's journalism is the focus of chapters 2 and 3, let us look briefly at its underlying assumptions and forms. His journalism is social, based on the assumption that he is having a dialogue with a friend who is interested in the life that he, Runyon, is leading. Not surprisingly, given how much time he spent listening, his journalism is an extension of conversation. Reading Runyon's columns, we feel as if he had spent some time listening while others talked, before responding with his thoughts for 750 words or so. Runyon assumes his readers will give him no more than about five minutes.

His journalistic pieces include his western fictions, where Runyon honed the technique of his Broadway stories. The "Grandpa Mugg" series in 1922 was soon to be followed by the more cynical 1923–24 series "My Old Home Town." He did not mention Pueblo, Colorado—the town in which he was raised by his alcoholic father—as the site of these fictions, but it was the inspiration for these Western tales. He originally signed the Grandpa anecdotes "A. Mugg." In his early experiments with fiction he uses the present tense and begins to develop his own special vocabulary and syntax, using such phrases as "more than somewhat." These stories provide a reservoir of images and themes for his later work.

If we can generalize, Runyon's imagined audience is a working class or lower middle class male who has a wife, a job that barely pays the rent or mortgage, maybe a second job on nights and weekends; he thinks of his audience as one of those he calls "muggs," a little guy who dreams of winning a number, who bets with a bookie, and who is also on the lookout for a way to make an extra buck. Even in the years before the Depression, nothing came easy to those whom Runyon imagined as his readers. They might be doormen or cab drivers. The most education they have is high school. They do not read Walter Lippmann or the *New York Times*.

One of his best known journalistic pieces is "The Insidious I." Typically the first sentence almost violently intrudes into the reader's interior space by grabbing his attention: "My autobiography, or life story, is one thing you can bet I will never write" (ST 1). Notice how, without patronizing his readers, he defines "autobiography." The second sentence reminds the reader that his special friend Runyon is something of an insider sharing—with a wink at his audience, that is, those he can trust—his insider's world: "If I told the truth a lot of persons, including myself, might go to jail" (ST 1). He uses simple words such as "bet" and "jail, " as if to assure his readers that they are in the right place—namely, the site of Runyon's column rather than the site of the book review or the editorial page. The column was a safe haven—a place to which one could go for a few minutes each morning or after work—where Runyon's readers could count on a respite from their complicated routines and their worries about dollars and cents. Every day they turn to Runyon, their surrogate insider, who knows important people, knows what is going on behind the scenes, knows the secret rites and rituals of New York City and the sports world, and reveals these mysteries and secrets to his readers. Yet at times he admits to holding back, with the promise that there is more to come.

The colloquial diction of his columns resonates with that of the narrators and characters in his New York stories. In the very next sentence, which begins one of his characteristic short paragraphs, he mocks the pretensions of his more educated colleagues by emphasizing the crass Runyonesque materialism that his regular readers recognize: "Of course an even more potent reason why I am never going to write my own tale is that there is no sure money in that tripe. It is purely speculative. It might sell but the odds are against it" (ST 1). The gambling metaphor is essential Runyon and locates the reader in his world. In a characteristic gambit he switches to speaking about himself in the third person as Professor Runyon, as if he were chiding those of lofty ideas and formal education: "I am aware that there are many other writing fellows, especially in the newspaper columning dodge, who write out of sheer altruism and who pick up their weekly wage envelopes merely as a matter of form. But not Professor Runyon. The professor wants his. I think I am less spurious than those muggs who let on that their journalistic pursuits are guided by motives far above mere gold" (ST 2).

Almost Iago-like, he flouts the expectations of his readers—at a time when the vast majority were churchgoers—that material quest is an evil or that education and writing are higher values. Runyon almost flaunts his economic success, but he assumes that because he writes as one of the common folk—one of the "muggs" who has known what it is like to scrimp and save and who has been one of the have-nots—they will side with him. In the following sentence he locates himself within the New York Broadway world in terms that his audience would smile at: "It is pretty difficult to find a bookie in New York nowadays to get a market on this proposition but I imagine the price of publication against any book selling to a profit is easily 50 to 1 and up, depending on the author" (ST 1).

After letting on that he has been invited to write his autobiography, he complains how boring autobiographies have become. Another reason he will not write is he does not have anything interesting to say, since he is no *better* than his readers: "I do not think my material would ever pass on the basis of importance. My life has been made up of trivialities. I have accomplished no great deeds" (ST 3). This is another case of his positioning himself on common ground with his audience, as if, notwithstanding his temporary place among the urban cognoscenti, he really is one of them.

His persona is that of a privileged insider who is on the lookout for interesting tidbits that he might hear in his nightly journeys through the Broadway area. Rather than, he claims, bore his readers with autobiographical details, he will instead gladly and generously share what he has learned. He concludes with one of his insider "trivialities" in the form of a brief tale of one of the "muggs" triumphing over more prosperous furniture dealers; this tale fulfills the fantasy shared by much of his readership of the little guy, who needs to worry about every nickel, making a small score. To support this implication that his world is their world, Runyon shares one of his anecdotes about a gambling coup in a dice game by a vaudeville performer named Butch Tower who was playing Grand Rapids when a furniture convention was taking place. In doing so Runyon establishes that indeed it is he who has something interesting to say, namely real stories about real people who have suffered gains and losses and dream about hitting a jackpot: "Why, Butch cleaned those furniture dealers from top to bottom. If they had been betting their own merchandise, he would have furnished a ten-room house" (ST 4).

Runyon's genius is understanding how to invite himself into the world of his readers and, once invited, to continue his welcome. His secret is tone and diction. In another striking opening, he implicitly asks the audience to identify with him, their daily columnist companion, against those who would usurp his and their interests: "There is the disquieting rumor going the rounds that the owners of the newspapers were contemplating an effort to take their publications back from the columnists. I want to be on hand to protect my interests" ("Is Write Right?" ST 4).

On other occasions he ingratiates himself with his audience by admitting his own failings. Thus, in the following self-critical opening he makes common cause with his readers who are regularly made aware of their shortcomings by their bosses and spouses: "I sized up some of my columns as they appeared in print and I said to myself, well, Runyon, I see you are up to your old habit of windifying. This, dear reader, is the habit of being too windy. I might say prolix or garrulous or verbose, which denotes an excess of words in proportion to the thought, but I prefer windy" ("Wind Storm," ST 12). Once again he is something of a teacher, sharing his love of words, even as by using several synonyms he is knowingly iterating the very process of "windifying" he is critiquing. With its play on breaking wind or farting, the word "windifying" conveys to his audience the concept of making noise without saying anything. He extends his metaphor to other recognizable sources of empty talk with which the audience is familiar, before returning to his own self-indictment: "Windifying is common to many of our public figures and private citizens. It prevails among officials and even the clergy but is more pronounced among writers than any other class, though radio announcers are commencing to be strong contenders for top place" (ST 13). Of course, by sharing his secret, Runyon's persona also earns his readers' confidence that they can rely on their columnist friend to tell them the truth.

We might locate Runyon within the tradition of American wisdom figures such as Ben Franklin, Ralph Waldo Emerson, and Henry Thoreau, all of whose essays use the occasion of local observations and personal experiences to examine paradoxes of life. Runyon writes as if he had a personal relationship with each reader and as if his writing fulfills an obligation to tell his readers how to separate the wheat from the chaff. To be sure, some of that obligation is tongue in cheek, but he often assumes the position of a man made worldly wise by life who will instruct his readers how to avoid pitfalls: "Among those I have checked and okayed for the purge is the fellow of whom it is said, 'He loves people.' I think we have gone along with him as far as we should" ("O, Careless Love," ST 18). Deliberately echoing Horace, he speaks about how his purpose is "to entertain and instruct my parishioners"; note how he playfully "converts" his readers, many of whom are churchgoers, into secular followers of his reporting on factual rather than spiritual matters ("The Discriminating Thief," ST 15). That he acknowledges how he uses Bartlett's *Familiar Quotations* as a source for his self-admitted "intellectual larceny" is another humorous deviation from how the upright minister or priest leads his parishioners.

Runyon conveys a sense of vulnerability behind his tough exterior and speaks as if he himself had been hurt by the behavior of others. He can be fastidious, judgmental, grumpy, and ornery, but also sentimental and even silly. Runyon's columns often begin by engaging a reader with a provocative insight, moving to a small example, expanding outward to a more important instant, and ending with a clinching anecdote illustrating his point or an observation that turns his original comment. Thus in "Tripping over Trivia," he opens, in the American tradition of self-improvement, by acknowledging the need to correct a fault: "I am trying to cultivate the habit of not being particular about little things. . . . I have come to the conclusion that I have been wasting an enormous amount of time in being particular" (ST 30). As examples, he cites his fastidiousness about how he wants his eggs boiled before moving on to his preferences for plays, movies, and restaurant seats. After revealing himself as a clotheshorse who not only fritters away time in hat stores choosing hats but hangs up his clothes fastidiously, he closes by asking: "Will the time I save in not being particular in this shedding [of clothes] stand off the time I will probably waste in household argument about me not being particular?" (ST 33).

Approaching life with a sense of wonder intermixed with an eye to the absurdity of some of our accepted distinctions, Runyon relies on a candid moral brashness as he tries to tell us what is *really* going on. His posthumous volume *Trials and Other Tribulations,* in which he edited columns about five trials and one Senate hearing into the failure of the financier J. P. Morgan to pay taxes, testifies not only to his skill as a court reporter but also to his sympathy with outsiders, including gangsters, and his disdain for the privileged. Similarly, in his tales of his hometown in the West in *Trials and Other Tribulations,* and in other columns and stories, those with money—such as J. P. Morgan—are usually viewed with disdain.

Runyon understood the role of the newspaper in the early decades of the information age and realized that the impersonality of cities and large corporations created the need for intimate columns and stories. As we have seen, he writes with the assumption that his basic experiences overlap with those of his audience and that his audience will be sympathetic to someone who has come originally from its provincial world. When Runyon describes and responds to the cosmopolitan world of Broadway, he combines wonder, folk wisdom, urbanity, American optimism, patriotism, and often quite traditional Christian morality. In his columns Runyon often takes an ironic stance toward some of the subjects he describes, including himself, but rarely does he adopt an ironic—or patronizing or condescending—relationship with his reader. Indeed, one of the central characteristics of his columns is his respect for his readers and his willingness to share his feelings, values, experiences, and idiosyncrasies. He often writes as if he were talking to a friend in the spirit of "This is true, isn't it?" His tone is rarely contentious or argumentative, even when he writes in the hyperbolic mode.

Irony is a rhetorical strategy for suggesting positions or nuances that you don't want to say directly, and Runyon often *shares* this kind of irony with his audience. But his is a broad irony that an unsophisticated audience can appreciate (although there may be touches of winking insider irony in his references to famous people he knows). On occasion in his most cynical moments—perhaps in some of the late columns on his illness and some of his columns on celebrity trials—he does use the kind of modern irony that questions not merely pretensions but the very nature of meaning. At times we hear in the narrative voice of the New York stories urban ennui, worldweariness, refusal to believe in human relationships, and cynicism about sincerity and authenticity. But, in the tradition of American transcendentalism, even there these attitudes are tempered by Runyon's wonder at the spectacle of modern life and a kind of refreshing gee-whiz quality of his writing.[24]

SPORTSWRITER TO CELEBRITY JOURNALIST ·

Runyon's ruling passion was a voracious curiosity, and his perspective was a medley of ingenuousness, skeptical humor, and an anthropologist's interest in diverse tribal customs beyond the ken of his experience. On one hand, by 1914 Runyon, schooled in the hardscrabble world of Pueblo saloons rather than in high culture, had his western frontier perspective. On the other, he dressed impeccably, was getting to know important people in the world of sports and journalism, and was becoming a fixture on Broadway. Runyon was sure that in America the rich had the best of it, and he did not hesitate to share this with his readers on countless occasions. Confident in his ability as a magician with words, he took aim at making a good deal of money; as he wrote later: "My measure of success is money" ("Get the Money," ST 58).

Runyon wrote during a period when sportswriters began to see athletes in mythic proportion—Grantland Rice, for example, called the Notre Dame stars who defeated Army on October 18, 1924, "The Four Horseman"—and when those sportswriters began to sell newspapers as stars in their own right. As Allen Barra has written, "The 1920s were the golden age of myth-making journalism. A handful of talented writers who found other paths to literary fame blocked began to notice, as indeed their editors had already noticed, that a rising middle class was responding more to the exploits of Jack Dempsey, Babe Ruth, and Bobby Jones than what would come to be known as 'hard' news."[25]

Runyon, Rice, and Ring Lardner were the preeminent sportswriters of the 1920s. But Runyon's sportswriting does not focus on the crystallizing play or give a narrative of what happened next. Rather, in his sportswriting—as in his reports of trials, politics, and city life—he focused on the human characters more than the actual event, the special language of each activity, and, particularly, its culture and lore. "Well, about 95 per cent of all sports tradition is pure fiction. Lies if you like. But harmless" ("The Havana Affair," ST 131). Recalling the exploits of a great black fighter named Sam Langford, Runyon discusses Langford's past boxing prowess and compares him to other black fighters; while we might today think of this as a racist column, Runyon was urging contemporary readers to acknowledge the classiness of a black sportsman. When Runyon takes a brief respite from boxing to place Langford in the poignant present, he gives the story its most human dimension: "Langford, now in his sixties, was found in a Harlem hall room blind and penniless not long ago and this called up the above memories" ("Sam Langford," ST 129).

Runyon's sports stories focus on the human rather than the athletic dimension. He enjoys the language of boxing and sharing insider information with his readers, including suggestions that champion's resumes are built by "sure-footed oversized" "watermen" taking dives or, put differently but meaning the same thing, "a header into the wash bowl" ("The Havana Affair," ST 121). Writing of the current players who want to renegotiate their contracts, Ira Berkow invokes Damon Runyon's "The Old Guy's Lament" in which the speaker is a down on his luck former baseball player who now takes tickets at the ballpark turnstiles. The player resents the current contracts being paid to players he regards as inferior to him: "But think of the dough that they're grabbin'/ Guys that can't hit a balloon—/I can see where my parents were crazy/By havin' me born too soon! . . . You talk of your Ruth, and your Meusel/ and Kelly—

don't make me smile!/Them guys hit 'em a furlong/Where I used to hit 'em a mile!"[26]

Runyon was enamored with the horse Seabiscuit, the wonder horse of the Depression years 1936 to 1938, and with his rivalry with War Admiral, a Triple Crown winner and Horse of the Year in 1937 whom Seabiscuit beat in a 1938 showdown. Jim Squires has described the reason for racing's popularity: "In the decade of the Depression the new motion picture industry was entertaining 85 million people a week with feel-good productions, but people were anxious for even more diversion from the desperation of the era."[27] Seabiscuit's history is a Cinderella story of a rather undistinguished-looking horse that lost his first sixteen races and was regarded prematurely as an underachiever only to be owned, trained, and ridden by an unlikely trio—respectively, Charles Howard, Tom Smith, and Johnny (Red) Pollard. Seabiscuit's life became a kind of Horatio Alger story, what Squires calls "an allegory for Depression era America."[28] Seabiscuit supposedly received more newspaper coverage than Roosevelt, Hitler, or Mussolini in 1938.[29] Runyon, who often read the world as a text for his own life, saw Seabiscuit's saga as a version of his own emergence from the obscurity of an outsider and of his cashing in on his second chance.

In the world of sportswriting, Runyon could combine his imaginative energy and inventive word play with his reporting skills. The first time he covered a major league team in spring training for the *American* in 1911, he coined the name "Bugs" for a pitcher named Raymond because the pitcher liked insects. Runyon abandoned straightforward inning by inning descriptions for a loosely organized idiosyncratic melange of feature writing, social commentary, and verbal pyrotechnics—which is what he also did in his court reporting of sensational trials, trials he regarded as sporting events with a different and perhaps less fair sense of rules. Thus, on July 22, Runyon opened a story of the Giants defeat of the Cardinals by a 4–0 score: "As for you, Roger Bresnahan with your oily voice and city ways— take that! Zam! Bumpety Bump-Bump! (Noise of villain falling off the front stop, bleeding from the nose.)"[30] Does he not brilliantly understand how we fans identify viscerally with our home team, how we transfer our emotional life to the players who represent us safely since we cannot "lose" but only "win," and how we revel in their victories? As we shall see in chapter 3, Runyon's sense of how spectators engage in transference also carries over into his reporting of celebrity trials. Apparently he had an encyclopedic store of baseball information but preferred to focus on the social aspect of the game. Thus he would write after a game of a safety issue at the Polo Grounds where thousands of people stood behind the top tier of seats and created "a decidedly dangerous congestion in the case of accident"[31]

Runyon enjoyed teasing New Yorkers about their New York–centricism and their inverse provincialism. Reporting on a game between the Yankees and the St. Louis Browns, he focused on a Denver citizen, Jack Krum, from "those mysterious wilds on the other side of the Mississippi River." Krum comes to visit a player he once knew, Roy Hartzell, with whom he plays cards and shakes "dice for things during the long hard winters which inhabit the mountain fastnesses," but Krum is baffled by the game of baseball.[32]

No sooner did Runyon begin sportswriting than he used the genre to become as much a performer as a reporter. For a newly hired sportswriter, Runyon was given a lot of space to define himself—his experience of what he observed—as the subject. Writing of the Harvard-Yale football game, he was fascinated by a world so different from that of his Colorado youth; this Ivy League world featured the singing of school songs, the carrying of pennants, the rooting sections of bluebloods: "At least half the crowd was made up of women who furnished the real color of the wonderful scene. They all bore crimson or blue pennants and wore great bunches of white chrysanthemums with blue or crimson laid across the tops—which is the latest idea in flower decorations. . . . Football songs are largely a matter of taste anyway, but all this melody was very soothing to the savage breasts of the rival sympathizers."[33]

Yet in his Denver days Runyon had been something of an idealistic crusading reporter. That crusading spirit carried over on occasion into his sportswriting, as when he excoriated baseball for burying evidence of the fixed 1919 World Series until a Chicago grand jury was convened. In a column on the top of the sports page section entitled "Read This Story" and signed with initials "D.R.," he reprinted a story by the *American's* sports editor, Harry Cashman, which had suggested that the Series was controlled by gamblers and had excoriated Major League Baseball for ignoring "a report that justified the greatest activity and closest investigation on the part of the men supposed to protect the great national game."[34] He was outraged that while the guilty players were banned from baseball, the bribers were going free.

Runyon was a national celebrity by 1920; he had a contract with Hearst that earned him close to $20,000 a year when $10,000 was a fine income in New York, and that was only for his daily column; he was paid extra for Sunday articles. He was increasingly driven by his materialistic spirit. His gambling, night life, investment in boxers' careers, compulsion for new clothing, and other aspects of his flamboyant way of living created a demand for money. For the *Sunday American*, Runyon wrote some autobiographical and uncollected "Chelsea McBride" stories, which anticipated the Broadway stories, especially in their use of the present—or historical present—tense.

Runyon became a celebrity at a time when a handful of writers and journalists—including Ring Lardner, Walter Winchell, and Westbrook Pegler—were the stars of their day. Although a keen social observer and willing speaker on behalf of what he believed needed improvement, he usually avoided direct political comment but seemed as the years passed to be increasingly suspicious of anything that challenged the political status quo. By both temperament and policy, he usually remained politically and emotionally detached and never criticized his employer, William Randolph Hearst. He frequently voiced the amoral credos: "Go for the money" and "Never bite the hand that feeds you," credos that inform the values of his persona in his columns and fiction.[35] Although he had male companions galore and hunted with men (and even fished without enthusiasm), Runyon recused himself from intimacy. Edwin P. Hoyt describes a rather unpleasant figure: "He slighted people and sometimes made enemies quite unintentionally. He was always the outsider, respected and wanting instead to be loved, but not loving, and respecting nearly no one."[36]

In his final years he did develop a close friendship with Walter Winchell, who was pleased that Runyon's fictional character Waldo Winchester was modeled on him. Winchell greatly admired

Runyon's immersion in his work: "He has the joy of accomplishment. . . . The newspaper game is fun to him. An exclusive piece of news is manna from heaven to him."[37] Yet according to Neal Gabler, Winchell was far more ambivalent about the Broadway world than Runyon.

In the later 1920s Runyon's worldview seemed to take a more cynical turn. Some of his acerbity came from his work as a court reporter in fall 1926, on the Hall-Mills case, where Mrs. Hall and her brothers—all of the Johnson and Johnson pharmaceutical family—were acquitted of murdering her husband despite strong evidence to the contrary. A subsequent April 1927 trial that affected his sense that justice favored the rich was the guilty verdict and execution of a corset salesman named Judd Gray and his lover, Ruth Snyder, who had killed Snyder's husband with a sash weight. In August 1927 he was outraged at the unfair trial and subsequent executions of the anarchists Nicola Sacco and Bartolomeo Vanzetti, who were hardly the threat to national security that the prosecutors alleged. More and more Runyon came to believe that, as Hoyt puts it, "[M]oney was the source of all power and pleasure in the world."[38]

Although Runyon was a womanizing narcissist who reveled in fancy and expensive clothes befitting a New York celebrity and insider, his sympathies, somewhat paradoxically, often lay with the outsiders, and he resented the inequities of the social system. Even in the minor matter of Bruce Caldwell, who was declared ineligible to play in the 1927 Yale-Princeton game because he had played for the freshman team at Brown before enrolling at Yale, he complained in a November 12, 1927 column of the special privileges enjoyed by the rich: "When a prominent citizen gets jammed up with the rules, there are always a lot of folks ready to turn on the brine for him, and to argue that he didn't know or that if he did know he really didn't mean it. But when some bezark that no one ever heard of gets found out they rush him off to the bar of justice and the sneezer, or jail, with never a sob gulped out in his behalf."[39]

Runyon's sympathy for outsiders, which sometimes extended to criminals, may have derived from his lack of formal education and his rough and tumble upbringing in a frontier town. Perhaps his attraction to outlaws went back to his saloon days in Denver, when he apparently had a six-shooter, and his days as a volunteer in the Spanish-American War. It is possible that his disdain for the wealthy and upper classes was a way for him to justify his friendships and sympathy with members of the underworld, including his friendships with Arnold Rothstein, Al Capone, and other gangsters. He felt sympathy for Rothstein, who had been murdered, and for Capone, whom he believed had been persecuted by the government. He not only consorted with Rothstein on a regular basis at Lindy's, but he also believed, contrary to accepted opinion, that Rothstein was not involved in fixing the 1919 World Series. Believing that the underworld preyed on the common man no more than did the so-called respectable, he did not see any difference among the ethics of businessmen, politicians, and criminals. Indeed, he seems to have been drawn to the outsiders who, like himself, burrowed into the social fabric with a combination of chutzpah, individualism, and disregard for social distinctions.

Runyon's cynicism may help explain his tolerance for the corrupt and often inept regime of the high-living New York mayor Jimmy Walker, who, after being in office seven years and using the office to feather his own nest, had to resign in 1932. Walker didn't subscribe to traditional morality and flouted the view that the mayor was required to be a paragon of upright behavior. As Ann Douglas notes, "The debonair Walker came from working-class Irish stock; however dilatory and scant his reform impulses might be, his sympathies were with the people and they knew it."[40] Walker had much in common with Runyon, and they admired one another. Both lacked formal education, sympathized with the common people rather than the social elite, combined flamboyance with discipline, reveled in New York night life—including socializing with showgirls while married—associated with dubious characters, loved clothes, and dressed ostentatiously. It is also possible that Runyon wanted to believe—but could not convince himself—that his impressive income was a bridge to a place among the elite. He certainly knew that his real status rested with his position in the ambiguous world of sports figures, touts, showgirls, boxers, and speakeasy owners who populated the area between Columbus Circle and Times Square. Perhaps he needed to have a place in both camps, the haves with whom he consorted and the have-nots—the "muggs" who do the best they can—who would judge that elite.

While Runyon was a keen observer of manners and behavior, he was—and his fictional narrator and characters are—unreflective about the intricacies of motives, impatient or oblivious to complex ideas, and barely aware of the nation's—or even New York City's— larger political debates. Runyon lived in a world where style, whether understated or overstated, dominated; with his fixation on clothes, he was the quintessence of a kind of ostentatious and flashy style. Revelation of the authentic self was not the mode in which the culture operated. Impenetrable surfaces deflecting audiences from penetrating their inner lives marked the public personae of larger than life characters such as Fred Astaire, Joe DiMaggio, and Joe Lewis. Runyon's often deadpan tone toward human behavior is bemused, cool, sly, matter-of-fact, but not without ingenuous moments of self-regarding charisma and self-aggrandizement. Indeed, at times, Runyon thinly disguises his marvel at the influence and position he himself achieved.

CHAPTER 1

RUNYON'S NEW YORK

Historical Contexts
and Fictional Universe

NEW YORK CITY BACKGROUND

In 1825 the Erie Canal connected the Hudson River to the Great Lakes and established New York as the most important city in the United States. Even in the eighteenth century New York Harbor had dominated trade and commerce. Walt Whitman celebrated the noise, variety, and erotic energy of the city. His optimistic vision of a nation of brothers—of a vibrant multicultural social mosaic—was an ideal challenged by private greed, dismal social conditions, and ethnic rivalries for manual labor and blue collar jobs. The variety of cultures combined with the density of population to cause difficulties. The ethnic tensions, dating to the earliest settlers in the seventeenth century, when Dutch merchants scorned Sephardic Jews, were exacerbated by the various waves in immigration in the nineteenth century, beginning with the Irish and continuing later with Italians, Jews, other Europeans, and Chinese and Japanese. Continuing waves of impoverished newcomers fleeing dismal conditions abroad—or, in the case of African Americans, the rural South—increased the population and emphasized the gulf between wealth in Fifth Avenue mansions and poverty in Lower East Side tenements. Stimulated by *How the Other Half Lives,* Jacob Riis's exposé of hunger, overcrowdedness, unsanitary conditions, and inadequate medical care in the tenements, reformers gradually sought an ethical calculus in which social justice would complement capital formation.

Manhattan is both island and seaport, and its geographical narrowness toward the port area did not allow much room for expansion. With Central Park, carefully planned by Frederick Law Olmsted, and its grid of streets, New York had a seeming underpinning of order. Indeed, Dell Upton has written of the grid of streets as "the embodiment of an economically informed vision of urban society" because it "envisioned commerce as an all-encompassing, impersonal systematic exchange of commodities rather than, as it had traditionally been regarded (and still was by many small traders) a series of discrete, highly personal, morally rigged relationships."[1] We shall see how beneath Runyon's idiosyncratic yet highly structured plots—a kind of metaphor for the grid of streets—exists a subversive demimonde where economic relationships are discrete, highly personal, and morally rigged.

New York took off in the 1890s and continued its growth as the brightest star of America's firmament through World War II. It was not until 1898 that the outer boroughs of New York were consolidated into one city. The opening of the subway in 1904 brought millions to Times Square and its immediate surrounding area. The subway itself was an image of speed and dynamism, of nervous energy and accelerating stimulation. By the end of the nineteenth century electrification had made New York a city of bright lights. As Edwin G. Burrows and Mike Wallace observe, "Electric nights drew throngs of festive boulevardiers to the streets, linking its big-city image indelibly to the bright lights of its avenues. This identification was fixed forevermore with the emergence, in the mid-1890s, of what people began calling the 'Great White Way'—a stretch of Broadway between 23rd and 34th streets that began to blaze with electric advertisements."[2] Glamorously lit, Broadway began to flourish at the end of the century as out of town tourism and business visitors vastly increased and public transportation improved. And the theatrical stars had an influence on public behavior; as Burrows and Wallace note, the theater's marketing of personalities "was directly tied in with the marketing of commodities. The daily doings of famous actresses were chronicled in the women's magazines, and their choice of clothes, jewelry, and millinery began to set national trends."[3] Later in his columns Runyon would exploit the public fascination with celebrity lives.

In part because songs like "The Sidewalks of New York" (1894) and "The Band Played On" (1895) kept New York life in America's aural consciousness, the rest of the nation wanted to learn more about the exotic megalopolis and in particular its amusements and entertainments. Thus readers eagerly devoured the daily columns of Runyon and Walter Winchell and their compatriots. By the end of the nineteenth century, as Burrows and Wallace observe, "[T]he growing vigor of a multiethnic popular culture, the rapid commercialization of entertainment on a hitherto unmatched scale, the emergence of novel kinds of mass amusement forms, the loosening during leisure time of constraints that governed elsewhere in the city" made New York an entertainment capital.[4] At the center of Madison Square was the Garden, with a diversity of events from circuses to horse shows.

As if it were announcing the onset of the "informational" city, the Times Square area was named after the new office building of the *New York Times* there. In Times Square, advertising and entertainment joined to create a center of consumer culture. With new public buildings and elaborate billboard displays, Times Square became the heart of the city. As Eric Lampard writes, "[A] symbiosis of commercial advertising and commercial entertainment prophetically juxtaposed the glittering theatre marquees and extravagant electrical billboards of Time Square."[5] By 1913 vaudeville houses, some serving one class, some another, had opened. Legitimate theater and movie theaters and nightclubs concentrated in this area, which by the late 1930s spread northward from Times Square to 52nd Street. The peak theatrical season was 1927–28, when 264 shows opened in the district.[6] The increasing costs for live theater coupled with the onset of the Depression and the coming of popular, accessible, and inexpensive cinema affected the legitimate theater. (Runyon loved films and went to about ten a week.) Many of the legitimate theaters were turned into motion picture houses and theaters for radio shows. Vaudeville departed by the late 1930s. Burlesque theaters flourished in the mid-1930s until the license commissioner of New York, Paul Moss, closed them in May 1937; while court victories enabled burlesque theaters to have occasional reprieves, their heyday was over. By the early 1940s, even the unadvertised strip nightclubs on 52nd Street finally were closed. The theater district narrowed to 44th and 45th Streets between Times Square and Eighth Avenue. Gradually, by the 1940s, the area became raffish and something of a cross between a carnival and an amusement park. The flash of modern advertising replaced architecture as the focus.

As newspapers became a crucial part of city life, the informational city became not only part of the commercial and industrial city but also in some sense its competitor. Newspapers helped their readers understand and decode the city. They provided readers each day with new chapters of continuing narratives while giving shape and form to political and social issues. Inexpensive newspapers replaced novels as reading material for many. Beginning in 1883, Joseph Pulitzer built his *New York World* on the premise that newspapers were entertainment. His competition included such penny newspapers as the *Sun* and the *Herald* as well as the less sensationalistic *Tribune*— later merged with the *Herald*—and *New York Times*. The *World* not only drew on working-class life for its content, but used a condensed vernacular style and multicolumn banners that appealed to a mass audience, including women. According to Burrows and Wallace, "Pulitzer understood, as did manufacturers and purveyors of consumer goods, that in the 1880s women did most household purchasing, and their patronage was therefore the key to attracting advertisers."[7]

Using a mixture of human drama, lurid sensationalism, celebrity events, and sports coverage, penny newspapers in turn-of-the-twentieth-century New York competed for circulation and advertising. The New York newspaper industry was in continual flux with new arrivals, purchases, mergers, and editorial makeovers. William Randolph Hearst's *Journal* emulated Pulitzer's successful *World*. While headlines grew larger, the clothes on the women in illustrations became skimpier.

Originating as penny papers in the nineteenth century but evolving into their present form in the early twentieth century, tabloids focused on celebrities—film stars and gangsters, the wealthy and flamboyant—and their scandals, and mingled the private and social spheres. Thus we can say that the penny newspapers were the parents of the modern American tabloid. In 1919, Joseph Patterson launched the tabloid the *Illustrated Daily News,* soon known as the *Daily News,* and Hearst followed in 1924 with the *Daily Mirror,* which announced it was 90 percent entertainment and 10 percent news and baldly copied the *Daily News.* A few months prior to the introduction of the *Daily Mirror,* Bernard Macfadden began another tabloid, The *New York Evening Graphic,* and recruited Walter Winchell to his staff as a gossip writer—a position which is that of the ultimate voyeur and spectator—focusing on illicit romances, births, and other social and political tidbits. According to Neal Gabler, the *Daily News* "employed a formula of screaming headlines, lurid tales and plentiful illustrations," and by 1923 had the largest circulation in the country at 750,000; its tabloid brethren—the *Daily Mirror* and the *Graphic*—were at least as sensationalistic.[8]

Wooed by Hearst—who by 1930 owned twenty-six papers in eighteen cities and whose King Features offered millions of readers—Winchell moved in 1929 to the *Mirror.* Runyon, who wrote for Hearst's *American,* already had this kind of readership. While there were sports columnists (such as Grantland Rice) and political and public affairs columnists (such as Bugs Baer and Westbrook Pegler) and gossip columnists (such as Leonard Lyons), none achieved the influence of Runyon and Winchell. The pugnacious Winchell varied his content from day to day to satisfy his diverse audience—Mondays were for gossip, Tuesdays and Thursdays he focused on anecdotes and jokes, and Saturdays he wrote about obscure facts. While in his columns Winchell did take on somewhat different personae, he did not do so in the wildly inventive way that Runyon did.

The growth of advertising was a major factor in the flourishing of magazines in which Runyon's work appeared. These magazines, as Eric Lampard put it, "disseminated the metropolitan 'way of life' and its consumer iconography into every provincial town and hamlet in competition with the enticements offered by local newspapers and direct mail catalogues"—including, we might note, the very unmetropolitan Sears and Roebuck catalogue.[9] The circulation of these monthly magazines increased at a much greater rate than that of daily newspapers from 1890 to 1905.[10]

With the increasing dominance of New York in literary culture, it is not surprising that a great many of the major American magazines were published in New York. As Neil Harris notes, "[A]s New York prospered and expanded, stories on the city's growth, accompanied now by artist illustrations as well as photographs, obtained particular prominence."[11] Although these magazines were national and international in coverage, they often stressed the glamour of New York, where celebrities, particularly those in the theater, resided.

Runyon's reputation was established in the period between the World Wars, especially in the 1920s, the decade that was, as Ann Douglas reminds us in *Terrible Honesty,* "the first age of the media, of book clubs, best-sellers and record charts, of radio and talking pictures; by the end of the decade, one of three Americans owned a radio and a record player, three out of four went to the movies at least once a week, and virtually no one was out of reach of advertising's voice."[12] Many factors, of course, went into the making of the world Runyon describes. From the outset, New York was a culture of *doing* not *being;* status was measured mostly in terms of what was accomplished, and virtually anyone could make his or her mark with ability and luck. "Making it" usually was defined as succeeding financially rather than social climbing; because success was measured in terms of money and power, there was great social mobility. While a self-styled, often Anglo-Protestant social elite looked down on *nouveaux riches,* that elite was far less important and dominant than in Europe or even other American cities. Certainly New York was far more pleasure-seeking, frivolous, entertainment oriented, and secular than New England. When it became the dominant cultural site, the rest of the country often followed in imitation. As Douglas writes of artists' and writers' attraction to New York, "For a few giddy and glorious moments in the 1920s, New York held out to its new inhabitants its extraordinary promise of freedom and creative self-expression."[13]

Runyon's city has strong parallels to Walter Benjamin's Paris or Milan, divided into arcades where merchandise is hawked, where a culture of consumption reigns, and where merchants depend on creating a desire to have. Benjamin's arcade was—as Herbert Muschamp explains—"a block long pedestrian passage nestled between two masonry structures. It was lined on either side with small shops, tearooms, amusements and other commercial attractions. . . . The arcade itself was a visual device: a spatial frame around the shop windows that inspired passersby with the desire to purchase *la vie en rose*. Behind the windows, novelties continuously appear. Parisians regard themselves in the reflective glass."[14] The city is a maze that one enters to get lost. The city is not only a challenge to understand, but the ultimate enigma. City dwellers live in a phantasmagoric dream state in which they are manipulated and seduced to purchase. As Muschamp, summarizing Benjamin, puts it, "Like the factories that produced the wares sold there, the arcade was an industrial machine. It relied on display, advertising, newspapers and the other new technologies of consumer manipulation."[15] Runyon understood, too, that the modern city depended on a culture of consumption rather than on one of production. Indeed, what Muschamp says about Benjamin's style in *The Arcades Project* is appropriate to Runyon's tales and particularly to his newspaper columns: "The project mutated into the literary equivalent of its subject; a discontinuous maze, composed of brief insights and digressions, along with quotations that glitter from the pages like wares in a shop window."[16]

Runyon believed that New York was special and that it took special talent and grit to succeed there. Yet he believed the measure of success in New York was money, and, as we have seen, he embraced materialism and respected wealth as a sign of status. A dandy in dress and a man of large income who loved to spend, he was ambivalent about the quality of mass-produced consumer goods, notwithstanding that such goods allowed the working American to share in the nation's prosperity. In his introduction to *Inventing Times Square*, William R. Taylor describes "the emergence of a new interest in mass-produced goods and standardized consumption by the end of the nineteenth century. . . . The ensuing changes in production, distribution, and consumption style, fired by the unleashing of consumer credit, created the first consumer culture during the 1920s."[17] In subsequent chapters, we shall see how in his Broadway stories Runyon both embraced and parodied this consumer culture.

Tabloids and their gossip columns were interested in those who spent money. Money rather than social position mattered; spenders were welcome whether they were athletes, entertainers, gamblers, or gangsters. Like the gangster, the star entertainer, making fabulous sums, living in luxury, was a democratic figure who often came from the lower classes; he or she offered the model of success to readers who aspired to a more exciting life than they had.

Runyon was in tune with the sensibility of his audience; as Taylor observes, "More and more, in interpreting what they saw and felt, urban people believed their eyes rather than scripture: They read the city in new and exciting ways. Besides printed ads, corridors of illuminated signs by night and colorful billboards by day created visual excitement about the products and locations they promoted. Strategies in advertising, such as the tie-in, encouraged consumers to see products in relation to other desired objects or constructs. Consumer products thus assumed their modern place in personal aspirations, personal dreams."[18]

Runyon's world owes a great deal to the development of urban culture in the 1920s, and Prohibition did much to shape that culture. As Lewis Erenberg writes: "Consumer capitalism was in the ascendant.... The war against alcohol expressed hostility toward big cities, but it focused on New York as the capital of the new social mores. Besides drink, moralists attacked the movies, jazz, cigarette smoking by women, and the saloons as un-American emanations of a mongrelized culture. Prohibition thus represented an attempt by urban, rural, and small-town Protestants to establish the hegemony of their familial values over the expansive values associated with a more cosmopolitan urban life."[19] By the late 1920s speakeasies, Greenwich Village dance halls, and Harlem nightclubs abounded. The young went to nightclubs to escape their parents. Prohibition drove night life underground and opened the door to gangsters. Arnold Rothstein, accused fixer of the 1919 World Series and the model of Runyon's character known as "The Brain," controlled many nightclubs.

Runyon, we recall, enjoyed his friendships with such diverse gangster figures as Capone and Rothstein. Burrows and Wallace remind us that the complicity in New York between politicians and criminals and police and criminals dated back to the post–Civil War Gilded Age: "Bribery and corruption of law enforcement officers became as commonplace as it was in the mainstream business world. The newly professionalized underworld nexus of criminals, fences, lawyers, police, and politicians would grow and deepen in coming generations, but the fundamental structure had been put in place."[20]

As Muschamp observes, "New York . . . is the capital of secular distractions. We accept worldly substitutions for ideas that once possessed sacred value. In architecture, concepts like innovation, progress, demolition, preservation, context and historical precedent have the aura of sacraments. Yet they lack the stability once assured by religious authority. Instead they are pegged to market value."[21] An aspect of Runyon pegged almost everything to market value. Another related aspect—his showy clothes, his second wife, his Florida home—pegged everything to its theatricality and performance value, specifically how some spectacle or person "showed" at any moment.

Martin Arnold has remarked on New York's "sense of excitement, the heady possibility that just around the corner something extraordinary could happen to you. Not the violence, which certainly has never been missing, but a roving and unabashed adventure that could connect with you suddenly and positively, leaving you caked with fun and joy."[22] Runyon reveled in the excitement and adventure of New York, and those qualities were crystallized in the Broadway area. Runyon's Broadway stretched from 37th Street to about 52nd Street on the West Side, but it was a state of mind as well as a specific location. Taylor notes, "It is probably more instructive . . . to visualize Times Square as a hub centered at Broadway and Forty-second Street with axes radiating in all directions than it is to try to conceive of it as a precise area."[23] As the hub of the mass transit system, Times Square attracted patrons and tourists. The area is the center of a nighttime world often revolving around Broadway in the streets known as the forties, especially the eatery Mindy's, a thin disguise for Lindy's, which was originally located between 49th and 50th on Broadway and named for its owner and manager, Leo Lindermann. It is a world in which chorus girls, gamblers, newspaper writers, criminals, and policemen mingle uneasily. Yet is also a contested space, where various interests—street vendors, taxi drivers, window shoppers, cops, and whores—are jostling for space supremacy. As Taylor writes, Runyon heard here the "rich and expressive argots" of the sporting world, the underworld, especially bootlegging, as well as vaudeville, show business, and carnival.[24]

Completed in 1925, the new version of Madison Square Garden was between 49th and 50th on Eighth Avenue. The sidewalk in front was called Jacobs Beach, after the fight impresario Mike Jacobs; it extended to the front of Lindy's. Sports figures and sports writers hung out at Jack Dempsey's two restaurants on Broadway and on Eighth Avenue. The lower Fifties were heavily populated with speakeasies—including Runyon's mythical 300 Club operated by his fictional Missouri Martin—many in basements and back rooms with peepholes.[25] As Lewis Erenberg observes, "gangster owners were tolerated because they challenged restrictions on personal choice."[26]

Runyon writes as if he knew everyone and everything about everyone in New York and, later, Hollywood and Miami. While he often took a sardonic view of New York excess, he understood that New York depended on a culture of pleasure and enjoyment. New York City's culture lived in the present and for the moment, and acknowledged the legitimacy of carpe diem rather than adherence to traditional religious strictures. Runyon's choice of the present tense is his verbal correlative for a world of the moment, for do not gamblers, gangsters, showgirls, and drinkers often live without thinking of the future or planning for the next day? In this world illegal shortcuts, flamboyant recreation, sensory pleasure, wild parties, bizarre intrigues, and instant vengeance are the counterparts to the supposedly respectable world of wealth and privilege.

Beginning in 1910 sexual restraints and Victorian morality began to crumble. Indeed, crystallized by the *Ziegfeld Follies* in the second half of the 1910s, the concept of palaces of pleasure at which nudity and sensuality were celebrated became part of the city scene. Including speakeasies and burlesque, Runyon's world is a masculine world in which ethnic and racial stereotypes proliferate, where disputes are settled by violence, and where many marginal characters carry guns. World War I itself may have encouraged excess; many of Runyon's characters, including the hit man nicknamed Asleep in

"Situation Wanted" (1936), learned about violence while serving in the military. According to Erenberg, "Defended as the savior of moral democratic civilization, the [first world] war destroyed the importance of civilization for ordering experience; the grim war undercut the idea of restraint of social passions for social duty by the excesses to which the idea had been put."[27] That many respectable citizens had fought in the Great War and had been exposed to combat may have increased fascination with tough guys and led some people to rely on violent solutions. Runyon had seen action in the Philippine Insurrection of the Spanish American War and was a war correspondent during the Great War.

Because of the Volstead Act of 1919, respectable restaurants and roof gardens were replaced by, as Laurence Senelick puts it: "nonalcoholic cabarets which, for a fifty dollar cover charge, provided chorus girls or walk-on actresses for each table; the customer could take it from there. . . . Wining and dining a chorus girl was a sport of the rich or at least the well-heeled; the sexual consummation was a private tête-a-tête . . . behind closed doors."[28] The Prohibition world of cabaret shows is an important part of the culture of sensuality and plays a prominent role in Runyon stories. With their flamboyance, speed, and pacing, nightclub reviews were dedicated to creating a pleasurable sense of excitement. The girls cavorted in front of the audience. Lewis Erenberg recalls, "Unlike burlesque, where enjoyment of the female form was permitted only at a distance and in a voyeuristic fantasy, the cabaret floor show brought the chorus girl into the intimate proximity with the audience and made the young women tangible models of youth. Working close to the customers, they enticed men with face, figure, and personality. . . . [F]riendly and personable, they were blank slates upon which members of the audience might write their hopes and fantasies. Their ever-present smiles invited customers to project their desires onto their faces."[29] As mentioned, Runyon's second wife, Patrice, was a Spanish nightclub dancer, and she was hardly the first chorus girl in whom he was interested.

"Chorus girls, dressed in playful and glamorous attire," Erenberg observes, "added to the appeal, boldly presenting themselves as consumer objects, as symbols of adornment and success, advertising the body as a locus of desire and personal transformation. Every Broadway café soon followed suit, focusing on the eroticized female body as the centerpiece of the cabaret business."[30] Prohibition in the form of the Volstead Act changed the way New York City night life was organized. According to Laurence Senelick, "The rapid sleazification of Times Square was due not to a moral breakdown but to a most moral experiment: the passage of the Volstead Act in 1919. . . . Throughout the 1920s and well into the 1930s, the revues were raided and the legitimate theaters regularly attacked by John Sumner and the Society for the Suppression of Vice."[31] The performing women became active participants in sexual fantasy, but the male was left to complete that fantasy either by trying to date the girl or by returning home with his companion, for women often accompanied men to these performances. Erenberg observes: "These were not old-fashioned small-town girls filled with moral constraints but women with the ability to attract their men and keep them interested, all the while enjoying life alongside them as companions and playmates."[32]

Combining nudity and mirrors, nightclubs appealed to the narcissism of both actors and audience. As Gregory F. Gilmartin has noted of Joseph Urban's designs for nightclubs in the 1920s and early 1930s: "They were so extensively mirrored that one suspects the basic point was to allow patrons to see themselves within the decor and within the crowd; both actors and spectators in a comedy of fashion and consumption."[33] The nightclubs homogenized status. According to Erenberg, the nightlife of the 1920s was "a culmination, building on the trends under way in social and sexual life since the 1890s."[34] The entertainment was increasingly more risqué. Sexuality was part of the appeal; dancers in explicit erotic costumes became part of the Broadway cabaret scene. (To a degree, the Broadway nightclub, with its sexuality and cosmopolitan ethnic mix, became mainstreamed and its entertainers found outlets on radio and later television.)

The Depression affected the nightclub scene. Nightclubs often were fronts for underworld money and hoodlums became the major patrons. "Prohibition," Erenberg remarks, "offered great opportunities for quick cash and . . . criminal warfare intensified over diminishing revenues."[35] By 1931, during the suppression and decline in the legitimate theater, the Minsky brothers arrived in Times Square with their racy shows. After Billy Minsky bought the Republic Theatre on 42nd Street, the International at Columbus Circle, and the Central at 47th Street, other burlesque shows began to flourish in the area until 1937, when they were vehemently attacked. Yet paradoxically after World War I public prostitution waned.

The repeal of Prohibition in December 1933, combined with the New Deal stimulation of the economy, led by 1936 to something of a Broadway resurgence, even if the Broadway scene now had to compete with a mostly non-Jewish East Side café society. After Prohibition, Jewish entrepreneurs (such as Billy Rose and Joe Moss) who owned a good many of the Broadway nightclubs wanted to provide a social evening at a reasonable price. The gangster influence waned, and many of the operators who had cooperated with gangsters sought to become more reputable and open their nightclubs to the middle class. (The subtext of Runyon's "Situation Wanted" is that when the killer for hire Asleep emerges from jail in 1936, he finds the scene completely changed.)

RUNYON'S NEW YORK

It is not too much to say that New York is both the protagonist and antagonist of Runyon's fiction. In a sense he brought to New York City his nineteenth-century pioneering belief that all things are possible; for behind his cynicism is an ingenuous belief in the city as an opportunity for the white ethnics to find a grander life. With its violence, possibility, and openness to diversity, the city was another version of the frontier to him. He enjoyed the diversity of its neighborhoods, the interaction of individuals, the flux, motion, and energy that permeated everyday life. What Margo Jefferson wrote about the photography of Berenice Abbott's New York and her mentor Eugene Atget's Paris applies to Runyon's New York: "[I]t is about how we live in (and with) an artificial world—the city—that is as intricate and overpowering, as impervious to our will, despite being designed by us, as the natural world."[36]

Captivated by the sheer wonder and power of New York, Runyon regarded New York as his Moby Dick, the great white whale he sought but could never quite capture. He reveled in the lurid side of New York: the sensational, ghoulish, incongruous, violent, terrifying, disruptive, jarring. Yet he also relished the struggles of individuals, obsessed, self-dramatizing, in pain, trying for transcendence yet threatened with self-obliteration. Like Kafka, he dramatizes moments of crisis when characters are aware of their plight, aware of what life has brought them, and yet still hoping in some way to wrench something—love, money, stature—from their situation.

Always something of a tourist, Runyon enjoyed the spectacle—the biggest, the tallest, the most—of New York, especially Manhattan. Curiosity was his ruling passion and he loved not only to record the telling details of the pulsating life of the city that swirled around him but to penetrate the mysteries beneath what he saw and heard. For Runyon, New York was the quintessence of the modern city, and Broadway was the quintessence of New York. As both sardonic observer and participant, he felt the excitement, responded to the uncertainty and incipient chaos, enjoyed the glitter, and thrilled to the challenge of a city impossible to comprehend in its infinite variety.

Stephen Kinzer comments on an exhibit entitled "View of the City: 1910's–1940's" (which is often focused on the New York that Runyon knew): "Looking for new ways to express the emotions of American life, [these artists] portrayed the city as a thrilling jumble of shapes, shadows, and vivid energy."[37] While living in New York, Georgia O'Keeffe wrote, "Today the city is something bigger, greater, more complex than ever before in history. . . . There is meaning in its strong, warm grip that we are all trying to grasp."[38] Opened at the end of the last century and linking suburbia to the metropolis, the Brooklyn Bridge carried a particular fascination for artists as diverse as O'Keeffe and Margaret Bourke White. Modernists as different from one another as Stuart Davis and Joseph Stella shared O'Keeffe's optimism and reveled in the city's promise and excitement. Like Runyon, these artists were trying to find the meaning of the city. As Kinzer puts it: "The city seemed to be exploding with possibilities as it hurtled from the stately era of the brownstone into the dynamism of the skyscraper age. . . . There are almost no hints of violence, crowding, pollution or other problems that afflicted the city."[39]

The population of New York doubled between 1910 and 1930. Dance and theater flourished in the 1920s. Perhaps influenced by Margaret Mead's popular anthropological study, *Coming of Age in Samoa* (1928), which strongly questioned the desirability of celibacy, some New Yorkers became less monogamous; Runyon's Broadway stories reflect this trend. Bohemian behavior flourished in Greenwich Village but, as Runyon's Broadway stories and journalism make clear, that behavior was not confined to that area. Modern photography and modern journalism—including the widely read syndicated gossip columns—seemed to capture the kinetic pace of New York. Photography found one of its ideal subjects in the variety of cityscapes and characterizations in New York. The Photo-Secessionist Group, influenced by Alfred Stieglitz and including such figures as Edward Steichen, Paul Strand, and Alvin Coburn, were, as Douglas notes, "all intent on pictorial and dramatic effects but eschewing the heavy cosmeticizing and touch-ups then in vogue."[40]

Runyon understood, as Herbert Muschamp has written, that "The New York City street is the social contract of modern democracy inscribed in space, the place where the Statue of Liberty's promise is fulfilled. In every street, public and private realms bump into one another a million times a minute. Thoughts explode. Emotions erupt. Inspiration comes. Despair is dispersed. Resolve is strengthened. Curiosity is rewarded."[41] Runyon enjoyed the ethnic diversity, the different customs and foods, and seemed to have a special fondness for what he saw as the flamboyance and idiosyncracies of the first and second generation Italians, Irish, and Jews. Nevertheless he was not immune from ethnic stereotyping.

Runyon's Broadway stories and columns, along with Winchell's columns and radio broadcasts, helped create the allure of New York. Runyon's fictional world entered the imagination of those who read his work and was certainly part of the magnet of glamour and possibility that drew young people to New York, especially Manhattan. Published in popular magazines, his stories came to occupy the inner space of denizens of the heartland, the small towns, the rural South, and later the English speaking world beyond the shores of the

United States. His audience shared Runyon's New York life, and, later, his Florida home and his Hollywood visits.

Runyon urged his readers to recognize that the history of New York was the history of America and that New York's perpetual efforts to resolve the pluralistic ethnic, social, sexual, and economic interests was a model for America's task. Runyon was fascinated not only by a city teeming with immigrants but also by neighborhood changeovers where hordes of people converged on and transformed the precincts of the wealthy. He chronicled the way the nouveau riche undermined rigid social castes, how different classes rubbed shoulders in their shared greed and desire, the wide gulf between wealthy and everyday people, and changes in individual fortunes from the prosperous 1920s to the Depression.

Runyon's New York is part of our cultural memory. Because of the reach of his writing, he created America's image of New York and especially Broadway, even more than Al Hirschfeld or the *New Yorker* or even the *New York Times*, which was not at the time a national newspaper. Of course there is the actual city and the one he constructed in his columns and fiction—and in the films he wrote and produced—but it is that fictional city most Americans came to know in the era before jet planes and inexpensive air travel. Runyon also exposed Americans to the dangerous, dark, demonic city where sharpsters prey on one another. (In the nineteenth century, too, images of the city of possibility—Haussmann's Paris and the 1851 London Great Exhibition of Victoria and Albert—alternated with images of the city as impersonal juggernaut and socially dysfunctional space breeding physical disease and emotional dissonance— Zola's Paris and Dickens's London.) Runyon understood the loneliness and exhilaration of the city, which the urban sociologist and political economist Max Weber defined as a place of "detachment and sophisticated cynicism ... political parties, bosses, machines, chambers of commerce, credit associations, labor unions, factories, newspapers, churches, schools, welfare agencies, philanthropic societies, humane societies, museums, art galleries, lodges, zoos, auditoriums, parks, playgrounds, slums, red light districts, riversides or park avenues, main streets, jungles, sanitation plants and taxi-cab companies."[42]

Runyon's world is a capitalist, secular world where money is important and bookkeeping—and bookmaking—are dominant activities. He is fascinated by how money is accumulated, whether it be legally or illegally. In his November 1935 article in *Cosmopolitan* on Kansas Governor Alf Landon, entitled "Horse and Buggy Governor," Runyon characteristically is taken with Landon's having made his own fortune as an oil operator before applying his economic principles to the state of Kansas. In Runyon's stories cost is almost always a factor in determining value, although in them we also find touching moments of sentiment. Yet his ideology—"Take the money"—is that of the ultimate capitalist, and he measured his own value in terms of how much money he made. Although he reached the top and remained there, would he not have seen in his dying with little means a kind of ironic parable of the difficulty of new money holding on to wealth?

Runyon's world is not an idealized one but one founded in a strong acquisitive spirit; after all, New York was the epicenter of the commercial spirit and contained both garish wealth displayed in the most ostentatious ways and searing poverty, often virtually side by side—especially in the Times Square and Broadway theater and nightclub neighborhoods that were his focus. Runyon's first Broadway story, "Romance in the Roaring Forties," appeared two months before the October 1929 stock market collapse and the onset of the Depression. When Runyon's hilarious but cynical stories began to appear, the grim melodrama of the Depression was dominating the news; New York, more than most of the country, was, as John Mosedale reminds us, devastated by the Depression with "bankers as suicides; jobless men; families without food; New Yorkers sleeping on subways, sleeping in Central Park, living in shanties called Hoovervilles."[43]

That for Runyon social validation in New York was often equated with the accumulation of wealth is highlighted not only by his treating crime—whether it be gambling, illegal liquor business, kidnapping, or murder for hire—as another industry but also by his stressing the respectable world's fascination with gangsters. While some of Runyon's characters are small-time touts and bookies, many are out and out gangsters—unscrupulous tough guys who rob and murder one another and on occasion innocents and even cops.

Bonnie Menes Kahn has observed, "The great city, the cosmopolitan city . . . is one where diversity has created a temporary tolerance, a thriving exchange among strangers. And the project of the place . . . is an attempt to benefit from the presence of newcomers and outsiders."[44] Except for African Americans—a regrettable blind spot—Runyon understood the relationships, including the tensions, between classes and ethnics in New York. He saw New York's incompleteness and its social and cultural instability, the unmaking of distinctions and customs and fortunes that had recently been made. The rise and fall of gangsters—due to a change in fortunes deriving from either the impact of Prohibition or the period that immediately followed, or gambling reversals, or violence—mirrored and satirized the turns of fortune in the legitimate world. He enjoyed the continual mixing of highbrow and amusement culture and the social homogenizing of a culture shaped by materialistic desires and the sirens of pleasure. Runyon understood, too, the downside of urban life, such as the chasm between the haves and the have-nots, crowded housing conditions, underemployment, and even the priggishness of the censorious.

Runyon's cynicism never fully undermines his ecstatic embrace of New York City and his reveling in its spectacle and flamboyance. He loved not only to record the telling details of the pulsating life of the city that swirled around him, but also to penetrate the mysteries beneath what he saw and heard. He understood that what Joseph Rykwert observes of the modern city is even more true of New York: "[T]he modern city is a city of contradictions; . . . it houses many *ethnes,* many cultures, and classes, many religions. . . . [I]t is too fragmentary, too full of contrast and strife: it must therefore have many faces, not one. . . . The lack of any coherent, explicit, image may therefore . . . be a positive virtue."[45] Runyon was a spectator of great and small events. He was the eyes and ears of his readers. It was as if sporting events and trials—and even the day to day lives of celebrities—were vaudeville acts for him to observe and report. His audience overheard his gossip and tingled at his name-dropping. They became spectators not only to the great sporting events and trials, but also to the daily hustle and bustle of New York, the quintessential modern city.

In the 1930s and 1940s the New York literary intellectuals—such as Edmund Wilson and Lionel Trilling and what became the *Partisan Review* crowd—had little interest in eye and ear, while by contrast Runyon's sensibility is aural and visual. While their sensibility is abstract, his is specific. Unlike them, he is alert to the New York theater and to vaudeville performances as well as to the commercialization of the Broadway area. Runyon's anti-intellectualism often shows in his satires of Freud and Marx, intellectual figures deified in the world of New York intellectuals. Lacking a formal education, Runyon developed a kind of inverted snobbery based on knowing the world and living among a wide variety of people. He represented the world of popular culture; he thumbed his nose at intellectuals and at the pretensions of magazines like *Vanity Fair, The American Mercury, The Smart Set,* and the *New Yorker.*

If New York intellectuals had a circle, Runyon had a public. Interestingly, the figures that dominated American journalism—most notably Runyon but also Winchell, Lardner, and Rice—are not mentioned in Thomas Bender's fine study, *New York Intellect: A History of Intellectual Life in New York City, from 1750 to the Beginnings of Our Own Time* (New York: Alfred A. Knopf, New York 1987). Bender accepts the distinction—deriving in part from Matthew Arnold (on whom Trilling wrote his dissertation and a major book)—of the *Partisan Review* crowd between the value of serious literature and the pedestrian nature of popular literature. The subjects of Bender's book and *Inventing Times Square,* edited by William R. Taylor, are almost mutually exclusive. Even though both purport to be the history of New York City culture, they occupy parallel universes.

CULTURAL CONTEXTS

Runyon's city is at the crossroads between the metropolis that was emerging in the first decades of the twentieth century and the dismal conditions of the late nineteenth century, defined, according to Anthony Vidler, by "lack of light and air, unsanitary and overcrowded conditions and congested circulation that demanded the opening up of narrow streets."[46] (Phillip Lopate remarked that New York "typified the struggle of Social Darwinism."[47]) We might recall not only the way that Herman Melville's Bartleby the Scrivener lives in "miserable friendlessness and loneliness," but, forty-seven years later, the city of Theodore Dreiser's *Sister Carrie* (1900). The city is a site where men and women often seem to be strangers whose feelings and motivations are hidden from one another and who are desperately seeking companionship. Kahn could be describing *Sister Carrie* when she writes: "Women wear masks of who they are supposed to be while hoping to attract someone for what they really are underneath. And in men impersonal behavior is lauded; all powerful men must resemble one another. They are reduced to a crowd."[48]

Runyon became an important figure when the Ash Can school, led by Robert Henri (1865–1929) and including such figures as George Bellows (1882–1925) and John Sloan (1871–1951), were prominent painters of realistic cityscapes, most notably New York. Influenced by the realism of journalism, these painters created neighborhood scenes, with a particular emphasis on working class life and grim depictions of poverty. They shared some of Runyon's reportorial curiosity about the modern city. Their emphasis on transmitting direct experience based on observation anticipated the pragmatic aesthetic of John Dewey in the 1930s that provided an alternative to cultural elitism.

Just as elitist book reviewers and highbrow intellectuals patronized Runyon, art critics in such surveys as Sam Hunter's *Modern American Painting and Sculpture* and Barbara Rose's *American Painting: The Twentieth Century* dismissed painters of the Ash Can school for not subscribing to modernist tenets.[49] Such critics were only interested in those who played a role in the evolving teleology of modernist formalism. For example, Rose dismissed the Ash Can school as "superficial" and indicted most of its artists for lacking "much knowledge or interest in modernism."[50]

Sloan, in particular, used illustration and caricature to give a sense of the modern city; like Runyon, he was attracted to small anecdotes of urban life that revealed how various subcultures lived. George Benjamin Luks (1867–1933) used his skills as an illustrator, developed on the art staff of Philadelphia newspapers, to capture the personalities of his subjects by exaggerating some details at the expense of others; he was interested in the working poor and ethnic

life. We cannot with any certainty know if Sloan's and Luks's interests in the immediacy of scenes, the moment of felt life, influenced
Runyon to use the present tense, but surely he would have been
aware of their work. Luks's painting "Allen Street" bustles with life
on Manhattan's Lower East Side and achieves its dramatic effect by
simple light and dark contrasts.

What Hunter wrote about Sloan could be said about Runyon,
although Sloan's haunts tended to be downtown—the Lower East
Side, the Bowery, the West Side below Fourteenth Street: "The fact
that he found vitality and human interest in the seamier pockets of
the big city was quite in tune with the spirit of the new realism, as
was his tendency to give human squalor the touch of romance."[51]
(Hunter, however, looks down at Sloan and calls his subjects "crude
caricatures."[52])

Runyon's tales of loneliness and alienation have much in common with the work of Edward Hopper (1882–1967), a painter influenced by Sloan. Both responded to the spiritual vacancy of the
modern city, but for Runyon the excitement and energy was usually
more than enough compensation. Runyon would have known Ben
Shahn's (1898–1969) acerbic depictions of the drabness and vacancy
of urban environments and been aware of Shahn's interest in political issues, such as the execution of Sacco and Vanzetti.

Sloan and Luks influenced Reginald Marsh (1898–1954), who
stressed the unsavory and congested aspects of urban life: the public
beach, subway, and burlesque halls, especially New York's popular
Gaiety Burlesque. Once a story illustrator, he used the narrative
mode in his paintings. In Marsh's 1930–1933 "(Gaiety) Burlesque
(Also Known as Irving Place Burlesque)" he focuses on the sordid
spectacle of women undressing for an all male audience; one grin-
ning character, recalling some of Runyon's mischievous narrators,
looks back at us to draw us into the world we are observing. In that
piece and in "Subway—11th Street" (1930), with its medley of raw
energy, ethnic variety, diverse classes, sexuality, tawdriness, isolation,
and loneliness among crowds of strangers, Marsh depicts Runyon's
world.

Educated at Eton and Cambridge, Philip Evergood (1901–1973)
returned to New York to depict in his paintings poverty and the

coarse underbelly of the urban poor. Evergood focused on the mundane amusements of those whose lack of money and education prevented them from pursuing more ambitious paths. In the carnivalesque canvas "Love on the Beach" (1937), Evergood cynically depicts distorted bodies seeking relationships based purely on sexual attraction. Runyon's view was not too different; he at once celebrated and condemned promiscuity. Evergood and Marsh were patronized by highbrow critics for similar reasons as Runyon. On first encounter, all three seemed more interested in subject matter than technique and used popular forms and seemingly unsophisticated techniques to communicate viscerally with a larger audience. Moreover, they relied on exaggerations and even grotesque and distorted perspectives.

Another painter who helps us understand Runyon is John Marin (1870–1953), especially his 1936 series of watercolors, including "City Movement, Downtown Manhattan #2" (1936), which had much in common with Runyon's rendering of the city's vitality and energy. Runyon would have understood Marin's 1913 letter to Alfred Stieglitz: "[T]he whole city is alive; buildings, people all are alone."[53] Marin reveled in the kinetic quality of the city, using the title "City Movement" for seven paintings and "Street Movement" for fourteen. Like Runyon, Stuart Davis (1894–1964) was captivated by the dynamic quality of American life and its lack of rigid class structures, and was influenced by jazz and popular cultural forms—in his case, by posters—and worked with a combination of ironic detachment and high spirited élan. Like Runyon, Davis satirized and celebrated contemporary American culture. Within paintings that tended toward the abstract, Davis enjoyed surprising his viewers with abrasive lettering or words, as if to suggest that advertising and headlines were as much a part of the world as nature or people. Runyon would have appreciated Davis's remarking, "I often use words in my pictures . . . because they are a part of my urban subject matter; . . . [my phrases are] as real as any shape of a face or a tree."[54]

Runyon's emphasis on the visual owes much to the commercial culture and signs of Broadway—color, glass, and light became features of commercial display and Times Square became the "white light district" and the "Great White Way"—and anticipates television in its rapid presentation of images. The appeal of his stories to

Hollywood surely owes much to the visual and kinetic quality of his imagination. Hollywood studios, as Taylor observes, "once provided a visual and musical conduit to Broadway for the rest of the nation," and anticipated early television in installing New York—especially Broadway—as the nation's cultural capital and mecca for "syndicated journalism, network radio, and Hollywood studios—all national media had used the entertainment district as a base of operations after the 1920s."[55]

Popular music was centered in New York's Tin Pan Alley, which by 1920 had gradually moved from West 28th Street between Broadway and Sixth—its site in the 1910s—to the Times Square area. Irving Berlin was a dominant figure, who, as Douglas writes, "headed a broad-based linguistic revolution as well as a musical one" and used a vernacular American idiom in his songs.[56] His early music was syncopated; he wrote the music and lyrics. According to Douglas, "ragging or syncopating came easily to Berlin, as to all Jewish composers, because Jewish music, with its Eastern and Mediterranean sources, its complex rhythms, and preference for minor keys, had something in common with the African-American sound."[57] Do we not hear those qualities in Runyon's style?

As his column entitled "The Greatest Song Writer in the World" shows, Runyon was very much aware of this world. Thus when writing of Grant Clark—an important figure of an earlier musical generation—he compares him to Johnny Mercer ("The Greatest Song Writer in the World," ST 232). Opening up to an anecdote about Broadway night, he recalls how Clark put his hand on the wrist of an Englishman who didn't appreciate "boogie woogie" and said: "I just have to feel the pulse of anyone who does not like ragtime" (ST 233).

RUNYON'S DEMIMONDE

Runyon was fascinated by those whose commercial dealings were on the edge of legality and by those whose activities crossed over into criminality. Just as the demimonde in his stories has an attraction for supposedly respectable people who are quite pleased to consort with gangsters, so, too, Runyon realized, the demimonde has an attraction for readers. Notwithstanding his own insecurities and anxieties—or because of them—he was repelled by the lonely and socially inept rich, especially males who preyed on showgirls. The respectable world even invites the underworld to parties to show off their "mixing" capacity, although "Broadway guys, such as will go to a party like this, are apt to just sit around and say nothing, and act very gentlemanly, because they figure they are on exhibition like freaks" ("Social Error," ROB 451). We recognize that post–World War II Las Vegas, where entertainers and politicians hobnobbed with criminals, was not so different.

"The Old Doll's House" (1933) provides an example of how Runyon juxtaposes the underworld with the respectable world to emphasize both similarities and differences. Lance McGowen, a liquor importer and gangster, finds refuge from an attack by Brooklyn gangsters in the house of the wealthy and brokenhearted Miss Abigail Ardsley (ROB 61). Runyon ostentatiously uses the epithets "Mr." and "Miss" for the wealthy. After Lance kills the rival gangsters, Miss Ardsley, appreciating his attention, testifies that he was with her at midnight, neglecting to mention that all the clocks in her house were stopped the last time she saw her beloved, who was chased into the snow by her father to freeze to death during the blizzard of 1888. Just as success and wealth breed respect in the criminal world, so they do in the respectable world: "Nobody ever sees so much bowing and scraping before in a courtroom. In fact, even the judge bows, and although I am only a spectator I find myself bowing too, because the way I look at it, anybody with as many potatoes as Miss Abigail Ardsley is entitled to a general bowing" (ROB 71). In contrast to Lance McGowen, who is held accountable by the legal system, no one tries Miss Ardsley's father for negligent homicide.

Runyon's Broadway is what Vidler calls "a site of interaction, encounter and the support of strangers for each other," Times Square "a place of gathering and vigil," Mindy's and its environs are "communicator[s] of information and interchange."[58] Yet dark shadows, popularized by Fritz Lang's *Metropolis* (1926) and other noir films, lurk in the form of poverty, greed, and various illicit activities and criminal intent.

Kahn observes, "All urbanites are strangers when they first enter the city. Each newcomer is a stranger long before he reaches the city gate, simply because he does not belong where he is."[59] Cities consist of strangers and outsiders, and Runyon always remembered that he arrived as stranger and outsider. Italian American culture fascinated him—witness the story "Too much Pep" (1931)—and he understood how difficult it was for Italians, particularly during the Depression years, when they suffered greater unemployment and more hardship than other European ethnic groups, to find their way into the professions and corporate America. Runyon enjoyed mingling with gangsters of various ethnicities, but enjoyed a special friendship with Al Capone. In "Social Error" (1930) Runyon's persona calls the respectable world's fascination with the criminal world an "underworld complex" and attributes the term to Waldo Winchester, a thin disguise for Walter Winchell: "Waldo Winchester says many legitimate people are much interested in the doings of tough guys, and consider them very romantic, and he says if I do not believe it look at all the junk the newspapers print making heroes out of tough guys" (ROB 450). Yet if anyone had an underworld complex, it was Runyon himself.

Taylor speculates, that Runyon's "success and the wide popularity of his stories about gangsters may, in fact, have been the result of the degree to which his work embodies a tension between respectability and prurience that was central to his time. In portraying petty criminals and hoods as sympathetically and engagingly as he did, he was catering to what Winchell once described as society's 'underworld complex,' a middle-class love affair with the underworld that began during Prohibition. In striking out at the ruthlessness of wealth and privilege as he did, he may simply have been inverting the class spectrum, leaving its pieties intact."[60]

We might call this *gangster chic*. Respectable working class and middle-class people enjoyed reading about those who do not work 9 to 5 and return to their family lives. As readers today do we not still participate in the same kind of voyeurism? Do we not also fantasize about settling scores with those we do not like or whose successes seem unjustified in relation to our merit? Perhaps Prohibition (1920–1933), which required many citizens to have a secret life on the darker side of the law, contributed to this affinity for criminals and enjoyment of the disreputable. As Ann Douglas writes: "White

New Yorkers defying Prohibition enjoyed flaunting in broad daylight the pretense of secrecy that lawbreaking involved. They loved the ultraslim hip flasks that eliminated the telltale bulge of a bottle, the passwords needed to open speakeasy doors, the proliferating slang and nonsense terms for booze and drinking."[61]

Citizens not only became lawbreakers but performers assuming roles and wearing masks. Owners of speakeasies visited by respectable folk often had criminal backgrounds; some of the patrons did, too. Betting with bookmakers and playing numbers were also illegal activities that made respectable citizens cross the border into the criminal world. Finally, the world of burlesque and showgirls attracted a varied male audience; respectable citizens and "wise guys" often patronized the same shows for the same reasons and competed for the same women.

In our era of instant fortunes and plenty—or at least the euphoric era prior to the terrorist destruction of the World Trade Center—it is easy to forget what New York was like in the 1930s. While some people had money, most were barely getting by. We can see indications of grinding poverty in a photograph by Irving Browning (1895–1961) entitled "Advertising (about 1930)": Three "sandwich" men dressed in shabby coats hover over a grate for warmth, each wearing signs advertising small merchants; one is for used trunks and luggage at "bankrupt prices," another is for reweaving garments, the message of the third is unclear.[62] In Runyon's New York (and occasionally Miami), selfishness and narcissism rule, but there are occasional acts of generosity and moments of tenderness. His New York is a world where conversation is both recreational and a way to get an edge—and yet are not his conversations with a purpose a foreshadowing of contemporary business lunches at the Four Seasons? His New York is a world of dreams—often seamy—where boxing managers, like Runyon's fictional Spider McCoy, never give up their hopes of owning a piece of the next heavyweight champ.

Runyon speaks ironically about the hard times on the New York streets, but his world is one in which virtually everyone, except perhaps the few large dealers in products banned by Prohibition and those born to wealth, suffers from what he calls "the unemployment situation" where "nobody is working and making any money"

("Breach of Promise," ROB 16). Many of these men are touts, trying to give someone a winner in the hopes that in exchange, the recipient will give the tout either a tip from the winnings or a few dollars to bet, or both. The chorus girls looking for husbands are often exploited by married men—wealthy or pretending to be—when they are not themselves taking advantage of infatuated hangers-on who steal to support the girls' desire for jewelry and nice hotel rooms. Women are beaten by their husbands, and girlfriends by their lovers; children are abandoned. In "Little Miss Marker" (1932), Runyon's narrator observes, "[I]t is by no means uncommon in this town for little kids to be left sitting in chairs, or on doorsteps, to be chucked into orphan asylums by whoever finds them" (ROB 300).

Runyon's stories often focus on this narcissistic, pleasure-orientated world where gangsters, chorus girls, and the well-to-do intermingle. While Runyon enjoys the rich ethnic and class diversity of Manhattan, gay life and Black life are ostentatiously absent from his world. Yet homosocial bonding between males to whom women are little more than sex objects is an important aspect of this culture. As Taylor writes of Runyon, the transplanted Westerner, "Homoerotic bonding remained . . . a regular feature of what might be called 'the West of memory.' As incorporated into Runyon's fiction this version of the West acquired a New York accent."[63] In a New York version of homosocial bonding, various aggregations of gangsters, gamblers, traveling businessmen out on the town, drinking men, and politicians mingled in speakeasies, cabarets, sporting events, racetracks, and all-night restaurants like Lindy's.

Within Runyon's fictional world there is sex without explicit sexuality; chorus girls look for sugar daddies to help them out, and those sugar daddies often are successful gangsters like Dave the Dude and The Brain. Nor is Runyon unaware of the relationship between a character wielding his "big John Roscoe"—his gun—and his expressing himself sexually. Runyon writes about racy behavior in sly and suggestive ways. In fact, his stories are teeming with hormonal energy. In "Tight Shoes" (1936), Miss Minnie Schultz is fond of Rupert Salsinger, a political radical if not a malcontent, who "is really much better than a raw hand at making love, even though he is so conservative about speaking about marriage" (ROB 467). Certainly Runyon's speaker often calls attention to chorus girls and hostesses who wear hardly any clothes, or who might forget to wear underwear to Mindy's, and his world is rife with relationships between unmarried adults and hanky-panky. While he has much to say about his preferences in women, and what he has to say would now be considered sexist, he does not brag about specific conquests. He tells us his preferences are for women with little feet and ankles ("The Brakeman's Daughter," ROB 499), yet not too small: "I like my dolls big enough to take a good hold on" ("Social Error," ROB 448). He assures us, "I am a fairly good-looking guy" ("Madame La Gimp," ROB 248).

RUNYON'S HETEROGENEITY:
ETHNICS AND CLASSES

Runyon focused on social contrast and idiosyncratic variety. Like other great urban writers and artists such as Dickens, Conrad, Manet, and Joyce, Runyon had an eye for jarring details that provide contrasts and disrupt unity. Within his spare stories, he packed telling details that affirmed New York's vitality and diversity. He had an eye for social extremes. Runyon's stories show the heterodoxy of class in New York, show how diverse groups intermingle in the Broadway world. Broadway—and its extension to the racetracks, fights, and college football games—is a kind of social demilitarized zone where touts and small-time gangsters rub shoulders with the wealthy and privileged. Manhattan is a kind of symphony composed of subway roars, taxi sounds, shrieks, the odd gunshot, and even horses neighing. Thus Princess O'Hara in the 1934 story of that name is called "Princess" because her father, an alcoholic victoria driver who claims Irish royal blood, is called King O'Hara by the Broadway crowd. After her father dies and she inherits his business and the horse named Goldberg, she is looked after by the Mindy's crowd. When Goldberg becomes ill, the Mindy's crowd steals a horse from the track; the horse turns out to be a star racehorse whose speed saves her life when she witnesses a beer truck highjacking and murder and is in danger from the perpetrators. She falls in love with a descendent of French royalty who is her passenger. To help the marriage take place, the horseplayer Regret generously gives her $1,000.

While Runyon loved the ethnic variety of New York, his stories teem with ethnic stereotypes. The narrators use words like "wop" and "guinea" for Italians, call Chinese people "chinks," and in "The Lemon Drop Kid" (1934) the narrator speaks of a black man as a "big, sleepy-looking stove lid" (DRO 454). Characters have names like Wop Joey, Guinea Mike, and Little Yid. Runyon enjoys, in "Dancing Dan's Christmas" (1932), the incongruity of "a guy by the name of Ooky, who is nothing but an old rum-dum, and who is going around all week dressed like Santa Claus and carrying a sign advertising Moe Lewinsky's clothing joint around in Sixth Avenue" (ROB 258). (To apprehend the aggressively abrasive flavor of the phonics of this Runyonese—with its extra prepositions and consonant clusters—one must read it aloud.) The narrator in "Too Much Pep" claims never to speak of Italians "as wops, or guineas, or dagoes, or grease-balls, because I consider this most disrespectful, like calling Jewish people mockies, or Hebes, or geese" (ROB 632). The narrator in "Broadway Financier" voices clear if muted ethnic prejudices against Italians and Jews, especially unassimilated ones on the Lower East Side whom he refers to over and over again metonymically as "shawls and whiskers" and who are compulsive savers. Furthermore, in the Lower East Side "there always seems to be a smell of herring around and about" ("Broadway Financier," ROB 212). Not everyone will enjoy reading about a character named "Jew Louie" ("Hold 'Em Yale!") or "Mockie Max" ("The Old Doll's House") or seeing Sam the Gonoph from Essex Street on the Lower East Side described as "a short, chunky black-looking guy with a big beezer, and he is always sweating even on a cold day" ("Hold 'Em Yale!" ROB 147). In another instance, Runyon says of a gangster called Izzy Cheesecake, "he is slightly Jewish, and has a large beezer, and is considered a handy man in many respects" ("'Gentlemen, The King!'" ROB 171). In "Dancing Dan's Christmas" (1932), we have an ambiguous case where it is not easy to distinguish Runyon's prejudice from that of his narrator's; the narrator's antipathy to Good Time Charley Bernstein's celebrating Christmas after hosting him to a day and night of drinking could be attributed to Runyon's characterization of the increasingly inebriated narrator rather than to Runyon himself.

Notwithstanding his narrators' prejudices, Runyon enjoyed hearing and understanding some Yiddish. By 1910 the Lower East Side had a population of 500,000 Jews, and their influence penetrated the worlds that Runyon knew. Journalists and social reformers cast their eyes on the population density, and the neighborhood had celebrity status; as people left it they remembered it with nostalgia. Indeed, at times the grimy, teeming neighborhood became something of a legend, and references to the Lower East Side as it once was may even be one of the appeals Runyon's stories have for Jews who left those kind of neighborhoods for the suburbs and later Florida; as Paul Berman observes, "[I]f the modern American Jews, in gazing back on the tenements of downtown New York, have come up with one more exotic site to locate their Jewishness yearnings, it is not just because America's Jews have left their traditions behind, but also because America's Jews have not left their traditions behind. As the French historian Pierre Nora nicely puts it, 'To be Jewish is to remember being Jewish.'"[64] I suspect that this is not only true of the Jews but of the Irish and Italians—and of all of us who have roots in New York City. Part of the appeal of Runyon's stories is that they resonate with echoes of stories we have heard about New York, including ethnic New York, from our parents and grandparents.

Runyon understands the kinetic nature of the classes in a city driven by money. Money drives gangsters and businessmen alike. He realizes that business transactions—legal and illegal—take place in a no-man's-land outside arbitrary class and social distinctions. All that is required for a business deal is a buyer and seller, and the buyer might be a wealthy heir, a blueblood, while the seller may be providing entertainment as a dispenser of liquor or as a showgirl. Runyon also is aware of the continuing mix of ethnicity in the demimonde, and the tension that that mix creates.

Much of the humor in Runyon's stories depends on the ironic juxtaposition of two worlds and the border crossings between them. Thus figures like the abusive Mr. Justin Veezee in "What, No Butler?" (1933) use their inherited wealth to prey on showgirls. At times it seems that the only protection against predatory wealth is gangster intervention. In a strange way the gangsters often police themselves and intervene on the side of those who are being exploited by those whose rapacity exceeds accepted bounds. "Hold 'Em, Yale!" (1931) derives from the clash of the gangster and immigrant world with the blueblood world. The gangsters protect a young innocent from being preyed on by a cheat and fortune-hunter named Gigolo George.

Indeed, we observe in Runyon a recurring pattern in which the gangsters—like Big Jule in "The Hottest Guy in the World" (1930), Earthquake in "Earthquake" (1933), or Sorrowful in "Little Miss Marker" (1932)—rather than the police act as the primary figures in mending the cleavages and schisms in the social order and in reestablishing temporary social equilibrium. In part Runyon's sympathy for the demimonde derives from his awareness that its members can have similar, if not more genuine, feelings than the respectable world. Our response to his characters, including the narrator, like our response to the Soprano family in the HBO series *The Sopranos,* is based on our sharing this sympathy.

As a journalist and fiction writer, Runyon was interested in the dark side of city glamour: the restless and the isolated, the loners living in one room in seedy hotels, the screams in the night. He was fascinated by the social dementia of the city, including the lives of criminals. It is a paradox that Runyon's bread-and-butter realism has much in common with surrealism in its insistence on freeing the mind from traditional assumptions about class and social hierarchies and from self-imposed repression. Many of his characters have a kind of demented rationalism that undermines the logic of the narration as well as the logic of rationalism's generic cousin, realism. Thus in "Too Much Pep" (1937), Don Pep', the ultimate Sicilian assassin, frightens his adversaries to death. Runyon catches the balance between paranoia and euphoria and oscillations between those poles that form the underpinnings of urban life. Underneath the facade of order is, at times, turmoil and chaos.

When we remember that midtown Manhattan is still a world of contrast between the rich and poor, with the middle classes in the outer boroughs, we realize that Runyon's world is our world. His characters played the numbers; now we play the lottery. Today's city population includes a multitude of those who live in the world of mutual funds and IRAs, today's respectable version of numbers. The same shocking events—domestic murders, spouse and child abuse, ruthless gangsters, abandoned children—are on our TV screens every night. Today not only do we have the alcoholic derelicts of Runyon's era—recall the title character of "Madame La Gimp" (1929) from whom sympathetic customers no sooner "buy" last week's newspapers and faded flowers than they leave them behind as worthless—but also drug addicts nodding off on Manhattan's streets.

RUNYON AND FITZGERALD

Neal Gabler observes: "While Fitzgerald plumbed the tragic depths of the Jazz Age, examining its ambivalence towards the money and the verve that enlivened it, Runyon, no less a twenties writer, skated over its shiny surface where there was no tragedy, only comedy, some sentiment and occasional rue—unless that *was* the real tragedy: that like so many others on Broadway, he had lost the capacity to feel and was left only with the capacity to perform."[65] However, F. Scott Fitzgerald's New York in *The Great Gatsby* and Runyon's New York have much in common.

Like Runyon and his narrators, Nick Carraway and his creator are fascinated by the texture of New York: "I began to like New York, the racy, adventurous feel of it at night, and the satisfaction that the constant flicker of men and women and machines gives to the restless eye" (GG 57). Like Runyon, both Carraway and Gatsby come East, only to be captivated by New York, although Carraway returns home and Gatsby is shot; as Nick puts it, "The city seen from the Queensboro bridge is always the city seen for the first time, in its first wild promise of all the mystery and the beauty in the world" (GG 69). As an excluded outsider, Nick is alternately fascinated and depressed by the excitement and glamour of Runyon's beloved Roaring Forties: "Again at eight o'clock, when the dark lanes of the Forties were five deep with throbbing taxicabs bound for the theatre district, I felt a sinking in my heart. Forms leaned together in the taxis as they waited, and voices sang, and there was laughter from unheard jokes, and lighted cigarettes outlined unintelligible gestures inside. Imagining that I, too, was hurrying toward gayety and sharing their intimate excitement, I wished them well"(GG 57–58). Like Runyon, Fitzgerald's Nick was taken by the restlessness and mystery, the secrecy and scandal of New York. Of the apartment on 158th Street that Tom Buchanan has for his adulterous relationship with Myrtle Wilson, Nick recalls: "Yet high over the city our line of yellow windows must have contributed their share of human secrecy to the casual watcher in the darkening streets, and I was with him, too, looking up and wondering" (GG 56). Runyon would have identified with Nick's lurking voyeuristic imagination.

Runyon's narrators, like Nick, claim to "reserve all judgments," and yet on many occasion Runyon's narrators do intrude (GG 1). For one thing, although from far different social classes, both Nick and Runyon's speakers are amazed at the infinite variety of New York. As Nick puts it, "I was within and without, simultaneously enchanted and repelled by the inexhaustible variety of life" (GG 36). But except for his racial animosity toward Blacks, Runyon is more tolerant of ethnic variety and certainly would not buy into Nick's rather ostentatious anti-Semitism.

From all the internal evidence in Runyon's stories, he knew *The Great Gatsby* well. Like Fitzgerald (and his creation Gatsby), Runyon was fascinated by money. Fitzgerald's fictional Meyer Wolfsheim, a gambler who fixed the 1919 World Series and who in many ways recalls The Brain, eats lunch with Nick and Gatsby, at a 42nd Street restaurant. Unlike Runyon's narrators, Nick is an innocent in this world of the demimonde, a world in which Gatsby is comfortable. Of the fixed World Series, Nick remarks: "It never occurred to me that one man could start to play with the faith of fifty million people— with the single-mindedness of a burglar blowing a safe" (GG 74).

Wolfsheim seems a man of pervasive influence; at one point Gatsby replaces his servants with a family that used to own a small hotel and whom "Wolfsheim wanted to do something for" (GG 114). Indeed, Nick wonders if Gatsby had been part of the fixing scandal. Described as "a small, flat-nosed Jew . . . [with a] large head," Wolfsheim recalls the night a cohort named Rosy Rosenthal was shot outside the old Metropole at four in the morning after he and Wolfsheim had a long dinner there with four others (GG 69). Reading of Wolfsheim, do we not think of Runyon's gangsters hanging out in Mindy's?

While it is possible Runyon's present tense usage pays homage to Fitzgerald's use of that tense when describing Gatsby's parties, in some ways Runyon's stories are a response to Fitzgerald's snobbery. Runyon would have enjoyed Fitzgerald's mixture of hangers-on, scoundrels, and the upwardly mobile who attend Gatsby's parties and how that social mixture—along with the dark influence of the Broadway world in the person of Wolfsheim—"begot" West Egg and its "raw vigor that chafed under the old euphemisms and by the too obtrusive fate that herded its inhabitants along a short-cut from nothing to nothing" (GG 108).

Everyone but Nick is someone other than he pretends to be, and Nick is in love with both Daisy and Gatsby, and does not know it. Gatsby is all the more a Runyonesque character because of his assumed name. He reinvents himself and attaches himself to disreputable characters. He invents his past. He seems to be a confidence man and a bootlegger. He is very much of the gangster world about which Runyon later writes. Coming from the Midwest and reinventing himself by changing his name from James Gatz to Jay Gatsby and associating with disreputable Broadway types, he also resembles Runyon himself. Indeed, qualities like "resourcefulness of movement" and "restlessness" that breaks "through his punctilious manner" could describe Runyon (GG 65).

Runyon would have understood Gatsby's observing of the manipulative and amoral Daisy: "Her voice is full of money" (GG 120). Although Gatsby took the fall for her errant driving, Daisy does not even respond to his death. Not only is Daisy as cynical and tough as Runyon's predatory women, but so also is Jordan, the less wealthy of the two women from Louisville, who is also without scruples or values. Jordan seeks a husband as zealously as Lily in Edith Wharton's *House of Mirth*. When Nick throws her over, she lies about being engaged to someone else to increase her currency in his eyes.

THE DEPRESSION WORLD
OF RUNYON'S FICTION

Runyon published his first four Broadway stories in 1929. As the prosperity of the 1920s gave way to the Depression years of the

1930s, Runyon's world is not the fantasy world of Fred Astaire and Ginger Rogers, where the right girl and guy get paired up in a world that the Depression seems not to have touched, where everyone wears elegant clothes and lives in expensive hotel rooms, and where characters open their mouths and sing Irving Berlin and George and Ira Gershwin tunes. Berlin, in particular, as Stephen Holden notes, "could touch on a common chord of feeling. . . . Often wistful but never bitter, his lyrics embodied a bedrock faith in hearth, home, and country that transcended sentimentality."[66]

No, Runyon's is a world where grinding poverty and economic humiliation are facts of everyday life, and where the rich are treated differently from the poor and a woman awaits a man who will take her away from the humiliation of the chorus line to "a little white house with green shutters and vines all around and about" ("Pick the Winner" [1933], ROB 323). For women, marriage is the one bridge from poverty to economic comfort, but more often interminable engagements end finally in disappointment. At the racetrack the difference between a tout and a handicapper is whether or not one is broke; the one who is not broke is a handicapper "respected by one and all, including the Pinkertons, for knowing so much about the races" (ROB 311). Indeed, money gets respect; even the doormen at nightclubs give "a very large hello" to those who have money and "a very small hello" to those who do not ("The Big Umbrella" [1937], ROB 550).

In Runyon's world, selfishness often prevails, even when the anticipated result is physical harm to others. That few of his characters care about the community's interests may be symptomatic of a world in which there was a fissure between the public world and, as Erenberg puts it, "the private personal world," a split that "permitted the exploration of greater impulse and passion."[67] While Runyon's stories have quite a few destitute teenage girls who become chorus girls and are promised marriage by unscrupulous characters who may even beat them, often women take advantage of and even betray gullible men. In "That Ever-Loving Wife of Hymie's" (1931), even though Hymie gives his wife every nickel he has to support her in style, she is cheating on him. When her lover bets her husband $500 and the husband puts her up as his bet, she pretends to root for her husband's horse while actually rooting for her lover's horse.

In Runyon's world, jobless men haunt the streets at four in the morning in the hopes of borrowing a few dollars for their rent money at shabby hotels—or, more often, for gambling—and often awaken in the afternoon. Runyon's denizens expectantly await the smile of lady luck, but luck smiles rarely. Nor is murder out of the ordinary, for in this macho world violence is never far from the surface, and people are not infrequently shot. While the musical comedy *Guys and Dolls* generally makes these folk lovable characters, some are murderers and use their revolvers and machine guns without compunction.

Runyon has a wonderful eye for detail, the sounds, smells, and tastes of New York. He writes in the present tense as if to capture the immediacy of every conversation and the life of every story. Perhaps his most fantastic fiction is that his narrator remembers every word he hears. His eye is the eye of a camera—the camera of tabloid newspapers for which he wrote—and his imagination is a visual one. No wonder that twenty of his stories became motion pictures and two, *Lady for a Day* (1933)—based on "Madame La Gimp"—and *Little Miss Marker* (1934)—were major successes. His ear hears gossip, street lingo, and the cacophony of city sounds. The stories depend on a crisp slang that quickly reveals crucial information—as a journalist, Runyon was taught to put the essential information in the first paragraph—and he eschews glittery phrases. He presents the facts. Runyon does not often refer to jazz, but his expressive style, his verbal rifts, his improvisation certainly owes something to it.

In Runyon's New York, the criminal justice system is often helpless in the face of gamblers, whiskey runners defying Prohibition, and ruthless gangsters. Schizoids like Cecil Earl who "is subject to spells of being somebody else besides Cecil Earl" and psychopaths go untreated ("Broadway Complex" [1933], DRO 268). Bank failures hurt little people. In "Broadway Financier" (1932), Silk is a tiny seventeen-year-old orphan who has to work as a showgirl; her mother died heartbroken after losing her life's savings earned from scrubbing floors. People do not bathe every day or use deodorants and often have smells carried over from what they eat or do. Thus in "It Comes up Mud" (1933), the Runyon narrator says of Little Alphie, "what with hanging out with his horses most of the time, he never smells like any rose geranium" (ROB 534).

The police and even the racing authorities are far more concerned with protecting the wealthy than the class of citizens who are just trying to get by. The police are complicit with the gangsters; if someone complains about how a mobster puts his enemies in sacks in such a way that the victim strangles himself when he awakes, the mobster reports the complainant to Police Headquarters, as if it were the mobsters making the rules rather than the police ("Sense of Humor," ROB 273). Nor do the police seem able to intervene to prevent public or private mayhem.

CONCLUSION

In a piece written for the *New York Times* series "Writers on Writing," Russell Banks recalls meeting a "connected" old gangster named Jocko, a man whom he knew when he was a young, aspiring writer. Jocko is a Runyonesque character who says he does "little a this, little a that, same as always." In response to Banks's question about why the gangster "hung around with all those poets and artists and musicians," Jocko, echoing Oscar Wilde in *The Decay of Lying,* responds: "Yeah, well, artists are a lot like gangsters. They both know that the official version, the one everyone believes, is a lie."[68] Runyon would have loved Banks's tale, for Runyon writes about how gangsters make up identities; how they often masquerade and have nicknames and disguises; and how they either pretend to be legitimate businessman or consider their criminal activities as another form of business. He himself knew a good deal about criminal activities, including fixed fights and manipulated baseball games. He often implies that gangsters are in many ways radical versions of all of us, trying to do the best we can both economically in our work life and romantically in our private life, while hoping to find a way to connect our work world and our private world.

THE EYES AND EARS OF THE CITY

Runyon's Collected Journalism

INTRODUCTION

With his plain-speaking prose and slang, Runyon could write about the elite—entertainment and sports heroes, political and social figures—but he helped define aspects of the popular culture that belonged to white collar and blue collar workers. He played an important role in the creation of democratic language and in breaking the barriers between a middlebrow and an elite culture.

Runyon enjoyed writing about his nonintellectual life. While he admitted to not being "any more of real 'bo [hobo] than one of the Rockefeller kids," he enjoyed stealing "rides on freight and passenger trains" ("Some Hoboes," ST 265). Characteristically, he spoke of his attraction to the special language hoboes used: "I picked up much of the lore of the road through contacts with real rovers and I accumulated considerable of their patter of that long-gone time" (ST 265).

Runyon himself wrote of many New York subcultures: sports, the often simple and even idyllic outer borough world of his fictional Turps family, the gangster world during and after Prohibition, the world of theater. He wrote, we must remember, when a group of

New York intellectuals were using a different kind of journalism—the high-brow literary magazine, especially the *Partisan Review*, founded in 1935—to try to define high culture in opposition to Runyon's popular culture and create what Terry Cooney calls "a rich and inclusive American culture—and especially an American literature—that could measure up to the traditions of Europe."[1] The *Partisan Review* crowd found its center in Greenwich Village; Runyon's world was Times Square to Columbus Circle, mostly on the West Side. While Runyon wrote for the mass media, the intellectuals wrote for little magazines that had influence—or so they hoped—beyond their circulation.

Interestingly, the same kind of masculine clubbiness and homosocial behavior was inherent in both Runyon's crowd and the *Partisan Review* crowd. Each looked down at the other from a steep and icy peak. Each group was composed of outsiders—in the case of the New York intellectuals, Jews from ethnic neighborhoods—and each had left-of-center sentiments. But while the intellectuals often were attracted to Marxism, Runyon admired the rugged individualism of the West from which he came and considered capitalism a wonderful system by which someone like himself could become a well-to-do somebody by dint of his own labors, ambition, and genius. According to Cooney, the New York intellectuals brought from their backgrounds "a direct polemical style, a concern with identity and a need to establish a place for themselves; a belief in their own centrality and that of New York City; a commitment to Western culture, to secular thought, to critical intelligence; and an eagerness to engage the world that their worst detractors could hardly find unappealing."[2]

Runyon shared many of these features with them, except he might have substituted the middle-class phrase "common sense"—a term used by the parents of the New York intellectuals—for "critical intelligence." Runyon's lowbrow colleagues were not educated at Colombia with Norman Podhoretz in the literary masterworks of Western culture, which were regarded by intellectuals as "a repository of the universal, existing not in space or time but rather in some transcendental realm of the spirit."[3] But each group maintained a secular vision. Each judged the rest of the country and even the world from their New York perspective—although in his columns

Runyon often wrote as one fellow sharing his observations with his neighbors who, by accident of geography, did not live in New York (or, later, Miami and Hollywood), but lived in another world defined by the famous Saul Steinberg cartoon that sees Manhattan as the epicenter of the universe.

THE ROLE OF NEWSPAPERS
IN READING THE CITY

Bringing diverse groups together in a limited space, the city has potential for vast conflict and social disharmony, even as it requires social cooperation to make it work. As Lewis Mumford argues in *The Culture of Cities:* "The city is in a complete sense, then, a geographic plexus, an economic organization, an institutional process, a theatre of social action, and an esthetic symbol of collective unity. On one hand, it is a physical frame for the commonplace domestic and economic activities; on the other, it is a consciously dramatic setting for the more significant actions and the more sublimated urges of a human culture. The city fosters art and *is* art; the city creates the theatre and *is* the theatre. It is in the city, the city as theatre, that man's more purposive activities are formulated and worked out, through conflicting and cooperating personalities, events, groups, into more significant culminations."[4] For Runyon the city is theater and spectacle and his narrator is the observer.

We may think of the city in the early twentieth century as a site of pollution, overpopulation, and urban chaos, but we must not forget that the metropolis also was regarded as a source of promise and wonder. According to Walter Benjamin, "The City is reflected in a thousand eyes, a thousand lenses. . . . Mirrors are the immaterial element of the city, her emblem."[5] Runyon's present tense narrator of his stories are those eyes, those mirrors, but he dematerializes often into a voyeur, an observer.

In the early twentieth century, the city becomes the quintessence of industrial progress, a world dominated by clocks instead of the rural rhythms of nature. The Russian poet Aleksander Shevchenko wrote, "The world has been transformed into a single, monstrous, fantastic, perpetually moving machine. We, like some kind of ideally manufactured mechanical man, have grown used to living, getting up, going to bed, eating and working by the clock—and the sense of rhythm and mechanical harmony, reflected in the whole of our life, cannot help but be reflected in our thinking and in our spiritual life: in Art."[6] Certainly, as Fredric Jameson and E. P. Thompson have noticed, the introduction of time into the workplace changed the way urban life proceeded. Measurable time became a crucial part of urban life; for example, time was accentuated by half-hour radio shows.[7] Consider how often time is a factor in Runyon stories and how every second counts; for example, in "It Comes Up Mud" (1933), Veere rushes back to his bank to avoid disgrace and in "The Brakeman's Daughter" (1933), the elaborate plan to kill False Face depends on perfect timing.

Perhaps nothing reflected the focus on clock time more than the daily newspapers at the turn of the twentieth century; every twenty-four hours and more often where papers were published both in the morning and the afternoon, people were informed about what was happening. The morning newspaper gave each person a geographical range that had previously been available only to political leaders and wealthy world travelers. With the help of photographs tabloids exposed private affairs. And, as Stephen Kern reminds us, "The newsreel, invented around the turn of the century, threaded knowledge across class and frontiers."[8] Along with cinema and, later radio, the twentieth century columnist defined popular culture.

Let me recall the role of newspapers in my own life. Born in 1941, I grew up in a suburban home where I was exposed to multiple newspapers; as I followed sports, my father's stocks, and political news, the day was divided for me into the appearance of the various newspapers. Network TV news did not debut until 1963, and my family—like most families I knew in the New York metropolitan area—relied on newspapers rather than the radio for most of its news. My father rarely read books, but I remember him reading several newspapers a day in the 1940s and 1950s.

Either the *New York Times* was delivered—always on Sunday and some years, when my father chose to get the earlier edition, during the week—or my father brought it home from work. During high school I subscribed to and read the *New York Herald Tribune* and then brought it home for the rest of the family to read. My father arrived home between 6 and 7 P.M. with the *New York World Telegram and Sun* (a combination of three merged newspapers), which included the day's stock report until 3 P.M. and box scores and other updated sports data. He also picked up other papers he found on the train, such as the *New York Post*—then the only Democratic, leftist paper in New York and not the Murdoch tabloid it is today—and, on rare occasions, the supposedly anti-Semitic Hearst paper the *New York Journal American* where Runyon had once appeared, and that featured the despised alleged anti-Jewish Westbrook Pegler. To inform us about what was going on in Long Island and especially Nassau County, he had *Newsday* or the *Long Island Press* delivered in the afternoon—and both if one or the other were running a special. My father disdained the tabloids, *The Daily News* and *The Mirror.*

In *Reading Berlin 1900,* Peter Fritzsche uses the concept of "word city" to describe the preponderance of "small bits and rich streams of text that saturated the twentieth-century city, guided and misguided its inhabitants, and, in large measure, fashioned the nature of metropolitan experience."[9] While Fritzsche's focus is Berlin, much of his argument pertains to American cities and particularly New York. The daily newspaper continually revises our sense of reality and emphasizes the provisional and temporary nature of our perceptions. Each day modifies, qualifies, transforms, and revises the text of the prior day. Newspapers, by stressing eyewitness accounts, contributed to the modernist focus on perspective.

As Fritzsche notes, "the aesthetics of modernism and the culture of consumption distorted the city by embellishing its most fantastic characteristics."[10] The "word city" is not merely a reflection of the actual city but contributes to the creation of the image of the city that we know. In other words, the actual city and the "word city" are in a symbiotic relationship. Or as Fritzsche writes, "Truly an elaborate fabrication, the word city should be regarded a social text that simultaneously reflected, distorted, and reconstituted the city."[11]

Newspapers came to prominence in the very late nineteenth and early twentieth century. At this time the literacy rate had increased. More homes had adequate lighting for reading, first with the introduction of gas lamps, then of electricity. The accessibility of parks, waiting rooms, hotel lobbies, and cafés made reading a way of relaxing in comfortable public places easier. Railroads rapidly transported newspapers and other reading material—catalogues, magazines, even books—that might otherwise become dated. The migration from country to cities after the American Civil War and a popular press catering to the needs and interests of city workers played a role in the increasing importance of newspapers. The daily newspaper became the source of information and, through its advertising, aroused the desires that consumer capitalism required. As David M. Kennedy writes of the 1920s, "For urban workers, prosperity was wondrous and real. They had more money than ever before, and they enjoyed an amazing variety of new products on which to spend it: not only automobiles but also canned foods, washing machines, refrigerators, synthetic fabrics, telephones, motion pictures (with sound after 1927) and—along with the automobile the most revolutionary of the new technologies—radios."[12]

Advertising, which grew explosively in the 1920s, enabled publishers to keep the cost of purchasing the paper low. Newspapers generally favored local news over political and diplomatic news, for that, along with advertising, was what readers wanted. Readers were interested in sports events, crime reporting, what was going on in theaters on Saturday night, and what job openings were to be found on Monday morning. They enjoyed reading about the growth and excitement of the city in which they lived. As Fritzsche writes, "Not until the newspaper reformulated itself as an encyclopedia of daily life . . . could it become a quotidian item in the people's inventory."[13] Cities teemed with newspaper sellers and newspaper kiosks. For readers, the city's spectacles, including sensational crimes and sporting events, became a part of the very essence of city life.

Newspapers were central not only to the dynamism of the modern city but to the city as something always in a state of becoming, a work in progress. In *Ulysses* (1922), the seminal text of modernism, James Joyce is highly focused on the role of newspapers, particularly in the "Aeolus" chapter—the "lungs" of the city—where Bloom responds to the sounds of the printing press as if it were speaking to him. Moreover, the headlines in the chapter do not merely reflect reality; they are a performance that creates its own reality. The perspective of modern journalism presents a moral anatomy of Dublin, but I want to stress the pun on anatomy because Joyce perceives the city as a living body and his schema assigns bodily organs to each part: kidneys ("Ca-lypso"); genitals ("Lotus-Eaters"); heart ("Hades"); digestive system ("Lestrygonians"), which ingests and excretes; brain ("Scylla and Charybdis"); ear ("Sirens"); muscles ("Cyclops"); womb ("Oxen of the Sun"); locomotion apparatus ("Circe"); nerves ("Eumaeus"); skeleton ("Ithaca"); flesh ("Penelope"); and a circulatory system in the form of the electric power station ("Wandering Rocks"). Thus the book Joyce conceived as "the epic of the human body" also implies that the city is an anthropomorphic breathing organism.

Despite their seemingly radical divergence, writers like Runyon and Joyce represented the physiognomy of the city and enjoyed ren-dering the city's physical shape. Almost as if he were a physician reading x-rays, Runyon mapped out the internal organs of the night-time city. Giving the lie to stereotypical images of an immense undif-ferentiated mass of concrete that was populated by an anonymous homogeneous aggregation of people, newspapers separated the city into its component parts. It was as if newspapers were acknowledged as the city's eyes. As Peter Fritzsche notes, "This attention to, and even celebration of, diversity and difference tended to undermine a coherent vision of the city."[14] At a time when Freud and other mod-ernists such as Oscar Wilde were teaching us that we do not have co-herent personalities, that we wear many masks and have many identities, the newspapers were showing us the diversity of our cities. The face of a large city has many different masks. Runyon's was the nighttime world, the world of pleasure and entertainment; of sensu-ality, desires and passions; of apathy and relaxation; of homogeneity in classes; of enemies lurking in shadows; of criminal violence.

The newspaper subsumes all the organs until it is the living, breathing androgynous gigantic body of the city. The newspaper is the essence of the circulatory system of the body of the city, and the term "newspaper circulation" plays upon this fact. As Fritzsche notes, "The publishing industry was widely regarded as the last word in the organization, automation, and distribution of goods."[15] Through elaborate distribution systems, the newspapers organized their readers into an accessible audience. Reading the same paper about the same events created a community with a shared experi-ence. Or, as Fritzsche puts it, "[T]he word city organized the city by creating a like-minded readership."[16] That, of course, would include a like-minded consumer desire created by advertising. The anthropomorphized city suffers downtimes when money dries up, for much of its circulatory system is driven by the availability of money.

Seducing their prospective clients with newspaper ads, the city's commercial clothing interests, Runyon understood, invite each of us to consider not only our own bodies, but also to how we wish to present our body as a component part of the community or neighborhood body. The neighborhood streets in the area in which the Turps live—the subject of Runyon's series of anecdotes about a Brooklyn middle-class couple discussed in chapter eight—are a kind of coherent body in terms of a collective aggregation of human skin covered by clothing; those bodies are in turn clothed by the buildings in which the neighborhood residents reside. And this is true of each neighborhood. Just as a neighborhood can be imagined as a physical body in which money and news circulate, so can the city composed of neighborhood bodies be considered a larger body with its component parts and the nation a giant body consisting of the component parts of its cities, towns, and villages.

Photography responded to individual bodies in various states of dress and undress and to the neighborhood and the city as body. Interest in photography, stimulated by Charles de Forest Fredericks (1832–1894) and Mathew Brady (1823?–1896), was particularly pervasive in New York City. That interest stimulated the increasing demand by the 1880s for newspapers and illustrated magazines in New York, a demand that contributed to New York's becoming the Mediaopolis. The first halftone photograph appeared in the *New York Daily Graphic* in 1880. As Michael Kimmelman notes, "Photography also dovetailed with the new concept of the city as spectacle, as an endless producer of exceptional, theatrical images, a shifting who's who of people and things."[17]

RUNYON'S COLLECTED COLUMNS: PERSONAE AND AUDIENCE

From the 1920s until Runyon's death, he and Winchell were the two most important columnists in America. Winchell had a far-flung political influence, in part because of his radio broadcasts, in part because of his taking strong political stands in favor of Roosevelt, and in part because of his sheer egotism. Runyon usually eschewed the polemical in favor of a curiosity about human nature. While both contributed to glamorizing the gangster world and both had friends among gangsters, Winchell was a confidant of the FBI's J. Edgar Hoover and arranged in 1939 to deliver Louis "Lepke" Buchalter of Murder, Inc. to the authorities.

While Winchell wrote in one voice, Runyon invented a variety of personae in his columns. He enjoyed the kind of narrative ventriloquism whereby he spoke in another voice. Perhaps because of their inventiveness and diversity, Runyon valued his newspaper columns as much as or more than he valued his short stories. In 1946, when Runyon was too ill to do much more than write his columns, two collections brought together some of his highlights: *In Our Town,* a collection of early Sunday pieces—echoing the title of Thornton Wilder's 1938 *Our Town*—was published with wonderful illustrations by Garth Williams, and *Short Takes* brought together some of his best daily columns. *Runyon From First to Last,* a mélange of Pueblo, Colorado stories, nineteen Broadway stories, and late columns collected under the rubric "Written in Sickness," was published posthumously.

Although the Broadway stories owe much to the columns and vice versa, the columns are often narrated in the past tense and lack the dramatic immediacy of the present tense Broadway stories. This is certainly true of the "My Old Man" columns, most of which were written during the 1916–26 period and were collected in 1939 under the title *My Old Man;* some were republished in *Short Takes* in 1946. The columns are narrated by A. Mugg—first introduced as a character in 1916—who not only repeats My Old Man's views but sometimes interjects his own. The brief stories of *In Our Town* and the three very short stories published separately in 1936 in *Collier's*— "Lou Louder," "Joe Terrace," and "Burge McCall"—as well as the homespun wisdom of *My Old Man* and other anecdotes collected under the title "Our Old Man" in the volume *Short Takes* all drew on the popularity of dime novel Westerns in urban areas, where rugged individualists—sometimes desperadoes—were in control of their lives and where, unlike the city, as Burrows and Wallace put it, "masters of property and capital were not in control."[18] As they note, in the later part of the nineteenth century, "Western adventures" were a "wildly popular genre . . . churned out en masse in the metropolis."[19]

Particularly effective was the deadpan practical advice in the My Old Man and Our Old Man anecdotes. The old man's wisdom derives from Runyon's life in Pueblo. Thinking about how his stories had become repetitious, Our Old Man "could see that he must have told the same stories hundreds of times. He said he wondered why he had not met with foul play" ("As Time Goes By," ST 102). At times the iterative "he said" in those stories becomes inadvertently distancing, as when Our Old Man, outlines in "The Sobbing System" a taxonomy of how to get ahead in the world: those "who cried their way through life," those who hollered, those who flattered ("the oil system"), the "quiet bluff system," "the connection system," and the one he most admired, "the hard work system" (ST 103–6). Yet the categorizing does at least partially work because Our Old Man becomes a wisdom figure summarizing the conclusions of a lifetime of experience, one that includes hard knocks. With considerable irony at the expense of Our Old Man whose wisdom does not seem to have done him much good, the piece concludes: "Somebody asked Our Old Man if he had a system and he said no, but if things did not get better for him he was going to try two of them at once—crying and hollering" (ST 106). In the Broadway stories, to place the reader in the immediacy of the strange world he is presenting, Runyon omits the cumbersome "he said," uses direct quotes from narrators, and relies on the present tense.

Our Old Man is also a mask for Runyon, who fully understood the discrepancy between what we profess and how we behave. In "Live and Let Live," "Our Old Man said it was truly remarkable how much good advice he could think of to give his fellow men and how little of it he took himself. He said no man or woman who followed his advice to the letter could possibly fail of success in life, yet he remained pretty much of a failure because he was unable to take his own medicine" (ST 81). The advice he uses as his example is "do no favors and trust no one," and those are essential Runyon views (ST 81). But Our Old Man's cynicism is tempered with gentleness and forgiveness; even when women betray his trust, he never completely loses the illusion of trust and faithfulness, and "he considered the crossing-ups he had received at their hands just so many beautiful experiences" (ST 83). Runyon shares this mixture of feelings. He himself has some antediluvian ideas about the commodification of women. For example, his own behavior shows that he agrees with Our Old Man's thought in "Pleasing the Wife" that spending money to make one's wife beautiful was a worthy pursuit: "He said he feared many men regarded their wives as the least important of their possessions, else why would they take works of art like women and let their loveliness deteriorate through want of care and adornment?" (ST 92). While Runyon can be a male chauvinist, he often is quite sympathetic to women, as when in "Humoring the Little Women" he argues that "there were more bad husbands in the world than bad wives" (ST 86).

The Western stories bear great similarities to the Broadway stories. The Greenlight saloon, where disreputable characters hang out in "My Old Home Town," anticipates the New York hangouts. The psychology of character and the grammar of motive are the same. Greed, desire, love, and revenge drive the stories in both places. Reading in the Young Squirt stories about the excesses of "Halloweve Spirits" when property is stolen and damaged and people injured, we think of Runyon's rather jaundiced view of the mayhem wrought by supposed practical jokes in the Broadway stories: "Of course all this is nothing but youthful humor, and it is considered quite a laugh by one and all, except maybe a few parties who find their property eight or ten miles away from where it ought to be, and who feel a little bit crabby about it for a time" ("Halloweve Spirits," RFAL 228).

Runyon's persona has many aspects, from innocent spectator observing a small town in the West to a rogue. In the guise of a rogue, he is an inveterate gambler, consorts with gangsters, knows everyone's private secrets, and has a store of revealing insider anecdotes about corruption and double-dealing. He assumes that his audience is interested in this rogue world. His diverse audience has many components: those who would intimately know the characters and places of whom he speaks; those other New Yorkers and perhaps outer borough readers who would recognize them; those in the hinterlands for whom this world would be exotic, but who might yearn to be part of the New York world by visiting or who know something about those who live there; and those whose lives take place in a different world. At once an immigrant from the outside world and an established member of the inside world, Runyon does a masterful job at building rhetorical bridges to all these audiences.

Some of the occasional columns in *Short Takes* give us a sense of the audience for which Runyon imagined himself writing. He thinks of America as a vast aggregation of neighborhoods of which Broadway, Hollywood, Saratoga, and Brooklyn are just four. He assumes a commonality among these neighborhoods. My father, now ninety, is always saying "People are alike," meaning that we need to accept differences of personal and cultural behavior. Was that not the essence of the Roosevelt ideal in the 1930s? Defending in a hilarious piece entitled "Forceful Remarks" his view that "the good old-time punch-in-the-nose" was an excellent means "of settling arguments and differences of opinion," Runyon argues that rather than spreading violence, after "a brisk exchange of punches in (or at) the nose, the wind-up [was] a handshake and a renewal of friendship that rarely again suffered a fracture. The punch-in-the-nose was a wonderful cement and a great spreader of mutual respect" (ST 318). Advocating nose-punching subverts the expectations of respectability, as does the pun on "fracture." Runyon aligns minor macho violence not with division but with unity. Runyon's tongue-in-cheek hyperbole appeals to the sentiments of his imagined average Joe, but also reveals a subversive self that finds violent solutions appealing. Indeed, Runyon begins "Forceful Remarks" with his expression of regret on learning that Stalin did not bop his windy general over the head with a vodka bottle when the latter spoke at great length: "It would be a wonderful innovation if the toastmaster at every banquet was supplied with vodka bottle and given *carte blanche* by law to pass among the orators and belt them bow-legged at his discretion. It would make for shorter and perhaps more interesting banquet speeches" (ST 316).

Part of Runyon's appeal is that he says what his readers think, subverts respectability, and in his folksy, matter-of-fact way suggests that the unthinkable and outrageous may be worth considering. Runyon realizes that while his readers may not go to high-toned banquets, they have their own diet of retirement parties, family gatherings, mandatory holiday office parties, union meetings, bowling award nights, church and temple occasions, and monthly Elks and Lions club events.

In his daily 800-word columns, Runyon was a miniaturist in terms of the personal essay. He can take the most pedestrian subject and turn it into a subject of verbal peregrination. A typical comical subversive column is "Talking Turkey." Here he claims that America has been gulled to think of this bird as a holiday delicacy whereas chicken, duck, or goose is better: "[O]ur supposed national taste for turkey is the result of some intimidation. I mean our people who would rather be dead than out of fashion have been induced to believe that at certain seasons you either eat turkey or you are plumb out of style" (ST 304). Written during the war, this column puts him on the side of A. Muggs, the average Joe—including G.I. Joe—who is being told what he should eat: "Just now the newspapers and magazine vogue in turkey pictures is of soldiers nibbling at turkey meat with an implied relish that I can scarcely reconcile with what I hear of Army cooking . . ." (ST 304). Yet after making common cause with those who eat turkey, he then steps away and reports as an insider about how baby turkey is elegantly and deliciously prepared in elite restaurants such as the Colony in New York—"It is served at the Colony with a sauce composed of mustard and applesauce which may strike some of my readers as slightly bizarre but which I assure them is quite the thing" (ST 305)—or at Mike Romanoff's in Beverly Hills, as if these were just other neighborhoods he happened to frequent. But he wants not only to wink at his fellow insiders, but to share his experience—after assuring his audience that he still belongs to their world—of the elegant world he has the opportunity (because this is America!) to observe and take part in. Moreover, Runyon, gourmet and gourmand, was sure that love of food cuts across class and wealth lines.

Within the nonfiction columns the Runyonesque slang is the same as in the fiction. But the nonfiction columns are monologues driven by the persona's voice rather than the narrative and interspersed with the briefest of anecdotes. By his words, in his short columns he depicts himself as a man with a vast array of acquaintances from diverse walks of life as well as a theater and movie aficionado and a gambler. At times contemporary readers will find him a misogynist if not an abusive rascal, as when he speaks (even if jokingly)—as if he approved of such behavior—of a man giving his wife "a good rousting around" ("Leave Them and Love Them," ST 19, 25). His columns define a strong egotistical "I," but one whose audience is assumed to be working folk who share his perspective. Indeed, he gave voice to his readers—those he calls the "muggs"—who were often working-class people struggling to get to the middle class. Usually the humor is broad, as would befit a columnist who expected to be read by tabloid readers on a subway. In Runyon's acceptance of his own limitations, he writes in an appealing way with which his readers could identify: "[N]othing makes me madder when I am up against something I know is a physical or mental impossibility for me to accomplish than to have someone say: 'Oh, you can do it all right'" ("There Are Limitations," ST 64)

Runyon has a double optics; he sees himself as one of the naive common people who compose a large part of his imagined audience, and as someone who is sharing experiences that they have not had an opportunity to share. "Muggs" is an elastic term moving from all humans except the privileged social and economic elite to a specific group with whom he identifies. In his columns Runyon is materialistic—in "Magnificent Mammon," his advice to young people is "Get the money" (ST 55)—and cynical about human behavior: "Trust no one," he counsels the imaginary young man seeking advice and abstract values (ST 61). Defending his materialism, and thinking perhaps of his fellow transplanted Coloradian journalist Gene Fowler, who claimed indifference to money, "I am less spurious than those muggs who let on that their journalistic pursuits are guided by motives far above mere gold" ("The Insidious I," ST 2). (To be sure, it is just as likely that he does not have anyone particular in mind other than those colleagues who speak about journalism as a higher calling.) He contends that the materialistic standard of cultural quality rests with the public rather than the experts: "My measure of success is money. I have no interest in artistic triumphs that are financial losers" (ST 58). Yet "get the money" turns out to have some poignant wisdom beyond greed: "[T]hat is what I am talking about, money as a defense—a defense in youth against that irksome love in an attic or a housing project[,] in middle age against the petty laws and regulations that annoy Mr. and Mrs. Mugg, and in old age against fear and disrespect" (ST 57).

Thus, supposed freedom of speech is something one can enjoy if one has plenty of money, but otherwise, Runyon counsels, it is better to be quiet. Both freedom of speech and freedom of worship "are largely figurative and . . . carry restrictions" (ST 37). In "Free-loading Ethics," writing on free-loading from an extremely knowledgeable if not world-class perspective, he plays on the word "free." Indeed, he purports to be reporting on a discussion of free-loaders in which he took part or on which he was consulted as an authority: "A free-loader is a confirmed guest. He is the man who is always willing to come to dinner. . . . As a rule, a host likes to be agreed with or he would not be a host" (ST 306). Once again, within his reductive dichotomy and hyperbole, he speaks to recognizable neighborhood and experiential truth with which the audience can identify. We do not quarrel with our hosts, particularly if they are our bosses or ward or church leaders and are inviting us out of some sense of *noblesse oblige.* Runyon puts himself in the position of one who needs to toady to get the desired result, namely further invitations: "When the host is at the head of the table giving off gas, the free-loader should listen as attentively as possible, confining his own remarks to a few terse observations" (ST 307). Once again he opens up his microcosmic perspective—a discussion of a group of free-loaders—to a macrocosmic perspective when he turns to free-loading customs of Hollywood—a place that, prior to television and jet travel, might as well have been Frank Baum's Oz to most of middle America. But Runyon maintains a condescension that puts him with a foot in both the insider's and outsider's world: "The free-loading in Hollywood is supposed to be the best in the United States, especially in the private homes of the inmates of the movie capital. It is said that Hollywood preserves to a higher degree than any other community in the country the true science of cuisine in the home" (ST 308–9). Note how the passive tense of the second sentence and the dismissive term "inmates" separates the speaker from the veteran "old-time free-loader" who is Runyon's supposed firsthand source on Hollywood. This free-loader takes us back to the city where he has made his reputation and gives his readers a glimpse of his home base: "He said New York City is absolutely the tail-ender, bar Brooklyn. His mother lives in Brooklyn" (ST 309).

RECURRING THEMES IN RUNYON'S COLUMNS

Runyon's reporting and columns reflected his sense of how history's large and small events affected the middle class and working people. Americans in the 1920s favored spectacles, from heavyweight fights to Charles Lindbergh's flight, from the 1920 political conventions to horseracing, and Runyon lent hyperbole and color to most of the major ones. As John Mosedale puts it, "The war . . . left Americans avid for sensation and release. Some of that was restlessness."[20] Runyon helped create the legend of Jack Dempsey; in 1922 he intermittently wrote a series of pieces called "A Tale of Two Fists: The Life Story of Jack Dempsey." In the series he not only glorifies Dempsey but makes much of his former hobo life, a life that had something in common with Runyon's own youthful memories. Runyon's descriptions of the September 22, 1927, second Dempsey-Tunney fight in Chicago was part of the massive chorus of attention it received: "Down on the canvas for the first time in his boxing career, sniffing at the resin dust there, with the murderous old Manassa Man Mauler glowering over him with evil intent, Gene Tunney, the fighting marine, got up and carried to victory. . . . Once he got to his feet, Tunney began running backward as only a skillful boxer in distress knows how to run, back, back, back he went with the glowering Dempsey fairly growling in anger."[21] It is as if the boxer were the coward and the slugger the aggressor whose desserts are undermined by wily skills barely appropriate for a heavyweight champion: "Then, as calmly as a delicatessen owner slicing up his bologna he proceeded to cut Dempsey up with his spearing left."[22] Runyon favored his friend Dempsey—in 1922 he had been the only reporter invited on Dempsey's European trip—over the educated and socially connected Tunney.

Runyon was not only fascinated with racehorses and gambling on them but also with the naiveté and stupidity of horseplayers, including himself. Gambling on horses was a source of some of his most humorous columns. For Runyon horseracing is a metaphor for life; the effort to predict the future—effort motivated by greed—is a major focus. We develop elaborate systems for beating the odds, when, of course, finally, we all surrender to the condition of mortality and aging. "Just Dreamers" begins: "A fellow has come up with a system for beating the races based on dreams"; if nothing conforms to the dream, one does not bet. Runyon then segues into an "adviser" (a euphemism for tout) friend of his, now in the armed services, named Horse Thief Burke who used to give tips supposedly based on his nightmares; of course, Burke never runs out of horses for each race. Runyon concludes the piece of about 600 words with how he himself stabbed a pin into a list of Kentucky Derby entries only to pick a terrible horse; on the other side of the page was a bank advertisement: "Save your money" (ST 172).

Characteristically the piece unfolds from a somewhat impersonal discovery to a memory of a racetrack friend who at first appears to have done something similar except the friend was illegally hustling others to bet for him. In telling us about Burke, Runyon reminds us that America is at war but that Burke is not much of a soldier, in part because his focus is on horses and "burlesque beauts" (ST 171). Runyon then returns to systems of beating the horses. A rather loose association holds the piece together until we realize that even in the army Burke seeks an advantage, writing in praise of his "officers" just in case they are reading his mail (ST 171).

A gambler himself and someone familiar with the gambling culture of western saloons, Runyon assumed that his audience of blue- and white-collar working people hoped to win a bonanza by a stroke of good luck in gambling. He assumed many of them visited racetracks or regularly bet with bookmakers. In "Where to Find the Common Man," Runyon concludes with his friend Good Time Charley Friedman's comment: "I often wondered why people go broke at the race track. . . . Now I know. It is because they are always trying to pick something to beat the best horses" (ST 161). In "No Justice," subtitled "Monologue of a Horse Player (*transcribed from life*)," Runyon begins: "What did I ever do to anybody? Why can't I win? . . . I try to live right. I never stole nothing. Why can't I win?" Job-like, the player pathetically seeks answers to his plight, returning to the refrain: "What did I ever do to anybody? . . . Why can't I win?" (ST 167–68). Following Jonathan Swift, Runyon enjoys the irony of anthropomorphizing horses, as if bettors could win more if they could discover the way horses behave: "Race horses, like human beings, are creatures of habit. They are easily taught to do certain things in a certain way and most of them (horses and humans) go on doing those certain things in that certain way all their lives, without questioning" ("The Thinking Equines," ST 179). In "Horse Sense," Runyon imagines an old racehorse speaking poignantly about his plight as he moves from one owner to another because his original owner will not let him retire gracefully as a successful stakes horse: "I had earned retirement. But he ran me in a claiming race and since then I have gone from barn to barn, always dropping lower in racing class as my legs got worse. I hope that owner feels ashamed when he sees me now. I wish him all the humiliation I have felt myself as I have gone lower and lower. But none of my physical pain. I would not wish that on a dog" (ST 177).

In his later years Runyon became a high stakes gin rummy player, perhaps in part because he recognized and embraced the strong element of luck: "Gin Rummy is scarcely the game the old-fashioned pro gambler would pick as a specialty because the element of luck figures in it so strongly that even a rank sucker at cards has some sort of a chance if given as square rattle" ("Two Gamblers," ST 189). Note how Runyon writes as an insider familiar with the discourse of gambling, even as he shares these terms and wisdom with the audience of his nationally syndicated column, an audience for whom this kind of talk is exotic: "I think the real advantage in high stakes gin is with the player who best carries weight, which is to say who plays just as calmly for two dollars a point as he would for a penny a point" (ST 190). It may be that Runyon helped export gin rummy to the rest of the country.

Runyon enjoyed risk; he gambled illegally in the back rooms of restaurants and enjoyed recalling how, when he and his friends were tipped off, they knew how to destroy evidence ("The Law Elbows

In," ST 193–96). Always impressed with the sight of large amounts of cash, he enjoys sharing his insider's knowledge of high stakes gambling at which he had been at least a partial participant: "Another friend of mine (my goodness, Runyon, what strange friends you have!) was sneaking a wheel into a Park avenue apartment some years ago, meaning he was operating a roulette game for a few selected customers . . ." (ST 195). Always on the side of those who flummox the police, he is amused that "the boys" are tipped off in advance.

In the 1930s and 1940s, Runyon began to express strong political opinions in his columns, perhaps in response to his rival Winchell's interest in politics. He always favored what he thought of as the interests of the little guy, represented, as we shall see, by his fictitious upwardly striving Brooklyn couple the Turps, who, in fact, discuss whether Roosevelt should run for a third term in a January 1940 column. Winchell was a Roosevelt and New Deal booster in the 1930s, but by the 1940s he became increasingly skeptical of big government when he thought it was intruding on the individual's rights. Runyon's characteristic mixture of cynicism and idealism inform his politics. But Runyon realized that, as Kennedy put it, "the conditions of life and work were markedly better at the decade's [the 1930s] end than at its beginning, and the improvement was due in no small measure to the success of the union movement"—and Runyon knew that his columns were read by union members, the little people with whom he sided.[23]

Runyon's children's stories are really adult stories; they are an outlet for his fantasy and perhaps rehearsals for the rapid plot reversal of his more sustained stories. Although Runyon occasionally idealizes children in his Broadway stories, the dramatized persona of his hilarious tongue-in-cheek anecdotes about children is deliberately a streetwise figure who has little idea of what children are about. Yet these columns are also wonderful spoofs of conventional children's stories and of the kind of nonsense some adults tell children. Indeed, in *Short Takes,* within the section entitled "For Children Only" is a fable of how the Stork Club got its name. A man named Billingsley (the Stork Club's real owner) found Louie the Stork drunk in the street with a leftover baby that he had not delivered to the right address; Billingsley set up a place for Louie to organize more efficiently his baby-delivering assignments under the auspices of Walter Winchell. Of course, Runyon's fable of Louie the Stork as a heavy drinker who delivers babies to the wrong address is, as he well knew, hardly what children need hear to help them feel loved and to build their self-esteem. But isn't that the point of a Runyon children's story that mocks the very sentimental and silly essence of some contemporary children stories?

In "Phooey and Louie" Runyon writes about a pigeon who poses as Louie the Stork to get a reward for delivering a baby, and chooses a larger baby than he can carry to be sure he gets the reward he expects. The baby is too large for Phooey, who collapses; with a wink at how to bet on horses by keeping in mind the weight of the jockey, the speaker concludes: "So the moral is, kids, never try to carry too much weight" (ST 353). Isn't Runyon's sardonic point that any child old enough to read the kind of prose he is writing should have other explanations than a stork for procreation?

Another of the columns collected in *Short Takes* under the title "For Children Only" is about a Paul Bunyansque soldier named Algernon who makes other marines resentful because he kills all the enemy troops before the other soldiers get there: "[I]t seems when he landed on an island where there were Japs Algernon would first uproot a coconaut tree of perhaps 100 feet in height, trim it neatly, leaving just a sort of natural crotch in the shape of a hook at one end and then as he nabbed the Japs would string them on this tree as he used to string catfish on a willow twig when he was a boy living in a town on the Big Muddy" ("Algernon," ST 355). Choosing for his Herculean hero the most effeminate and least likely name, Runyon is undoubtedly thinking of Oscar Wilde's Algernon in *The Importance of Being Earnest* and perhaps the first name of the British poet Swinburne. Runyon's high-spirited hyperbolic humor is in the American (and especially) Western tradition of the tall tale; he imagines rural America in reductive terms. In the second Algernon incident, Runyon's hero has a confrontation with "Stuporman" and "Trash Boardman" and, after feeling their muscles, sits down to laugh at their pretension. Not only do they go away, but Algernon's Bunyanesque—Runyon would have enjoyed the homophonic resonance between Runyon and Bunyan—laughter causes a slight earthquake.

Runyon's illness revealed a poignant yet attractive vulnerability. His columns on his illness, some of which are collected in *Runyon From First to Last* as "Written in Sickness" and in *Short Takes* as "On Being Sick," are excruciatingly honest and moving. He is everyman asking for sympathy, even while knowing it will not help. Indeed, Runyon's eloquence and directness as his life slowly ebbed would have been particularly striking to an audience that was, as many of us born in the 1930s and 1940s recall, culturally educated not to speak about such things.

Yet his prolonged final illness is also the cause of his retreating into himself. For example, in "A Dog's Best Friend," he uses the occasion to express his anger, bitterness, and, yes, self-pity by comparing how his dog "did not sidle away when I was ill, in the manner of many human beings from whom I thought I had the right to expect at least an inquiry. Their desertion made me a little sour for a time " (ST 279). Since humanity is composed "of 80 per cent jerks," and since "the first law of human nature is self-preservation," "I should have known what would happen because I have seen it happen to others a thousand times before, not only in illness but in other bad luck" (ST 279). He speaks misanthropically of "human rats," like real rats, deserting a sinking ship; real rats, he cynically observes, are better guessers, for the human rats "often go tearing away from a ship that manages to stay afloat and then they have to sneak back and ingratiate themselves into a berth again" (ST 280). If dogs are man's best friends, he suggests, it may be because man rarely is up to the task; indeed, dogs, he implies, should not count on man. But he keeps Nubbin, his "very sick little dog," with him because "I too have been very ill and I know how lonesome one can get in illness" (ST 279). Rather poignantly, Runyon identifies with the dog, whom he has objectified as a version of himself: "I remember how she has always loved the company of human beings, the sound of human conversation, and how responsive she has always been to a word or even a look" (ST 279).

Reflecting his Western individualistic heritage, Runyon believes less in community projects than in how individuals treat one another. "A Dog's Best Friend" lacks irony and is a scathing indictment of those who allow friends to wither on the vine when they need help. Comparing humans unfavorably to dogs and even rats expresses Runyon's dismay at how humans treat their fellows. More and more, Runyon cynically believes that a good deed will generate resentment in someone and that humans behave badly when their fellows most need them. Thus, "A Dog's Best Friend" ends not only with a recollection of how the "great theatrical producer" Charles Dillingham was "broke and commencing to be forgotten along the big street"—that is, Broadway—but also with a reference to someone he felt had been wrongfully maligned and deserted by all but one of his friends (ST 280).

Runyon shared with his readers the space of his mind for years in his columns; he is a friend, an average mugg like themselves, who has been reporting about the cosmopolitan world in columns and stories. He has been a part of their fantasy world, and suddenly he becomes a man in deep trouble. "Why Me?" begins: "When physical calamity befalls, the toughest thing for the victim to overcome is the feeling of resentment that it should have happened to me" (ST 364). He enlarges the horizon of the question "Why Me?": "It is a question that has been asked by afflicted mortals through the ages. It is being asked more than ever just now as the maimed men come back from war broken in body and spirit and completely bewildered, asking 'Why me?'" (ST 365).

Although Runyon was twice married to Catholics, he was not interested at all in religion or spirituality (even though he once flirted with the idea of converting before learning how difficult it would be). Yet in "Why Me?," he invokes the story of Job, concluding with Job's words of humility: "*Therefore have I uttered that I understood not; things too wonderful for me, which I knew not*" (ST 367). In these columns he made common cause with all who suffer and dropped his ironic mask to share with his readers his humble, frightened self. In "Why Me?" we have no references to cosmopolitan doings; Runyon's verbal world—now spare and sparse without his usual digressions—like Job's world of things, is stripped bare.

At times Runyon can barely force himself to look beyond his own plight. In "The Doctor Knows Best," he writes of the loneliness and isolation of illness. He speaks of a man in pain going to a doctor who cannot find the pain and thinks after seeing the x-rays and offering a variety of cures that the man is a hypochondriac. His wife, too, is sure the pain is in the man's imagination. When the man dies, his wife and family are indignant; in the concluding line, Runyon adds, "The doctor is in a bit of a huff about the man dying that way" (ST 369).

In his final columns, Runyon becomes preoccupied with dying. In "Sweet Dreams," he writes, "A man is usually born in bed, and spends at least half of his life in bed. If he is lucky, he dies in bed. We used to think that the best place to die was on the battle field, face to the foe, etc., but that was when we were much younger and more casual about dying" (ST 379). In "No Life," he writes about gradually receiving a doctor's stipulations—no orange juice, or grapefruit, or coffee, or sugar, or candy, or any sweets, or spiced food, no herring, gefilte fish, goulash, salami, seasoned Italian food, and, finally, cigarettes. Runyon was a man who lived on coffee and cigarettes. He poignantly concludes, "Doc, a guy might as well be dead, hey?" (ST 372).

After Runyon's April 1944 operations to remove his malignant larynx, he could no longer speak. His frankness about his disability takes place in a world where such infirmities either are not discussed or are discussed only in whispers behind the victim's back: "Since I lost my voice or about 90 per cent of its once bell-like timbre, I have discovered many inconveniences as well as some striking conveniences" ("Passing the Word Along," ST 382). A man who had once the cachet of a movie star, Runyon is reduced to virtual silence. He takes the position of one who is handicapped: "The hale and hearty shun the afflicted and I cannot say I blame them much" (ST 384). On one hand, we hear Runyon's irrepressible spirit—a sense that we start where are. But on the other hand, we also hear some self-pity and bitterness: "Maybe it would be better for all concerned if I did not try to talk at all because everybody else is talking these days and I would not be missed" (ST 384). He poignantly describes how he communicates by note pad and how his friends begin searching for spectacles while "[T]hey invariably have some fatuous remark to make about getting old as if I did not know by just looking at them or remembering how long I have known them" (ST 386). His misogynist strain peeks through in his final months, as he snidely concludes that he doesn't use pad and pencil with "dames," because most are "near-sighted since infancy and too vain to wear cheaters" and "not all of them can read"—perhaps thinking bitterly about his second wife Patrice's separating her life from his and eventually divorcing him when he most needed her (ST 386). Surely even in the 1940s, his women readers would have found this more offensive than funny.

On occasion, especially when the subject is an anecdote about celebrities, one might wonder what was so appealing about some columns. But that is to forget the star quality of Runyon as performer and entertainer sharing his glamorous world. Living in a world of glitter, lights, and excitement, he was a surrogate for his readers. His are the words of a man of vast experience sharing with acquaintances—or indeed friends developed from years of one-way dialogue—what he has seen. And one can understand the excitement of his audience when hearing about a celebrity like Al Jolson, a megastar who captivated audiences in every city in which he appeared and who, at the age of forty-one, was the star in 1927 of the first talking motion picture, *The Jazz Singer.* Even a rather pedestrian column about an interview with the aged champion boxer John L. Sullivan in which Sullivan often fades into the background evoked a legendary name for his readers. Runyon's newspaper friends were figures in their own right whose names elicited curiosity: Arthur Brisbane, the front page columnist of the *American,* whom he calls "Mr. Brisbane," or Irvin Cobb, whom he met first as rewrite man and who became a minor literary figure and was known among writers as a great trencherman. To be sure, some of his columns, such as "Breakfast at Lindy's," seem as much name-dropping as substance (ST 207–210). Perhaps the latter is interesting because "Little Nig" from that column turns up in the Broadway stories. While for us such a column is dated, no doubt sharing his New York world was a source of excitement to his audience.

MY OLD MAN

My Old Man (New York: Stackpole Sons, 1939) is a collection of the columns with that title on a variety of subjects, from "On Literature," the opening advisory column, to "On Indulging Wives," the final one—with thirty-three others in between. They purport to be the advice given to Amos Mugg by his father. Each begins with the phrase "My Old Man." These anecdotes have a naive utopian strain that contrasts with the worldliness and cynicism of Runyon's New York stories and columns.

The My Old Man columns alternate homespun philosophy and ingenuousness with toughness and cynicism, but the tone is more gentle than in the *In Our Town* stories. As Patricia Ward D'itri puts it, "Whereas My Old Man derides pretension and exposes hypocrisy with a sham *mea culpa* attitude that the narrator occasionally exposes, in *In Our Town* he makes no attempt to excuse or explain the violence, greed and hypocrisy that are only occasionally interspersed with acts of kindness, generosity, or courage" (*Damon Runyon,* New York: Twayne, 1982, 47–48).[24] My Old Man is the closest Runyon comes to a version of the myth of the American pastoral, the notion of the West as a simpler world of, to recall "America the Beautiful," "spacious skies" and "amber waves of grain." The concept of "Homespun" represented a mythic pastoral version of an orderly premodern way of life based on household production: the farmer in his field; his wife at her spinning wheel or in her kitchen; craftsmen, like cobblers and blacksmiths, in their small shops; and children in little red schoolhouses. But Runyon also realized that this pastoral myth ignored the poverty and harshness of much rural life in the West.

The old man concludes the opening essay of *My Old Man* entitled "On Literature" by asserting that the most "beautiful" sentence that he had read was "The Lord is my Shepherd; I shall not want," a sentiment that sounds a far different note than we hear in Runyon's stories and many of his columns (MOM 14). The anecdotes in *My Old Man* have considerably fewer slang terms and neologisms than many of Runyon's columns and especially the stories narrated by Runyon's Broadway voice. My Old Man dislikes all kinds of hypocrisy, including claiming someone who recently died was better than he was and forgetting that he was "petty and mean" ("On the Dear Departed," MOM 19). In his war against nonsense, My Old Man attacks foolish proverbs and shibboleths such as "everything happens for the best" (IOT 28) or that "early to bed and early to rise . . . would make men healthy, wealthy, or wise" ("On Sayings," MOM 28–29).

The narrator recounts: "My Old Man said many old sayings had established false hopes and wholly erroneous impressions of life in the minds of a lot of people" ("On Sayings," MOM 29). My Old Man also has a macrocosmic view of politics: "[H]e knew from reading history that there never had been a time when the country was not teetering on the brink of an abyss and never a time when free government was not on the wane on account of that fellow, whoever he was, in the White House" ("On Teetering," MOM 31).

The My Old Man stories remind us that Runyon had many masks. Like Oscar Wilde, he knew we are most ourselves when we tell lies about our own exploits. Runyon would have agreed with Wilde that imaginative writers are wonderful liars: "[A] good colorful liar . . . was just a fiction writer who never got a chance to immortalize himself in print" ("On Liars," MOM 35). However, he exempts from his generosity to liars both mean-spirited lying that hurts others and lies in political campaign.

My Old Man is Runyon's mask for moral rectitude without humbug. My Old Man is a resident of Pueblo, Colorado, but in these stories is often a kind of gentle Norman Rockwellian small-town philosopher rather than a ruffian from a violent frontier outpost. The very qualities for which Runyon praises Alf Landon in his November 1935 article in *Cosmopolitan* entitled "Horse and Buggy Governor" are some of the qualities that My Old Man exemplifies and admires in others—and indeed qualities to which Runyon himself aspires: "He employs human language, often interlarding his speech with slang expressions and occasionally a good solid oath. He is a essentially man of the people and of sound American background. . . . He knows what he wants to say and says it without forensic flourish" (*Cosmopolitan* 173). While Runyon enjoyed ethnic variety, his barometer is the often idealized West in which he grew up.

My Old Man gives Runyon a chance to share his homespun wisdom and to define his values by creating an alter ego and moral surrogate. Runyon is most at home when he is debunking. Often after his Old Man pontificates, Runyon pulls the rug from under him. Thus after the narrator reports his father's wisdom on conscience and his leniency toward sexual peccadilloes, he concludes: "Somebody asked . . . how he came to be such an authority on conscience, and he got sore. He said he was not on the witness stand" ("On Sinners," MOM 49). And we learn that some homespun fellows are frauds for whom "that homespun stuff" was put on to hide an inferiority complex, while the genuine homespun—presumably including himself, although he is amazingly well read (as we learn in "On Literature," the first entry of the volume)—"might be illiterate" but had dignity and pride in his appearance ("On Homespun Fellows," MOM 65). The Old Man's wisdom is a strange conflicted combination of Puritanism and tolerance, and at times his son, the narrator who approvingly reports his father's wisdom, represents that conflict within both the father and son.

In "On Cowardice," My Old Man's point is that everyone is afraid, and most men are glad to find a fellow coward who does not want to fight. He himself admits to being afraid of the Boogie man as both a child and an adult. But it is hardly credible, as he claims, that he "never went out in public except wearing thick eyeglasses and one hand in a sling and limping a little" because he was afraid someone would think he was brave and want to fight him (MOM 86). His hyperbole is often qualified by self-knowledge and humility; while it is doubtful, as he claims, that he has read billions of words, he does know from the Pueblo library that "he had little more than nibbled at the world's output of words"; of course we know that the library had more than a tiny fraction of the world's English words ("On Literature," MOM 11).

In *My Old Man,* Runyon also enacts troubling events from his past. After the narrator's father is particularly harsh if not pontifical toward those who abuse wives and children—for them, he "favored a revival of the pillory and the stocks of Puritanical days as punishment"—the narrator reveals Runyon's own resentment ("On Sinners," MOM 49). Runyon himself knew what it was to live with an irresponsible parent after his mother died. When the Old Man's son reminds his father that "I could not remember that he had busted any suspenders looking after my welfare," his father does acknowledges his culpability (MOM 49).

Indeed, family values and relations between husbands and wives as well as children and parents—neither Runyon's nor his father's strong suit—occupy much of My Old Man's attention. In "On Cuteness," My Old Man "used to say that one thing he hoped was that he would not live long enough for his children to go around telling 'cute' stories on him" (MOM 99). Like Runyon, My Old Man is often disillusioned with women and the likelihood of successful marriage and successful parenting, but he does hold out the possibility of good marriages and child-parent relations.

Much in the My Old Man columns and the Turps stories is antithetical to the criminal chic of the Broadway stories. In the former, violence more likely takes the form of a punch in the nose than killing enemies with guns. The macho gangster code of the stories takes a back seat to an honest awareness of fear. When the speaker's father was in the army, "He said he used to fashion in his frightened fancy, sinister figures out of every distant bush. He said when there was any fighting he was always too benumbed from fear to recollect afterwards what had occurred" ("On Cowardice," MOM 8). The variety of Runyon's personae and the diverse kinds of intimate sharing create a bond between Runyon and his readers.

Characteristically, Runyon intersperses opinions with brief anecdotes in the My Old Man columns, often in this case anecdotes from his own life. My Old Man is not a consistent character, but he is attractively human with flaws and foibles that are often in disjunction with his absolutist advice. He speaks in the past tense; on the whole, he is not as lively as Joe Turp or as funny as Joe's wife, Ethel. Due to the Old Man's self-criticism, humility, optimism, and tolerance, these columns lack the combination of wordiness, cynicism, and high spirits of the Runyon voice in other columns and stories. These columns express an underlying seriousness with a strong scent of morality, especially in the one entitled "On Growing Old."

Runyon's own complexity enacts that of Times Square, which, contrary to its earthy image, includes, according to William R. Taylor, "polarities of piety and prurience, of clergy and impresarios, of gimlet eye reformers and starry-eyed performers—each using the other for inspiration."[25] My Old Man's preachiness and piety represent that other side of Broadway culture, the one we see dramatized in the Salvation Army presence on Times Square.

IN OUR TOWN

In Our Town spoke to the postwar nostalgia for a simpler America, one that could make simple moral distinctions. Murray Schumach of the *New York Times* praised the short collection of twenty-seven brief anecdotes, some as short as 400 words, few longer than 800 words: "The cynical humor that spoofs at stuffed shirtism and simplicity of style, the sympathy for the underdog and the plots that break like a fast curve—they are all here. . . . There is a quality of the good vignette to these tales, which, in sum, gives a better picture of small town life and pace than many weightier sociological tomes."[26] Even the spare, laconic prose speaks nostalgically to a time when, within Runyon's mythic West of yore, excessive verbiage was not necessary.

Yet, as if the Depression and international turmoil had polluted innocence, the third person narrator has a bitter edge. This omniscient narrator, intimately aware of the goings-on in Our Town, writes as moral historian of the foibles of his fellow denizens, and he does so mostly in the past tense. Interestingly, Runyon usually uses the characteristic present tense of his Broadway stories when the characters move to New York City.

The brief caricatures of small-town life in "Our Town" recall the world of Norman Rockwell. Runyon looks back nostalgically to a simpler world, but—unlike Rockwell's and following a tradition in American literature that included Mark Twain, William Faulkner, and Sherwood Anderson—his nostalgia is qualified by a hard-edged and cynical perspective. Runyon is amused by but not unsympathetic to the way that dreams provide sustaining fictions in a difficult world and how dreams are manufactured on the thinnest thread of evidence that a horse will come in or that a scheme will come to fruition.

Runyon's nostalgic evocation of the American frontier and its simpler world at first seems to give his readers a pastoral myth. Like the Turps stories, the Western stories depend on implicit juxtaposition to the world of sophisticates in New York. Yet Runyon reveals that underneath people are similar, some decent, some predatory, and many a mixture of both. Based on a fictional version of Pueblo, Colorado, a world he evokes without New York hype but with his characteristic sardonic hyperbole, Runyon focuses on the small virtues, idiosyncrasies, and vices of the title figures of his anecdotes. While many of these figures maintain their integrity in the face of trying circumstances, others act mean-spiritedly after they reach their breaking point.

Each anecdote is given the name of its principal figure, beginning with the one entitled "Our Old Man"—published in *My Old Man* as "On Good Turns"—which revolves around the credo of the fictional narrator's father: "Never Blame the Booster for What the Sucker Does"—a motto that informs the entire collection: "[Our Old Man] said it meant that you should never hold a fellow responsible for the consequences of an effort to do you a nice turn" (IOT 3). It turns out that the folk of Our Town are just as corrupt and venal as in any city, and that people are no different in one place from another. In Runyon's small-town world women are abused, good deeds often go unappreciated, misers hoard money, and violence never lurks far from the surface.

The world of Our Town has a full share of wife-beaters, weasels, cheats, hypocrites, and eccentrics as well as a relatively few decent people who care about others. In the second story we hear about Samuel Graze, a huge man who beats his wife until "he wore her down to sixty pounds"; one night after he came home drunk, beat her, and fell asleep, she tied him up and beat him to death (IOT 10). She was given a reprimand, "although some thought it was setting a bad example to the other women in Our Town whose husbands like to give them a beating now and then" (IOT 11).

Coming from an impoverished background and requiring a good deal of money for his gambling, clothes, homes, and travels, Runyon believed in the power of the dollar to pave the road to happiness. In "The Happiness Jones," the rest of the town resents that the Joneses not only won the lottery but also, contrary to expectations, do not quarrel over the money even though different family members had contributed different amounts toward the winning ticket: "In fact, they were happier than ever, because they now had enough money for all their needs, and they did not have to scrimp and save" (IOT 28). Runyon had a strong distaste for penuriousness. In "Jeremiah Zore," because Jeremiah Zore's miserly father wouldn't pay the cost of lighting up the building that he constructed as a monument to himself, his son, Jonathan Zore, a famous aviator, crashes his plane when coming to visit his father and dies.

The anecdotes are often parables and folk tales that illustrate a point, perhaps a cynical one about human nature. For example, in

"Doc Brackett," the doctor was a "fine man" who doctored the poor, even taking care of a sick Mexican child on his wedding day with the result that his bride canceled the wedding in a pique. He remained a bachelor who "liked to drink whiskey and play poker in the back rooms of saloons" (IOT 36). But Brackett never turned anyone away for lack of means, and when he died and discussion dragged on about an appropriate tombstone, the Mexican child's parents put on his grave his sign, "Dr. Brackett, Office upstairs."

With "Doc Brackett," Runyon found himself accused of plagiarism; in 1946 he received a letter telling him that the story originated with Dr. James Bell Naylor.[27] In fact, Runyon often gave shape and form to anecdotes that he had been told as a boy.

Many of the citizens of Our Town, like Pete Hankins, the subject of the third anecdote, migrate to New York. In Pete's case, because of the death of the laundryman for whom he was the driver, Pete becomes a New York City taxi driver, and a good and honest one. But with four children, he "has a tough time getting along" ("Pete Hankins," IOT 13). In Runyon's spare, understated style, he makes Pete the most sympathetic of characters. He has a sign in his cab, "honesty is the best policy," and preaches that motto to his son. Driving his car on a particularly cold night at 2:00 A.M. with icicles on his mustache, he picks up a wealthy couple who accuse him of trying to swindle them, even though he had gone only 6 cents of fare out of the way to avoid "bad streets." During the dispute the woman of the couple called him "ignorant" (IOT 15). After finding a purse with $2,000 in his car belonging to the very couple who insulted him, and seeking to return it, Pete goes in vain to the club where he dropped them off; finally, he drives around from club to club "all over town" until he finds them (IOT 16). When he gives her the purse, the woman suspiciously counts her money without saying thank you or giving him a small tip: "He thought they should have offered to pay him for the gas he had used up looking for them" (IOT 15).

Because the migration from Our Town to New York mirrored his own life change, Runyon was fascinated with it and retold it in many forms. Even in the *In Our Town* stories, Runyon's Broadway world is often present. Pete Hankins drops his wealthy fares off at

Jimmy Kelly's in Greenwich Village, pursues them uptown to El Morocco, and finds them at Club 18. Others who migrate to New York include the policeman Freddie Lipscomber, who ruefully learns the folly of "putting himself in the other fellow's place" before making an arrest ("Officer Lipscomber," IOT 40). He learns the lesson of being overly charitable after being tricked and humiliated by a burglar who convinces him that he, the burglar, is the storeowner making a withdrawal from the cash register.

Another anecdote focuses on a move from Our Town to New York by the sisters Marigold and Maidie So. Marigold misses her chance for love because she lives in a fantasy world—what Runyon calls elsewhere Dream Street—while Maidie lives in the here and now and marries a roughneck with money but a roughneck she apparently can manage. That the sisters have the odd last name So plays on the proverb "We reap what we sow." In another anecdote of a change from Our Town to New York, the forty-year-old widow Mrs. Pilplay no sooner moves than she goes to places to rumba and even pays the tab for her male partners. When she is running out of money, she finds Julius, a sixty-six-year-old millionaire. After she teaches him the rumba, he runs off with a cigarette girl. Runyon's cynical lesson, perhaps applicable to both Julius and Mrs. Pilplay: "[I]t is silly to teach an old dog new tricks" ("Mrs. Pilplay," IOT 62).

Runyon not only believed in the power of money, but he also was certain of the ingratitude of most people, particularly when it came to monetary generosity. Dr. Davenport arrived in Our Town fresh from medical school with a little money. He treated needy patients for free and never pressed the others. When the Depression came and his resources were wiped out, he tried to collect on the more than $123,000 he was owed, but his bills were ignored. Finally, near starvation, he borrowed a gun from a policeman and "went around to the citizens who owed him money, and told each and every one that he would blow their heads off if they did not pay him at once" ("Dr. Davenport," IOT 74). The narrator bemusedly reports that by nightfall Dr. Davenport had collected $6,876.70.

Of course, Dr. Davenport's reputation suffered among "the better class," who "said a doctor who expected to get paid for his services must be crazy" (IOT 75). In a typical cynical Runyonesque ending, the narrator reminds us that good intentions and generosity may have odd consequences. Mr. Wheeler had borrowed seventy cents from Dr. Davenport to purchase rat poison to commit suicide; Mrs. Wheeler was "always felt grateful to Dr. Davenport for that even though she had neglected to pay him back the money" (IOT 75).

COLLIER'S SKETCHES

In summer 1936 *Collier's* published three very brief sketches about local characters that were not published in *In Our Town* but in *More Guys and Dolls:* "Burge McCall" (July 11), "Lou Louder" (August 8), and "Joe Terrace" (August 29). All three have the hard-edged cynical humor of the *In Our Town* sketches. Perhaps because they were slightly longer than the *In Our Town* pieces, Runyon could sell them to *Collier's.* Among other things, they reveal something about gallows humor during the Depression and the willingness of a popular magazine like *Collier's* to cater to that humor with sketches that are far less funny to us than Runyon's other stories.

Twice married and twice divorced Burge McCall, another citizen of Our Town, hates his wife, comes home drunk, and spends his ample salary on himself and other women. After Burge slaps his wife, she gets her brother-in-law to tell Burge that she bought a pound of rat poison "to poison a big rat" (MGAD 51); seeing that his house has no rats, Burge completely changes his behavior. He begins to eat out for fear of being poisoned at home; he stops drinking because he "wanted to be in full possession of all his faculties at all times" (MGAD 52); and he begins to take his wife out so he can have her in his sights. The comic result it that the McCall couple becomes close and affectionate. The story is a reductive parable about how fear and self-interest on the part of both Burge and his wife—who in fact hadn't bought poison—drive not only proximity but intimacy.

In "Lou Louder," a story that reminds us of the Broadway noir world of Runyon's most violent stories, sexual intimacy is tightly linked to death. Ill with tuberculosis and expecting not to live long, Lou went out West to Our Town. The bartender of the Greenlight saloon there, he is the target of a planned killing by the Baker brothers, each of whom wants to kill him because they have both been told by Pabalita Duke—the young Mexican wife of Shalimar, the much older and well-liked owner of the Commercial Hotel—that Lou has insulted her; the brothers don't know that Lou, like themselves, is having an affair with her. Lou has been warned by friends to be on the ready. Since the Baker brothers aren't speaking to one another, their plans to kill Lou are separate. While both Bakers are drinking at the bar in the Greenlight saloon, Shalimar is killed by a thrown knife. After the brothers are jailed, the citizens hang Joe Baker; thinking he is saving his brother Sid, Joe accepts the vigilante action, saying to the mob, "I deserve my fate" (MGAD 55). At the same time another mob hangs Sid; hoping to save Joe, he confesses. It turns out that the knife that killed Shalimar—who was at the bar with a gun to kill Lou—was thrown by Pabalita after Lou had written her that he didn't want to see her any more. Lou survives another thirty years.

"Joe Terrace," the final dark story in the *Collier's* miniseries, is the name of a linotype operator at the town newspaper, the *Morning Chief.* He took his wife, who always tried to please him, out to Lover's Leap and "hit her on the head with a rock and knocked her off the cliff" (MGAD 58). Everyone in Our Town thought it was an accident until, while setting the type for the Reverend John Clee's weekly sermon, Joe bizarrely inserted a line, "Please, Lord, forgive me for what I did to Tubby" (MGAD 59). Everyone besides the humorously named Sheriff Letch—in this case resonating with the vernacular "ketch" as in "ketch" or "catch" a culprit—who was regularly denounced by Clee as disreputable, finds Clee's sermons too boring to read. But Letch, because he made a bet with a friend that he would find a typographical error, sees the confession, arrests Joe, and gets reelected. Runyon the newspaperman enjoys the joke about the sheriff who reads the sermons for typos, not for content. If Runyon's moral is about how a guilty conscience reveals its secrets, the story is none too convincing because it fails to probe Terrace's psyche.

That in each of these three cynical sketches someone—the McCalls, Lou Louder, the sheriff who discovers Joe Terrace's crime—emerges better off than at the beginning shows Runyon's touch of sentiment. Perhaps in "Lou Louder" and "Joe Terrace," we can see Runyon's smiling at the law of inadvertent consequences. And indeed that law applies to our view of Runyon, whose macho stories often reveal a hint of a softer and what his readers would regard as a more feminine side.

RUNYON'S POEMS

Written primarily for his blue-collar and lower-middle-class, white-collar, working-class audience, Runyon's poems were basically part of his journalism. His intended audience, as with much of his writing, seems to be more male than female, and his poems in particular take up male subjects of sports and gambling. They belong to an oral tradition of tale-telling and ballads and are often written in dialect. Runyon not infrequently incorporated his verse into his newspaper columns. In his last days, he was editing *Poems for Men* (1947), and the book was published posthumously. As Clark Kinnaird notes in the preface, "It is possible that if Runyon himself had determined the contents, some of the verses would have been replaced with others that were omitted, or a smaller number included."[28] Runyon dashed off poems with little literary merit, but because of his name and their accessibility in newspapers and magazines, they found an enthusiastic and large readership. Their wisdom and folk humor appealed to a readership who turned to Runyon each day for a moment's pleasure and wisdom.

While he didn't even list in his collected works his early books of poetry, *Tents of Trouble* (1911) and *Rhymes of the Firing Line* (1912), in *Poems for Men* he and Clark Kinnaird—who completed the volume after Runyon's death—acknowledged and reprinted some of the earlier poems. The best known of his poems is his paean to Sande the jockey entitled "A Handy Guy Like Sande," where the speaker—perhaps a Runyon surrogate—nostalgically recaptures a feeling of his own youth in writing about the jockey's comeback in 1930: "Maybe he's gettin' along,/But the ol' heart's still a-tickin',/An the ol' bean's goin' strong./Roll back the years! Yea, roll 'em!/Say, but I'm young agin,/Watchin' that handy/Guy named Sande,/Bootin' a winner in!"[29]

Runyon called his poems "ballads" or "songs." D'Itri observes: "[I]n some way they have the simplicity and untutored form of traditional ballads."[30] Runyon wrote in the vernacular, trying for a voice in which one man spoke to another. It is the oral tradition of folk poetry: limericks, rhymed couplets, easy poems, and anecdotes in verse. Often a speaker is responding to a particular event that he recalls.

The appeal of these poems is the universality of their themes—blighted hopes, frustrated desires, awareness of mortality—in a discourse that is accessible to anyone who can read. They are adult poems in language that someone who has had a few years of high school education or even less can read. At Runyon's best, as in "The Old Horse Player," often circulated as "All Hawss Players Must Die Broke," he captures the weight of collected experience and the speech patterns and rhythms of a character whose wisdom strikes a chord in his readers. The interrogative "I" who questions and learns from the insistent if not obsessive speaker who returns to his refrain line, "All hawss players must die broke," is a surrogate for all of us who hope the world will shine on our dreams (PFM 100). Isn't Runyon's point in part that all of us—not just horse players—are finally trumped by time and *must* die?

"The Spender" is a tale told by a narrator who has heard from Kahoe, a money-grubbing waiter and "a liar of local fame," about a generous tipper, named Daffy Moore, who made money as a war profiteer but whose conscience was tortured by guilt: "I see/The shredded bodies of noble men,/And all of them killed by me!" In the poem, we see not only Runyon's lifelong disdain for those who profited from war but also perhaps an awareness that reporters and writers, like profiteers, have a parasitic relationship to those who actually fight in wars. We also see in the poem some self-inquiry into the motives of a man who is, like Runyon himself, a profligate "spender." After a night of listening to his ravings, Kahoe showed Moore to the door; the next day Moore was locked up in an asylum by his family (PFM 69). Of course, since Kahoe is a liar, we don't know how much is true or whether he tells the tale to entertain the narrator, whom he thinks is "a man of means/And conjures quarters out of my jeans" (PFM 70); indeed, perhaps Kahoe's telling a tale about a big tipper who always gives bills rather than change is a lesson for the narrator.

"A Diamond Ditty" is told by a frame narrator who reports to us readers the responses of an old baseball scout who watches some of those he thought would be stars make cameo appearances in baseball's major leagues and realizes that he drastically overestimated their abilities. The poem is not only about how our evaluations of abilities and expectations are fed by our fantasies, but also how our judgments are reflected through our desires and how optative becomes indicative. "Oh, the Old Scout slumped down in his chair,/ And said: 'I'm wondering how/They could look as good to me 'way down there,/And look so different now'" (PFM 139).

Runyon wrote frequently about the pain of aging and the loss of energy and ability. In "The Old Hop Horse," a horseplayer speaks to a horse that in the past had been able to win by being fed stimulants; the horse, not realizing that aging is his problem concludes: "And I 'member when one jab/Would make a wolf o' me—/No, Chief, you bet your life the hop/Ain't what it used to be" (PFM 105). Even as we understand that the horseplayer has lost a large bet ("quite a chunk,/ And same I kinnot blow"), we realize that the horseplayer too has aged and like the horse, his life has come to nothing (PFM 104).

Often the poems, like the short stories, express the melancholy fatalism of a man who has spent countless hours and days at the track and usually come up a loser. Thus in "Can You Keep a Secret?," a poem told by a narrator who has bet on three separate horses on which he has received tips and still lost, Runyon concludes: "They dropped in an added starter,/And the sucker—he won by a mile./ . . . No matter how many you're playing,/There ain't no way you can win" (PFM 89). In "The Honest Bookie," Runyon uses the third person to describe a bookie who pays off when he loses but, when he wins—and after advancing money to his customers—waits in vain for "the guys who said they'd pay" (PFM 92).

Another motif that recurs from the stories is an ironic look at the good old days. Unlike Norman Rockwell's nostalgic eulogies for America's past, Runyon's poems show how memory often distorts facts and leaves a residue of bitterness for opportunities missed or imagined merit unappreciated. For example, in "The Old Guy's

Lament," a former baseball star, now reduced to working as a ticket taker for the bleachers, recalls the days when he was a dominant star nicknamed "Murderous McGarr." Regretting that in those days salaries were not what they are now, he concludes his poignant and self-pitying monologue: "Look up my monicker, Mister,/And see what I have done with my bat!/But think of the dough that they're grabbin',/Guys that can't hit a balloon—/I can see where my parents were crazy/By havin' me born so soon!" (PFM 142). Resenting that he now must work at what he feels is an unworthy job with little compensation, the speaker's complaints become more and more strident until in the final lines his envy—when he accuses his parents of conceiving him a few decades too early—becomes at once ridiculous and pathological.

While doing his job, the ticket taker is talking either to the narrator or to himself so loudly that the narrator overhears him; the more the ticket taker recalls the distinction between how he remembers himself and how he is now, the more he ups the rhetorical ante. That he is a fictitious character makes his hyperbolic claims about stardom in the 1880s all the more ironic. Yet perhaps Runyon's point is that the speaker's distorted, if not delusional, reminiscence of the good old days when he was more powerful than current stars like Babe Ruth is a reductive version of how the past looks to all of us as we age: "The guys hit 'em a furlong,/Where I used to hit 'em a mile!" (PFM 141).

Runyon often used his poems to impart the wisdom of his life experience, but in a poem entitled "A Jew" in the November 1922 *Cosmopolitan*—a poem not included in *Poems for Men*—he is a teacher reminding his readers of the folly of anti-Semitism. Making little effort to create a dramatized persona, Runyon presents a speaker who is more like himself than usual. It is a poem in praise of a real hero, Sam Dreben, a Jewish soldier who emigrated from Russia and who was much decorated for his World War I service by France and the United States. Underneath the poem in italics is a brief description presumably written by Runyon that concludes: "Sam Dreben, patriot, soldier and gentleman known throughout the army as 'The Fighting Jew,'"—an epithet we might find less appealing than Runyon meant it. Indeed, today's audience would object to the stereotypical physical description of the Jew: "He is short, and fat, and funny./And the nose upon his face/ is about the size of Bugler Dugan's horn/But the grin that plays behind it/ Is wide, and soft, and sunny."[31]

Yet it is as if Runyon proposes the stereotype only to debunk it: "And there's a heart beneath the medals/That beats loyal brave and true—/That's Dreben,/A Jew!"[32] Runyon's persona presents the case of the heroic Jew as rebuttal to a story he mentions at the beginning of the first stanza that speaks of prejudice against the Jews, a story that he has thrown in disgust on the floor. Runyon's America, we realize once more, is not Norman Rockwell's idealized America. Beginning with the very next lines, Runyon evokes in each stanza a photograph of Dreben wearing his medals: "There's a photo on the table/That's a memory of the war/And a man who never figured in the news." In the third and final stanza, he writes: "Now whenever I read articles/That breathe of racial hate,/or hear arguments that hold his kind to scorn, . . . think, God Almighty/We will always have a few/like Dreben,/A Jew!"[33]

RUNYON AND ROCKWELL

We live in a world where intellectuals have discovered not only the value of popular culture in understanding the history of a period, but even the pleasure of popular culture. In the 1930s, 1940s, and 1950s intellectuals patronized popular culture; the patronizing term "kitsch" to describe artistic work of little value pandering to popular taste was much in vogue. It was Clement Greenberg who gave the term currency in a 1939 *Partisan Review* piece entitled "Avant-Garde and Kitsch," and Norman Rockwell was one of his examples of kitsch.

Some of the same intellectuals favored Marxism in politics. New York intellectuals like Clement Greenberg, Dwight McDonald, Philip Rahv, and others associated with the *Partisan Review,* including Lionel Trilling, thought mass culture was antagonistic to modernist experiments in literature, painting, sculpture, music, and dance and that realism had been co-opted by the cultural industries of capitalism. They did not quite see that American individuality and boldness and even quirky behavior was an ally of modernist experimentalism and that figures like Runyon and Jackson Pollack had similar roots in the West and shared the Emersonian celebration of the individual. As Peter Schjeldahl puts it, "American populism has always differed in political character from its European counterparts. It celebrates the individual, steering closer to condoned anarchy than to forced solidarity."[34]

We better understand Runyon by comparing him with Rockwell (1894–1978), another major figure whose contribution to popular culture between the World Wars shaped the American psyche. While one might argue that Rockwell spoke more to an upwardly mobile middle-class audience and Runyon, at least in his daily columns, to a working-class and less mobile lower-middle-class audience—government workers such as postal workers, policemen, and firemen—they have much in common. For one thing, Runyon's stories, like Rockwell's illustrations, appeared in magazines read by the middle class. Moreover, Rockwell and Runyon inherited the optimistic assumption from prior eras that we Americans have the ability to know, make sense of, and control our lives and our communities; for the most part, they eschewed anxiety and dubiety. They refused to be overwhelmed by technology and political differences, and they shared a belief that there is an American audience that transcends religious, ethnic, and gender differences. Each in his own way often simplified not merely the confusion of growing up but the obsessions, compulsions, and dimly acknowledged needs that drive human behavior. The very psychological complexity that they ignored becomes not only the text for the modern sensibility but the sensibility for modern texts.

Compared to Runyon, Rockwell depicted a simpler, less frenzied life on the covers of *The Saturday Evening Post,* a magazine that had a circulation of three million in 1937 and for which Rockwell did 321 covers. He often idealized American life, especially in that publication; he wrote, "I guess I have a bad case of the American nostalgia for the clean, simple country life as opposed to the complicated world of the city."[35] Just as Runyon's cynical view shaped our sense of what America, often to our dismay, had become, Rockwell's idealized sense of the past shaped our view of what America had been—

and perhaps should be. As Deborah Solomon observes, Rockwell "did more to visualize the aspirations of Americans than any other artist of the 20th century. . . . [H]e painted a country whose spirit remained intact despite two world wars and the Great Depression."[36]

It is worth remembering that in the 1920s the popular magazines like *Collier's* and *The Saturday Evening Post*—the very ones for which Runyon wrote—played an important role in bringing to a mass middlebrow audience important writers like F. Scott Fitzgerald, Willa Cather, and John Dos Passos. Anne Knutson has argued that "The *[Saturday Evening] Post* sought out and defined and spoke to what is now called middle America. The *Post*'s and Rockwell's America was one that was rooted so firmly in the ethics of the past that it could accommodate and internalize the changes of the twentieth century without being overwhelmed by them."[37] Under George Horace Lorimer's leadership from 1898 to 1936, *The Saturday Evening Post* had an enormous influence on American beliefs and attitudes, and Rockwell's covers played a leading role. Rockwell felt that the United States lacked a unifying consciousness and wanted to provide in the *Post* a paradigm for people to measure themselves against.[38] As Knutson put it: "The articles, fiction, illustrations, and advertisements functioned as how-to guides for living in twentieth century America: they taught readers how to make sense of the vast and rapid changes in their new century."[39] By 1929, the *Post*'s circulation was 2 million and its readership 20 million.[40] Gradually, beginning in 1908, the *Post*'s audience included more and more women, and in response advertising revenue and circulation dramatically increased.

Runyon saw America as chaotic, disruptive, exciting, and violent. While he, like Rockwell, espoused patriotism, he not only promoted American values of upward mobility, but also endorsed taking advantage of opportunity, aggressive behavior (often but not always male), even ruthlessness, self-interest, and greed. At times it is as if Runyon's black humor was refuting Rockwell's fantasy world. But, unlike Runyon, Rockwell rarely depicted poverty, degradation, envy, or malice. Rockwell's was a world of virtues; Runyon's often was a world of vices. Yet the similarities in their brief sketches, the clarity of their presentations, their avoidance of complex psychology, and their kinship with popular film (think of Frank Capra's *Meet*

John Doe [1941], *It Happened One Night* [1934], *Mr. Smith Goes to Washington* [1939]) and radio serials, which often celebrated the dignity of common man, is similar. Like Rockwell and Capra, Runyon believed it is the individual who mattered and that each person could make a difference. He shared with them an appreciation of American good humor and humility when it occurred, but was also very much aware of selfishness and narcissism. Yet Runyon could write in the Rockwell/Capra vein, and his sentimentality and warmth toward the Turps and the life he describes are not so different from that of Rockwell's folk.

Rockwell's drawings refer to a tradition of realistic portraiture beginning with Rembrandt and place him squarely in the Western humanistic tradition. His attitude is the obverse of Runyon's cynicism, yet it is Runyon who is the actual realist, showing us the grim world of Prohibition and the Depression, of gambling and hustling, albeit in an accepting and often high-spirited way. While Rockwell looked nostalgically back to a idyllic past that never was, Runyon often alerted his readers to the failure of Prohibition, the complicity of the police with criminals, and the terrible effects of the Depression. Runyon's stories never appeared in the issues of *The Saturday Evening Post* for which Rockwell created covers, although Runyon's more optimistic and good-humored Turps stories—including the 1937 "A Call on the President," the one Turps story that appeared in the *Post*—would not have been incongruous with Rockwell's covers.

Interestingly, it is Rockwell, not Runyon, who was born in New York City. Rockwell showed us an America that we wanted to see, a world where kids grew up without pain and where neighbors cared for each other in a small town. In "Shuffleton's Barbershop" (1950), he idealizes the musical group that plays after hours in the back room of a barbershop and by doing so extols small-town customs, innocent pleasures, the rhythm of rural life. He wanted to let people look at themselves and enjoy the way they lived; for that reason he depicted people he actually knew, and also drew himself and his wife.

Like Rockwell, Runyon based his characters on actual people he knew, some of whom—like Waldo Winchester as Walter Winchell—were easily recognizable by those in the Broadway neighborhood.

Perhaps Runyon would have subscribed to Rockwell's words: "Commonplaces are never tiresome. It is we who become tired when we cease to be curious or appreciative. . . . [W]e find that it is not a new scene which is needed, but a new viewpoint."[41]

Like Runyon's persona, Rockwell is an insider in the world he depicts. Runyon's narrator resembles the figure in some Rockwell paintings who is a surrogate beholder, namely, "a character within the painting's space whose response to the action we may take as a cue to our own responses and through whose eyes we are presumed to see the scene portrayed in its optimistic configuration."[42] In "After the Prom" (1957) that role is performed by the soda jerk. By extension a surrogate beholder within a painting or story is in an analogous position to us the audience, but of course he or she is also acted on within the imagined ontology. In this case, the soda jerk is observed and responded to, even as he observes and responds to the young couple, and as he and the young couple are observed by the older working man whose costume suggests that he is a war veteran. The subject of "Saying Grace" (1951) is in part the secular onlookers—our surrogates—who respect what to them is the eccentricity of public prayer. In both "Saying Grace" and "After the Prom," is not the man on the left perhaps a second, more jaundiced observer of the playful youths?

Both Runyon and Rockwell are democratic in their appreciation of the historical processes taking place in America and in their appeal to a popular audience. In the 1950s urban life became a foregrounded subject in American culture, perhaps with a considerable debt to Runyon. As Neil Harris puts it, "[C]hampioning the American city's pedigree as a legitimate historical category and glorifying the immigrant experience as a quintessential national subject reached unprecedented levels after World War II."[43] Yet Rockwell rarely found room in his work for urban America ("Union Station" [1944] and "Roadblock" [1949] are notable exceptions).

Rockwell's work is a paean to America and expresses the optimistic vein of Whitman or Emerson. His sequence paintings, "Day in the Life of a Little Girl" (1952) and "The Gossips" (1948), have a narrative element that remind us that Rockwell is interested in telling a story and that indeed virtually all of his magazine covers compose a story about the human comedy. As with Runyon, seemingly incidental details are carefully selected and serve the larger purpose of the narrative. In "The Gossips" (1948), the object of the gossip hears the story and in the last image accuses the person who started the process. As in Runyon, human telling as opposed to electronic telling via radio, TV, or the Internet is the major source of information.

In "Girl at Mirror" (1954) Rockwell suggests that as we move into the complex postwar world, it is the doll, the nineteenth-century chair, and even perhaps the old slightly yellowed cotton slip that give the girl a refuge, but he also suggests the incipient preadolescent sexuality that cannot be arrested—in the magazine on the girl's lap, Rockwell depicts the picture of an older woman—and the element of narcissism that reminds us of the popular nineteenth-century French painter William Adolphe Bouguereau.

If for Runyon mischief is kidnapping someone at gunpoint, for Rockwell mischief is young boys, in his cover "No Swimming," swimming without clothes in a forbidden area. Rockwell's hopeful idealism often ignored the devastating historical events like the Depression and the World Wars, to say nothing of the Holocaust. Ethnic variations are absent, and we see—even in the 1943 wartime "Four Freedoms" series, based on a 1941 Roosevelt speech—little about the place of blacks in America or the emergence of Jews, Italians, and Irish. To be sure, later in his career Rockwell included ethnic variety in such covers as the 1961 multicultural "Golden Rule." After he moved to *Look* in the 1960s he depicted social change and expressed his support for the Civil Rights Movement; for example, "New Kids in the Neighborhood" (1967) stresses the common interests of black and white kids. In "Southern Justice (Murder in Mississippi)" (1965) he aroused the conscience of the nation with graphically violent images.

The fact that, in "Freedom of Speech," the working-class man is accorded a chance to express his opinion in a room full of men in suits shows Rockwell's fascination with men who do the physical work—the mailman or milkman or electrician—on which the rest of us depend. (Runyon shares this interest in the working man in "A Call on the President."). Rockwell shows America as an organic community in which each man plays his part, while the women—except during the war effort, when they take jobs out of necessity—are usually the nurturers. Rockwell's persona is not a hard-boiled Broadway character familiar with gamblers and bootleggers but the pipe-smoking innocent of the "Triple Self-Portrait" (1960), a figure who does his part by rendering the ideal world he observes.

Rockwell and Runyon appealed to an audience with a brief attention span who wanted a smile, even if in Runyon's case it is a grim smile based on black humor. For the most part, Runyon's noir small-town world of *My Old Man* and *In Our Town* and his jaundiced view of human behavior and motives differ from Rockwell's optimism. Rockwell made social change seem comfortable and continuous with the past. As Judy L. Larson and Maureen Hart Hennessey put it, "Rockwell's art reassured the nation that cherished values would not disappear, for the nation needed them to meet its new challenges. . . . Particularly during times of crisis, Rockwell created images that communicated patriotism and unquestioned allegiance to the United States. Rockwell's stories promoted American values such as industriousness, fair play and decency."[44] Normalcy prevails in "Freedom from Fear" (1943): Solomon observes, "It shows two children snug in bed, their mother stooping to pick up their blanket, their father looking on, holding a newspaper whose partially visible headline announces news of 'bombing' and 'horror' abroad."[45] After the terrorist attacks on September 11, 2001, *The New York Times* printed an updated version, changing only the headline. Would not the cynical Runyon have understood that tucking in one's children could not protect them from life's complexities? The idealist in Runyon longed for the simpler world of this and other of Rockwell's illustrations, even as he regretted its absence.

CHAPTER 3

RUNYON'S TRIAL
REPORTING AND THE
SPECTATOR CULTURE

B y the 1920s modern urban life created a spectator culture, where the morning newspaper reported on sensational events, especially crime scenes and trials, to feed the insatiable voyeurism of the public. In this chapter we shall examine how Runyon's reporting of major trials had an important effect on the transformation of these trials into crystallizing media events. What distinguishes the modern spectator culture is its focus not only on the act of observing but on the interchange between those looking and those being looked at. In thinking about the evolution of spectator culture, we need think not only of the aforementioned penny newspapers and tabloids but of the invention of photography, Edward Muybridge's stop-action photography (depending on taking the same picture from three separate positions), and early cinema.

"The technology of speed," Stephen Kern observes, "affected newspaper reporting and modified the language of journalistic communication."[1] Operating since the 1830s, the telegraph opened the door to speedy transmission of vital information. First used in 1887, telephones followed as a major means of proliferating information. The telephone changed the way people communicated in personal relations and the way that they were part of a community. Indeed, shared "party" lines may have whetted the appetite for the kind of gossip the popular columnists served up. They legitimized interest in other people's lives; even if listening in was bad manners, who could restrain one's natural curiosity to know one's neighbor's business? Runyon presents himself as someone who listens in and reports in columns or various narratives—in the Broadway stories, the Turps stories, the stories of *My Old Man* and *In Our Town*—on what he purports to have heard. As the very concept of privacy in the home changes, boundaries of what is sacrosanct in terms of voyeuristic observing and prying change.

In 1903, wireless telegraphy enabled messages to reach ships and allowed political leaders to communicate across the ocean. Kern describes the journalistic world in which Runyon came of age: "Because economy of expression produced monetary savings, reporters were inclined to write their stories with the fewest possible words. The telegraph encouraged the use of unambiguous words to avoid any confusion, and the language of journalism came to be more uniform as certain words came into more frequent use. . . . Information tended to be written with a minimum of punctuation."[2] Runyon's columns appeared across the nation because they could be telegraphed into communities. The assassination of Archduke Francis Ferdinand was the shot heard 'round the world because of telegraphic communications and the newspaper stories resulting from those communications. The age of electronic communication not only reflected but created events, giving new meaning to the idea that language is constituted and constituting. The reporter as spectator becomes not merely the person who detachedly observes the effects of events but the person whose perspective creates those effects.

The railway and later subways or street railways not only enlarged cities but created new sources of motion and energy. Thanks to electricity and the automobile, speed was an increasing factor in American urban life. Runyon loved it, but Henry Adams complained that the speed of modern life had made people "irritable, nervous, querulous, unreasonable and afraid," and William Dean Howells complained about the "uproar" in New York.[3] In a sense, Runyon's use of the present tense owes something to his experience of instantaneously transmitting his news reports.

As Kern observes, the early cinema—cinema fascinated Runyon—"reproduced the mechanization, jerkiness, and rush of modern times."[4] Irwin Panofsky has observed that the enjoyment of moving pictures had less to do with subject matter than with "the sheer delight in the fact that things seemed to move."[5]

Runyon renders not only the public commotion and circus atmosphere revolving around spectacle trials, but the kinetic quality of city life, auto travel, horses running, and sports events. He renders a world where the concept of privacy changes; while the narrator of the story might be eating in a public place, acquaintances join him and even help themselves to part of his dinner. Even in more suburban outposts of metropolitan areas, privacy gives way to a world where everyone knows where people live, and think nothing of stopping by to badger them about buying something, joining a religious group, or making a contribution to a cause. One symptom of the lack of privacy is how newspapers transform criminal trials and legal proceedings into community gossip.

Some of Runyon's columns of major trials are collected in *Trials and Other Tribulations,* a volume compiled after his death.[6] With excited spectators contending for seats and hordes of reporters and photographers, major trials seemed like important sporting events: "The trial is a sort of game, the players on one side of the attorneys for the defense, and on the other the attorneys for the State" ("Postscript," (TT 282). Trials became performances where the judge, prosecutors, and defense attorneys were reviewed as if they were actors. As readers browsed the papers, reporters browsed the city. Thus reading the newspaper was not only secondhand spectatorship if not voyeurism, but also a course on how to observe firsthand while walking or taking a bus or tram, especially on weekends when there was time for sightseeing and strolling. Of course, we see this spectator culture today in the obsession with the O. J. Simpson trial, the killing of JonBenet Ramsey, or the disappearance of Chandra Levy.

"THE HALL-MILLS CASE"

Runyon's articles collected in *Trials and Other Tribulations* under the title "The Hall-Mills Case" focus on a 1926 trial for a murder that took place four years earlier. Members of the Johnson and Johnson pharmaceutical family—Mrs. Frances Stevens Hall, her two brothers, William (called "Willie") and Henry Stevens, and a cousin, Henry de la Bruyere Carpender—were acquitted of the murder of Hall's husband, Edward W. Hall, an Episcopalian clergyman whose body was found along with that of Mrs. Eleanor Mills on a farm outside New Brunswick, New Jersey. Both victims were shot, Mrs. Mills's throat was slashed, and their love letters were scattered about.

Reverend Hall had been having an affair with Eleanor Mills, a married woman of modest circumstances. During the four years before the case reached trial, the tabloid journalists of the *Daily Mirror* kept it in the public eye. While an initial attempt by police to identify a suspect had produced little more than a theory that a botched robbery had taken place on the night of the murders, the New York papers—especially Hearst's *Mirror*—desiring a more sensational story, competed fiercely for information that could seize their readers' interest.

While radio was beginning to play a role in this growing circus atmosphere, it was primarily newspapers that kept the events in the spotlight. Playing on and further fueling society's lust for exciting stories that provided intrigue on a daily basis, as well as on the public's fascination with the wealthy, the Hall-Mills case was transformed into a phenomenon far beyond the realm of mere reporting. In the spring of 1926, editor Philip Payne of the *Daily Mirror* sent newshounds to uncover any potential leads in the almost static investigation. Only a few months later, in July 1926, the *Mirror*—purporting that it had uncovered new evidence nearly three and a half years after the murder—broke a story with the headline: "Hall-Mills Mystery Bared."[6]

The *Mirror* alleged that Louise Geist, the parlor maid, who had originally corroborated Mrs. Halls's story, had been bribed by her employers to give false evidence. Furthermore, the newspaper accused some police officials involved with the investigation of taking bribes and destroying evidence against Mrs. Hall.[7] As a direct result of the pressure created by this supposed new information, New Jersey police authorities were forced to indict Mrs. Hall and her two brothers on two counts of murder. Yet four years earlier, when the memory of witnesses would have been fresher, the authorities had claimed that there was too little evidence to proceed with a trial. After their acquittal, the defendants sued the *Mirror* for $1.5 million but apparently settled for $50,000.[8]

The public's unceasing fascination with the murders revealed as much about society's insatiable appetite for scandal as it did about the willingness of publishers to sell newspapers, even if it meant creating news in the guise of transmitting facts. As Damon Runyon observed about the pending trial: "The Halls-Mills murder case is now an old, old story to newspaper readers. It has probably been argued and debated at every breakfast table during the past few years. It can be recited to its smallest details. . . . But they [the residents of New Jersey] are all eagerly awaiting the rehash of the tale that will begin tomorrow, expecting it will produce some new and hitherto unpublished chapter that will answer definitely the questions that have been asked over and over and over again—Who killed 'em? Why?" (TT 12).

Although the verdict for Mrs. Hall and her brother eventually came back as not guilty, the intense mediathon was a prime example of the transformation of the media into a vehicle for sensational journalism and an acceleration of newspapers' playing a more visible role in criminal cases. As Runyon noted: "[The trial] has taken on some of the aspects of a big sports event. In fact, the telegraph switchboard used for the Dempsey-Tunney fight has been installed in the court house. . . . An enterprising radio outfit will unofficially broadcast the proceedings, play by play, so to speak" (TT 12).

According to John Lofton, "the *Daily Mirror* openly championed the side of the prosecution and the *New York Evening Graphic* took the side of the defendants."[9] In siding with the prosecution, Runyon, writing for Hearst's papers, played a leading role. Believing the defendants were guilty, he shaped his narrative to give us the impression that wealth and privilege played a crucial role in the verdict. He is sympathetic to the kind of folk whom he knew in Pueblo, Colorado, like Mrs. Mills's husband, a working man, and Jane Gipson, a rural woman whom the prosecution claimed had witnessed the crime and whom both sides refer to as the "pig woman."

Runyon had a visual imagination, and he evokes the players in terms of their physical appearance, dress, mannerisms, and idiosyncrasies. Notwithstanding newsreels, the reporter, in the days before television, showed us events that we could not witness directly. Thus in "The Halls-Mills Case," Runyon presented the prosecutor, State Senator Alexander Simpson, as "a small jockey-sized, fox terrier-like, little man with a wheedling voice. . . . He dresses like a small town sport, fancy colored shirt, black leather spats and a dark suit with a pin stripe" (TT 13). Gradually, with his aggressiveness and relentless search for truth and disdain for class, Simpson emerges in his closing arguments as something of a hero in Runyon's eyes: "A little man with oily gray hair and a very blade of a voice stood before the bar of 'Jersey justice' yesterday and made it listen" (TT 92). Runyon's perspective merges with that of the prosecutor when he refers "to the Hall-Stevens-Carpender clan as the reigning family of the Johnson and Johnson aristocracy of New Brunswick, whose crest is a mustard plaster" (TT 92–93).

Runyon is as puzzled and disturbed by the acquittal as many of us were by the result of the O. J. Simpson trial, and shares the prosecutor's sense of outrage at the miscarriage of justice unfolding. He sympathizes with Prosecutor Simpson, who accused the jury of a wide range of improper behavior, from gossiping about the case and sleeping in the courtroom, to calling Simpson names among themselves. Demanding a mistrial, Simpson presented affidavits to support his contention that "on the second day of the trial before the evidence was clearly under way some [members of the jury] practically said they would not convict if the murder was committed before their faces" (TT 81).

In Runyon's trial reporting, we see his debt to political and social cartoons, and we see an anticipation of the illuminating distortions of the Broadway stories. Did not media interest in the criminality of the supposed wealthy and respectable help create a market for those of his short stories focusing on the machinations of the elite—"A Job for the Macarone," "Cemetery Bait," "What, No Butler?"—especially since Runyon's byline was associated with the mediathons, and he was thought to be among the cognoscenti?

Runyon knows how to show rather than tell. His dramatic personae are the stuff of novels, and each one—even the most minor—is drawn individually to stress what makes each character a unique player in the drama. By focusing on Mrs. Hall's courtroom response to the testimony of the doctor who performed the autopsies and used a dummy to illustrate his points, he gradually makes clear where his sympathies lie: "Not once did her eyes turn to the dummy, as her ears heard the doctor tell how the singing voice of the woman who stole her husband's love had been literally carved from her throat, tongue, windpipe, and larynx, that black night . . . when the State says Mrs. Hall was present" (TT 34). When her brother Henry weeps in response to the rhetoric of the defense, he describes Mrs. Hall sitting "stiff and proud. . . . It strikes me as determined repression" (TT 86).

Not only does Runyon have an eye for distinguishing details, but he has an ear for the words and intonations of each witness, defendant, and lawyer. Later, when Mrs. Hall is being examined and having a tough time explaining her response (her words: "'They have met foul play, they are together, they are dead'") after learning that her husband and his lover were missing but not yet discovered as dead, Runyon draws upon a metaphor from one of his favorite spectator activities: "It was almost as if a chap in the prize ring had been reeling around, a bit groggy under a punch, only to be saved by the bell" (TT 77, 78).

Runyon's narrative power and sense of drama inform his reporting: "But not by one change of muscle in the pallid mask that is her face, not by one gesture or change of attitude did Frances Noel Stevens Hall indicate she heard the words other than some recital of ordinary phraseology" (TT 45). What he does not lose is his sense of humor or his ability to laugh at himself; when a man called Dr. Runyon, who is brother Willie's physician, testifies, he cannot resist describing Dr. Runyon as " bald and a bit belligerent, and not entirely up to the Runyon type in pulchritude." But Damon is also making a point about stereotyping on the basis of family and appearance (TT 69).

The Hall-Mills trial reveals a great deal about the culture of the 1920s. For example, one of the prosecution strategies—one that Runyon refers to as "ugly inference" on Simpson's part—was to imply that one of the defendants, Willie Stevens, who was somewhat mentally impaired, had "Negro" blood because he had different features from those of his brother, Henry (TT 60). We also see how the wealthy believe they can control the processes by hiring their own detective "in what the State conceives to be an effort on the part of Mrs. Hall to choke off any evidence damaging to her and her brothers in connection with the massacre of the parson and his sweetheart" (TT 73). (Note the graphic verb "choke off," another of Runyon's masterly verbs that resonate with meaning for his middlebrow audience.)

But Runyon's perspective on the trial was hardly shared by C. E. Bechhofer Roberts, also known as "Ephesian," who argued that the "mystery of the murders remains unsolved" and that the tabloid newspapers created a hysterical environment in which innocent people were accused and tried on "baseless charges."[10] The grand jury assembled ten weeks after the September 16, 1922, discovery of the two bodies failed to indict Mrs. Hall or any other member of the Mills or Hall family. But "the higher judge in the Hall-Mills case was the sensational press in New York which, reluctant to leave this juicy mystery while a drop of sensation might still be squeezed from it, re-opened the whole affair some three and half years later."[11]

Because the drive for a trial was orchestrated by the Hearst paper, one could argue that Runyon's reporting was slanted against Mrs. Hall and her family. But he believed that justice was slanted when it came to the privileged classes; often he could barely disguise his anger and resentment toward those people: "[A] pig is a pig, even when it wears evening clothes."[12] According to Edwin P. Hoyt, "Damon was angry with the so-called 'good people,' the bankers, lawyers and particularly the Wall Street brokers, who bought the swill of the speakeasies, collected their imported champagne in carload lots, corrupted the chorus girls of Broadway, and cheated in public in a manner the underworld considered downright disgraceful, in the manipulation of business. These were Damon's pigs, not the Broadway types who went around and about, doing this and that."[13]

"'DADDY' AND 'PEACHES'"

Runyon understood that curiosity was his ruling passion and that he shared it with most of his readers. Somewhat iconoclastically, he looked at the foibles of the wealthy as revealed by sensational trials that dominated the tabloids. His trial reporting opened the doors and windows to a world small-town America did not know.

In "'Daddy' and 'Peaches'" he writes about the 1927 trial of Edward W. Browning, who married Frances Heenan Browning (Peaches) when she was fifteen. He sued for divorce, claiming he had been abandoned, and she countersued. Both sides sought a private trial, but when the request was denied, the trial became what Runyon calls a "sextravaganza" (TT 117) observed by a full courtroom of voyeurs "almost rioting in their desire to get a peep at the principals in a duel of defamation": "The Gods on Mount Olympus, or wherever it is the gods assemble, must have held their sides with laughter today—and probably their noses, too—as they looked down and watched the earthworms wriggling in the muck heap of a modern-day matrimonial squabble" (TT 107).

Notwithstanding that there is some evidence that Peaches and her mother were not indifferent to Browning's wealth when agreeing to this marriage, Runyon does express some limited sympathy for the child bride: "Even a case-hardened old sinner, such as your correspondent, must feel a little sympathy for Peaches" (TT 114). Before she was married, Peaches had been disfigured by having acid thrown on her face by another lover of Browning's named Mary Spas. Now Peaches is rather obese. Browning's lawyers do their best to discredit her character before she was married, while her lawyers do their best to expose the oddities of his personal life, including Browning's requirement that Peaches appear "before him *au naturel*" and his bringing into their home, for some not quite explained purpose, a large live goose (TT 120).

Defending the elaborate coverage of the trial against editorial criticism from a rival newspaper, which had taken a sanctimonious view, Runyon concludes his commentary on the trial by arguing, perhaps facetiously, that the coverage is a "good thing": "[A]s long as such cases are permitted in the courts of law they ought to get plenty of publicity, if only because it mirrors to the rest of humanity the sappiness of some of its representatives, and perhaps of the law, too, and thus may possibly act as deterrent to other saps" (TT 136).

Runyon not only stresses women as sexual objects, but at times he exhibits a nasty misogynist strain. Tongue in cheek but nevertheless revealingly, he expresses sorrow for poor officers on guard in the courtroom who "were viciously assaulted by infuriated women trying to shove past them to listen to the testimony and determine for themselves if it is as terrible as they hear. . . . The more dangerous were mainly women past thirty and they stepped on the cops' corns and snatched buttons off the cops' jackets, and threatened to tweak the cops' noses if the cops got too gay with them" (TT 121). In the context of this description of women in an irrational voyeuristic frenzy, Browning becomes a bit more sympathetic.

"THE ETERNAL BLONDE"

Runyon's misogyny and sexism are especially on display in the columns collected under the title "The Eternal Blonde," his reports on the 1927 trial of the gruesome murder by Ruth Snyder and her lover, Henry Judd Gray, of her husband. Both had admitted to the murder before the trial, confessing that they had hit Snyder with a window sash and strangled him with picture wire. But Mrs. Snyder recanted before the trial; during the trial Snyder and Gray each accused the other of primary responsibility. Both were found guilty and sentenced to the electric chair; they were executed January 13, 1928.

Despising both principals, Runyon opens his coverage of this sensational trial with characteristic hyperbole befitting his efforts to pique the interest of his audience. Runyon claims that the circumstances of the case "for sheer stupidity and brutality have seldom been equalled in the history of crime" (TT 139). Unlike the underworld figure Arnold Rothstein, whom, as we shall see, Runyon grudgingly admires for refusing to name his assailant, Mrs. Snyder and Gray "have been 'hollering copper' on each other lately, as the boys [the gangsters whom Runyon knows] say" (TT 142). According to the informal criminal code, what happens within their alternate world remains in that world; one does not betray one's criminal colleagues for one's own benefit or involve the police in settling disputes. As in "Undertaker Song" (1934), those who violate this underworld code are dealt with violently.

From the opening lines—not a sentence but a casting of characters for the courtroom drama to unfold—Runyon focuses obsessively on Snyder's appearance, with a strong focus on her blond hair:

"A chilly looking blonde with frosty eyes and one of those marble, you-bet-you-will chins, and an inert, scare-drunk fellow that you couldn't miss among any hundred men as a dead set-up for a blonde, or the shell game, or maybe a gold brick" (TT 139). Assigning the origin of the epithet to other nameless observers, he calls her "The Bloody Blonde" (TT 182). When Snyder testifies that she knew Gray was in her home to kill her husband, Runyon observes with bitter humor: "Three gentleman contemplating marriage to blondes hastened to the telephone booths to cancel their troth, shivering in their boots as they went" (TT 180).

Snyder is more cold-blooded than Gray; while he, according to Runyon, makes "public confession, perhaps by way of easement to a sorely harassed conscience" (TT 184), she has been the instigator, "the blond magnet" (TT 190). At the end, when Runyon says he couldn't condemn a woman to death, a woman whom he describes as "a blond throwback to the jungle cat" (TT 198), we realize her blond hair has become a metonymy not only for Mrs. Snyder, but for the threatening potential of women to use their wiles to undermine men by seduction and subterfuge.

The trial gives Runyon space to play with prose and develop his characters. Each report that he files is like a scene in a play, a chapter in an evolving novel. At his best Runyon can write memorable sentences that appeal in substance to middlebrow audiences and in style and allusion (to *Macbeth*) to the cognoscenti: "Bloody apparitions rising out of his memory of that dreadful night in Queen's Village probably gibbered at the window of Henry Judd Gray's soul yesterday afternoon" (TT 181). Runyon summarizes Gray's testimony in scathingly ironic terms: "She-she-she-she-she she-she-she. That was the burden of the bloody song of the little corset salesman . . ." (TT 152).

"ARNOLD ROTHSTEIN'S FINAL PAYOFF"

Runyon also covered the trial of George C. McManus, who was charged with shooting Arnold Rothstein, whom Runyon knew, at the Park Central Hotel on November 4, 1928, after losing a large sum in a poker game in which they both participated. In this particular game Rothstein was also a loser, but it was assumed—perhaps correctly—that Rothstein couldn't or wouldn't pay McManus some money he owed him. Because the state could not prove that McManus was the gunman, the judge ordered a verdict of "not guilty" and didn't allow the jury to deliberate.

In the 1929 (the year of his first Broadway stories) series of columns collected in *Trials and Tribulations* as "Arnold Rothstein's Final Payoff," Runyon gives us a preview of the world of his fiction. As John Mosedale notes, Runyon "admired Rothstein. Part of this represented the simple-minded tendency to find glamour in crime, to feel important knowing the dirty little secret."[14] Runyon was impressed by money, and Rothstein had plenty.

Runyon's opening column is quite brilliant: "If the ghost of Arnold Rothstein" hovered over his trial, it would have been "a violent shock to the enormous vanity of the dead gambler. . . . He lived in the belief that he was widely known. He had spent many years establishing himself as a landmark on old Broadway" (TT 206). His final payoff is to be a corpse. Life goes on without him; gamblers find other bookies and sources for their loans. The man who dominated the Broadway streets Runyon called the Roaring Forties is just another dead gambler; those summoned for jury duty didn't know him or know anyone who did, although perhaps some are falsely denying that they consort with such notorious figures.

While not at the level of Runyon's best trial reporting, his pieces comprising "Arnold Rothstein's Final Payoff" reflect some of the hard-boiled cynicism and tough irony that he brings to observing the trials as social spectacles and cultural commentary. The dying Rothstein becomes who he is—not a "millionaire gambler" or "the money king, with property scattered all over the Greater City, a big apartment house on fashionable Park Avenue, a Rolls-Royce and a Minerva at his beck and call, and secretaries and servants bowing to him," but "a man of the underworld. And as one of the 'dice hustlers' of the dingy garage lofts, and the 'mobsters' high and low [Rothstein] muttered, 'I won't tell'" (TT 222).

When the dying Rothstein refuses to identify his assassin, he confirms his identity as man of the underworld. Runyon grudgingly admires Rothstein's adhering to a code—even though Rothstein had always said, "If anyone gets me, they'll burn for it" (TT 221). Runyon's ironic comment is in gambler's argot: "Then another 'sure thing' went wrong on Broadway, where 'sure things' are always going wrong—the 'sure thing' that Rothstein would tell" (TT 222). Rothstein knew to which world he belonged and in dying shed his pretensions and embraced that world.

Indeed, within the narrative of the trial Runyon establishes sympathy with those who, like himself, gamble. Not one of the "big towners"—New Yorkers—being considered for jury duty thought a gambler was "a low character" and, in a remark to the prosecutor that Runyon clearly endorses, "One mumbled something about there being a lot of gamblers in Wall Street who didn't excite his prejudice" (TT 208). Runyon uses the term "boys" to refer to Broadway characters with whom Rothstein consorted. His humor also gives insight into the world in which the Broadway characters live and their routines: "It is a severe handicap to summon a man to such a remote quarter as the Criminal Courts Building along toward [horseracing's] post time"; or: "Some of the boys were wondering if Judge Nott would entertain a motion to switch his hours around and start in at 4 P.M., the usual hour of adjournment, and run to 10:30 A.M., which is a gentleman's bedtime" (TT 211).

"AL CAPONE"

In the columns collected under the title "Al Capone," we see Runyon's sympathy with the gangster on trial in 1931 for income tax evasion. Runyon never reveals that he knew Capone quite well or that he was taken with the splendor of Capone's lifestyle, including his Palm Island house. If in the Rothstein piece Runyon at times emphasizes the distance between himself and a gangster he knew well, here he somewhat bridges the distance by humanizing Capone as "Al," a victim of big government. He implies that citizens of America might expect more from their government—whom he refers to as "your Uncle Sam"—than its pursuit of Capone for $215,000 in back taxes. Runyon's calling Capone "Al" has the effect of making him a regular guy being pursued by a predatory government that wants to imprison him: "Your Uncle Sam argues that if a man spends a raft of money he must necessarily have a raft of money to spend, a theory that sounds logical unless your Uncle Sam is including horse players" (TT 235).

At the trial Runyon emphasizes the human beneath the cartoon stereotype: "[H]e was a terrific disappointment to the strictly seeing-Chicago tourist who felt that Al should have been vested at least in some of the panoply of his reputed office as Maharajah of the Hoods. Perhaps a cartridge belt. Some strangers felt this Chicago has been misrepresented to them" (TT 227). When asked by reporters whether he was concerned about his trial, the man Runyon calls "Al" responded: "Who wouldn't be worried?" (TT 228). While Runyon doesn't quite make a case for him, he does not demonize or mythicize him into a larger-than-life figure; in fact, Runyon brings him down to human size by acknowledging his own kinship with Capone as a fellow gambler: "Your correspondent cheerfully yields the palm he has borne with such distinction for lo these many years as the world's worst horse player to Mr. Alphonse Capone" (TT 242).

"MORGAN THE MIGHTY"

When Runyon covered the 1933 investigation of the Senate Committee on Banking and Currency of J. Pierpont Morgan's business empire, he showed no mercy. Runyon's scathing view of Morgan's arrogance and of the favoritism shown to insiders who accumulated stock at a special price before others could purchase it helped create the political environment for the establishment of the Securities and Exchange Commission (SEC). Ultimately, the Security and Exchange Commission was empowered to regulate how stocks were issued and sold.

The columns assembled under the title "Morgan the Mighty" begin "Morgan, the mighty, is on the spot!" Writing during the high tide of the Depression, Runyon the populist revels in the revelation that Morgan himself paid no taxes in 1931 and 1932 and that Morgan's partners paid a mere $48,000 in 1930 and nothing in 1931 and 1932. Using his characteristic technique of iteration to create caricatures of his figures, Runyon repeats the epigraph "the mighty" after Morgan's name as if Morgan were conquering royalty, the despot of

Mammon, descended from an ancient line of kings and emperors: "Morgan—Morgan, the Mighty—son of Morgan, the Magnificent" (TT 253). Early in his first dispatch he proposes a telling comparison: "It turns out to be an income tax inquiry, something like Al Capone's or any of the other boys" (TT 252).

Like Simpson in the Hall-Mills Case, Ferdinand Pecora, the staff lawyer for the Senate committee, is an aggressive attorney not cowed by privilege; Runyon uses him to generalize his own antipathy for Morgan's ingenuous and sanctimonious evasions: "Pecora is trying to clean all the windows in the great House of Morgan so he can get a good peek inside" (TT 254).

Runyon plays on isolationist "America First" sentiments when he reports that Morgan pays taxes to England but not the United States: "There sit the great J. Pierpont Morgan, proud overlord of the financial world, and his faithful henchmen, all damp with perspiration—the great Morgan who admits he pays Great Britain income taxes in the same years he pays nothing to his own United States" (TT 258). None of this hostility is present in Runyon's description of the trials of Capone or Rothstein.

By using the stiffly formal "there sit," Runyon distances himself from the privileged and Ivy League–educated Morgan and places himself within the ken of those who do pay taxes, including the family from which Pecora comes. The very next sentence, like its predecessor a separate paragraph, juxtaposes Pecora with Morgan: "And there the swarthy Ferdinand Pecora, son of Italian immigrant parents, patiently bears his way through a weird jungle of high finance until the twisting trails around him are alive with all manner of strange things in the form of disclosures that will astound this nation" (TT 258).

Unlike the columns on Capone, Runyon eschews disdain for "Your Uncle Sam" as a zealous prosecutor of the innocent, but rather almost gloats about how "a great democracy has [Morgan] in hand and is divesting him of so many sacred secrets" (TT 261). Yet the prior sentence is not without irony, for we learn that many Senators are rather tepid in their enthusiasm for Pecora's "efforts to spade up all the financial skeletons in the house of Morgan that he can locate" (TT 265).

Like the anecdote discussed in chapter 2 of the "lady and gentleman in evening clothes" who mistreated Pete Hankins, the Morgan piece in *Trial and Other Tribulations* crystallizes Runyon's class resentment ("Pete Hankins," IOT 14). Runyon's acerbic cynicism is central to his persona. At once a parvenu and a prominent member of the newspaper establishment, he is the ultimate insider who identifies with outsiders and who rebels against the position of the wealthy and prominent. Since money was the way Runyon proved himself an equal to the privileged class he hated and resented, he both accumulated and spent a great deal. Runyon, the nattiest of dressers whose taste tended toward the flamboyant, is a keen and often critical observer of the clothes worn by the trial principals.

Runyon sometimes regretted that he had not remained a rebel, but rather had become domesticated into the establishment and the prerogatives of success. That Capone and Rothstein flaunted their wealth in the face of old money was something that drew Runyon to them. He consorted with gangsters in part because he was in awe of their audacity at flouting social standards. Like Runyon, they often mirrored the values of the very class they despised.

RADIO DAYS

Before turning to the Lindbergh kidnapping trial and stressing its continuity with the sensational trials Runyon covered in *Trials and Tribulations,* we must examine the rise of radio as a complementary media to print journalism. By the 1920s, radio linked rural, small-town America to the great metropolitan areas. David Kennedy notes, "The political and social effects of radio were only beginning to be felt in the late 1920s. . . . Radio assaulted the insularity of local communities. It also, not incidentally, catalyzed the homogenization of American popular culture."[15] And, as Runyon understood in his Turps stories, radio also had a profound political effect. As Kennedy puts it, "Radio provided a means to concentrate and exercise power from the top, to bypass and shrink the influence of leaders and institutions that had previously mediated between individuals and local communities on the one side and the national political parties and the national government on the other."[16] And of course listeners, unlike participants in the give and take of town meetings, can't answer back and in some respects become children at the feet of their political father. No one understood this better than Roosevelt. In his nationally broadcast Fireside Chats, he articulated his credo and the New Deal philosophy of which, as Kennedy writes, "Security was the touchstone."[17] (Roosevelt, Kennedy elaborates, "breathed new meaning into ideas like liberty and freedom. He bestowed new legitimacy on the idea of government."[18]) Thus while aware of district leaders, the Turps take their major grievance about the firing of their mailman directly to President Roosevelt, who, because of his Fireside Chats, had become to them and others a kind of Superdaddy who empowered his listeners to believe that they mattered and that he would fix their local problems.

Thus, along with newspaper columns and news stories, radio helped create national unity and a common culture. National spectacles such as sporting events, political speeches, and sensational trials were transported into the homes and workplaces of the entire country. One didn't have to be a reader to experience vividly an entire world beyond one's own experience. Listeners, as Susan Douglas puts it, got "a more immediate sense of their nation as it was living and breathing, and talking right then and there."[19] Interestingly, in the early 1920s men and boys brought radio into homes, often as ham hobbyists, just as the male often returned home with the daily newspaper. At first, radio information was something of a male prerogative, but that soon changed.

Radio exploded in the 1920s as a form of entertainment. Susan Douglas observes: "But with the exception of the movies and nightclubs in urban areas, there also seemed to be the beginning of a shift in desire among some, especially in the middle classes, for the security, ease, and privacy of the home during leisure hours."[20] As Americans seemed to retreat into the domestic sphere, Runyon's Broadway characters, living economically on the edge and often in physical danger, provided entertainment for a domestic culture. The Turps, however, come home at a decent hour and enjoy domestic pleasures unknown to the characters of his Broadway stories. The desire to recuse oneself domestically created not only a readership for magazines and newspapers but also perhaps an audience for the surrogate reality found in the more exciting world of the Runyon stories.

Douglas proposes the following reasons for radio's boom: "Technical novelty, the thrill of hearing voices and music from so far away, hunger for entertainment and diversion, and the emerging desire to withdraw from public spaces, all these fueled the boom. . . . The turn to listening . . . was one of the important ways some men and boys navigated the changing definitions of masculinity and their increased presence in the domestic sphere in the 1920s. . . . [F]or men and boys of many ages in the early 1920s, tinkering with radio combined technical mastery with the chance to explore another strange but compelling dimension inaccessible to those without expertise and determination."[21] Just as newspaper readers could scan a paper to decide what they wanted to read or if and when they wanted to put the paper down or return to it, listeners also could listen when and how long they pleased.

By the early 1920s several radio stations had been established in New York and its surroundings. The first networks were formed a few years later: NBC with its New York flagship station WEAF in November 1926 and CBS with its New York flagship station WOR in 1927. The purpose of networks was to broadcast the same show at the same time to a wide audience. Just as sporting events—the World Series, the Kentucky Derby, major boxing championships—drove the circulation of newspapers, they also gave the networks their popularity. These networks also broadcast Duke Ellington and Cab Calloway from the Cotton Club in Harlem. After 1928 radio programs engaged a wider range of entertainers and musicians, including ethnic humor that was also popular on the vaudeville stage.

Radio exported to the rest of the nation Al Jolson, George Burns and Gracie Allen, Ed Wynn, Jack Benny, and Fred Allen, among others, as well as the musical talent of Bing Crosby and Rudy Vallee. Radio entertainment, just like Runyon's stories and Rockwell's drawings, often provided a world of make-believe during the Depression. One of the most popular shows was Martin Block's "Make Believe Ballroom," where he played selections from several bands.[22] Consequently, argues William R. Taylor, "a Broadway style, including everything from neon lights and publicity hype to dress and manner of speech, had somehow worked its way beneath our skins as a nation by sometime in the 1930s."[23] Runyon helped create that style. Because the radio had become the source of instant news bulletins, Orson Welles's notorious 1938 radio drama, "War of the Worlds," purporting to be a newscast about the invasion of Martians in New Jersey, caused hysteria in the New York area. Indeed, radio's instantaneousness—communicating synchronically as events unfolded with its listeners—pushed newspapers more and more away from strict reporting and toward featuring columnists like Runyon. Indeed, Runyon's use of the present tense in the New York stories that he first published in 1929 may be an effort to imitate the immediacy of radio.

Compared to print media, radio news was more dramatic and emotional and brought the information more quickly. Radio relieved suspense about what happened even as it intensified excitement. It also created a sense of intimacy as voices from distant wars and disasters entered the home. It reached a lower-class audience who might not be fluent readers or have adequate time—or lighting—to carefully peruse newspapers. As Susan Douglas writes, "[R]adio cultivated, especially among women, people of lower income levels, and those living in rural areas, a greater interest in the news, and for many of these groups an interest they didn't previously have."[24]

In the 1930s radio's impact on American culture increased dramatically, in large part because of its coverage of the 1932 Hoover-Roosevelt presidential election and of the Lindbergh baby's kidnapping. Broadcast radio stood vigil outside the Lindbergh estate near Hopewell, New Jersey, for seventy-two hours until the baby's body was found—and provided the first nationally broadcast radio trial. Radio could provide virtually immediate information. It could give listeners a sense that they were on the spot during trials or an election rally without their having to leave their homes. So threatening to the newspapers was the radio that newspapers demanded a December 1933 pact—entitled the Biltmore agreement—that radio would not broadcast news less than twenty-four hours old to protect the "freshness" of the daily papers. But, not surprisingly, within a year the pact was ignored.

With hourly news reports, the extra editions of newspapers lost their excitement and appeal. At a time when radio was becoming the favorite recreational activity, according to a *Fortune* poll, and was displacing newspapers as the major news source, Walter Winchell became a major radio figure.[25] Winchell, like Runyon, glamorized gangsters as simply pursuing what we would now call a different lifestyle from respectable folk, although later, in a highly publicized event, he became a confidante of J. Edgar Hoover and delivered to Hoover the notorious Louis "Lepke" Buchalter. He became a significant force in defining the political landscape. Winchell was born in 1897 into a Jewish family named Winechels. By eighteen he was part of a vaudeville act with Rita Green, who became his first wife. He conducted a snide but serious campaign against the Nazis beginning in the early 1930s, before Nazism was identified as a major evil in the United States. In the face of Hearst's resistance, Winchell exposed Nazi sympathizers in his columns; in March 1938 Hearst instructed his editors to excise from Winchell's columns "dangerous or disagreeable paragraphs."[26] To be sure, some of Winchell's asides were deplorable, as when he used the brush of homosexuality to tar the Nazis, whom he called Ratzis.[27]

Drawing upon the period's interest in slang—an interest cultivated in part by New York journalists like himself and Runyon—Winchell in 1930 brought his own brand of slang and wordplay to radio. Winchell was a great supporter of Roosevelt, and the administration fed him news tips and inside information. Until the fall of 1940 Winchell preached preparedness without intervention, but in the late 1930s he vigorously attacked isolationism. Indeed, he was an early critic of appeasement and took the lead in opposing Hitler and the Nazis. As Douglas writes, "His notorious staccato style conveyed a barely repressed hysteria. He was a shameless self-promoter, determined to make the news as well as announce it."[28] Yet he did much to garner support for Roosevelt's programs for economic and social justice and for a united patriotic front as the United States faced the inevitability of war.

Radio brought World War II into homes, including that of Runyon's fictional Brooklyn couple, the Turps. Americans learned about Europe, Hitler's conquests, and the Munich conference via radio; they heard live or instantly translated speeches by major world figures, and their interest in politics and international affairs increased in direct proportion to their knowledge. As Douglas notes, radio had obvious advantages: "[I]t was often first with breaking news, it was 'free,' you could get the news while doing something else; and listeners often felt transported to the scene of the event."[29] Between 1940 and 1944, due to the international events and World War II, the hours devoted to news rose dramatically, and by 1943 listeners tuned in an average of four-and-a-half hours a day. Although war correspondents were limited in expressing their opinions, especially before the United States entered the war, reporters such as Eric Sevareid, William Shirer, Charles Collingwood, H. V. Kaltenborn, and Cecil Brown became the kind of celebrities and stars that the columnists once were.

THE LINDBERGH TRIAL AS CULTURAL EVENT

With his first successful solo nonstop flight over the Atlantic to Paris on May 21, 1927, Charles Lindbergh captured the popular imagination. An enormous parade on June 13, 1927, followed his return to New York. The newspapers gave the entire event enormous attention. When Lindbergh visited Washington shortly after his return to America, Runyon caught the spirit of the euphoria of Lindbergh's triumph, a spirit that crystallized the optimism of the later 1920s before the Stock Market Crash. As John Mosedale writes, "The man, the event, the times came together in an outburst of adulation without parallel. The technology of communication made instant mass hero worship possible."[30] With characteristic ambivalence and with tongue in cheek, Runyon mocked the hero worship of a young man by an audience desperate for something larger than itself, even as he understood the captivating appeal of the handsome youth who had flown the Atlantic:

> A bashful-looking, long-legged, gangling boy, with cheeks of pink and with a cowlick in his hair that won't let the blond locks stay slicked down, came back to his home folks today one of the biggest in all the world.
> *Lindy!*
> *My heart, how young he seemed!*

And how weighty, how absurd the Colonel Charles Augustus Lindbergh seemed as you gazed at him sitting there, as slim as your finger.[31]

Hitler was an admirer of Lindbergh as a paradigm of the blond Nordic hero—clean cut, hatless, and a teetotaler—and the attraction proved mutual.

The March 1, 1932 kidnapping of the Lindbergh baby dominated the media. Even the elite *New York Times* devoted thirteen columns of its March 2, 1932 issue to news and photographs. Finally, on May 12, 1932 the baby was found in a shallow grave near the Lindbergh home. Bruno Richard Hauptmann, the alleged kidnapper and murderer, was arrested on September 19, 1934. The guilty verdict came in on February 13, 1935, and he was sentenced to die in the electric chair on March 18, 1935.

The kidnapping captured the attention of the nation. Not only had one of America's heroes been hit by tragedy, but a whirlwind of drama seemed to surround the case as it developed. With themes of celebrity, suspense, ransom money, and murder, Lindbergh's case truly became the trial of the century. Thus, it was not surprising that on January 2, 1935 such famous reporters as Damon Runyon and Walter Winchell descended on the small town of Flemington, New Jersey, to observe and report on the trial. H. L. Mencken called it "the greatest story since the Resurrection."[32] Indeed, many observers were at least as interested in getting a glimpse of media celebrities attending the trial such as Dorothy Kilgallen, Ford Maddox Ford, Edna Ferber, Alexander Woollcott, and Heywood Broun, along with Runyon and Winchell, as they were in the principals in the case.

As we have seen in our discussion of the circus trials covered in Runyon's *Trials and Tribulations,* the media—newspapers, magazines, radio, newsreels—not only reported on events but participated in creating events. The Lindbergh case was a litmus test for the power of the media and gives an idea of the world in which Runyon was working. Using techniques that had boosted the importance of major sporting events and employing reporters like Runyon, who had made his mark in sportswriting, the media created a performance and spectacle that captured the imagination of the American public. Either without the court's knowledge or with tacit approval, newsreel companies brought cameras into court and concealed microphones; the resulting films were shown in theaters. Only near the end of the trial did the judge object. As Ludovic Kennedy notes, "The demand for copy was staggering—the coverage given to the trial exceeded any comparable event in American history, including the Armistice and the Olympic Games. It was estimated that an average of half a million words spewed out of Flemington daily; the trial transcript alone took sixty thousand."[33] Clearly there is a direct line to the Simpson trial some fifty years later and to the kind of sensationalistic journalism that became the stuff of television. As Albert Friendly and Ronald L. Goldfarb have observed: "The enormous growth of the press, the extent and vividness of its impact (compounded through the pervasive medium of television), its ability to blanket not merely a community but the whole nation with its views, its opinions, and the force of its reports have made its potential for injury more overpowering than ever before."[34]

William Randolph Hearst remarked of the Lindbergh trial: "The public is even more fond of entertainment than it is of information."[35] The term "media circus" aptly describes the Lindbergh trial, but the spectacle trial as media entertainment and "infocircus" has its origin in the Hall-Mills and Snyder-Gray trials, both of which Runyon covered extensively, as well as in the 1924 Nathan Leopold–Richard Loeb trial for the kidnapping and killing of a young boy named Bobby Franks. Frank Rich defines the mediathon as "a relentless hybrid of media circus, soap opera and tabloid journalism."[36] The term "mediathon" applies to the coverage of the Sam Shepherd trial and the Kennedy assassination, including Jack Ruby's killing of Lee Harvey Oswald. Rich's contemporary examples are the Lewinsky-Clinton scandal, the Simpson trial, Woody Allen's private life, and the TV marriage and annulment of Darva Conger as well as other "reality" television. (How often in his Broadway stories, from "Romance in the Roaring Forties" [1929] to "Tight Shoes" [1936], is Runyon aware of the power of the press to make the news!)

The Lindbergh kidnapping was also a turning point in the ascendancy of radio as a medium for news and for mediathons of the kind that paved the way for the continuous coverage of the Kennedy assassination, the Iraq war, the O. J. Simpson trial, and the Gore-Bush postelection marathon. While newspapers certainly could seize national attention with captivating and sensational stories, they were, finally, asynchronic with events and thus reported on events that had already occurred. Radio, on the other hand, was synchronic and thus offered a vital element of intimacy, vividness, and immediacy, as if the listener were there. By 1935, nearly 67 percent of households owned radios.[37]

When the Lindbergh baby was kidnapped in 1932, the news was transmitted almost immediately, solely as a result of radio. Both the WOR and CBS stations in New York interrupted their programs within an hour of each other to announce news of the kidnapping. By the following morning, two of the major networks, CBS and NBC, established special lines of communication to reporters on the scene in Hopewell, New Jersey, near the Lindbergh estate. As Douglas noted: "Both networks kept a constant vigil for seventy-two days until the baby's body was found. On-the-spot reporting had been established technically and journalistically."[38] The nation took part in a public ritual of sadness and sympathy, a ritual orchestrated by radio sounds and choreographed in the press.

The Lindbergh trial marked the beginning of nationally broadcast murder trials. With rampant competition among newspapers and radio, restraint in a case such as Lindbergh—that spanned some three years before reaching trial—took a backseat to attracting readership and listeners by offering "breaking news," often in the form of biased headlines and flamboyant commentaries. Because the media had achieved such a profound impact on society, it also came to be seen as capable of hindering justice.

Winchell, perhaps like the majority of his counterparts in the media, held as his creed that the defendant, Hauptmann, had acted alone in the kidnapping and murder of the twenty-month-old Lindbergh baby.[39] While Winchell seemed to have preceded the jury in finding the defendant guilty and made no attempt to hide his bias during his reports on the trial, Runyon—said to be "the best-dressed journalist at the trial"—gradually put aside his own prejudices and began making keen cultural observations.[40] Noel Behn has argued convincingly that some of the evidence was quite dubious and that supporting witnesses for Hauptmann, especially several handwriting experts, were discouraged by the threat of being ridiculed and pilloried by unfriendly media.[41]

Although Winchell never wavered in championing Hauptmann's guilt, Runyon became increasingly detached and thoughtful. While waiting for the verdict Runyon described in detail the "litter of milk cans and paper bags on the floor" and the precise reactions and garb of participants.[42] Of one participant who wore a white hat every day, the clothes-conscious Runyon wrote, "His best friends and severest critics should inform the dapper gentleman from Perth Amboy that the white lady is all right for Tom Mix, but not for one of Jersey's well-dressed gents."[43]

In general, Runyon's thoughtful comments on the Lindbergh trial contrast to the qualities that marked his columns collected in *Trials and Tribulations.* For the most part he eschewed the sensationalism, cynicism, and provocative descriptions of predatory women that marked several of the pieces in that collection and not so incidentally contributed to the feeding frenzy of media hysteria that accompanied those trials. Yet early in the Lindbergh trial he had milked the sensationalism, beginning his report January 3, 1935, the day the trial began, with a characteristically precise description in terms that would arouse the sympathy and anger of his readers: "They hand slender, gentle, little Anne Morrow Lindbergh the stained, torn garments that her baby wore the last night she saw him alive in the crib, as she sits on the witness stand this afternoon, bravely fighting back tears."[44] And he juxtaposes the woman on the witness stand to Hauptmann's wife—with the Hauptmanns' "own little son"—while telling us "Hauptmann himself stares at the lovely figure on the witness stand out of his deep-sunken eyes, his face impassive."[45] Runyon often creates sensation and spectacle for the consumption of readers who purchase the papers. In this column, he organizes his story around the mother's testimony rather than the father's, whom he calls Colonel Lindbergh; he speaks of the "day of drama which reaches its peak when his wife is on the witness stand facing the staring eyes of the spectators, with half the women in the courtroom sobbing in sympathy with her."[46]

Contributing a short piece to a May 1935 *Cosmopolitan* article entitled "Why They'll Never Forget the Trial of the Century," an article that invited ten notable writers who were at the trial to comment, Runyon wrote in favor of abolishing the death sentence:

> My chief impression of the Hauptmann trial is this: It was the strongest argument for the abolition of capital punishment that our nation has seen in years. The fact that a human life is at stake is always responsible for the morbid curiosity of the mob in a murder trial. . . .
>
> Bruno Richard Hauptmann may be guilty. I don't know. I heard all the evidence and I still don't know. If guilty[,] death perhaps seems too small a punishment. But the possibility that he may be telling the truth slight as it may appear to some, would deter me from putting him to death.
>
> It is the lingering doubt in my own mind in this particular case and the knowledge born of long experience and observation, that the death penalty has not served to minimize capital crimes and that at best it merely arouses the worst human instincts when a big murder is afoot, that causes me to recall the trial as a tremendous brief against the legal taking of life. (*Cosmopolitan*, May 1935, 36)

In his book on the Lindbergh trial, Ludovic Kennedy has contrasted Runyon's mode of reporting—his description, for example, of the surroundings and personalities while a verdict was awaited—with Winchell's partisan role: "Winchell, who from an early date had proclaimed Hauptmann's guilt, had a privileged position near the balustrade and was sometimes observed passing notes to the prosecution. He habitually wore dark glasses, uncommon at the time, said one reporter, and unknown in winter, which made him easily recognized, if that was their purpose. He began his broadcasts against a chatter of telegraph keys and with the words, 'Good evening America, and all the ships at sea.'"[47] If anything showed Winchell's celebrity and influence during this time, it was when the twelve jurors were being selected. According to Kennedy, prospective jurors were asked whether they had "formed any firm view about the guilt or innocence of the defendant, had they been unduly influenced by anything they had read in the papers, especially the *Daily Mirror* column of Walter Winchell?"[48] This reference to Winchell is highly indicative not only of the influence of the media but also of the effects of biased reporting.

Radio played a major role in keeping the case in the public imagination. When the ransom money—gold certificates that were no longer accepted as legal currency—began to surface around New York City, Winchell excoriated bank tellers: "Boys, if you weren't such a bunch of saps and yaps, you'd have already captured the Lindbergh kidnappers."[49] Convinced that Hauptmann had acted alone, Winchell, according to Behn, ignored evidence to the contrary and shaped the verdict before the trial began: "Radio was coming of age with trial. An estimated forty million Americans were listening to on-the-scene broadcast reports from Flemington hours before the first headlines could hit the streets. In addition to regularly scheduled newscasts, New York City alone had nine special reports on eight different stations in just the afternoons of each trial day. Even in the area of 'special features,' radio held its own with print. The papers had contracted a series of experts, including psychiatrists and legal scholars, to write about the trial. Their commentaries had proved to be very popular with the readership, and very influential. Radio was putting on its own specialists with equal success. . . ."[50]

On January 2, 1935, the day the trial began, over 100 photographers and between 300 and 350 reporters were on hand to report the Lindbergh trial. As Susan Douglas describes it, "The local sheriff sold tickets to the trial; vaudeville performers offered witnesses contracts to go on stage; tourists by the busload descended on the small town. There was daily coverage of what went on in court. . . . In the courtroom [Winchell] was as much an actor as a reporter, giving tips to the prosecution, mouthing comments to Hauptmann, sitting next to Hauptmann's wife during testimony."[51]

Friendly and Goldfarb observed: "The enormous growth of the press, the extent and vividness of its impact . . . its ability to blanket not merely a community but the whole nation with its views, its opinions, and the force of its reports have made its potential for injury more overpowering than ever before."[52] Reading about the trial, we realize that the press's ability to shape public sentiment and influence a criminal proceeding was a significant part of the trial of Bruce Hauptmann.

The media stigmatized Hauptmann as a criminal prior to and throughout the trial. With such tremendous interest in the case and subsequent vast coverage, Hauptmann had little chance of receiving a truly impartial trial. In the face of such a tragedy surrounding one of America's heroes, the public desperately wanted closure; the media had no qualms about providing such closure by convicting Hauptmann on a seemingly daily basis. Throughout much of the trial, Runyon appeared to have a strong dislike for Hauptmann, while offering a very sympathetic portrayal of the Lindberghs. As he wrote in a front-page story in the *New York Daily American* following the first day of the trial: "Bruno Richard Hauptmann, cold, silent, morose type of the Old World criminal with a record as a 'bad guy' behind him, goes on trial for his life in this quiet little town [of Flemington, New Jersey] tomorrow morning. . . . [He] faces a chain of circumstantial evidence that seems strong enough to bind him in the electric chair in the state prison at Trenton."[53]

Given such highly negative portrayals in which popular columnists were already sentencing him to death, there was little chance for Hauptmann to convince the public of his innocence. Further evidence of his conviction by the media can be extracted from an article that appeared in the *New York American* on the second day of the trial by a psychiatrist, Dr. Edward Cowles. He had apparently studied Hauptmann's facial structure and features and had been able to formulate conclusions that would reinforce Hauptmann's image as a cold-hearted criminal. As he proclaimed: "In studying Hauptmann one is struck by his floppy ears. Eyebrows are well curved but his eyes are deeply set. The back of his head is rather flat. Hauptmann is distinctly psychopathic. This means his nervous system has never fully developed and his standard of thinking is of a lower order."[54]

CONCLUSION: THE SPECTATOR CULTURE

Well before the Lindbergh trial, Walter Winchell created the business of turning gossip into *commodity* by covering scandalous behavior of public figures and embroidering sensational trials. We might say he understood the materiality of gossip, or, put another way, of how human curiosity could be transformed into currency by the sale of newspapers. Runyon among others followed his lead in churning words as *material*. Indeed, gossip became an entity of its own; the mention of the famous and near famous within the most mundane column about a restaurant or an event elicited interest. Winchell saw the trial as a chance to prove to his peers that he was a reporter rather than simply a gossipmonger. Yet even while he complained of the circus atmosphere, he as much as anyone contributed to it by, as Gabler puts it, "forcing himself into the trial as a protagonist. . . . Thereafter, the media would be as much participants in an event as reporters of it, shaping and sensationalizing on a new scale and turning events into occasions, national festivals."[55]

What had begun with the Hall-Mills case—and, perhaps before that, the 1924 Leopold-Loeb trial—as an overly intense and competitive battle for public attention had given way to one of the most poignant displays of sensationalism in a criminal case: the Hauptmann trial. In 1937, a group representing the American Bar Association and the American Society of Newspaper Editors reviewed the media behavior during that trial and concluded: "The trial of Bruce Hauptmann . . . exhibited, perhaps, the most spectacular and depressing example of improper publicity and professional misconduct ever presented to the people of the United States in a criminal trial."[56] As a consequence of the circus-like atmosphere that surrounded the Hauptmann trial, the American Bar Association convened in January 1936 to form an eighteen-member special committee comprised of members of the press, radio, and bar to set "standards of publicity of judicial proceedings."[57]

The newspapers in the Hall-Mills trial and the media in the Hauptmann trial played upon their readers' desire for a neat denouement. Thus, in a dangerous cycle, the media kept pumping out more of what the public wanted: more evidence, witnesses, stories, and hype. Anticipating our own media trials, some conducted on television without courtrooms, the trials became public spectacles in which the newspapers created their readers' need for a sense of an ending—and, for some tabloid readers, the need to find that ending in the neat solution of a public ritualistic execution.

As always, we see a conflict between Runyon the reporter who wrote for money and fame and Runyon the idealist. With his strong visual imagination focusing on physical appearance, dress, manner-isms, and idiosyncrasies, Runyon helped transform the figures in his trial reporting into cartoons and thus contributed to simplistic media feeding frenzies. Yet perhaps in response to the hysteria surrounding the Lindbergh kidnapping and murder as well as the role that Winchell's radio broadcasts played, Runyon the idealist recoiled at the excesses of the Hauptmann trial. Although Runyon understood the appeal of stories of lust and greed, we often see, in his covering of trials, his sympathy for the have-nots. Runyon characteristically takes the part of the underclass. The only Runyon story Hearst ever rejected was one he wrote in August 1927 about the anarchists Nicola Sacco and Bartolomeo Vanzetti, whom Runyon believed were unfairly convicted of murder because, as Italian immigrants and self-proclaimed anarchists, they offended the moneyed and power classes; his unpublished story began: "They're frying Sacco and Vanzetti in the morning."[58]

THE ART AND ARTISTRY
OF RUNYON'S FICTION

INTRODUCTION

In a later edition of *The American Language,* H. L. Mencken observed of Broadway language at the end of the 1930s: "[I]t is from this quarter that most American slang comes, a large part of it invented by gag-writers, newspaper columnists, and press agents, and the rest borrowed from the vocabularies of criminals, prostitutes and the lower orders of show folk. There was a time when it was chiefly propagated by vaudeville performers, but now that vaudeville is in eclipse the torch has been taken over by the harlequins of movie and radio."[1] Of course, Runyonese was a significant variation. Above all, Runyon wrote to amuse himself, and we should never forget that words are his drug of choice. He savors the juice of his own language. Runyon has his own voice and style. He puns and plays with words as if they were mental putty. He also knew gangster argot from his time on the city desk. *Variety* called his language "slanguage," which, according to William R. Taylor, "reflected, among other sources, the richness of Jewish humor and the Yiddish Theatre. . . . It more closely resembled a distinctive manner of speech, in effect an amalgam of languages highly expressive of the historical moment: jokes, an inventive punning and toying with words reminiscent of vaudeville, new ways of representing speech in dialect, a distinctive syntax and temporal mode (i.e., Runyon's historical present tense), a repertoire of characters unmatched since the early days of Western humor, a colorful array of 'monikers' to designate them, and anecdotal lore and narrative configurations that sealed the locality in myth."[2]

Like the recently deceased filmmaker Billy Wilder, Runyon invented a gallery of swindlers, opportunists, and manipulators. Yet like Wilder he had a romantic and idealistic side. Runyon's anecdotal realism is often a disguise for surrealism and cartoon. When describing what he considers moral decrepitude—especially older men preying upon innocent young women, as in "The Lily of St. Pierre" (1930)—his realism goes beyond necessary specificity to the point where its excess and overdeterminism approaches what we might call hyper-realism. Note, too, how Runyon anticipates the cartoon universe of Art Spiegelman's *The Wild Party*—itself a commentary on the excesses of the 1920s—and even *Maus*. The rapid reversals in fortune and discontinuity in plot may owe something to a number of genres: vaudeville; popular shows like the 1938 *Hellzapoppin* with Ole Olsen and Chic Johnson; popular cinematic forms such as Charlie Chaplin's films and later, those of the Three Stooges and the Marx Brothers. As Edward Rothstein notes, "[T]he silent-film version of America is saturated with sensation and physical energy, playful inventiveness and human possibility."[3] While not all of Runyon's characters triumph, those who do remind us of Rothstein's view of early film stars and film producers: "These were the same qualities [i.e., sensation and physical energy, playful inventiveness, and human possibility] associated with the great stars of the era, ranging from Mary Pickford to Rudolph Valentino, who themselves began in poverty and replicated, at least publicly, the triumph of their characters. The same was true of the early film producers, many of whom, like Adolph Zukor were immigrants. . . . [T]hey enacted the American myth in their own reinvented lives as much as in their films. [T]he American idea of material prosperity and individualism has become generalized. It has become associated with the nature of modernity itself."[4] The appeal of American culture, including Runyon's stories and his autobiographical anecdotes, may rest in part on what Rothstein calls "its promise of unbounded possibility."[5]

Runyon's early Western tales exhibit the mixture of cynicism and sentimentality that marks the Broadway stories. An anecdote like the early "In One Ear" effectively shows Runyon's sympathy for the outsider. In that story, a man named Johnny Wingfield is committed to an insane asylum for life because he put a skunkweed wreath on the casket of Mr. G. H. Pendleton, the town's richest man. Pendleton was Wingfield's former partner and had euchred him out of his share of their business. As Runyon writes in "Christmas Revenge," "A no-account guy without money, and a no-account guy with plenty of it, are two entirely different matters in my old home town and everywhere else" (RFTL 221). Character psychology is never Runyon's forte, and these early tales do not explore the characters' and narrators' grammar of motive as deftly as the best of his Broadway stories. Often the plotting is weaker and the endings flaccid.

Since to Runyon people are people, it is hardly surprising that the values of his rural hometown mirror those of his current hometown, New York. In the 1907 "The Defense of Strikerville," he is on the side of the have-nots—both the strikers and the men, desperately needing employment, hired for $2 a day by the Colorado National Militia; he also enjoys the special language of the males in the squad room discussing "that despised arm of the military resources" (RFTL 61). Sent to suppress the strikers, the militia befriends them and protects them.

Runyon's world is one where folk of modest means or less are trying to get along by winning at the horses or at cards or dice. Many if not most of them live on what Runyon calls "Dream Street" in "Dream Street Rose" (1932); much like Kafka's characters, they are trapped in a claustrophobic world from which they cannot escape, even while dreaming of a transformed state or metamorphosis—in Runyon's stories by marriage, fame, or money. That transformed state rarely arrives, and when the transformation does occur, it is often in the form of a grotesque joke.

Runyon understood the materialistic basis of life in the city and often chronicled that, but he also looked for personal stories that ran against the grain of the underlying commercial spirit and greed. As we shall see in stories like "The Lily of St. Pierre" (1930), "Little Miss Marker" (1932), and "Johnny One-Eye" (1941), Runyon had a strong sentimental streak, particularly regarding children and animals. Yet reversals often flout expectations that all will come out well. After being temporarily transformed into an ebullient and generous man by loving a little girl left as a marker in "Little Miss Marker," once the girl dies, Sorrowful reverts to his gloomy former self, a self that was selfish, stingy, lonely, and unresponsive to others.

Since the narrator is a Broadway character in all the longer stories after 1929, I shall use the term "Broadway stories" even for those that take place outside Manhattan. Derived and shaped in part by Runyon's coverage of trials discussed in chapter 3—coverage that continued as he was writing his early Broadway stories—the narrator of the Broadway stories reports to us on the spectacles he has seen or heard. As Taylor notes, "In this world of mayhem, it is the function of the narrative voice to exercise a slightly distant controlling influence. The historical present in which he addresses us is a measure of his narrative control."[6] Perhaps, as Taylor argues, Runyon's verbal style owes something to radio drama. Runyon interweaves redundancy; repetition not only reinforces the dramatization of telling but gives the presentation the feel of New York speech rhythms. For example, in "For a Pal" (1932), the narrator—one of the few Runyon narrators who does not let on how he knows the story and does not describe his own dialogue with a principal character—speaks of Little Yid's family owning a factory where "they make caps such as some citizens wear on their heads" or "a Chinese ducket being a complimentary ducket that is punched full of holes like Chinese money, and which you do not have to pay for" (DRO 497).

Runyon understood the difficulty of rendering the city and chose to render its smallest component parts. As Rothstein has observed, "[T]he city is not an autonomous object: it is itself the effect of complex cultural transfixions."[7] As a human construct in which myriad conscious and unconscious factors play a part, "the city is potentially a large-scale metaphor, a landscape that mirrors the cultural physiognomy of its creators. Yet if the city is to a great extent a cultural mirror, it cannot be easily evaluated simply by observing its effects. Its appearance may itself be an effect rather than just a cause."[8]

RUNYON'S STYLE

Let us examine some of the major ingredients of Runyonesque style. Runyon, as we have noted, began his career in New York as a sportswriter and never lost his fascination for the sports world. Thus also influencing his style was the fast pace of sportswriting: early deadlines, description of action in the present, and the need to open strongly and move to a grand crescendo. Sportswriting also taught him how to structure a story so that the early moments anticipate the account of winners and losers in terms of an absolute result. Many of the agons of his stories are about who wins and who loses, and the pace of events could be broken down into rounds and innings.

Runyon is a master at capturing in breathless sentences the movement and confusion of the crowded city: "A traffic copper takes a peek at the situation, and calls for the reserves from the Forty-seventh Street station, and somebody else sends for the fire truck down the street, and pretty soon cops are running from every direction, and the fire-engines are coming, and the big guy in his shirt-sleeves is more excited than ever" ("The Hottest Guy in the World" [1930]. ROB 363). What gives this sentence its energy is the accretion of independent clauses with present tense verbs emphasizing action, while the concatenation of these visual—indeed cinematic—clauses are linked by the increasingly excited series of five "ands."

Runyon's language is secular, particular, and derived from what he saw and heard. His language has the hyperbole and excess of the confrontational and aggressive people who inhabited the world in which he lived. His style is created from a dialogue of styles; certainly his neologisms depend for their effect on their place in sentences with ordinary words. His language mixes gangster argot, the rhythm and sounds of jazz, and the pace and tempo of burlesque comedians. The gangster argot was probably homogenized from Jewish, Italian, and Irish immigrants who did not have much formal education. The heavy consonant clusters—almost metallic in hardness and reflecting a New York dialect that enunciates consonants, especially the final one, with emphasis and panache—reinforce the jazziness of Runyon's prose.

Runyon's use of vernacular, slangy, and even boozy, heavily accented Broadway speech inverts the expectations of high art and expresses his underlying skepticism about wealth, social position, and respectability in a world where wealth and power get affirmative action. As if mocking locutions of the polite world, Runyon uses odd archaisms, like "dast" for the past of "dare" as in "I dast not leave John Ignatius Junior for a minute" in "Butch Minds the Baby" (1930; ROB 245). When we read aloud, we see how Runyon has invented a style that is noisy, tumultuous, cacophonous, brassy, and shrill—a phonic metaphor for Broadway. While he not only uses slang and flagrantly ungrammatical language, he also uses grammatically lax conversational speech that was characteristic of discourse heard in the Broadway beat he knew. His stylistic play—violating agreement in terms of verbs and subjects—subverts our expectations in the way that the behavior of his subjects often does; both transport us from our respectable world.

Like Spike Lee's films, which also capture the hurley-burley and intensity of the modern city, Runyon's Broadway stories have a blunt hard edge. His style is quite deliberately not the nuanced, subtle high-culture style of a Jane Austen or Henry James, who establish a deft grammar of motives in which we understand behavior from carefully established verbal codes making distinctions within a tradition of manners. Indeed, Runyon subverts this high cultural tradition. The discrepancy between the street parlance with which the narrator or characters describe behavior and their actual motives and intents is part of the humor. The narrator inverts the expected meanings of words. For example, he uses "joke" and "laugh" ironically because these terms disguise the malice and the joke will be lost on the victim. He uses words normally applied to behavior in the respectable world to describe the career trajectory of gangsters, such as "prominent," "promising," "up and coming," and "from a modest beginning."

One of the underlying themes of Runyon's work is the elasticity of language as well as class and social distinction. Runyon's own invented and elastic language not only reflects the world he describes but enacts and creates it: "Prominent" can mean that one is the object of public attention from the police, as when we are told, in "The Hottest Guy in the World" (1930): "[C]oppers always blame everything no matter where it happens on the most prominent guy they can think of, and Big Jule is quite prominent all over the U.S.A." (ROB 355). Thus Frankie Ferocious, whose real name is "something in Italian like Feroccio . . . builds himself up until he is a very large operator in merchandise of one kind and another, especial alcohol" ("Sense of Humor" [1934], ROB 269). To be "considered a handy man in every respect" does not mean that someone fixes small appliances but that he is a reliable gangster, probably one not averse to using a gun in a pinch ("Gentlemen, the King!" [1931], ROB 171). In Runyon argot, to go to "college" is to spend significant time in prison, as if Runyon were parodying how respectable people get their education in contrast to how those in the underworld get theirs.

Runyon's style depends on the reader's understanding the ironic discrepancy between what he says and what he means. As the narrator frequently observes, when one has "potatoes" (money), one is treated differently—and the narrator in virtually every story is one of the marginalized have-nots. His characters, and often the narrator himself, measure people in terms of what they are "holding" in terms of money. In "Princess O'Hara" (1934), the oft-repeated phrase "a little off-hand guzzling" describes not social drinking but rather those who wish to use a horse-drawn victoria for sexual petting—and perhaps metonymically tasting one another's fluids; this phrase sets the scene for a romance between the young woman victoria driver known as "Princess O'Hara" and a Frenchman named Prince Georges Latour (ROB 433).

Like James Joyce, Runyon uses musical sounds to reinforce meaning. Take, for example, "The Lily of St. Pierre": The speaker sings baritone in a quartet in Good Time Charley Bernstein's speakeasy, and many of the quartet's songs are about unrequited love, the subject of the story. Phonics become part of the texture not only in the quartet's "ho-hum-hum-ho-hum-hum," "bum-bum," "bay-hay-ay-ay-BEE!" (ROB 132–33) but also in the jarring sound of Jack O'Hearts shooting of Louis the Lug, the tenor of the quartet: "whangity-whang-whang" (ROB 134). Runyon had almost an infinite variety of phonic terms for the sound of guns, from the "big whoom" (ROB 352) and a "big blooey-blooey" (ROB 543) to "root-a-toot-toot" (ROB 655) and "tooty-toot-toot out across the water" (ROB 529). These sounds are the sounds of comic strips and movie cartoons. Indeed, Runyon's tales are often farcical, highly visual, full of mayhem and pratfalls such as we might find in Disney cartoons— or, as we have noted, in Chaplin or Marx Brothers films.

Drawing on ethnic sources and the freewheeling saloon culture of his Western heritage. Runyon contributed to inventing a peculiar American English in contrast to the WASP upper-class language that mirrored the stultified discourse of the English genteel class. His creative neologisms imply an alternative American homegrown culture, one that recognizes without embarrassment or disguise ambition and the pursuit of money. Runyon's language is as rich in its surprise and inventiveness as that of James Joyce, another great twentieth-century writer of urban life who had a wonderful ear. It is as if Runyon were on a verbal trampoline, showing off how he can shape and twist and reinvent language and looking for clever variations on terms he has heard and/or used before. His language reflects the odd combination of incipient chaos, glitter, and promise of excitement that constantly percolates in New York. In Runyonese, a gun is a "Betsy" or a "John Roscoe." Someone carrying a gun has "that certain business on him." Sometimes called "that thing" that one "takes out" in emergencies, the gun almost becomes a metonymy for penis (see "Situation Wanted," ROB 659).

Other recurring terms include: "put the zing on" for attracting a man or "make a powerful play" for a man courting. Other examples of Runyonese: "to have many coconuts" is to be wealthy; "as clean as a jaybird," is to be without any means; "to scrag" or "to guzzle" is to kill—but "to guzzle" also can mean to make love; a "pancake" or a "looking pancake" is an attractive woman. An unattractive woman is a "blouwzola" or an "old komoppo"; "puts his checks back in the rack" means to die; "deals them off the arm" is to wait on tables; a "boat race" is a fixed horserace; "make a scratch" is to get a little money one way or another; "the old ackamarackus" is a confidence game, as when the Lemon Drop Kid in the story of that name pretends his lemon drops are really a secret medicine that has cured him of arthritis.

Runyon would have subscribed to Oscar Wilde's view that we are most ourselves when we wear a mask or disguise our identity. Runyon invents names that speak to the ruling quality of character. (Even today the Mafioso have names like the Dapper Don for John Gotti.) Thus a kvetch named Philly the Weeper "is such a guy as will go around with a loaf of bread under his arm weeping because he is hungry" (DRO 3). Madame La Gimp is an alcoholic woman who walks with a limp; Foots Samuels has large feet. His characters often lack last names, as if to hide their real identity from the criminal justice system or as if poverty and social class had deprived them of full names; the appellations "Mister," "Mr.," "Mrs.," or "Misses" are rarely used. Of a character named "Regret," who obsessively bemoans how his horses barely lose, the narrator of "The Bloodhounds of Broadway" (1930), writes: "What this guy's real name is I never hear, and anyway names make no difference to me, especially on Broadway, because the chances are that no matter what name a guy has, it is not his square name" (ROB 90). The wealthy—like Paul D. Veere, Justin Veezee—or those with a respectable position—like Cap Duhaine, the head of Pinkertons, the private security company hired to police racetracks—are more likely to have full names or at least last names, while the economically and socially marginal carry appellations such as that of the racetrack hanger-on "Hot Horse Herbie." While Silk, whose smoothness serves her self-interest in "Broadway Financier" (1932), is denoted by a single four-letter name, other women have found replacements for their first or last names. Miss Beaulah Beauregard's real name is Benson, and her supposed "ancestral" estate home is a very poor farm dependent on one old mule ("It Comes Up Mud," 1933). We can be sure in "Pick the Winner" (1933) that "Cutie" Singleton's given name is not Cutie.

Runyon's present tense style speaks to the moment of an action; his sentences are unfolding temporal events. His characters live in the present tense as if they were sealed hermetically from past and future. In style and substance Runyon relies on what might be called, from one perspective, an aesthetics of insubstantiality. That in his world everything is not merely kinetic but ephemeral is emphasized by the present tense. Tom Clark has argued that Runyon's present tense derives from the dialect of Broadway; he cites as evidence the testimony in the Rothstein murder trial.[9] The characteristic present tense also may owe something to tabloids, where the present moment seduces readers and where the unseen flash camera catches a momentary event. It may be that the popularity of radio plays, dependent on listeners hearing words arriving by voice, sharpened Runyon's interest in the oral quality of his speakers. The speaker is an on-site reporter giving outsiders the inside information. The present tense suggests a cinematic camera, a rolling and roving eye recording and synthesizing all it sees. Yet the tense also conveys an omniscient historic sense of the subculture it describes. The narrator writes of Asleep, a murderer who puts people to sleep permanently in "Situation Wanted" (1936): "For several years along in the late 'twenties, he handles all of the late Dave the Dude's private business when Dave the Dude is at war with the late Big Moey, and when somebody finally takes care of Dave the Dude himself, Asleep is with Big Moey for quite a while" (ROB 658). Typically this sentence is more loaded in what it reveals about the gangster subculture than it seems; for one thing, there is a hint that Asleep may have killed Dave the Dude at the behest of Big Moey; for another, within the story's context, the war between Dave the Dude and Big Moey is not different from and is just as important as the Spanish Civil War where Asleep sells his services—perhaps once again—to the highest bidder. For Asleep is the ultimate capitalist, selling his services to whomever will do him the most good. As an aspiring entrepreneurial capitalist, he sells his services for a piece of land in Miami, which he appropriately turns into a cemetery where his customers sleep; his first customer is none other than Benny, a rival for his fiancée, a rival whom Asleep murders. Asleep is not only still in the death business, but by killing Benny, he has broken his own rule of killing only "for professional purposes, and when I am paid for the same" (ROB 659).

The *now* matters in urban culture where nature's rhythms play a reduced role. Appropriate to characters who take names that are not their own, use language in odd ways, and invent their own language to match self-created reality, Runyon playfully coins new words and reconfigures existing ones. Slipping a word in here, repeating it there in the company of another new word, Runyon gradually invents his own vocabulary or slang. At times his style is the hyperbolic ironic style we associate with New York, a style that makes a telling point by saying more than it means and depends on an audience recognizing that, as Oscar Wilde observed, nothing succeeds like excess. Thus the narrator in "Lillian" (1930) describes "an old burlesque doll" named Mimmie Madigan, "who is not working since Abraham Lincoln is assassinated" (ROB 279). This verbal inflation owes much to the one-liners of burlesque comedians. We see the influence of these one-liners and Runyon's slang in Woody Allen's films; indeed, Allen examined aspects of Runyon's world in *Broadway Danny Rose* (1984).

Runyon's style, like that of Piet Mondrian's "Broadway Boogie Woogie" (1942–43), is exuberant, energetic, and urgent. Like the city life to which they are responding, Runyon's and Mondrian's styles teem with life, move in several directions at once, and overflow with intensity. For both, the subway—with its noise, anonymous crowds, swaying cars, abrupt stops—is not only the circulation system of the cities but also its unconscious. When New York's subway opened on October 28, 1904, it was celebrated as a major public event. According to the next day's *New York Times*, "All the afternoon the crowds hung around the curious-looking little stations, waiting for heads and shoulders to appear at their feet and grow into bodies."[10] Often Runyon's involved sentences barreling along—moving first one way and then another—but finally coming into the station like a subway are miniatures of his plots. The structure of his stories—and perhaps even of individual sentences—reflects a fascination with emerging from a clandestine world where the narrator is an intrepid explorer of the city's underground mysteries. One might say that the structure of his stories and sentences gives spatial dimension to his fascination with the underworld.

Runyon not only listens with his magnificent ear to the slang of these New York streets but embroiders and transforms it until it becomes his own special inimitable discourse. Sentences seem to wander away, as if they had a drink or two, or as if they were fatigued at four in the morning, but eventually they get their bearings. They have the circumlocutiousness of a culture that loves talk for its own sake. Of The Louse Kid, a "promising young guy in many respects," the speaker in "The Old Doll's House" (1933), the narrator observes: "He is supposed to be a wonderful hand with a burlap bag when anybody wishes to put somebody in such a bag, which is considered a great practical joke in Brooklyn, and in fact The Louse Kid has a burlap bag with him on the night in question, and they are figuring on putting Lance McGowan in the bag when they call on him, just for a laugh" (ROB 62). We know from other stories that a certain way of putting people in a bag—so that they are unable to escape without strangling—can be a way of killing them; in fact, The Louse Kid is accompanied by friends with "a couple of sawed-offs" (ROB 62). This sentence proceeds tangentially yet incrementally, until it locates victim and intent. The speaker, like a jazz musician, plays upon a central theme but diverges into solo flights or riffs that are variations of the theme, in this case that mobsters are looking for their prey. Repetition of the word "bag" is the sound—the note—that holds the sequence together; rereading, we see it becomes a metonymy for a way of hunting humans as if they were animals of prey. We think of hunters bagging game.

By the 1920s, Tin Pan Alley—the popular music industry—had moved its center from West 28th Street to Times Square and was part of Runyon's world. Irving Berlin's early music was ragtime, and he had much to do—even if anticipated by George M. Cohan—with bringing the vernacular into popular songs. Runyon's style owes something to ragtime; "ragging" or syncopating, meant emphasizing the off beat; as Ann Douglas notes, "Ragtime scored for the piano was built on a syncopated, rhythmically inventive, right-hand treble played against a steady 2/4 march rhythm on the left-hand bass."[11] What Runyon does is stress the off syllable—the usually unaccented minor words—against the expected pattern of iambic stresses, creating a prose in which every word carries a pronounced stress. Transitional words like "who," "when," and "whom" in the following sentence, even the seemingly innocuous "and"s and "for," become part of the "ragging rhythm"—a kind of complex duet—that breaks the expected stress pattern and creates a hard-driving urban sound: "[S]ome very unusual things often happen to guys who get money off of The Brain and fail to kick it back just when they promise, such as broken noses and sprained ankles and other injuries, for The Brain has people around him who seem to resent guys getting dough off of him and not kicking it back" ("A Very Honorable Guy" [1929], ROB 417). That the iteration of the term "kicking back" refers to paying back a loan, even as it playfully resonates with what happens to those who fail to pay The Brain in a timely fashion, is an example of the richness and dark humor of Runyon's style.

Runyon's hardboiled, heavily stressed, consonant-loaded style owed as much to the sounds of American entertainment as it did to gangster argot and popular journalism. In the New York accent of Runyon's characters, the consonants are always articulated and the final ones are enunciated fully; the speech slows down as the sentence ends, and the final consonant is orated like a long closing note. New York culture emphasized talk as performance and is often accompanied by head and hand gestures, almost like a jazz pianist who plays with flourishes of his hands, head, and feet. New York conversation is often restless, with the participants intermittently looking around, glancing at their watches, making eye contact and looking away, and, finally, moving away from the person to whom they are talking as they think of going to their next destination—or their next conversational opportunity within a room or dining table—as their fellow conversationalist finishes. To some outsiders this is rude, but this is the essence of the style in Runyon's stories.

Runyon often uses traditional kinds of verbal play. For example, in "Big Shoulders" (1936), the narrator is ironical toward nostalgia as a mode; when Blooch begins to talk about "the good old days," the narrator epigrammatically remarks: "[A]s near as I can make out, Blooch's good old days are about the same as everybody's else's good old days, and most of the time he is half starving" (ROB 586). Verbal humor takes the form of malapropism when Runyon has his narrator misuse words, as in "Cemetery Bait" (1936); in that story, when the narrator is anxious to remove himself from visiting prisons, Runyon expects us to see the fun in the narrator's confusing "epitomize" with "summarize": "I do not care to remain in such surroundings listening to reminiscence, so I request George to epitomize as much as possible, and to omit all reference to low characters and sordid situations" (ROB 516). This passage also mocks the Puritanical element in the second half of the 1930s, which advocated aggressive censorship of vaudeville and fiction.

Just as the stories often end with surprises and reversals, so do the sentences. Indeed Runyon often inverts grammatical expectations or uses a sequence of clauses to gradually undermine the original premise of a sentence's first independent clause. The last sentences of a story are memorable for their twists and turns, their wheedling and seduction of the reader into accepting as logical what is in fact outrageous. Take the last sentence of "Situation Wanted":

"Well, afterward I hear that the first lot Asleep sells is to the family of the late Benny Barker, the bookie, who passes away during the race meeting in Miami, Florida, of pneumonia, superinduced by lying out all night in a ditch of water near the home of Miss Anna Lark, although I understand that the fact that Benny is tied up in a sack in the ditch is considered a slight contributing cause of his last illness" (ROB 673). All the apparent circumlocutions at the outset are, on our second reading, informative and without fluff. Perhaps Asleep found Benny Barker with his fiancée. Indeed, many sentences are like dances in burlesque and even vaudeville with their playful teasing, arousing of expectations, and surprise reversals. Entire stories bear some relation to the stories of comic burlesque entertainers, stories that depend on punch lines. The rhythms of delivery owe something to stage comedians, often Jewish, whose stories are almost always narrated in the present tense.

The unity of Runyon's stories as a collective corpus derives in part from the consistency of the narrator's hardbitten ironic style and in part from recurring characters, such as Ambrose Hammer, the drama critic, who is an amateur detective (and may owe something to Raymond Chandler and Dashiel Hammett) and is always falling in love; Waldo Winchester, another scribe, whose name, as we have noted, suggests Walter Winchell; Dave the Dude; the Brooklyn hoodlum Harry the Horse and his friends Spanish John and Little Isadore; Sam the Gonoph, the ticket broker, and Hot Horse Herbie; John Brannigan, the cop who comes from the same neighborhood as Big Jule and who has his own code in enforcing the law; and Spider McCoy, the fight manager, who is always searching for the next heavyweight champion of the world.

RUNYON'S NARRATORS

Runyon's desire to change his clothing several times a day suggests not only exceptional fastidiousness and narcissism but a chameleonic side that finds an outlet in his imagination. Given Runyon's penchant for inventing personae in his columns, it is hardly surprising that he enjoys inventing a range of narrators to tell his stories. Indeed, his inventing various masks was a kind of cross-dressing. Runyon creates narrators familiar with the demimonde to tell us stories of that world. His speakers subscribe to an informal code of honor; while valuing loyalty to friends and keeping one's word in terms of debt payments, they despise those who rat to the cops. Runyon enjoys the occasional triumph of the outsider at the expense of those who break the behavioral code to which he subscribes. While generally sympathetic to the travails of the demimonde, Runyon enjoys telling of the comeuppance of those who break that code or are physically abusive to spouses and girlfriends.

Runyon's narrator is characteristically a good listener, an acute observer, and has a wonderful ear for dialogue. He hears the rhythms of speech of those who tell him their anecdotes and tales; he feels the glances and gestures that make a conversation and understands the dynamics of transference and countertransference in tale-telling and listening and the potential power that words give him to shape and manipulate his audience. Runyon's narrator is almost always an insider, one of the characters about whom he writes, but very much an outsider to the world of wealth, power, and criminal moguls.

Talking is a kind of action in Runyon's world, a resource for manipulation, an outlet of aggression, a way of showing affection, a kind of comic routine for oneself and one's listeners. Runyon understands that by agreeing to listen to a tale, the listener becomes somewhat complicit. Indeed, at times the teller relies on his source to tell the rest of the story, as in "'Gentlemen, the King!'" (1931) or "Big Umbrella" (1937). Often one of the characters accidentally runs into the narrator sometime after the main events have taken place—perhaps at Mindy's—to tell the narrator a surprising anecdote that gives the story's plot a final striking reversal.

In his many guises, Runyon's narrator hangs around with an assortment of characters, many of them gangsters and wannabe gangsters. What the narrative personae have in common is poverty, joblessness, economic anger, and economic envy—the very things of concern to Runyon's working- and middle-class audience during the Depression years. Runyon depends upon our subversively identifying with gangsters rather than—as in the work of his contemporaries Chandler or Hammett—those trying to solve crimes and apprehend criminals. Runyon understood that gangsters made up identities and wore masks, like actors, and journalists—indeed, like all of us.

Self-knowledge and introspection are rarely found in these stories, and the narrator is heavily ironic about almost everything. Runyon's narrator is not entirely a consistent figure, and it would be a mistake to think Runyon invents only one speaker. Often he is rather passive, willing to be a hanger-on in a variety of dubious enterprises, such as hawking tickets for Sam the Gonoph, or, as in "The Three Wise Guys" (1933), going with two hoods to search for hidden loot from an armed robbery. At other times he speaks as if he might initiate illegal importing of alcohol: "I am greatly interested in his story, and especially in what Kitty says about the pre-war champagne, because I can see that there may be great business opportunities in such a place if a guy can get in with the right people" ("'Gentlemen, The King!,'" ROB 185). If in "The Three Wise Guys" he is a quiet drinker, in "Dancing Dan's Christmas" he is quite rambunctious: in others he is more abstemious or claims to be so. Particularly since it closely follows a 1932 story, "Dancing Dan's Christmas," in which the narrator drinks himself into oblivion, there is no reason in the 1933 "The Three Wise Guys," in which he also drinks heavily, to take seriously the narrator's claim (using a locution mocking legal discourse) that "I am by no means a rum-pot and very seldom indulge in alcoholic beverages in any way, shape, manner or form" (ROB 397).

At times the narrator seems to be wary of involvement with gangsters; at other times he seems not only to consort with them but also to be in league with them, as when, in "Lillian" (1930) he warns a beer runner named Crutchy that "some of our citizens do not like his face and that it may be a good idea for him to leave town, especially if he insists on bringing ale into their territory" (ROB 286). That the subordinate clause beginning with "especially" is not an afterthought but the material that gives this sentence meaning is a characteristic Runyon technique. To have his narrator withhold information until it is absolutely necessary, Runyon understands, is an appropriate narrative style for a demimonde site in which one says as little as possible to those seeking information and where most exchanges between acquaintances are likely to have a strong dissembling component. Thus the speaker remarks early in "'Gentlemen, the King!'": "[I]t is never good policy to rap to visitors in this town, especially visitors from Philly, until you know why they are visiting" (ROB 171). As in this play on variations of "visit," Runyon will exploit a word's ironies until that word becomes a leitmotif. In "'Gentlemen, the King!'" the concept of *visit* is quite special; the story is about three gunmen who are hired to visit a small country in Europe not as tourists, performers, or journalists but to murder the king.

In Runyon's stories, we never know the first person narrator's name, but he emerges as a complex figure with a subtle range of emotions. Sometimes he is the insider's insider; at other times he is only allowed in Mindy's on Fridays because, as he says in "Situation Wanted," "the night manager does not care for me, either, and in fact he hates me from head to foot"(ROB 657). Depending on his economic circumstances or resulting from his anxiety if he is in a physically dangerous tight spot, we see pronounced mood swings. He is at the bottom rung economically; thus in "Pick the Winner" (1933) he accepts a proposition to go to Florida because he doesn't have a good coat—a "flogger" to protect him from winter chill. In "Undertaker Song" (1934) the narrator accepts Meyer Marmalade's offer to pay his expenses to Boston to keep Meyer company, explaining: "I have nothing on of importance at the moment and, in fact, I do not have anything on of importance for the past ten years" (ROB 327). At times his poverty seems close to overwhelming him; when he can't pay his rent during a grim racing season in 1931, he morbidly thinks about buying "myself a rope and end[ing] it all in the park of Biscayne Boulevard": "[T]he only trouble with the idea is I do not have the price of a rope, and anyway I hear most of the palm trees in the park are already spoken for by guys who have the same notion" ("Pick the Winner," ROB 316). He is a not-so-young bachelor who likes women. He seems to have an unusually large range of friends and acquaintances, some of whom are violent criminals who scare him and whom, he says, he tries to avoid—although sometimes he accompanies them on criminal enterprises, as in the safe-breaking caper in "Butch Minds the Baby" (1930). He is a guest in "Social Error" (1930) at one of the mixers where the rich entertain the Broadway guys in a criminal chic anticipation of radical chic.

Runyon himself, as we have noted, was enormously successful and was a great spender, but he knew the economic netherworld, knew its resentments at the immense gulf between the haves and the have-nots. Usually looking up from the bottom, his narrator has a frog's perspective on money and class. When in the company of Yale and Harvard students and alumni and their girlfriends and wives, his narrator is like an explorer encountering a different tribe. In "A Nice Price" (1934) his narrator rubs shoulders with an ostentatious Ivy League fantasy world from which he is excluded: "the young guys with the stir haircuts, and many beautiful young dolls wearing blue and red flowers, and old guys in sports pants and flat straw hats, and old dolls who walk as if their feet hurt them" (ROB 194). (The short "stir" haircut, Runyon expected us to know, is a mandatory crewcut given to prisoners in a stir, or jail.). Economic bitterness, Runyon implies, is pervasive among these have-nots who see this fantasy world across a huge economic chasm. In the aforementioned "A Nice Price," a story whose title uses the word "price" not only to indicate the odds for the race but as a metonymy for a lifestyle beyond the Broadway, Benny South Street, a member of a ticket-scalping crew, "tells me that what it costs to keep up these private yachts is a sin and a shame when you start to figure out the number of people in the world who are looking for breakfast money. . . . [S]ometimes I think maybe he is a dynamiter at heart" (ROB 195).

RUNYON'S CARNIVALESQUE IMAGINATION

Runyon stories partake of the essence of Bakhtinian carnival where hierarchical rank is suspended and special speech and communication that would be impossible under different circumstances can take place. From "Princess O'Hara," where the title character marries royalty—although not solvent royalty—to "The Hottest Guy in the World," where Miss Kitty Clancy (who seems a quite proper young lady) can love the gangster Big Jule before marrying the cop Johnny Brannigan, nothing homogenizes social distinction like sexual desire. We may think smilingly that after Jule leaves New York to escape capture, Kitty was a fast worker; after all, Jule has been away about a year and she has not only married but had a child; indeed, since we are not told how many months old the baby is, we might even wonder whose child she has, Jule's or Brannigan's.

Runyon's city is a labyrinth with hidden social connections between police and criminals, high society and mobsters, wealthy men and showgirls. His role is to make the connections in the fiction so his reader can understand the maze. To cite the title of one of his stories, "A Story Goes With It" (1931), the intricate, often implausible plots reveal these hidden connections. Plot often depends on coincidence and is subservient to character. But plot is not arbitrary. Often it is in the service of a cynical view of a hard city where, all things being equal, things turn out badly. That some endings are virtually non sequiturs may be how Runyon dramatizes his continuing surprises of everyday life within the bustling, ever changing metropolis, including the fact that in this world violent death is a ubiquitous possibility. In two moving noir stories, "The Brain Goes Home" (1931) and "Johnny One-Eye" (1941), Runyon dramatizes the process—the loneliness, desperation, despair, and physical pain—of such deaths to criminals who have become victims of their violent world. While we see Dave the Dude get married to Miss Billy Perry in "Romance in the Roaring Forties" (1929) and we see him in his heyday as a powerful gangster, we also learn of his death in "Situation Wanted" (1936), a story about a killer for hire by gangsters.

In the subterranean street culture, there are codes of behavior. Even in the worst days of the Depression, one pays one's bookmaker and one's markers (debts), one does not snitch on comrades, and one does not physically abuse women. Plots enact these code. Those who violate the code are "wrong gees" or "stinkers" or "hundred per cent" heels, and they are apt to end up dead, as does Joey Perhaps in "Undertaker Song" (1934), Frank in "Dream Street Rose" (1932), and Justin Veezee in "What, No Butler?" (1933).

Runyon's Broadway and Times Square fulfill Bakhtin's paradigm: "This temporary suspension, both ideal and real, of hierarchical rank created during carnival time a special type of communication impossible in everyday life. This led to the creation of special forms of marketplace speech and gesture, frank and free, permitting no distance between those who came in contact with each other and liberating from norms of etiquette and decency impossible at other times."[12] Thus characters of every class partake of Runyon's special slang and argot.

The sites of Runyon's stories are part of the recreational and carnivelesque city: speakeasies, the racetracks, strip shows ("Neat Strip" [1938]), Central Park at night ("Princess O'Hara"), and even the circus. From the outset when Jule looks out of the narrator's window and sees the annual appearance of the circus at Madison Square Garden, "The Hottest Guy in the World" is linked to the circus, a recurring modernist metaphor, from Picasso to Joyce, for the moral confusion and role-playing of twentieth century life. We realize that the real circus mirrors the city circus and that Runyon expects us to see the joke of the kind of criminal known as a "gorilla" shooting Bonzo, a real gorilla that has seized a baby and taken it to the roof. Implying the interchangeability of sports and circus and of scheduled and serendipitous occurrences within the city, Runyon's narrator first assumes the person on the roof is a prizefight manager on a bet. He then thinks that perhaps the gorilla with the baby is part of the merging of commercial and entertainment culture: "Naturally I figure it is some kind of advertising dodge put on by the Garden to ballyhoo the circus" (ROB 361). Moreover, the seemingly disorganized response to the situation resembles the chaotic pantomime of circus clowns or silent movies.

Runyon was what Charlie Chaplin called "high lowbrow," a category of artist that Ann Douglas defines as "eager to capture mass acceptance and elite adulation at a single stroke."[13] "Formed by an older tradition of live performance and broad but limited and cohesive audiences, the early media stars had a vivid cultural identity that antedated any identity the media could bestow; they shaped the media as much as they were shaped by them. Their work, whatever its artistic merits (and they were usually high), had historical importance in forming the genres that still dominate mass culture today: the *New Yorker* 'casual,' the syndicated editorial page, the gossip column, the smart urban comedy for stage and screen, the gangster movie, the talk show, the ad layout, the continuity of the comic strip, the hit-single record, the sexually explicit novel, and the packaged public persona of mass celebrities whether sports heroes, actors, literary stars, or politicians."[14]

While we might think of the *New Yorker*, first published in February 1925 under the auspices of its founder and editor Harold Ross, as a highbrow alternative to this world, almost every week the column "Talk of the Town" mentioned a ribald and disreputable speakeasy manager who called herself Texas Guanin. To be sure, the *New Yorker* cultivated a different style from the "slanglese" and the off-the-cuff or indirect but usually obvious opinions of Runyon, but its subject was often the world of popular culture. Douglas describes its trademark style as "a mix of high standards, no pretensions, and infinite discipline, irony to the fore and emotions to the far rear," but I am not sure that Runyon and his circle would not have agreed with Douglas's "no pretensions."[15]

Runyon creates a city that is a place of frenetic motion—a city that depends on speed for going from one place to another in terms of ambition, desire, and actual geographical movement. At times he implicitly measures New York's space against a larger Western concept of space, one defined by mountains, highways, and scenery. By contrast, New York seems to be teeming beyond the imagination with fascinating and magnetizing speed as well as energy and confusion. Yet he observes the city with a kind of sensual, almost tactile pleasure, as if he could feel its every pulsating rhythm. Many of his stories depend on coincidence and approach the unbelievable as if the plots were rhetorical rolls of the dice expressing his naive gambler's faith that he can make things come out all right notwithstanding the odds. At times they owe something to the slapstick plots, with the exaggerated characterizations and rapid reversals of the Marx Brothers and Charlie Chaplin. Drawing upon the energy of the way life is lived in a commercial, industrial society and celebrating celebrity, he anticipates the Pop and Conceptual art of Jasper Johns, Robert Rauschenberg, and Andy Warhol.

Perhaps Runyon's wordplay, farcical plots, and rapid transitions were influenced not only by vaudeville but by shows derived from vaudeville like *Cocoanuts* (1925). Written for the zany Marx Brothers by George S. Kaufman with music by Irving Berlin, the show contains high-spirited characters who use their wits to make money unscrupulously. Chico and Harpo play rogue brothers, Willy and Sam, who are gangsters, and Groucho is Schlemmer, an unsuccessful and shady hotel owner who tries to auction off undeveloped lots he owns on nearby land, with the help of Willy, who makes bogus bids to raise prices. Plot and logic take a backseat to entertainment and performance. Subverting every sentence with a wise remark based on willfully misunderstanding what he heard, Groucho was the archetypal New York smart aleck. Runyon would have reveled in Minnie Marx's response to a query about why she sent her sons into show business: "'Where else can people who don't know anything make so much money?'"[16]

Runyon's art is also aligned with another hyperbolic style, that of the popular singers Al Jolson and Sophie Tucker, rather than with what Ann Douglas calls the "crooner" style of Fred Astaire and Bing Crosby: "ultra-sophisticated, upper-crust cool, an intimate yet bland sexuality very different from the tears-and-laughter-drenched raw cravings of Jolson's belt-it-out style."[17] By contrast, Jolson's exaggerated ethnic style was far different and one that had close resemblances to Runyon's. As Ted Gioia wrote, "Above all, [Jolson] used every resource his body could muster to deepen the impression he made, orchestrating his face, his eyes, his limbs, his voice to amplify the intended effect. . . . His gestures were sometimes so dramatic that they become almost inseparable from our image of Jolson: the out-stretched arms, palms facing outward, the genuflection on one knee in front of his fans."[18]

As his career progressed, Irving Berlin's favorite vocalist for whom he wrote songs was the Nordic patrician Fred Astaire (born Frederick Austerlitz). A London favorite before becoming an American star, and a sophisticated WASP who appealed to upper class Fifth Avenue and East Side audiences—although much of his art is indebted to black singer-dancers—Astaire represented an alternate sophisticated tradition to Runyon.[19] Yet the very exaggeration of Astaire's cinematic gestures and language also had something in common with Runyon's plot choreography and diction. Nor should we forget that in films like *The Gay Divorcee* (1934), Astaire's ability to get the girl of his choice appealed to Depression-era moviegoers seeking escape and a fairy tale ending of the kind Runyon sometimes favored.

Bing Crosby, a dominant figure from 1927 to 1956, spoke, like Norman Rockwell, to the American desire during the Depression and wartime for simple truths and heartfelt sentiment. His heyday was 1931 to 1940, but he remained a paramount figure through the 1940s; in 1946 three of the five top-grossing films (*The Bells of St. Mary's, Blue Skies,* and *Road to Utopia*) were escapist Crosby vehicles. His radio program was a huge hit from 1931 to 1962 with 50 million listeners at its wartime peak. According to Gary Giddens, "He is the ideal figure for tracking the rise of American popular culture. He played pivotal roles in the development of the recording, radio and film industries while virtually defining the microphone as a singer's instrument.... He understood instinctively the modernist paradox: electrical appliances made singing more human, more expressive, more personal.... He managed to maintain his popularity during several major cultural upheavals in 20th century American history: Prohibition, Depression, World War II, the cold war and the affluent society."[20]

While Crosby's mellow voice and gentle lyrics were quite different from Runyon's cynical words, guttural sounds, and often-abrasive tone, Runyon also had a softer sentimental side. Runyon looked for human connections that were an alternative to the aches of modernism: displacement, uprootedness, imminent loss, and personal memory detached from cultural memory. We see the quest in his Joe Turp stories and some of his fictional tales of Pueblo, Colorado, but even in some of the Broadway stories where lonely men living on the edge, like Benny and Little Yid, desperately seek common bonds. Especially but not exclusively in the Turp stories, we see how optimism and resilience are coping mechanisms, and how neighborhoods are an antidote to a world where technology, industry, and progress dominate and cause alienation and insecurity. Before it became fashionable, Runyon was interested in unsung men and women—those people labor historian Debra Bernhardt and Rachael Bernstein spoke of as "ordinary people" with "extraordinary lives"—who collectively compile the social fabric of the city and are responsible for making its history.[21]

RUNYON'S SOCIAL CRITIQUE

As in Coppola's *Godfather* films, where the hierarchical structures parody the conventional world they flout and where the Mafioso are the heroic figures around which the world revolves, we sympathize with

Runyon's underworld characters in his Broadway stories, in part because they are the naughty boys we cannot be, in part because they live by their own rules. They are our dark side, our shadow selves acting out fantasies of dispensing revenge on the spot to those who threaten us, or, as the gangster friends of Sorrowful do in "Little Miss Marker," getting the best doctor when we need it by insisting on it with guns.

Always suspicious of respectability, Runyon satirizes dogma, class pretension, and complacency of all kinds. But even among the demimonde, the enthusiasm of the personal greeting one gives or receives often depends on perception of the means or importance of the person—or of the fear generated by the person being greeted. Thus in "Barbecue" (1941), Homer gives two gangsters "not a large hello and, in fact, it is a very small hello and they hello him back just as small and maybe smaller" (MGAD 348). Money is privilege. In "The Old Doll's House" (1933), when the wealthy Miss Abigail Ardsley testifies on behalf of Lance McGowen, "Nobody ever sees so much bowing and scraping before in a courtroom" (ROB 71). Runyon engages us to think not only about the outsiders and marginalized but about their necessary relationship to the world of money and power. He is a subversive showing us a world that defies bourgeois conventions, even while showing us that the demimonde, like the respectable world it mocks, is obsessed with the need for money. Runyon has a particular fondness for horseplayers who always lose because they think they have an edge from information received from supposedly reliable sources; he syntactically illustrates this oblique connection in a series of increasingly remote relationships, such as speaking of a guy who might be a "pal" of a close friend of the jockey's valet.

An insider who is part of the world that he presents to us outsiders—who presumably do not know this world—Runyon's narrator takes us into his confidence, even while he withholds vital information until the end. But these are not O. Henry stories and often the narrator leaves tangible verbal clues of forthcoming violence; take, for example, "Sense of Humor," where Joe the Joker is furious about Rosa's leaving him when he comes on tough times while Frankie Ferocious is prospering: "I have to laugh every time I think of how the big greaseball [Frankie] is going to feel when he finds out how expensive Rosa is" (ROB 271). Runyon, we discover, is a deft psychologist of character who eschews analysis for showing. But laughter, we understand, disguises hostility when Joe the Joker gives Frankie the hotfoot. Rereading, we see that Joe the Joker's sense of humor—a quality he ascribes to himself and the narrator oft repeats—is a displaced way of dealing with hostility and rage.

Runyon's stories track cultural and social changes. In "Situation Wanted," we see how the underworld has been affected by the end of Prohibition and a concomitant more aggressive policing of gangsters; thus when the hit man Asleep returns from "college" in Dannemora in 1936, the need for his services is severely diminished. That Asleep finds in the Spanish Civil War a site where his services as a ruthless killer are needed suggests Runyon's cynical view of the kind of men who thrive during wartime; more specifically, Runyon implies that some of those who went to Spain for reasons of political idealism may be social debris and unemployed sociopaths.

RUNYON THE POSTMODERNIST

Runyon has both modernist and postmodernist aspects. As a modernist, he responds with irony and enthusiasm to the excitement of the modern city, including its technological advances; develops a unique sensory style appropriate to his immersion in the world he observes; enjoys the expansion of personal and social freedom; and provides an idiosyncratic, good-humored, and tempered critique of society. But as a postmodernist, he offers a devastating social critique and is deeply skeptical of traditional social and economic hierarchies.

Fredric Jameson has written about how "a once-existing centered subject, in the period of classical capitalism, has today in a world of organizational bureaucracy dissolved. . . . [T]he end of the bourgeois ego, or monad, . . . means the end of much more—the end, for example, of style in the sense of the unique and the personal. . . . [T]he advanced capitalist countries today are now a field of stylistic and discursive heterogeneity without a norm."[22] Do we not see something of this postmodernist heterogeneity in the homogenization of language and attitudes in Runyon's stories? While he maintains a distinct personal and literary style, Broadway culture *speaks* generically rather than as a unique psyche, and words and responses

seem interchangeable not only from story to story but from character to character within stories. And the oppression of the Depression
might be cited as an important cause within the Runyonesque universe. Notwithstanding his cynicism about the commodification of
life, he himself weighed almost everything in terms of its worth in
dollars. Notwithstanding his hard-boiled attitude toward Broadway
culture, more than anyone he was responsible for making it into a
secular mecca for opportunity and self-fulfillment, including pleasure. Within his writing is what Taylor calls "a deeper uncertainty over
the play between spiritual longing and commodity fetishism at the
heart of those processes transforming cultural value into profit."[23]

As Edward Rothstein writes in "Modern and Postmodern, the
Bickering Twins": "Postmodernism refuses to take anything too seriously. Its mode is play, its attitude ironic."[24] With their reductive resolutions of implausible circumstances, Runyon's plots send up the
idea of narrative unity. With their chameleonic voice, they flout the
idea of the coherence and logic of narrative voice. With their oscilla-
tion between noir and sentimental pastiche, they often dissolve unity
of theme and tone as well as undermine and modify what seems the
prevailing and overriding perspective.

Runyon the postmodernist embraced popular culture and
flouted his disdain for elitist culture, although he was not above displaying his self-taught learning, as when he invents a place in Pennsylvania in "Tobias the Terrible" (1932) called Erasmus. Rather than
use references to a richer past as his normative standard for giving
shape and order to the futility and anarchy of the urban world he observes, he occasionally plunders it, as in "The Three Wise Guys" or
"The Melancholy Dane" (1944). Providing more information than
the reader needs or wants, Runyon's overdetermined hyperrealism—
in "A Piece of Pie" (1937) listing details of excessive and disgusting
overeating or cataloguing almost encyclopedically who is in a room at
the time of a police raid in "Tobias the Terrible"—anticipates postmodernism's occasional focus if not obsession with collections of
trivia. Like Jasper Johns or Robert Rauschenberg, Runyon appropriates cultural detritus—in Runyon's case, the world of speakeasies,
gangsters, racetracks, boxers—to show that the subjects of art do not
necessarily belong to the highbrow or elite.

CHAPTER 5

THE GENRES OF RUNYON'S FICTION

Noir and Sentiment in a Male-Dominated World

INTRODUCTION

Runyon's success took place in a world where intellectuals and critics despised and patronized popular culture. I grew up in a world where serious people didn't read the comics, go to musicals, or read popular fiction. Our teachers and professors taught the cult of intellectual elitism. I began reading the *Peanuts* comic strip on rare occasion in our local Ithaca newspaper only after Charles Schulz died. Yet the paperback editions of *The Best of Damon Runyon* and *Damon Runyon Favorites* sold over a million copies each! His stories boosted the circulation of the magazines in which they appeared. Runyon's own attitudes flew in the face of the credo of the suffering artist in the service of art: "My measure of success is money. I have no interest in artistic triumphs that are financial losers. I would like to have an artistic success that also made money, of course, but if I had to make a choice between the two I would take the dough. . . . Maybe what the experts say is perfection is not perfection at all, except in expert theory. Maybe it is the approval of the public that is actually the mark of real perfection. Anyway that is what counts with me . . ." (ST 58–59). If we think of Mark Twain, Bret Harte, O. Henry, and Ring Lardner, we realize Runyon was not the first newspaperman without sustained formal education to achieve literary fame.

Runyon's genius was to know the economic and cultural values and the taste of his reading audience. He wrote as if he were a member of that audience and created in his readers a sense of intimate friendship. He understood their curiosities, desires, and fantasies. He realized that his stories of the underworld gave his readers a way to escape their daily regimen and to indulge in fantasies of revenge, insubordination, adultery, and the possibility of quick wealth. Yet Runyon usually reminded his audience that acting on passion and intuition had its consequences. Indeed, often he redefined respectability and moral behavior to show that the real barbarians are those given social prominence. As Jean Wagner writes in *Runyonese* (the best monograph on Runyon), sometimes "the strain of gentility in the underworld characters is italicized while respectability is gently, but effectively disrobed of its aureole and luster."[1] Wagner further observes that for Runyon, "[T]he notions of respectability or dishonor which we currently associate with individuals from opposite ends of the social spectrum have no foundations at all in reality."[2]

Runyon's fiction takes many forms. In this and the next chapter I shall examine some of Runyon's fictional genres to understand the kind of stories he wrote. While discussing in detail some of Runyon's paradigmatic stories, I shall inclusively mention virtually all of them. My taxonomy has an arbitrary aspect, employing genres depending on the atmosphere within the imagined world of a story and genres depending on theme and subject matter. In this chapter I will arrange stories into genres where noir and sentiment are foregrounded; chapter 6 organizes genres around specific subjects and themes; and chapter 7 focuses on the genres of the later fiction but also on occasion uses as organizing principles atmosphere, subjects, and themes.

Clearly some of the stories belong to more than one category, but I have tried to provide a classification that does justice to Runyon's accomplishment. However, we should not forget that Runyon not only resisted the categorizing sensibility but also had something of a postmodernist sensibility in understanding that absurdity and nonsense help make sense of things.

In virtually all of Runyon's stories, some events disrupt the initial equilibrium. These destabilizing events usually make it difficult to restore the equilibrium in the expected form of traditional narrative but allow restoration as parody—often quite absurd—of the original equilibrium. His is the exaggerated cartoon perspective where hyperrealism meets surrealism. In that sense Runyon's tales are often parodies of traditional narratives, and his plot resolutions are often subversions of the unity and order we might expect in the kind of popular magazines in which he published. Thus not only is his subject matter—gangsters, gamblers, showgirls, money-making without scruples—subversive, but so are his form and language.

NOIR

Runyon's New York is far from the glamorous city of Fred Astaire or Woody Allen. Runyon enjoys surprise endings, and endings that often have a strong noir effect. The noir tales take place in the evening; petty swindlers and liars are everywhere. The colors are dark; people have names that disguise their identities. With human predators lurking in hiding, carrying weapons, and hoping to do harm to their prey, violent death and injury are never far away.

"Dark Dolores" (*Cosmopolitan,* Nov. 1929) is the first of the noir stories and the fourth, last, and darkest of the first four Broadway 1929 short stories—following "Romance in the Roaring Forties," "A Very Honorable Guy," and "Madame La Gimp." Runyon is obsessed with predatory women betraying men and avenging women murdering the men who wronged them. Dolores is the girlfriend of St. Louis gangster Frankie Farrone, who was killed by three other St. Louis gangsters—Black Mike, Scoodles, and Benny. They perform the murder on their way to Atlantic City for a peace conference presided over by Dave the Dude, a major and respected figure in the gangster world not only in New York but throughout the country.

The beautiful Dolores arrives in Atlantic City anonymously and gets a job as a hostess the same day as the St. Louis gangsters—

called "gorills" by the narrator—arrive. She captivates all three and gets them to woo her simultaneously, even as they get "more and more hostile toward each other" (DRO 111). Finally she gets her revenge on the men who murdered her boyfriend when she deliberately swims out to sea with all three following until they drown. A champion swimmer, she is a modern yet parodic version of a siren luring the males to their destruction. As a backup method for her revenge, she also had bought cyanide, presumably to drop in the three gangsters' drinks.

The reader is prepared for noir revelations by the narrator, who in a prelude links Dolores Dark, later called Dark Dolores because of her complexion, with women who killed guys. The tale begins ominously with Waldo Winchester's regretting that the newspapers have "no dolls around such as in the old days to make good stories for the newspapers by knocking off guys right and left" (DRO 102). He refers also to the *Odyssey* where Circe, who, as Winchester puts it, "is quite a hand for luring guys to destruction" and transforms her captives into swine before Odysseus gets them turned back to men (DRO 102). Runyon's Circe (Dolores) does not have to transform the men into swine, since they already qualify by means of their behavior; nor is there a figure to restore the men to their prior living condition. What Runyon is satirizing is the utter disregard for human life on the part of the newspapers and their desire for sensational news at any cost. That murders are commodities to be sold as news is underlined by Winchester's allusion to the Hall-Mills and Snyder murder cases—trials of which Runyon covered in all their lurid detail in 1926 and 1927: "The best we get nowadays is some doll belting a guy with a sash weight, or maybe filling him full of slugs, and this is no longer exciting" (DRO 102).

"Dream Street Rose" (*Collier's,* June 11, 1932) is a noir story of a wronged woman's revenge. Rose is an alcoholic and lives in a kind of fog, spending much time on West 47th Street between Sixth and Seventh Avenues on what is known as Dream Street "because in this block are many characters of one kind and another who always seem to be dreaming of different matters" (ROB 46). Strongly insisting that the narrator listen to her story, Rose speaks in the third person of a "friend" from Pueblo, Colorado (Runyon's hometown), but, we soon realize, the "friend" is a disguised version of herself and the story is her story. Rose uses the disguise of a friend to describe her own life because she is embarrassed and ashamed; she is distancing herself from her own sordid life by creating a fiction that she is merely reporting someone else's biography. She recalls that her dreams once had included a simple life with a loving husband, "a nice little home, and children running here and there . . . and [she]believes that everybody else in the world is like herself" (ROB 50). But she has been ruined by an abusive scoundrel named Frank McQuiggan with whom she falls in love and who is forced to marry her at gunpoint by her former boyfriend; the latter resents how McQuiggan has misused Rose. McQuiggan not only beats her but sells her to Black Emanuel, the owner of a dance joint in San Francisco, where, it is implied, she has to whore. She keeps track of the man she blames for permanently polluting her life, vows to get even, and is obsessed with revenge. She waits for the husband who abandons her to reach the zenith of wealth and fame before she takes his life as he has taken hers. When Frank is at his peak, she stalks him, steals a servant's key, gets into his house, and, according to what she tells the narrator, threatens to expose Frank unless he commits suicide. Do we in any other Runyon story hear such words of pure hatred as hers when recalling how Frank had shattered her idyllic dreams? "On top of the world. . . . It is where I am when you kill me as surely as if you strangle me with your hands. . . . I want to find you liking to live, so you will hate so much to die" (ROB 56)?

When the newspapers headline the story and mention the gun still in Frank's lap, Runyon expects his reader to assume that Rose murdered him. Moreover, the transference of sharing the story with our narrator in Good Time Charley Bernstein's speakeasy, where Bernstein also overhears her story, is a moment for Rose of ecstatic validation and self-definition, a moment that she requires to complete her vengeance.

A noir story in which a cynical and ruthless gangster is hoisted on his own petard, "The Brakeman's Daughter" (*Collier's,* July 8, 1933) is one of Runyon's most tightly and intricately plotted stories; every word and nuance matters. After Prohibition is lifted, Big False Face, who "comes from the Lower East Side" (which Runyon's audience would have understood as meaning he is Jewish), becomes a major beer brewer. To protect his interests, he calls a conference of independent breweries.

By using the respectable language of the business world to describe career progress in the gangster world, Runyon ironically implies that perhaps the criminal and business worlds are not so different: "In New Jersey, Big False Face secures a position with the late Crowbar Connolly, riding loads down out of Canada, and then he is with the late Hands McGovern, and the late Dark Tony de More, and also the late Lanky-lank Watson, and all this time Big False Face is advancing step by step in the business world, for he has a great personality, and is well liked by one and all" (ROB 503). But we realize that he has climbed on the backs of his various deceased employers. The repetition of the word "late" implies that Big False Face has had something to do with their deaths. We note with grim amusement that all his former employers and partners have, rather coincidentally, become "the late." Indeed, the fate of his former associates arouses our expectation that False Face will initiate further violence and makes us rather unsympathetic when the violence is directed at him. As if the narrator were telling a rags to riches Horatio Alger story at a testimonial dinner, he tells us about Big False Face's remarkable success. In fact, we know he gets his name because he "is often smiling when he is by no means amused at anything" (ROB 502).

A womanizer who assumes every woman is infatuated with him, The Humming Bird—whose nickname obscenely if obliquely suggests that he is always sniffing around women—is one of the guests Big False Face has summoned for his meeting of independent brewers. With the ploy of arranging for the vain and egotistical Humming Bird to meet a beautiful woman, supposedly the daughter of a brakeman who is a protective father, Big False Face thinks he is playing a practical joke called "the brakeman's daughter."

The story revolves around the power games of violent gangsters. Big False Face seeks to dominate and control the independent brewers until Cheeks Sheracki, a gangster guest, turns the tables on him. Playing the brakeman's daughter trick gives Cheeks—who pretends to be part of the trick and is in the group awaiting The Humming

Bird, the butt of the prank—an opportunity to kill False Face. Instead of scaring the victim with the sounds of breaking incandescent lightbulbs—sounds that mimic gunshots—Cheeks, who himself wears a false face by agreeing to be part of the "the brakeman's daughter" scenario, plays his own noir practical joke on False Face, a joke that is fatal. During the violent gunplay, The Humming Bird is protected by a woman he has met earlier that day and whom he has saved from being run down by one of False Face's beer truck drivers.

In Runyon's stories, common words—like "joke" in the preceding story—often take on a different coloration, as if subversive characters not only undermine laws and social conventions but subvert the conventional meaning of language. Indeed an earlier victim of False Face's version of the brakeman's daughter joke got lost in the woods and froze to death. Stressing Big False Face's sadistic sense of humor and disregard for the lives of others while preparing readers not to regret Big False Face's demise at the hands of Cheeks, the narrator remarks with bitter irony: "The biggest laugh that Big False Face ever gets out of the brakeman's daughter joke is the time he leaves a guy from Brooklyn by the name of Rocco Scarpati in the woods one cold winter night, and Rocco never does find his way out, and freezes as stiff as a starched shirt" (ROB 509). Thus it is a noir reversal of the concept of "joke" when Big False Face, who is always smiling, no matter what his real intentions, becomes the victim of false faces and mask wearing.

Runyon's wordplay adds to the grim humor. Runyon not only exploits the pun on the word "brakeman" as arresting or "braking" the victim of the supposed joke as well as "breaking" the victim's sexual fantasy, but he also plays with the word "brakeman" in the final noir reversal; putting a "brake" on Big False Face's life both "breaks" and "brakes" his elaborate joke and his seeming control. Just as The Humming Bird is a captive of his desire, Big False Face is a captive of his desire to control and arrange, and both figures allow their obsessions to cloud their better judgment; certainly False Face should have been wary of Cheeks's notorious reputation as a killer and Cheeks's resentment about the meeting. Because The Humming Bird has captivated the woman in the house where Cheeks plans to murder False Face—a house she and her father had just moved into—she takes care of him, but no one looks after Big False Face. It is also possible that False Face's driver, Ears Acosta (note the name implying hearing everything and "accosting"), is in on the plot to kill him.

In "Ransom. . . . $1,000,000" (*Cosmopolitan,* October 1933), Runyon's second-longest story (after the 1934 "Money from Home") and approaching a novella in length, the narrator participates in a major kidnapping of recent Yale graduate John Withington White III before returning to his profession of driving a cab. In this story, even more than in "Butch Minds the Baby" (1930), the self-dramatizing narrator is an active part of the criminal world rather than just an observer or hanger-on. Indifferent to human life, lacking morality, and immune to nuances of feelings, the narrator is much more of a lowlife than the usual hanger-on who narrates Runyon's stories. He seems to buy into a gruesome scheme that will involve the murder of young White if the ransom is not paid. In prior times the narrator had been a consort of Dan the Devil. The speaker has a reputation as a killer. His racial epithets—he calls his fellow kidnappers "wop" and "Heeb"—do not endear him to readers. That the narrator is one of the principals in the kidnapping is a necessary fictional device to retain the reportorial verisimilitude that Runyon desired in his stories. Writing for an audience concerned about realistic explanations, Runyon characteristically covers his tracks in terms of how the narrator knows what he knows.

Typical of the noir stories is the "Sense of Humor" (*Cosmopolitan,* September 1934) in which the narrator tells of Joe the Joker, a sadistic gangster who enjoys causing the pain of others; thus he enjoys giving people a "hot foot" by putting lit matches in the shoes a person is wearing. His wife, Rosa, a former nightclub singer, has left Joe for Frankie, whom she had known before her marriage; she runs out on Joe when, because of the Depression, he doesn't have as much money as he once had and Frankie is prospering. In this story Runyon does not glamorize gangsters but reveals them as moral dwarfs. Nor does he juxtapose gangsters with the respectable world. "Sense of Humor" creates a moral hell from which there is no exit. Indeed, this is one of Runyon's darkest stories, one strewn with corpses and people motivated by hatred and revenge.

Mobsters kidnap their enemies by "sacking"—that is, knocking them out and stuffing them in sacks trussed up in a bundle with a cord or wire tied around their neck in such a way that when they try to straighten out their knees as they try to escape, they strangle themselves. In a cycle of mob violence, Frankie has killed a couple of Joe's associates by sacking them; no sooner does Joe retaliate by machine-gunning Frank's henchmen than Joe's brother is found dead in a sack. Joe lets it be known that he will arrive in a sack at the home of the "rising citizen of Brooklyn," Frankie Ferocious, and when the sack is opened, he will come out shooting (ROB 271). The sack supposedly carrying Joe the Joker but actually carrying Rosa does arrive; thinking he is shooting into a sack carrying Joe the Joker, Frank finds to his dismay that he has killed Rosa, his own girlfriend and Joe's estranged wife. When the narrator grimly remarks, "Joe's sense of humor comes right out again," we realize that, after surviving the loss of his brother and the humiliation of losing his wife, Joe—a borderline psychotic—sadistically wanted to inflict as much pain as possible upon Frankie (ROB 277).

Like the given birth names of Joe the Joker and Frankie Ferocious (for Feroccio, who is Sicilian), words in this world become disguises for subterranean motives. Joe speaks of "my friend Frankie Ferocious" and pretends he is amused by Rosa's departure (ROB 270). What the narrator does demonstrate is that because of one psychotic person's warped sense of humor, others can be badly harmed, and this point has some relevance for the world beyond gangsters. Indeed, Runyon's story begins with the example of Joe the Joker's bad practical joke, the hot foot, which may be part of some of his male readers' experience. Everyone laughs with Joe because they are frightened of him.

Runyon examines the term "sense of humor," a term turned inside out by Joe to mask his thirst for revenge on both Frankie and his wife, Rosa. By using "sense of humor" in relation to Joe the Joker's behavior and its consequences, the narrator ironically redefines the term to mean a self-immersed narcissistic disregard of others approaching sadistic psychosis. Engaging the reader intimately in the second person as if he were talking to him directly, the narrator reports how Joe likes to fire tin foil pellets with a rubber band from his car with the occasional result of putting out someone's eye: "But it is

all in fun and shows *you* what a wonderful sense of humour Joe has"
(ROB 272; emphasis mine).

"Too Much Pep" (January 10, 1931; *Collier's*) is a tough noir
story that takes place in what was once the 114th Street to 116th
Street Italian enclave in Harlem. As David M. Kennedy reminds us,
"Everywhere immigrant communities banded together in ethnic enclaves, where they strove, not always consistently, both to preserve
their old-world cultural patrimony and to become American. They
were strangers in a strange land awkwardly suspended between the
world they had left behind and a world where they were not fully at
home. The Jewish ghettoes and Little Italys and Little Polands that
took root in American cities became worlds unto themselves. . . . Isolated by language, religion, livelihood, and neighborhood, they had
precious little ability to speak to one another and scant political
voice in the larger society."[3]

Runyon was fascinated with New York's ethnic diversity and the
physical and psychological borders of ethnic enclaves, in this case of
Italians. After being harassed by a vicious extortionist, Ignazio
Varderelli, called Ignaz the Wolf, who demands payment in exchange
for protection from his bombing businesses, his Italian Harlem "customers" decide to retaliate. Called by the narrator "Moustache
Petes, who are old-time Italians with large black moustaches," Ignaz
the Wolf's "customers" are industrious and frugal shop owners who
sell various kinds of Italian food (ROB 631). Under the leadership
of Marco and his father, artichoke dealers who refuse to pay the
$5,000 demanded by Ignaz, the Italian neighborhood merchants
send for Don Pep', an unimposing, small, elderly Sicilian with "a pair
of black eyes like a snake's eyes" who is a specialist for "putting parties in their places"—here a euphemism for killing (ROB 638, 636).
In Italy, he has killed ten men and four horses. After Ignaz shoots
Don Pep'—or thinks he has—the latter reappears at the cigar store
where Ignaz is playing cards and gives Ignaz a hug. Ignaz, thinking
he has seen a ghost and not knowing that he has shot a straw-stuffed
effigy of Don Pep', dies of fright. Ironically, until Don Pep' dis-
patches the Wolf, it looks like all Don Pep' does—as if he lacked pep
or energy for action—is lurk around in the darkness wearing a long
black coat and a matching flat hat.

Runyon was captivated by the cultural practices and tight bonds of these Mafioso. The texture of the story renders a sense of the Italian ethnic presence in New York and, in particular, the Sicilian heritage underlying it. The relentless single-minded plot emphasizes how the neighborhood has become caught in a cycle of violence. While "Too Much Pep" could be considered an "all's well that ends well" story that rids a nice neighborhood of a ruthless scourge, it also shows how lawlessness reigns in this section of the city and how distrusted and inept are those who should be upholding law and order.

NOIR WITH A NUANCE OF SENTIMENT

On occasion, as with Francesca and White's love relationship in "Ransom . . . $1,000,000," Runyon introduces a touch of sentiment in his noir stories. One of Runyon's richest and most tightly plotted stories, "Situation Wanted" (*Collier's*, November 21, 1936), has a love theme intertwined with strong noir aspects. Asleep, a small harmless looking guy is a hired killer who has returned from five years in prison, where he had been imprisoned from 1931 to late spring 1936. He comes back to find that, in the post-Prohibition world, organized crime is no longer in its heyday and his services no longer in demand. The title is a play on a man looking for work and the kind of ad he might take in a newspaper to advertise his services—if his services were legal.

With the narrator watching Asleep being thrown out of Mindy's and recalling Asleep's prior prominence, the story begins on a nostalgic note: "Well, here is a spectacle that really brings tears to my eyes, as I can remember when just a few years back the name of Asleep strikes terror to the hearts of one and all on Broadway . . . and in fact he is generally regarded as a genius. Asleep's line is taking care of anybody that somebody wishes to be taken care of, and at one time he is the highest-priced character in the business" (ROB 658). The humor derives from the incongruity of someone being at the top of his profession in the art of homicide—as if his kind of "taking care" were simply another line of the hospitality or health service business—and, further, from that someone being a rather mannerly person who wouldn't hurt a fly were it not a business proposition. Indeed, when Asleep is tossed from Mindy's by the night manager because a potential customer, the bookie Benny Barker, gets anxious and begins to yell "no, no, no" when Asleep asks Bennie if he wants an enemy killed, Asleep does not, as the narrator thought he might, turn his gun on the night manager (ROB 659).

The sentiment of the story derives from Asleep's wanting to marry a bubble dancer named Miss Anna Lark and to make a new beginning in Miami, where her father lives. After reading about the Spanish Civil War in the papers, Asleep finds the job he needs by going abroad to fight in what he, with his gangster background, understands as "a war between two different mobs living in this Spain, each of which wishes to control the situation. It reminds me of Chicago the time Big Moey sends me out to Al"—and the Runyon reader knows he means Capone (ROB 662). Benny Barker stakes Asleep to a trip to Spain, allegedly because he feels bad about having no homicide business for him. But we learn later that the real reason Benny wants to get rid of Asleep is that he cares about Anna Lark; we also realize that Benny's misplaced anxiety in Mindy's may be related to his fear that Asleep knows of his interest in Anna and might use his professional skills on him.

In fact, Franco invaded Spain from Morocco in summer 1936 and began to overturn the election victory of the left-leaning Republican government. The left responded with armed resistance to Franco's Fascists. Like the members of the American left who volunteered and fought with the Abraham Lincoln Brigade, Asleep had to sneak into Spain because his passport, like theirs, would have been stamped "not valid for travel in Spain."[4] In a wartime tale that becomes a Runyonesque parody of the Spanish Civil War, Asleep finds in Spain a place for his skills as a trained killer. He sells his services to the highest bidder—probably, although the reader cannot be certain, the Royalist side, since they are holding a castle under the leadership of General Pedro Vega. Asleep takes a crucial hill overlooking the castle by killing twelve men with a file turned into a knife.

Runyon's story makes clear the human cost of war on both sides. Using some of his World War I experience, Asleep takes over a large gun and shoots the group trying to capture the castle. While he is sympathetic to a young woman in the castle who, like him, is in love—a typical Runyon double plot where one plot bleeds into the other—his main reason for siding with General Vega is that the latter offered him Florida land in return for his services. Nevertheless, before the general comes up with the deed to his land, Asleep says: "Of course business is business in this case, and I cannot let sentiment interfere" (ROB 668). Does not this echo and parody of corporate practices anticipate the ethics of *The Godfather* books and films?

That neither Asleep nor his henchman, a former Spanish boxer named Manuel—who is "unable to find out what he is fighting about" (ROB 663)—seems to know on which side he is fighting may indicate Runyon's indifference to the Spanish Civil War, which was a cause célèbre to the intellectual left. David M. Kennedy reminds us that, while in America "some impassioned idealists saw Spain as the arena in which the great moral confrontation between fascism and democracy was being fought," most Americans in January 1937 "could not have cared less" and "two-thirds of the American people had no opinion about the events in Spain."[5]

It is something of a coup that Runyon can humanize Asleep, a professional killer. We readers are pleased that Asleep fulfills the American dream of a new start in Florida with his fiancé; we are pleased in part because Asleep in a parody of a romance plot frees the castle and the beautiful woman separated from her lover and pleased in part because Asleep is a man of feeling who responds with full heart to female tears. Asleep uses the land he has received from Vega to open a cemetery, a rather ironic denouement for the man who is so good at putting people permanently to sleep. Nor has Asleep forgotten the profession at which he excelled; the narrator tells us that the first cemetery plot is for the family of the late Benny Barker, who is found in a sack—we learned earlier that Asleep brought "the idea to Brooklyn of putting [people] in sacks"—in a ditch near Anna Lark's home (ROB 660).

"The Hottest Guy in the World" (*Liberty,* November 8, 1930) is another story where the seeming focus on the criminal world gives way to a sentimental turn of the plot, while revealing the common humanity of criminal and police. Although the policeman Johnny Brannigan and the criminal Big Jule grew up in the same neighborhood, and both have a propensity for violence, Johnny's is sanctioned and Jule's is not; Johnny "never misses a chance to push Big Jule around, and sometimes trying to boff Big Jule with his blackjack" (ROB 357). Finally, Brannigan, "the strong-arm copper" (ROB 357), lets Jule go after he saves the baby and Brannigan's wife, the former Miss Kitty Clancy—whom Jule loved before leaving town—by shooting the circus gorilla that has grabbed the baby and run onto the roof of Madison Square Garden. The "B" of Big Jule's nickname and of the strong-armed cop Brannigan tightens the link between the criminal and the cop who love the same woman. Jule's final joke after he learns whose baby he has saved underlines the *metaphoricity* of the circus, where city and circus represent one another figuratively and each is an image of the other: "[F]or a minute, Johnny, I am afraid I will not be able to pick out the right face between the two on the roof, because it is very hard to tell the monk and your baby apart" (366 ROB).

In "Baseball Hattie" (*Cosmopolitan,* May 1936), Runyon's lesson is that everyone is not for sale. The title character, Baseball Hattie, is a baseball groupie as well as a madam and hooker who falls in love with a splendid but illiterate left-handed pitcher, Haystack Duggeler; the latter is a drunken scoundrel—his name rhymes with guzzler—who gives Hattie "a slight pasting now and then" (ROB 650). The story ends with Hattie deliberately shooting Haystack in his pitching arm to prevent him from disgracing himself and, more important, the name of their son—although she doesn't really know the sex of the baby she is carrying—by throwing a game with the Brooklyn Dodgers at the behest of a gambler named Armand Fibleman (playing on feeble man), to whom Haystack owes money. While Duggeler's arm is amputated, "The newspapers," according to the narrator, "make quite a lot of Baseball Hattie protecting the fair name of baseball"; Hattie and Duggeler move to Los Angeles, where he becomes a respectable grocer until he dies (ROB 656).

Runyon has his narrator begin with an anecdote locating himself at the scene—in this case as a spectator at the Polo Grounds with Fibleman, who upon seeing Baseball Hattie, bolts and leaves. One of Runyon's characteristic and most effective techniques in the Broadway stories is to have the narrator set us in the present (in this case his seeing Baseball Hattie, whom he hasn't seen in years, at the

Polo Grounds) before taking us back in time to a sustained tale (in this case her relationship with Duggeler, which began more than twenty years ago and which ends in Hattie's shooting Duggeler) and then finally bringing us back to the present for a coda. In this case Runyon adds that the reason Baseball Hattie is now back at the Polo Grounds is to watch her son, "the new kid sensation of the big leagues, Derrill Duggeler, shut out Brooklyn with three hits. He is a wonderful young left-hander" (ROB 657).

Runyon juxtaposes the narrator's laissez-faire attitude with that of the idealistic Hattie, who understands what Fibleman is about. Rereading we wonder what kind of character the narrator must be if he hangs around with Fibleman, whom he describes as "a friend of mine," even though he has tried to fix a baseball game. (Of course Runyon himself was like a moth to a flame when it came to associating with disreputable figures.) The 1930s audience would have recognized Fibleman—with a Jewish last name and a first name close to that of Rothstein—as a fictional version of Arnold Rothstein.

"Johnny One-Eye" (*Collier's,* June 28, 1941) is a late noir story, qualified by a sentimental touch, about a badly wounded gangster named Rudolph who has been shot by another gangster named Buttsy Fagan. While in hiding and losing strength, the virtually friendless Rudolph befriends a cat. The cat, which we learn later is named Johnny, has been kicked in the eye by Buttsy, the man who has shot Rudolph. Rudolph also befriends the cat's owner, a young girl named Elsie who comes looking for the cat and allows Rudolph to keep it. Buttsy is her mother's live-in boyfriend; he terrorizes them and steals from her mother. Buttsy (is Runyon playing with the pun on "butt's eye?" as well as recalling Dickens's Fagin?) comes looking for Rudolph. Mistaking the cat for Rudolph in the dark room, he not only shoots the cat in the other eye but kills the cat. Finally, by killing Buttsy, the now-dying Rudolph avenges himself, Elsie, her mother, and the cat. In a sentimental ending, Rudolph arranges for Elsie not only to summon a policeman and claim the reward for capturing him, but for her to get a new cat.

The speaker is more an omniscient narrator than in any of Runyon's other stories, even to the point of penetrating the mind of the dying Rudolph. He is also part of the underworld, for he explains that Rudolph's "protection" business is "very respectable work," although the police regard it as extortion (MGAD 298). Not without some sympathy, Runyon shows us again how the underworld and demimonde ethic often redefines language according to its code.

Rudolph's warm response to the cat and the child rescues the story from noir. As Rudolph says to a man in the pet shop, "He is the only living thing that ever comes pushing up against me warm and friendly and trusts me in my whole life" (MGAD 302). He also cares about Elsie, the young girl who is caught in the maelstrom of the macho gangster world dominated by the intrusive and violent bully Buttsy who, according to Elsie, and in contrast to Rudolph, does not like "little girls," or "little kittens," or "little anythings" (MGAD 305).

Runyon's fears of approaching death find expression in this story. Writing in the early 1940s, he is very much aware of his own aging and deteriorating health; his throat began to bother him in 1938, although he had his tonsils removed in 1931 and was told to take care of his throat, which had been abused by cigarettes. Rudolph—whose name has homophonic resonances to that of his creator, Runyon—is now fat and in his forties. Recalling earlier times when he was shot and recovered, Rudolph "gets to thinking that maybe he is not the guy he used to be" (MGAD 301).

In Runyon's stories, at times violence has almost a sensual dimension with homosocial and, on occasion, sadomasochistic implications. When Rudolph shoots a former ally known as Cute Freddy, he gives him "a little tattooing. In fact, Rudolph practically crochets his monogram on Freddy's chest" (MGAD 299). The D.A. "wishes to place [Rudolph] in the old rocking chair in Sing Sing" (MGAD 299). When Rudolph shoots Buttsy, the police find "two bullet wounds close together in his throat" (MGAD 300). It is as if violence binds victim and perpetrator in a bizarre physical union.

The 1950 black and white film *Johnny One-Eye* (directed by Richard Florey, produced by Benedict Bogeous, screenplay by Richard Landau, a United Artists Film) is based on the story. Taking place in the shadows, it is so dark that at times the action is barely visible, but it does capture the grim predatory world of these gangsters. *Johnny One-Eye* reflects the aura of the early 1950s, the heyday of film noir. It presents the postwar 1950 audience with a vision of New York as a corrupt and violent city.

In the film Rudolph becomes Martin, and Martin and his antagonist kill each other. In the story "Johnny One-Eye," the tale is told by a detached third person anonymous narrator, but in the film version Martin becomes the narrator. (With the exception of the long 1933 story "Ransom . . . $1,000,000," when Runyon's narrator is engaged in illegal actions, the narrator is usually no more than a passive participant in criminal activity.) We first see this engaged self-dramatizing first person narrator on a ferry, in a barely visible night scene, killing a man called the Dutchman who has withheld money from him. Martin is joined in the murder by another man who, many years later, is about to turn him in so as to avoid criminal charges against himself. The cat is replaced by a dog, and, unlike in the story, the animal is not killed while serving as a decoy.

The film plot is complicated by a blackmailer named Ambrose, who is a corrupt member of the D.A.'s staff. The film is gentler than the story; the child Elise has a much larger role, particularly in terms of her relationship with Martin, and, in a sentimental turn, she is by his side when he dies. The film also takes a more moralistic view of gangster behavior; for example, when the man at the pet store—in the film a more professional and authoritative figure in the person of a veterinarian—removes a bullet from Martin, he condemns the animalistic behavior of men who kill each other.

"Earthquake" (*Cosmopolitan,* January 1933) is the name of both the title character, an exceptionally vicious and strong man who has killed a New York City policeman named Mulcahy, and the major event in the story, which allows this worst of all characters—seemingly a sociopath without a redeeming quality—to act heroically. Causing mayhem in New York, Earthquake has been given that name "because he is so fond of shaking things up" (ROB 161). Indeed, the narrator's ironically reductive summary of Earthquake's behavior "when he is in real good humor" reminds us of the noir figure Joe the Joker in "Sense of Humor": "[S]o you can see Earthquake is a very high-spirited guy, and full of fun" (ROB 162). The policeman Johnny Brannigan follows him to New Orleans and then to Nicaragua; as he is about to arrest Earthquake, an earthquake occurs, and Earthquake volunteers to hold up a collapsing building (he acts as if he were Samson—or Atlas, with whom he is specifically compared by Brannigan, who describes the story of Earthquake's heroic behavior to the narrator). By this act, he allows children and nuns to escape. Knowing the building will collapse on him, he chooses to die this way rather than face the electric chair for killing a policeman; he even lets Johnny Brannigan, who has been leading the children and nuns out through his legs, escape.

This story accentuates Runyon's lack of interest in interiority of character. We don't know the source of Earthquake's violent rage and can barely guess why he becomes, as he puts it, "soft-hearted," and doesn't let the building fall on Brannigan, the cop who has not only pursued and captured him but hit him on the head with a blackjack. In fact, he has told Brannigan that the bullet killing Mulcahy was meant for him. Yet right before the next ground tremor makes the building collapse on Earthquake, there is something touching about the way Brannigan and the now-humanized Earthquake, who have participated in the shared heroic rescue, bid each other "goodbye" (ROB 169).

Runyon's narrator is affected and modified by the characters and behavior he describes. As his opening words reveal, police are as anathema to him as they are to Earthquake: "Personally I do not care for coppers . . ." (ROB 159). It is as if Earthquake's hostility is transitive, for when the narrator meets a sickly looking Johnny Brannigan at Mindy's before he hears the story, he meanly remarks: "I am secretly hoping that it is something fatal, because the way I figure it there are a great many coppers in this world, and a few less may be a good thing for one and all concerned" (ROB 159).

NOIR STORIES WITH A SENTIMENTAL ENDING

In Runyon's world, often all is well that ends well. Particularly in the early stories, for the most part serious consequences do not follow violent acts, except when someone is so morally reprobate that our sympathies are with the perpetrator rather than the victim. In "A Very Honorable Guy" (*Cosmopolitan,* August 1929), Runyon's second published story, Feet and Hortense retire from Broadway and now live a different life "raising chickens and children right and left, and . . . all of Hortense's bracelets are now in Newark municipal bonds, which I am told are not bad bonds, at that" (ROB 429). Note the simple prose for the restorative ending, as if the couple's former troubles had been exorcised by magic and the world of hustling and gambling and violence forever put behind. Butch and the gangsters pull off their heist and crime pays in "Butch Minds the Baby" (1930); while we assume Butch flourishes from his gains and improves his domestic economy, we do know from the later "The Snatching of Bookie Bob" (1931) that Harry the Horse, Spanish John, and Little Yid will soon lose their money and need to try another illegal enterprise. In "Social Error" (1930) the reprobate Handsome Jack avoids being killed by his enemy and gets the girl of his dreams, and Basil Valentine, the writer and pretend tough guy, marries a wealthy woman who dotes on gangsters. Jack O'Hearts gets his righteous revenge in "The Lily of St. Pierre" (1930). In "The Bloodhounds of Broadway" (1931), Marvin Clay, apparently dead, is restored to life; Regret is released; Maud Milligan and Regret are not punished for their dalliance; and Miss Lovey Lou is not punished for taking a shot at Marvin Clay. In "Lillian" (1930), Wilbur suddenly stops drinking, marries the love of his life, who had left him, comes into money, and becomes a "useful citizen."

For every hard-edged story like "Ransom . . . $1,000,000," there is a sentimental one affirming the values of love and looking forward to the gentler and more sentimental tone of the anecdotes about a Brooklyn couple named Joe and Ethel Turp. Speaking in a sentimental but worldly tone that accepts human motives and understands human pain and reversals, the narrator of "Maybe a Queen" (*Collier's*, December 12, 1931) reveals how Ida Peters, who has been transformed by a series of marriages from a showgirl to the fulfillment of her dream to be a queen, renounces her title and angrily returns her jewels to her soon-to-be-king husband so that she can keep her yearly commitment to the one man she cares about, the neither bright nor successful Jack O'Donahue. By being true to her commitment, she is a Cinderella figure who after her clock strikes midnight reverts to her former identity. Destitute because her investments failed and at age forty lacking what it takes to find another wealthy husband, she is a head waitress at a place where she tells the narrator her story while serving him breakfast. The reader understands how within the Runyon universe, women are commodities that trade according to a changing valuation of their mix of wealth, age, beauty, and sexuality. Runyon's depiction of women reflects a culture where educational and professional opportunities were extremely limited.

When Jack first tells Ida he loves her and wishes to marry her, she is twenty-two and determined to marry guys with money so she will not be poor. Except for her relationship with Jack, money drives her feelings. Indeed, she can be sadistic in the way she casts off a man who has less money than she thought: "She always drops [that person] in as cruel a way as she can think of, such as looking right past him the next time they meet as if she never seen him before" (MGAD 41). Later as she becomes more prosperous she invents a family history "of old Revolutionary stock" and forgets that she came from Allentown (MGAD 40).

In a kind of Kafkaesque story, she flourishes as Jack declines, as if she were living off his life substance. The narrator describes him in his final years as "a very sorrowful spectacle, indeed. [Jack] is so thin you can scarcely see him when he is standing sideways, and he is stoop-shouldered, and his hair is quite gray, and his eyes are now away back in his head" (MGAD 46). By the time of their the last meeting in September 1930, more than nineteen years after they first met, he is suffering with tuberculosis and is too weak and sick to cross the street. In a scene of pure pathos, Jack is carried to their last rendezvous after he is hit by a taxicab; after asserting his love, he dies.

The sentimental ending is appropriate for a story published December 12, at the onset of the Christmas season. To the sentimental narrator, Ida, now a head waitress who retains her "cold and haughty [voice] as it ever is in the old days," is more a queen for her devotion to Jack. As she puts it, "I am the only head-waitress in the world who tosses off a throne just to hear a guy say, 'I love you,' although . . . personally I consider it worth it" (MGAD 49).

Written at the height of the Depression, "Broadway Financier" (*Collier's*, January 30, 1932) focuses on what almost everyone with any money at all most feared: the collapse of their bank. As David

M. Kennedy reminds us, "The more than five thousand bank failures between the Crash and the New Deal's rescue operation in March 1933 wiped out some $7 billion in depositors' money."[6] "Broadway Financier" is a story not only about the commodification of human relationships but about the precarious nature of the banking system and its effects on poor people. Runyon's plot has a self-regulating structure—typical of his all's well that ends well stories—that cleans up the mess and restores the lost money.

Although he is married, the Lower East Side banker Israel Ib steals from his bank to support an attractive Ziegfeld dancer, Silk, in a lavish lifestyle. Indeed, he meets Silk while allowing, at her behest, his employee Simon Slotsky, who has stolen from his bank to please Silk, to go to San Francisco and thus avoid prosecution. That Israel Ib has money and provides jewelry and real estate is enough to make Silk put up with him two or three times a year, even though he is fat and homely and she makes jokes about him. She may even milk him consciously or unconsciously because of her hatred for bankers due to the failure of the bank where her mother had deposited $300 she had earned from scrubbing floors. After Ib's bank fails and he is arrested, Silk, remembering how her mother's life had been ruined by a prior bank failure, makes up the bank's losses by selling her jewelry and real estate.

When she goes to the bank's neighborhood to tell the enraged depositors that with the help of the lawyer, Judge Goldstein (he reappears in "The Old Doll's House" a year later), she will make restitution for their losses, they, having seen her picture in the papers, begin to attack her. But she is rescued by Simon Slotsky's mother, who recognizes Silk, because Slotsky's mother has a picture of the woman who had intervened to save her son. Characteristic of Runyon's plot doubling, Silk's concern with Simon shows that she is tender-hearted, and what she does for the bank depositors and Israel Ib is in the same vein. Notwithstanding the negative publicity from the newspapers, which write about Ib's obsession with Silk and its effect on his bank's solvency, Ib continues to run the bank, and in one of Runyon's stories where at least superficial public and private equilibrium is reestablished, his wife returns and their marriage flourishes.

Runyon captures the hum and buzz of the overpopulated and predominately Jewish Lower East Side where, by 1900, people lived, "seven hundred per acre, a rate that topped Bombay's as the highest in the world. . . . Jews stayed packed like herring in a barrel in part because they couldn't afford to commute."[7] In this story about Jewish characters who steal from a bank, Runyon's ethnic stereotyping approaches what we now would regard as anti-Semitism—as in the narrator's metonymy "shawls and whiskers" to describe the Lower East Side inhabitants who lose their money (ROB, 215). Israel Ib—whose last named is clearly shortened—is described in terms of ethnic stereotypes: "He is a little short fat guy . . . with a pair of gold-rimmed cheaters hanging on a black ribbon across the vest. He has a large snozzle and is as homely as a mud fence" (ROB 210).

Taking Ib's money and restoring the bank to health, Silk is the Broadway financier of the title. But hasn't she deserved that title all along? When the narrator opens the story about huge scores woman have made off men and cites Silk "when she knocks off a banker by the name of Israel Ib" for over $3 million, we think we are going to hear about a predatory woman gulling a foolish man (ROB 210). And we do, but are we prepared for the reversal when she sells everything to make full restitution—especially when we learn she has been hanging around the Mindy's crowd since she was seventeen and thinks and talks like a guy "because she associates more with guys than she does with other dolls and gets a guy's slant on things" (ROB 205)? What she learns is the necessity for hard-boiled hustling in a world where money and the material things it buys matter and are the only things that matter. But perhaps she also learns to act boldly from the high rollers at Mindy's, and that gives her the courage to save the bank.

Focusing on how an abandoned young child changes the life of a sixty-year-old stingy, self-immersed, greedy bookie named Sorrowful, one of Runyon's most memorable stories, "Little Miss Marker" (*Collier's*, March 26, 1932), is a parable of how caring for someone is a transformative experience. According to the narrator: "This guy is always called Sorrowful because this is the way he always is about no matter what. . . . Any time you see him he is generally by himself, because being by himself is not apt to cost him anything" (ROB 298).

He informally adopts a three- or four-year-old girl left in his bookie shop by a father who supposedly has amnesia; learning how to care for another person, he becomes a happy, generous, free-spending person: "Sorrowful gets so he smiles now and then, and has a big hello for one and all" (ROB 302). "[B]ringing about such a wonderful change," the child becomes a joyous presence in his world and even lights up the Broadway world to which the narrator belongs (ROB 302). The girl is called Marky for two reasons: Sorrowful took her as a "marker," or deposit, for a two-dollar bet and, when asked her name, that is what the men in Mindy's hear. At odd moments she declares, "Marky dance," and "begins hopping and skipping around among the tables" (ROB 299).

Mindy's regulars take Marky under their wing and convince Sorrowful that the little girl needs a nice apartment; soon she has a chauffeur and a nanny. At one point Milk Ear Willie turns up at a nightclub to kill Sorrowful over a betting dispute, for Sorrowful does not always pay off expeditiously when he loses a parlay, but Marky jumps into his arms at the right time and Willie puts away his gun. The idyll concludes when the girl gets ill from running around in bare feet the very night she inadvertently saves Sorrowful. In a violent but hilarious scene, in which Runyon stresses that the best medical care—like the best justice—is available only to the wealthy and privileged, Willie even kidnaps a Park Avenue specialist "who does not practice much anymore, and then only among a few rich and influential people" (ROB 306).

The tale's intense, single-minded plot emphasizes its parabolic quality. If the story is about the restorative power of love, it is also about the depressive blight of loss. The idyll of Sorrowful turns into a sad, sentimental story, with a hint of noir when Marky's real father returns too late, and Sorrowful reverts to his former sour self and regains "the sad, mean-looking kisser that it is in the days before he ever sees Marky, and furthermore it is never again anything else" (ROB 310).

Runyon emphasizes the farcical nature of the mob encamped at the hospital. The newspapers assume because "there are so many prominent characters in and around"—"prominent" is Runyon's euphemism for well-known gangster—"that some well-known mob guy must be in the hospital full of slugs, and by and by the reporters come buzzing around to see what is what" (ROB 305). Indeed, at the hospital a hoodlum called Sleep-out "is looking around to see if there is anything worth picking up," which with his nickname could suggest not only money and valuables but women (ROB 305). The second meaning is emphasized by the narrator's next sentence: "In fact an old doll from Rockville Centre, who is suffering with yellow jaundice, puts up an awful holler when Sleep-out is heaved from her room"—supposedly because they are in the middle of a sexual encounter. (Since my family lived in the Nassau County suburban town of Rockville Centre for almost a century and I was born and raised there when the town pretended to be the image of rectitude, I find that sentence particularly amusing.)

The story has generated a number of films. The original black and white 1934 *Little Miss Marker* (directed by Alexander Hall, produced by B. P. Schulberg, screenplay by Leonard Spigelgass and Sam Hellman, and released in color in 1961) plays fast and loose with Runyon's plot without totally forgetting it. *Sorrowful Jones* (1949) (directed by Sydney Lansfield, produced by Robert Welch, screenplay by Edmund Hartmann) was a Bob Hope vehicle with Lucille Ball. In 1980 Walter Bernstein directed and wrote the screenplay for a star-studded *Little Miss Marker* with Walter Matthau, Tony Curtis, Bob Newhart, and Julie Andrews. Because he was older, less comical, and grumpier than Bob Hope, Walter Matthau as Sorrowful in the 1980 remake was more Runyonesque. Following the family oriented Hollywood values of the day, the 1980 film enacts the superiority of parenthood, the nuclear family, and religion over the Broadway world of race fixing, gambling, and cynicism.

These three well-known film versions of the story use Runyon's main ideas yet expand greatly upon the plot to increase its complexity. Each involves a young girl, Marky (Martha Jane), who is left by her father with Sorrowful as a "marker" for a racing bet. In Runyon's version, Marky dies before her father comes to claim her. However, in the films, the father commits suicide, and Marky does not die.

Beneath the tough exteriors are good-hearted folk with whom the audience empathizes. The original film is a feel-good fantasy without much psychological subtlety. For example, Little Miss Marker (Shirley Temple) very quickly seems to put her father behind her, although we know he has committed suicide. Rather than dying of pneumonia, the little girl is thrown from a horse. With the help of a transfusion from Big Steve (Charles Bickford), a mob figure bent on killing Sorrowful (Adolphe Menjou), her life is saved by the intervention of a famous doctor who is kidnapped on his wedding day. Steve is enraged because Sorrowful falls in love with Bangles, his girlfriend, in part because they both respond to Miss Marker. Sorrowful has a conversion experience and, after relearning how to pray—in part by teaching the little girl about prayer and God—pulls out of a racing scheme to dope a horse and agrees to marry Bangles and to adopt the young girl. The entire plot line about slipping Marky's horse a "speedball" was an addition to the story. We are left wondering what happened to the police search for the missing girl.

At times, as in "Little Miss Marker" or even "Breach of Promise" (1935), Runyon shows us how reprobate characters can do something good. For example, in "'Gentlemen, the King!'" (*Collier's,* April 25, 1931), hardened criminals are hired to assassinate a king of a small European country on behalf of the grand duke. Discovering that the king is a child when they break into his quarters, they befriend the child and turn on his enemies. The narrator hears from the three hoods—Kitty Quick and Izzy Cheesecake from Philadelphia, and Jo-Jo from Chicago—about a mysterious trip to Europe, but learns about the regicidal goal of the original mission and their taking the part of the child king only when he later runs into Kitty Quick. The latter tells the story of how the hoods change sides when they discover they have been hired for $200,000 to kill an innocent orphan child; as they leave the country they protect the child's political interests by having Jo-Jo throw a small bomb at the nefarious duke's house, killing him. (Recalling how the Kennedys apparently used Mafioso to try to assassinate Castro, we might be less shocked at this tale.)

On one hand, the narrator speaks of Izzy and Kitty as "old friends of mine," which positions him within a world where characters either know or brag about knowing Al Capone. On the other, he himself is intimidated by these violent bullies who eat dinner at his expense without being invited. Often the degree of the narrator's criminality or at least tolerance of nefarious behavior is a function of the world he describes, and this story begins with an unusually violent edge. For example, Jo-Jo is an extremely violent character who carries "pineapples"—grenades or small bombs—and who, the narrator asserts, "reminds me of an old lion I once see in a cage in Ringling's circus" (ROB 170). As if he were a circus sideshow act, Jo-Jo, the narrator continues, "is pointed out to visitors to the city as a very remarkable guy because he lives as long as he does, which is maybe forty years"—presumably because of Chicago gang wars and Jo-Jo's propensity for violence; but the narrator doesn't give reasons why forty years is a long life and expects the reader to smile knowingly about the underworld culture (ROB 171). Indeed, the seemingly psychotic Jo-Jo's idea of fun is to shoot animals as the criminal group drives to the small country where they are supposed to kill the king. Runyon's cast of characters are often oddities and freaks; in "The Hottest Guy in the World" (1930), Runyon actually uses the circus context when he creates an analogy between Jule and the ape seizing the baby.

If there is anything for which Runyon has a soft spot, it is for children, particularly orphans. At the center of the story is an idyllic reversal. After establishing that Kitty Quick, Izzy Cheescake, and Jo-Jo are hoodlums of the most dangerous kind, he humanizes them by showing how they are totally captivated by a child who reminds them of their own youth. After the three gangsters meet the king and his nanny, all three are charmed by the child and begin to play baseball; to impress the child-king, they recall (or fantasize) their glory as neighborhood baseball players. Indeed, Kitty claims that, when telling the story to the narrator, "the chances are I will be with the A's if I do not have other things to do" (ROB 183). Notwithstanding the violence done on behalf of the child-king, the story is transformed into something of a tall tale about male dissembling. From the representatives of the grand duke who set up the murder without mentioning that it is a personal power grab at the expense of an innocent child, to Jo-Jo's tales of knowing Al Capone, and, of course, the gangsters' exaggeration of their baseball prowess, these characters willfully disguise their motives, history, and, quite often, their identities.

As in "'Gentlemen, the King!'" children are usually exempt from the world of hostility. They are an oasis from the hustling world and can temporarily transform the hardest cases. Not only Sorrowful but the Mindy's crowd becomes attached to Little Miss Marker, and Jack O'Hearts is totally captivated by twelve-year-old Lily in "The Lily of St. Pierre" (1930), to whom he reads *Alice in Wonderland.* Nor in the latter tale should we miss the irony—whether Runyon intended it or not—that Jack O'Hearts is, like Lewis Carroll, infatuated with a very young girl, and that Lily is his Alice. For Jack O'Hearts, the house of Lily and her physician grandfather "is the quietest place I am ever in my life, and the only place I ever know any real peace" (ROB 36). In two stories in which crime does pay, the gangsters are protective of babies, and that protectiveness saves them from punishment: "Butch Minds the Baby" (1930) and "The Hottest Guy in the World" (1930).

IDYLLS AND SENTIMENT

Juxtaposed to the world of the noir stories are stories that validate romantic love and the possibility of transformation and transfiguration. In "The Idyll of Sarah Brown" (*Collier's,* January 28, 1933), the gun-toting gambler Sky Masterson not only falls in love with and marries the beautiful Sarah Brown, a soldier at the Salvation Army Broadway mission, but also joins the mission. Although drawing on bits and snips of a bevy of Runyon's stories, the wonderful 1950 musical comedy *Guys and Dolls* found its inspiration in "The Idyll of Sarah Brown." The ebullient musical lyrics by Frank Loesser, the mockery of religious certainty in "Sit Down You're Rocking the Boat," and the high-spirited relationship between Nathan Detroit and Adelaide place the musical version of Sky and Sarah's romance in a world of make-believe where romance and a kind of rough-edged gentleness always triumphs. The continued success of the musical by Jo Swerling and Abe Burrows and the film version with Marlon Brando as Sky and Frank Sinatra as Nathan Detroit have helped keep Runyon's name in the public eye.

Toward the end of the nineteenth century, the Salvation Army began to play a proselytizing role in New York—its national headquarters was at the Brooklyn Lyceum—among the urban immigrant poor. As Burrows and Wallace put it, "The Army promoted its orthodox Wesleyan message of grace, forgiveness, and love—and total war on drink—with novel methods. Stirring brass bands, drums, and tambourines, clearly audible over the din of city traffic, attracted passers-by. So did the rousing versions of religious texts set to popular melodies, including barroom ballads, love songs, vaudeville ditties, and minstrel tunes. . . . The Army displayed a Barnumesque flair for publicity."[8] Runyon probably enjoyed the irony of their using the hoopla and chutzpah of Broadway performative and advertising methods to win Broadway souls.

The opportunity for leadership positions in the Salvation Army also attracted young women like Sarah Brown. As Burrows and Wallace note, "Salvation Army girls, often alerted by bartenders, entered Bowery saloons or dance halls and rescued girls stupefied from drink or drugs, fighting off men who wanted to keep them there."[9] Sarah Brown's Broadway mission has little luck converting souls on Broadway, and when she finds out Sky is a gambler she denounces him and refuses his contributions. Gambling is anathema to her because it ruined her father and brother; that may explain why she and her grandfather, Arvide (note the play on the word "Avid") Abernathy, who runs the mission, are working for the Salvation Army in a place where gambling is flourishing.

Sarah manipulates Sky into adopting her religious perspective. Because he is a confidence man who has read widely in the Gideon Bible while moving from hotel room to hotel room, this is not so difficult a role for him to assume. Although Runyon was hardly a churchgoer, he knew the Bible, perhaps from the same source as Sky. Well before she wins her bet for his soul, Sarah has caught Sky's eye, arousing his interest and conveying to him that she is sexually interesting and interested. Indeed, if Sky opens up to Sarah's world, Sarah also joins his world of sensual pleasure. No sooner does he declare his love—and rather piously quote Paul in ways that remind us that he is, in gangster vernacular, a wise guy, if not wise ("If any man among you seemeth to be wise in the world, let him become a fool, that he may be wise")—than she asks if "maybe he remembers the second verse of the Song of Solomon" (MGAD 331). That verse gives the "idyll" richer meaning with its declaration of love in sensual terms: "For I *am* sick of love. . . . My beloved is like a roe or a young hart/ . . . For sweet *is* thy voice and thy countenance *is* comely. . . . For my beloved *is* mine and I *am* his."[10]

After Sky has lost his money by waging it against the souls of gamblers in a dice game, Sarah arrives at the very minute he is about to kill Brandy Bottle Bates, the man who is rolling the dice. Sky has figured out the dice are loaded; using the same dice without realizing they "are strictly phony" (and certainly unaware of how to manipulate them), Sarah rolls the dice for his soul and wins. Given the sly cheating of Bates, Runyon might have expected us to recall the next line from the second Song of Songs: "Take us the foxes, the little foxes, that spoil the vineyards."[11] Part of the story's fun is that Sky's given name is Obadiah, a prophet whose vision denounces the perfidy of Edom for betraying Israel after the fall of the Temple in 586 B.C. and for looting and massacring the Israelites in their weakened state; Obadiah predicts Edom's destruction and looks forward to an idyllic time for those who escape: "But upon Mount Zion shall be deliverance, and there shall be holiness."[12] Runyon is suggesting a playful parallel between the prophet Obadiah—the sound of whose name Runyon would have enjoyed—and the contemporary Obadiah, who is now denouncing Broadway, the corrupt contemporary Edom, which with its phonic resonance to Eden becomes an anti-utopia, an Eden manqué.

Some of the story's humor derives from how we are shaped by our heritage, for Sky's father was also a gambler and taught him a good deal about how to get on in the world. Indeed, his advice to his son provides one of Runyon's most memorable lines of skepticism and distrust: "Some day, somewhere . . . a guy is going to come to you and show you a nice brand-new deck of cards on which the seal is never broken, and this guy is going to offer to bet you that the jack of spades will jump out of this deck and squirt cider in your ear. But son . . . do not bet him, for as sure as you do you are going to get an ear full of cider" (MGAD 320). That advice informed Runyon's own skeptical and often cynical approach to life and observation of the world, whether it be sports, politics, marriage, or friendship. An inveterate and unsuccessful gambler, Runyon—who had a quixotic and resilient side—always was capable of thinking that he could control events and that if he kept his ears open and listened carefully, he might know more than someone else. He believed that caution, selfishness, and holding back trust would take him a long way. Yet he also knew from a lifetime of losing that someone might be even shrewder than he.

It may well be that when Sarah seeks Sky out at Nathan Detroit's crap game, challenges him to gamble for his soul, and wins his heart, she did squirt cider in Sky's ear. On the other hand, Sky's conversion might be an example of squirting cider in the ear of all those who thought they knew him as a gun-toting gambler and a rolling stone who avoided commitment. Or it may be that he has squirted cider in Sarah's ear—a wonderful sexual image that anticipates her citing *Song of Songs* as the text for their love, especially if we recall—as Runyon might have expected us to—from the second verse: "As an apple-tree among the trees of the wood, so is my beloved among the sons. I sat down under his shadow with great delight, and his fruit *was* sweet to my taste. . . . Stay me with flagon, comfort me with apples: for I am lovesick."[13]

In some of Runyon's early stories, perhaps because of his love for his second wife, Patrice, whom he married in 1932, the tone is lighter and the endings often include transformations to a better life for many of the characters. Runyon uses folk motifs such as versions of the Cinderella story—without the reversion to Cinderella's former state at the end—and of the pot of gold suddenly appearing to the deserving innocent. Often as in "A Very Honorable Guy" (1929), "Madame La Gimp" (1929), and "Lillian" (1930), marginal and broken figures—lonely, isolated, alienated, rejected, and powerless—are transformed in fairy-tale endings into people living comfortable bourgeois domestic lives. In "Social Error" (1930), the wealthy Miss Harriet Mackyle, who enjoys mixing with gangsters, finally marries the magazine writer Basil Valentine, who has pretended he is a tough guy to impress her.

Runyon began publishing his Broadway stories in the final years of Prohibition, which lasted from 1920 to 1933. Prohibition helped create a huge illegal industry of alcohol manufacture and transportation and a bonanza for criminals who captained that industry. In 1920 the Eighteenth Amendment—administered by the Volstead act—prohibited the sale, manufacture, export, and import of liquor; after a period of rampant illegal drinking, the Twenty-First Amendment repealed Prohibition.

Drinking during Prohibition plays a large role in the early stories. In this category we could place "Madame La Gimp," "Dream Street Rose" (1932), and especially two of the Christmas stories—namely "Dancing Dan's Christmas" (1932) and "The Three Wise Guys" (1933)—where the narrator does considerable drinking despite avowing that he "very seldom indulge[s] in alcoholic beverages in any way, shape, manner and form" (ROB 397). But let us briefly turn to his fifth published short story and the first to appear in *Collier's,* "Lillian" (February 1, 1930), a story in which the narrator is a member of the demimonde that hangs around Mindy's but is not a drinking man.

Wilbur, an entertainer who is also a drunk, finds, befriends, and adopts a cat—which, in his cups, he thinks is a leopard—and names her Lillian after his beloved Lillian Withington, who had been his partner in a singing and dancing act. That in his cups Wilbur lives in a haze in which reality is completely scrambled places him among a large number of Runyon's characters who have lost a grip on reality and suffer delusions if not mild psychosis and who live on what the narrator of "Dream Street Rose" calls Dream Street. After Lillian walks out on him because she "wishes money, and luxury, and a fine home," Wilbur begins to drink heavily (ROB 281).

He lives in a hotel room in a fleabag that catches fire. Completely drunk, Wilbur walks into the burning building—which he perceives as "a fairy palace all lighted up" (ROB 287)—to save the cat as well as a young child who has befriended the cat. Having been given whiskey regularly by Wilbur, the cat saves the boy by following the Scotch smell of a bottle that has been tipped over by the boy's father; the latter has died either from drink or from smoke inhalation or a combination of both. By the kind of Runyonesque coincidence that mocks the artifice of plotting even as it resolves the story, it turns out that the boy belongs to Lillian, his old girlfriend, whose husband has kidnapped their son. In a fairy-tale ending, reminiscent of Runyon's idylls, Wilbur is transformed when he marries Lillian, "falls into a lot of dough," stops drinking, and becomes a "useful citizen" (ROB 291).

That Lillian is the name of both the cat and the woman who leaves Wilbur plays on the traditional obscene term "pussy" to categorize women's genitalia. The metonymical relationship between cat and the woman he has lost is underlined—along with a kind of wink at his indiscriminate drunken sexuality—by Wilbur's keeping that name for the cat after he discovers the cat is male and could be named "Herman, or Sidney" (ROB 280). By recalling a cat and dog thief named Pussy McGuire, Runyon's narrator stresses the story's playful sexual nuances. As if she were the woman he has lost, Wilbur touches and fondles Lillian. Like the Lillian who has left Wilbur, the cat becomes erratic with his affections; as Lillian's affections depended on Wilbur's providing luxury, the cat's affections depend upon his generosity with liquor. Interestingly, when Wilbur regains his old girlfriend, he and the cat Lillian no longer need each other, and the cat attaches herself to a bootlegger who continues to serve it scotch.

The stories of the mid to late 1930s have fewer complete character transformations than the earlier ones, but the transformations still occur with some frequency until the stories of the late 1930s and 1940s. For example, in "Big Shoulders" (1936) Zelma Boodinski marries the Yale man she loves, Charley Flannagan, instead of the wealthy and presumably Jewish Jack Applebaum, to whom her father is in debt; along with her father, the couple prosper taking bets on football games, a sport that is Charley's specialty. In "The Big Umbrella" (1937) Margie McCoy, the orphan niece of Spider McCoy, the fight manager, is living in modest circumstances taking care of her uncle until she marries a king and becomes his queen. By marrying the sister of the dictator whom the king defeats in a fistfight to regain his throne, Spider finds a "wonderful and everloving" wife to take care of him (ROB 564). In "Neat Strip" (1938) a Yale law student of some means and seeming respectability wants to marry a stripper, but the student doesn't know that his mother was herself a former stripper. Bruno Bettelheim's discussion of fairy tales in *The Uses of Enchantment* aptly describes the fantasy strain of these stories: "[A] struggle against severe difficulties in life is unavoidable, is an intrinsic part of human existence—but if one does not shy away but steadfastly meets unexpected and often unjust hardships, one masters all obstacles and at the end emerges victorious. . . . Morality is not the issue in these tales, but rather, assurance that one can succeed."[14]

"Romance in the Roaring Forties," Runyon's first Broadway story, published in the July 1929 *Cosmopolitan,* is a high-spirited tale that begins as if it might be noir but concludes with a comic and even idyllic ending that marks Runyon's occasional "all's well that ends well stories." The story introduces Waldo Winchester—as we have noted, a comic version of Walter Winchell before Runyon and he became fast friends—and the prominent gangster Dave the Dude. Winchester is described by the narrator as "a nice-looking young guy who writes pieces about Broadway for the *Morning Item.*" In fact, he is something of what we now call a gossip columnist, writing "about the goings-on in night clubs, such as fights . . . and also about who is running around with who, including guys and dolls" (ROB 29).

Although Waldo Winchester is his rival for the affection of a club dancer named Billy Perry, Dave the Dude is apparently throwing a surprise wedding for Billy and Waldo, notwithstanding his former antagonism to Waldo or that he kidnaps Waldo as part of the surprise. But Waldo's wife, Lola Sapola, a woman acrobat so strong that she "juggles the other four people in the act," arrives, punches Dave, and carries off Waldo (ROB 39). Dave then marries Billy Perry. An acquaintance of Dave's and his gangster associates who has been invited to the wedding in a way he cannot refuse, the narrator confides that he is the one who telephoned Lola. Runyon surely knew about Winchell's own domestic situation—Winchell was married to one woman and living with another.

The story enacts Runyon's bemused fascination with the power of the press and his own enjoyment of using his column's influence to control not only public events but also private relationships. Billy seems to be fascinated with Waldo because he is "not a bootlegger and a gunman" and "puts lovely pieces in the paper about me, and he is a gentleman at all times" (ROB 33). Waldo not only woos Billy by putting nice things about her in the paper, but he intimidates club owners because he can write gossip that will hurt a nightclub. And the narrator reminds us that if Dave the Dude takes Waldo "out for an airing"—a euphemism for killing him—the newspapers will pay a great deal of attention since Waldo is something of a celebrity.

Runyon understood that celebrity incubates narcissism. In his depiction of Winchester and another journalist, Ambrose Hammer, he shows an awareness of how events are distorted by the individual eye of the teller and of the potential narcissism on the part of those who report the news. Runyon was aware that the media can present as well as obfuscate reality, and he knew how the media can reduce sociopolitical complexities into spectacular entertainment or what some now call infotainment. In fact, Runyon not only satirizes the power of the press, but reminds his readers with a wink of that power that he himself, as a journalist, possesses in full measure.

Runyon's third published Broadway story, "Madame La Gimp" (*Cosmopolitan,* October 1929), is also something of an idyll—another high-spirited all's well that ends well story in the mode of "Romance in the Roaring Forties." Dave the Dude arranges a party for a down and out drunk named Madame La Gimp—who, as her name indicates, walks with a limp—to help convince her daughter's fiancé's father, a Spanish nobleman, and his wife that Madame La Gimp is a distinguished citizen and a woman of substance. She had sent her daughter to Spain to be raised by her sister, and the daughter met the young Spanish man she loves. Dave's wife, Billy Perry, and Missouri Martin, the owner of the club in which she used to dance, take Madame La Gimp under their wing and dress her up so that she looks quite presentable.

Drawing on one of his characteristic themes, Runyon stresses the complicity between the respectable and the criminal world. For the party, Dave the Dude borrows the elegant apartment of a wealthy socialite, Rodney B. Emerson, who is "obligated to Dave the Dude" for supplying him with champagne. Dave's guests are mostly Broadway gangsters pretending to be important figures. Dave's ploy works and the young couple elopes. The idyll is underlined by the newly presentable Madame La Gimp's attracting as a husband Judge Henry G. Blake, a former suitor and Broadway character who is not a real judge but a well-dressed hustler. Lest we miss the irony of the mixing of respectable and criminal worlds, the story ends with Dave the Dude demanding stolen property be returned to the building where the party took place, "especially . . . the baby grand piano that is removed from Apartment 9-D" (ROB 254).

Runyon is often faulted because not only does every character talk the same way, but every character talks the way the narrator tells his tales. While at first characters seem barely individuated by speech, careful readers will find some distinctions. For example, in "Madame La Gimp" there are differences between Dave the Duke's aggressive intimidating style of speech, marked by a sense of presumptuous privilege, strong subject-predicate-object sentences, and a strong focus on himself—"I judge the proud old Spanish nobleman is none too bright. . . . I know how I will get the apartment"(ROB 242)—and that of Rodney Emerson, playing the role of the pompous, sequacious, and yet self-effacing Butler; the latter announces the names of his social betters such as "Willie K. Vanderbilt"—or famous show people—"Mister Al Jolson"—when various gangsters arrive at the party (ROB 250).

Rodney's periodic announcements remind us that no one is who he seems. The gangsters themselves—Dave the Dude, Little Manuel, Big Nig, Judge Henry G. Blake—live behind assumed names. Within this story, they exchange their assumed identities with celebrities. The Broadway characters, who themselves in their daily lives have shed their real names and identities, now put on an elaborate charade, claiming to be major American figures such as Al Jolson, Willie K. Vanderbilt, or Vice President Charles Curtis. Or put another way, in a house of mirrors, where the narrator and others stress that it is dangerous to ask questions about someone's past or to ask too many questions, characters not only wear masks to disguise who they are but also exchange one mask for another. It as if the Broadway theatrical world and the Broadway street world were interchangeable, for the street characters are playing parts everyday. But isn't Runyon the modernist implying that, rather than have coherent identities, we all play different roles at different times in our lives—even within each day—and these masks are radical versions of that? And yet Dave the Dude and his cohorts do not really cease to be themselves;

they steal from the other apartments; carry guns, as Wild William Wilkins does when he arrives at the party; drink excessively, as Judge Blake does; and shoot craps, even using, as Skeets Bolivar a.k.a. the Very Reverend John Roach Straton does, dishonest dice.

Pocketful of Miracles is a 1961 Frank Capra film that is an upbeat version of "Madame La Gimp"; in the spirit of *Guys and Dolls,* it is a remake of Capra's *Lady for a Day,* based on the same story. *Pocketful of Miracles* takes the nameless apple lady who takes care of the Brain in "The Brain Goes Home"(1931) and fuses her with Madame La Gimp, an alcoholic street person who sells old newspapers and faded flowers; while no one takes her merchandise, kind-hearted guys like Dave the Dude give her a little money. To the story of making the street person known as Apple Annie presentable to her Spanish in-laws, *Pocketful of Miracles* not only adds the notion that Dave the Dude requires for luck one of Annie's apples before any important event, but also creates the story of how Dave marries a showgirl named Queenie Martin, although in "Romance in the Roaring Forties" he marries Miss Billy Perry. The film also includes other events emphasizing Dave's power that are not found in Runyon's "Madame La Gimp"; in *Pocketful of Miracles,* Dave not only bests a Chicago gangster known as the King, but he also manipulates the mayor and governor into going to the party he gives to show how prominent a figure Annie is. Despite posturing with guns, no one gets hurt in this feel-good film, which shows the gangsters as comic figures with a capacity for love and decency.

"The Old Doll's House" (*Collier's,* May 13, 1933) depends on the juxtaposition of the gangster world and the blueblood world of New York wealth. Lance McGowan, a gangster described as "a coming guy in the business world," finds refuge from an attack by Brooklyn gangsters, who resent his intrusion into their borough, in the East Side house of the wealthy and brokenhearted Abigail Ardsley (ROB 61). Abigail no sooner welcomes him than she tells him how her beloved had died in the blizzard of '88; her father had discovered the couple passionately engaged in his house and tossed her love out into the storm. Whatever his motive, Lance allows her to rekindle her life for an evening, praising her looks, sharing sandwiches and wine, and giving her an evening of congenial companionship. Indeed,

Lance is a kind of playful Sir Lancelot engaged in an ironic version of pure chivalric love in service to Abigail. Runyon's depiction of Abigail's house and her living in the past may have been influenced by Charles Dickens's Miss Havisham in *Great Expectations*.

The noir gives way to an all's well that ends well ending, in part because we sympathize with Lance's desire for retribution against the Brooklyn gangsters after he wins our sympathies by participating empathetically in the lonely world of Abigail Ardsley. After leaving Abigail's house, Lance stops by Good Time Charley's place and kills two of the Brooklyn gangsters, Angie the Ox and henchman Mockie Max, and injures the third, The Louse Kid, who seems to be a master at stuffing people in burlap bags. With the newspapers clamoring for arrests and complaining about lawlessness, Johnny Brannigan arrests Lance, and it looks as if he will be convicted.

A recurring Runyon theme is the corruption and ineffectuality of the legal and judicial system, a system that in this and other stories completely fails to do its duty. When Abigail testifies that Lance was with her at twelve, and therefore has an alibi, the judge dismisses the case without allowing further questions. Of course, Abigail neglects to mention that all clocks in her house are stopped at the very hour decades ago when she last saw her beloved. On one hand, the legal system suffers from obeisance to the privileged and wealthy; the narrator cynically notes that for Lance McGowan's trial, Abigail arrives surrounded by "the biggest lawyers in this town, and they all represent Miss Abigail Ardsley one way or another, and they are present to see that her interests are protected, *especially from each other*" (ROB 71; emphasis mine). Even newspapers toady to the rich and describe Abigail's appearance in bogus terms—"she looks like she steps down out of an old-fashioned ivory miniature and . . . she is practically beautiful," even though she is what the narrator calls "an old chromo"—a Runyon term for old hag (ROB 71). On the other hand, the legal and judicial system allows gangsters to stalk the streets with impunity, to commit acts of violence upon one another without being convicted, and thus to flout the supposed standards of the respectable world; here Lance McGowan and his attorney, Judge Goldstein—who had been Silk's attorney in the 1932 "Broadway Financier"—manipulate the legal system to their own advantage.

In this violent world, words are often appropriated and distorted to mean something entirely different from their conventional meanings. The violence to language is as much the subject as the violence to humans. For example, when Lance sees Abigail, he thinks he needs to "guzzle" her before he realizes from her voice that she will not call the police. Indeed, the narrator again, as he had in "A Sense of Humor" and elsewhere, uses terms from the world of play to describe violent and homicidal behavior. Putting Lance in a burlap bag "just for the laugh" in an effort by rivals to kill him is ironically described as a great "practical joke" (ROB 63).

CHRISTMAS STORIES

Runyon published a number of stories that appeared in popular magazines in late December and revolve around Christmas: "Dancing Dan's Christmas" (*Collier's,* December 31, 1932), "Three Wise Guys" (*Collier's,* December 23, 1933), and "Palm Beach Santa Claus" (*Collier's,* December 24, 1938). While they contain some noir elements, they have a strong sentimental if not at times idyllic aspect befitting their Christmas themes.

"Dancing Dan's Christmas" has a less complicated plot than most of the stories. Despite the presence of gangsters, it is a breezy fairy tale that begins with the narrator transporting us to a simpler world by the use of a version of the fairy tale convention "Once upon a time": "Now one time it comes on Christmas, and in fact it is the evening before Christmas" (ROB 254). An all's well that ends well story, it has even less grammar of motive than is usual in Runyon. After much drinking of Tom-and-Jerry rum drinks with the narrator and Good Time Charley Bernstein in Bernstein's speakeasy, the high-spirited Dancing Dan borrows a Santa Claus outfit from Ooky who, dressed as Santa Claus, is advertising for Moe Lewinsky's clothing store.

With a nuance of anti-Semitism, the narrator enjoys the irony of celebration—or, at least recognition—of Christmas by Jews like Bernstein and Lewinsky. The narrator is alternately respectful of and irritated by Charley Bernstein's participation in Christmas festivities: "[P]ersonally I always think Good Time Charley Bernstein is a little out of line trying to sing a hymn in Jewish on such an occasion, and it causes words between us" (259). After they all are in their cups, Dancing Dan, accompanied by Charley and the narrator, goes to the home of the aged and dying grandmother of Muriel O'Neil—the woman whom the gangster Heine Schmitz and Dan both love—and puts the diamonds he has stolen into the grandmother's Christmas stocking. Dan is a rather intrepid fellow considering that Schmitz "will just as soon blow your brains out as look at you" (ROB 257).

A year later on Christmas eve the narrator learns from Shotgun Sam, a member of Schmitz's mob, that the Santa Claus outfit saved Dan from being killed by Heine Schmitz's henchmen because they thought he was Ooky. As a result of that Christmas present, Dan is alive this Christmas and in San Francisco "figuring on reforming and becoming a dancing teacher" so he can marry Muriel (ROB 266). Of course, it is hard to believe, as the narrator implies, that she does not know the details of Dan's criminal career to say nothing of Schmitz's.

"The Three Wise Guys," an exceptionally rich and well-crafted tale, is a Christmas fantasy in which gangsters and demimonde characters do the right thing. A substantial story that includes intimations of aging, loneliness, chance, and poverty, "The Three Wise Guys" reflects some of Runyon's own emotions at a time when he was well into his early fifties. Notwithstanding his second marriage, he still spent a good deal of his time in male bonding situations.

After much drinking at Good Time Charley's, the narrator accompanies two tough guys, Blondy Swanson, a now-retired and broke former major bootlegger who foresaw the end of Prohibition, and a safecracker, known as the Dutchman, to Bethlehem, Pennsylvania, to retrieve a large sum of stolen money that the Dutchman left behind when fleeing a crime scene. The Dutchman has invited Blondy to go with him and share half the loot; the narrator, who comfortably consorts with gangsters, enthusiastically volunteered to go along. Safecracking, according to the narrator, who apparently is familiar with such professions, has come back "during the Depression when there is no other way of making money, until it is a very prosperous business again" (ROB 403).

Once again the narrator is a member of the world he describes, using stock images like "colder than a deputy sheriff's heart" (ROB 405) to place himself within the criminal orbit, even as he juxtaposes that illicit orbit with a conventional world that eludes him and his two companions. Like Blondy and the Dutchman, he too has nowhere to go on Christmas Eve except a speakeasy and, indeed, tells us, as they drive to Bethlehem, that "none of us happen to think of it being Christmas Eve until we notice that there seems to be holly wreaths in windows here and there . . . but the chances are I will not be seeing any Christmas trees even if I am home" (ROB 405).

Without comment, he listens to Blondy's attributing his retirement to his patriotism before acknowledging the real reason is that he can't make money anymore. He satirically compares Blondy to respectable business moguls like John D. Rockefeller, J. P. Morgan, and Henry Ford—who also, his readers would have known, mask their profit motives in rhetoric about the good of the country and wrap themselves in the flag. Sounding as if Blondy had closed down a large part of the banking or car or oil industry as Morgan or Ford or Rockefeller might, the narrator says facetiously of Blondy's retirement announcement: "I consider Blondy's statement the most important commercial announcement I hear in many years, and naturally I ask him . . . what is to become of thousands of citizens who are dependent on him for merchandise" (ROB 399).

The dominant motif is regret and loss. Blondy regrets losing his girlfriend and the chance for a conventional life with a wife and children because he wouldn't give up his bootlegging. Like Blondy, the Dutchman is past his professional prime. He has lost some confidence now that he is in his fifties ("[H]e finds he is about half out of confidence, which is what happens to all guys when they commence getting old"), and this has been exacerbated by his being shot and taking a long time to recover (ROB 404). When we also learn that the Dutchman is a widower with eight children, seven of whom he delivered himself because he couldn't afford a doctor, we become more sympathetic.

Slowly and effectively Runyon's narrator reveals that it is Christmas and develops the parallel between his contemporary tale of three underworld and demimonde figures and the three wise men going to visit the Christ child. To get to the barn where he has hidden the money, the Dutchman and his passengers need follow a big star, which turns out to be "a light shining from the window of a ramshackle old frame building" (ROB 406). Recalling Chekhov's "The Student," an Easter story with ironic reminders of the persistance of poverty and misery, the narrator's references to poverty and the Depression remind us that Christ's coming has not eradicated human misery.

It turns out that Blondy's former girlfriend, the very morally upright Miss Clarabelle Cobb, a dancer in White's Scandals who "comes of very religious people," is in dire straits and lives in the very barn where the money is hidden and is in the process of giving birth. Her husband has been unfairly implicated as the insider who told the criminals where the money was in the very robbery in which the Dutchman participated and in which his three henchmen were killed by the police. But the guilty insider is in fact no other than Ambersham, the factory manager, and one of her husband's enthusiastic accusers. With the suffix "sham" and its play on the "ampersand," the typographical mark for "and," Ambersham's name has the kind of appropriateness Runyon loved to give his characters. If at first Ambersham's participation places him on the same side of the moral divide as the original robbers, we realize, to Runyon's amusement, that Ambersham, the supposedly respectable participant in the capitalistic economy and the demimonde trio actually reverse moral positions because the latter not only summons a doctor for Clarabelle but return the stolen money.

When the trio of Blondy Swanson, Good Time Charley, and the narrator is leaving Bethlehem, a policeman stops their car for speeding; finding only an empty bottle of rye whiskey but not the stolen money, the policeman snidely calls the trio "wise guys"—a term that had, and still has, criminal associations. But by letting them go because it is Christmas, the policeman saves the Dutchman from having to shoot him and get into major trouble. The Dutchman concludes that they have indeed been wise in their generosity: "We are wise guys. If we are not wise guys, we will still have the gripsack in this car for the copper to find" (ROB 413). One of the wise men who has journeyed to Bethlehem on Christmas Eve, the Dutchman, delivers Clarabelle Cobb's baby. Another of the wise men, Blondy, arranges to get her husband out of jail.

Revealing Runyon's views of the inherent nastiness and superficiality of those with inherited wealth, a later Christmas story, "Palm Beach Santa Claus" (1938), stresses both the underlying disparity of wealth between rich and poor and between the powerful and less powerful. An overweight, down on his luck, and, indeed, very hungry horseplayer named Fatso Zimpf agrees to play Santa Claus at a party for wealthy and arrogant Palm Beach, Florida, residents. But in this story Runyon continually builds Fatso's stature as a decent person in contrast to the world of Palm Beach wealth, where even the children are boorish and misbehaved and treat Fatso's Santa Claus as an inanimate toy, pulling his beard and kicking his ankles. A patient man, he nevertheless becomes impatient at spoiled children who abuse him and thinks that "maybe President Roosevelt is right about the redistribution of wealth" (MGAD 375).

The story also focuses on the cynical relations between men and women. The bogus Count Gregorio is wooing a beautiful wealthy young woman named Betty Lou Marvel, although she loves Johnny Relf, a younger man, who is being much wooed by the oft-married Mrs. Mimm, who is "two face-liftings old" (MGAD 371). Johnny is in his twenties and will inherit much money, but he is recognized as not very bright; in fact, Betty Lou loves him because he is "fun and good-looking" even though she knows he is a "lightweight " (MGAD, 372). Like Mrs. Mimm, Betty Lou regards Johnny as a boy toy, a commodity.

After learning how people in this world treat one another, Fatso intervenes in intimate relationships on the side of those who are getting the short end of the stick from husbands and lovers. He is a kind of Falstaffian Lord of Misrule who switches the intended recipient of valuable gifts with a distinct purpose. Finally by giving Mrs. Mimm's gift to Johnny but changing the donor's name to Betty Lou and by giving Johnny's gift to Betty Lou rather than to Mrs. Mimm, he brings Johnny and Betty Lou together.

While at first Fatso seems not only lazy and unattractively obese to the point of disability, but also completely self-immersed in his hunger, we gradually realize that this lonely but sensitive and perspicacious man who cares about people represents the concept of Santa Claus in a very corrupt world that doesn't appreciate him. Fatso turns out to be a Santa Claus who makes the world a little better. For this is a Christmas story with a considerable Runyonesque sentimentality that takes the side of the good-hearted and generous. When Fatso has a few dollars, he remembers to give a nickel to each of the Black kids—called "stove lids" by Runyon's narrator, using one of Runyon's offensive terms for Black people—who are hovering near him (MGAD 370). Even though he remembers that Gregorio, a gold-digging former busboy, had stolen $36 from the Italian restaurant where he worked in New York, he does not denounce the bogus "Count" Gregorio, who calls him a "fat bum." His code does not permit him to "holler copper" and, unless it is absolutely necessary to keep the count from marrying Betty Lou, he won't do so.

Because it is known that the enraged Mrs. Mimm (playing on "minimum") had reneged on her promise to pay him $50 to be Santa Claus at her party, whenever people from the Palm Beach party see Fatso they give him money. When a year later Fatso is telling his tale to our narrator—a fellow destitute horseplayer ("things are by no means dinkum for Fatso and me at the moment")—a women he has befriended as self-appointed Lord of Misrule comes up to Fatso and gives him $50 (MGAD 379). The tale ends with Fatso and the narrator rather touchingly saying Merry Christmas to each other.

We might consider "The Lily of St. Pierre" (*Collier's*, December 20, 1930) as a fourth Christmas story because of its sentimental evocation of domestic values in juxtaposition to gangster cynicism. In 1924, Jack O'Hearts went to the French isle of St. Pierre to run Scotch "for the Christmas trade" (ROB 136). While there he contracted pneumonia and recovered under the care of Dr. Armand Dorval and his twelve-year-old granddaughter, Lily. Jack returns to St. Pierre when he can because it is "the only place I ever know real peace" (ROB 136).

In thinly disguised rage at the exploitation of an innocent young woman by a predatory gangster, Runyon reminds us of his sympathy for children who are prematurely rushed into adulthood by poverty or exploitive behavior. When the story opens, the narrator is no sooner singing with a quartet including Louie the Lug than Jack O'Hearts walks in and shoots Louie, who eventually dies. Notwithstanding the violence, the reader's sympathy is with Jack because Louie had trifled with Lily. After Jack had introduced her to Louie in 1928, Louie, under false pretenses, convinced Lily to go to Halifax. There he mistreats her and leaves her to die in a hospital, wasting away because of an illness resembling but not identified as tuberculosis or pneumonia. What this story retrieves from our cultural memory is that prior to the invention of various antibiotics, sanitary living conditions, and better diet, people died or nearly died in North America of flu, pneumonia, and tuberculosis in far greater numbers than today.

CONCLUSION

As we have seen, Runyon's Broadway has its own customs and language. He gives personality to individuals within the impersonal juggernaut of the modern city. The city is manageable if one knows how to manage it, and sometimes the gangsters and other members of the demimonde have as good a take on managing that world as anyone. As if Broadway were a small village like that of the *In Our Town* anecdotes, everyone knows everybody's name.

As a frontier journalist descended from a father who was also a frontier journalist, the tall tale was part of Runyon's heritage, as it was of Mark Twain's; hyperbole is a way of seeing for Runyon. It may be, too, as William R. Taylor argues, that Runyon's work, like that of Alfred Henry Smith (1858–1914) and O. Henry (William Sydney Porter), derives from a Western American tradition of storytelling going back to Twain and Bret Harte; as Taylor puts it, "Runyon's world is preeminently a world of men; women figure in it as obsessions, as hostages, as prizes. . . . In the transformation from the West to Broadway, one is tempted to view them as replacing the cattle in these earlier fictions. . . . Homoerotic bonding was at the very heart of Runyon's fiction, as in his associations at work. Homoerotic bonding remained, of course, a regular feature of the celibate cowboy. . . ."[15]

Runyon saw himself in part as a rube and outsider from Manhattan, Kansas, by way of Pueblo, Colorado, and in part as a kind of Horatio Alger who transformed his economic fortunes by hard work. He no doubt felt a kinship with other Westerners like Edgar Lee Masters, Sherwood Anderson, Sinclair Lewis, and especially Mark Twain, all of whom wished to, as Wagner puts it, "lift at least a corner of the veil of sanctimoniousness and self-satisfaction behind which moneyed respectability was hiding its corruptions, perversions, and tragedies."[16] What unites Runyon's Broadway tales of noir and sentiment with his Broadway idylls are an awareness of the common humanity of class, ethnicity, and geography; sympathy with the marginalized and demimonde; and high-spirited enjoyment of the energy and humor of the Broadway world.

CHAPTER 6

THE GENRES OF RUNYON'S FICTION

Gangsters, Gamblers, and Boxers

INTRODUCTION

As a reporter who became a short story writer, Runyon's stance is that of an observer rather than a participant. He began writing his Broadway stories at the age of forty-nine, but his reporting was the laboratory in which he perfected his technique and developed the cool, ironic, detached voice of the stories. In talking about the underworld, whether in his reporting of the Capone trial or in his stories, he at times adopted the gangster's moral perspective; or as Stephen Fox puts it, "Yet despite the measured sociological clarity and ironic laughter audible in the distance, the moral perspective was faithfully internal. . . . In these stories cops were abusive, troublesome and worse than useless."[1] Sometimes one wonders if Runyon would endorse his narrator's disdain for the police and tolerance for robbery.

Fox has argued that the newspapers gave the aura of glamour to the mob: "In soaking up the Broadway scene, [Runyon] had displaced his own moral sense and picked up another. . . . [T]he romanticized soft-focus image of mobsters he created would survive permanently in his stories and movies."[2] Does not our fascination with the Mafia and with criminal life derive in part from the way

Runyon humanized them? What Runyon said about being coopted by the sports activities about which he was writing is applicable equally—if not more so—to his writing about the underworld and the demimonde in his short stories: "To be a great sports writer a man must hold himself pretty much aloof from the characters of the games with which he deals before his sympathy for them commences to distort his own viewpoint. . . . The very nature of nearly all professional sports and some amateur sports, too, makes them subject to influences and practices that are harmful to public morals. . . . [I]t is the duty of [sportswriters] to severely police their field" (ST 145).

In a June 1932 article, "The Twilight of the Gangster: An Interview with the Police Commissioner," Runyon argues that because of the falling off of sales of the whiskey they produce and the nightclubs they run, the underworld has been just as affected by the Depression as the so-called legitimate world. Runyon speaks of the relationship between the criminal world and the respectable one: "[S]upposedly respectable, decent citizens connive with lawbreakers. These are citizens who frequent the speak-easies and who buy liquor for consumption in their homes, all of which is assuredly connivance with lawbreakers and lawbreaking. . . . Certainly our American people remain amazingly indifferent to the pilfering of some of our cities, and to the exposure of felonies by trusted public servants and to moral turpitude that would have horrified us at other times" (*Cosmopolitan,* June 1932, 179). A cynic who knows Runyon's history of friendship with the likes of Arnold Rothstein and Al Capone might say that Runyon is blaming the public as much as the perpetrators. Until the Lindbergh kidnapping, there was little "public outcry" about a spate of kidnappings: "The public was as apathetic in its attitudes toward the snatch as it had been in its attitudes to other crimes" (*Cosmopolitan* 180).

Given Runyon's association with gangsters, his interview with the New York City Police Commissioner Mulrooney has to be taken with a grain of salt. Since Runyon played such a strong part in the newspapers' glorification of gangsters, it is rather ironic, as he surely recognized, that Runyon quotes Mulrooney on that subject: "I would say the young gangster is largely the result of a lack of spiritual guidance and parental care and of the glorification of the gangster in newspaper and magazine stories. The widespread suggestion that the gangster is a heroic figure and lives the life of Riley hasn't been helpful to our youth" (*Cosmopolitan* 179). Could Runyon, we wonder, have kept a straight face when he heard that wisdom from the Commissioner? Runyon hardly would have believed that if Harry the Horse and his fictional companions—and those gangsters he knew—had spent more time in church, they would be respectable citizens rather than kidnappers and gangsters. And Runyon would have smiled at Mulrooney's endorsement of mob ethics of a prior era and would have enjoyed the implicit parallel between criminals of an earlier generation and legitimate businessmen: "The old-time criminal rarely killed. . . . He was not infrequently a man of mature years and considerable experience in his criminal pursuit, and he went about his job with care and caution" (*Cosmopolitan* 179). In this chapter I discuss gangster stories before moving to stories of horseracing and boxing, sports that have full measures of illegal chicanery.

GANGSTER STORIES:
HARRY THE HORSE AND COMPANY

As if to distance himself from the ruffians he describes, in the following gangster stories, the narrator shares with us a story he has learned on two separate occasions. Knowing that he was presenting a narrator that the audience would take as a surrogate, Runyon wants to straddle the line between the narrator as a passive insider and one who crosses the line into criminal behavior. Except for "Butch Minds the Baby" (1930), where the narrator is at least a passive participant in robbery, Runyon recuses his narrator from active criminality. Thus in "Breach of Promise" (1935), after he recommends Harry to Goldfobber, he is out of the loop until Harry comes and tells him the story. After the prelude of "Delegates at Large" (1932) in which Harry announces that he is going to Chicago without telling the narrator why, the story jumps forward to Little Isadore telling the narrator what happened in Chicago. And in "The Snatching of Bookie Bob" (1931), he hears from Harry before and after the kidnapping.

Introducing the Brooklyn-based gangster Harry the Horse and his coterie, Spanish John and Little Isadore, "Butch Minds the Baby"

(*Collier's*, September 13, 1930) is an early and rather gently comic story about a successful safecracking that sentimentalizes criminal behavior. At the outset of "Butch Minds the Baby," Harry, Spanish John, and Little Isadore approach the narrator to help find Butch because they need a safecracker to steal money that has been set up for them by the company paymaster with the compliance of the watchman. The narrator is unenthusiastic about locating Butch, but after Spanish John and Little Isadore intimidate him by voraciously eating his dinner at Mindy's and Harry directly threatens him, he agrees to do so. He takes the three gangsters to visit Butch on a stifling evening when Butch is out on the stoop.

That the narrator emphasizes the heat of the city, as the narrator will do at the opening of "Delegates at Large," makes us remember that in the days prior to air conditioning, summer heat even more frequently exacerbated passions, undermined self-control, and contributed to desperate behavior. A three-time loser facing life imprisonment if he is caught a fourth time, Butch is at first reluctant, claiming that he has retired from such activity; moreover, while his wife is at a wake, he has the responsibility of looking after his son, John Ignatius Junior. Following some drinking, Butch is tempted by the promise of more than $10,000 as his share—with 5 percent of the heist to go into his son's bank account—and he takes his baby with him. After having trouble opening the safe before finally blowing it up and taking the money, he and the narrator run into cops with the baby. Thinking no one with a baby could possibly be robbers and showing a gentle interest in the baby, they let the men go. Although the cops and Harry and friends exchange shots without much injury, the heist of $20,000 is successful for all.

Later stories focus more on Harry and his cohorts as gangsters who do such things "as robbing people, or maybe shooting or stabbing them, and throwing pineapples [hand grenades]" (ROB 339), but this story uses Harry and his men to illustrate the juxtaposition of Butch's domestic values with those of criminal life. Runyon's forte is knowing how to manipulate his readers, and he uses his jaunty narrator to create a kind of moral free zone where safecracking is allowed if it involves a baby as beneficiary. Although the narrator claims to be more an onlooker than a participant and does not seem to benefit from the robbery, he certainly is an accomplice who consorts with criminals and who goes along on the heist without undue pressure. (Indeed, even though Runyon's narrators often say that those who know too much or ask too many questions can get into trouble, curiosity is the narrator's ruling passion in many of Runyon's stories.)

Because of the presence of the baby and the emphasis on how Butch meticulously takes care of him, the story becomes a sentimental tale without a noir mood. While the baby is crying in the cops' presence, Butch exclaims, "[T]here, there, there Daddy's itty woogleums" (ROB 353). Butch's worrying about the baby's colic while he hides the stolen money not only fools the cops but also engages our sympathy.

Part of the tale's fun is how words are comically redefined; take, for example, "honest," which is redefined to mean doing what one does well in one's own interest. Butch is an "honest citizen" now that he has retired from safecracking to become a bootlegger; when approached by Harry, he reluctantly turns the safecracking offer down at first: "I like to turn a few honest bobs now and then as well as anybody" (ROB 344–45). The term "personal friend" refers to an insider who cooperates with Harry to make the robbery easy; the term applies to the paymaster who tells him where the money is and the watchman who disappears when the men arrive for the robbery (ROB 343, 347). To Harry and the narrator, the word "kosher," as in "Everything is very kosher," means not that everything is legitimate or legal by community standards but that Harry and his friends are not out to trick or injure Butch but rather to make him a partner in an illegal proposition (ROB 341).

Before the release of the film adaptation, also entitled *Butch Minds the Baby* (1942)—which he produced—Runyon was called on the carpet by the board of censors, who didn't understand his slang. Another successful film adaptation of a Runyon story is a thirty-minute British production of "Butch Minds the Baby" (1982), in which the narrator is depicted as Runyon the journalist, who inadvertently gets involved in the robbery. The narrator's explanatory prelude containing a little background from the Depression is absent from the original story. But his and the characters' New York accents and Runyonese dialect, period dress, and the background of 1930s jazz combine to make this film a nice transformation of Runyon's story.

In the aforemetioned June 1932 interview with Police Commissioner Mulrooney, Runyon writes with some disdain about the recent spate of "snatchings" that culminated in the kidnapping and death of the Lindbergh baby, whose body was discovered May 12, 1932. Kidnapping is the province of desperate gangsters whose other businesses have suffered during the Depression. Yet "The Snatching of Bookie Bob" (*Collier's*, September 26, 1931) is a high-spirited tale about the "snatching," or kidnapping, business. The clever plot revolves around the kidnapping of Bookie Bob, a prosperous and wily bookie, who has been fingered, we learn at the end, by his wife, who resents his stinginess and will get a 25 percent cut of the $25,000 ransom. As the narrator, quite knowledgeable in these affairs and characteristically taking on some of the personality, values, and even economic conditions of those whom he describes, puts it: "The finger guy must know the party he fingers has plenty of scratch to begin with, and he must also know that this party is such a party as is not apt to make too much disturbance about being snatched, such as telling the gendarmes" (ROB 119). While they await the ransom payment to be delivered by his partner, Bookie Bob takes the kidnappers' losing bets with markers (or loans) he gives them for $50,000, which is $25,000 more than the ransom requested and paid. This results in Harry, Spanish John, and Little Isadore owing Bookie Bob $25,000 and his wife $6,250. According to their code of ethics, they never fail to pay off debts to bookies for fear of losing their reputation; as Harry puts it, "A guy must pay his bookmaker no matter what" (ROB 121).

Containing not only betrayal on the part of Bookie Bob's wife but also blatant sadism in the form of tickling Bookie Bob's toes with matches to encourage him to get a prompt ransom payment, the story has its noir aspect. The story also gives a brief reprise to Waldo Winchester, "the newspaper scribe" based on Walter Winchell, who is, we recall, a principal character and a kidnapping victim at the hands of Dave the Dude in Runyon's first published Broadway story, "Romance in the Roaring Forties"; here Winchester, not surprisingly given his experience in the prior story, takes a dim view of snatching, which he calls "kidnapping," and says "it is all a very wicked proposition" (ROB 120).

"Delegates at Large"(*Cosmopolitan,* July 1932) is, for some unaccountable reason, one of Runyon's least anthologized stories and is the only one absent from *Runyon on Broadway, The Damon Runyon Omnibus,* and *More Guys and Dolls.* When Harry the Horse and his cronies encounter the narrator, who is sitting on the steps of a bank on 48th Street and Seventh Avenue, they are extremely intimidating presences. Meeting them makes the narrator "more nervous than somewhat" (RFTL 211). Little Isadore and Spanish John do what Harry tells them to do, which is to rob and shoot people, "and sometimes Harry the Horse personally takes a shot or two himself" (RFTL 213).

On the train to Chicago, where Harry and his friends are invited to kill a gangster for hire named Donkey O'Neill at the behest of other Chicago gangsters, Harry falls in love with Maribel Marlo, a wealthy delegate to one of the 1932 presidential nominating conventions, although the political party is not identified; Miss Marlo assumes Harry and his coterie are "delegates at large."

Runyon stresses the incongruity of two groups of delegates to Chicago: Harry and his fellow assassins—a delegation of New York gangsters called in because "nowadays when anybody is to be taken care of in any town it is customary to invite outsiders in"—and the delegates to the political convention (RFTL 214). Much of the story's humor depends on Runyon's characteristic intermingling of the respectable and gangster worlds. Because O'Neill is a delegate to the political convention, Harry and his friends are told to wait until the convention is over before doing their work.

Much hilarity derives from Harry's getting delegate badges to the political convention, where he confuses the roistering and clamor of the convention—especially people fighting over signs during demonstrations—with gang fighting and begins to hit people who are opposing Miss Maribel Marlo. Indeed, he is not only a delegate at large but a large—in the sense of imposing—delegate. The demonstration Harry and his friends try to break up is in favor of legal beer, because, as we learn from Little Isadore's tale to the narrator, "[I]t seems that Miss Maribel Marlo is one of the most notorious

Drys in the country" (RFTL 226). Yet Runyon knew that it was a moot point whether legal beer was good for Harry and the underworld, which thrived on illegal alcohol during Prohibition.

In "Breach of Promise" (*Cosmopolitan,* January 1935), Harry the Horse is engaged by Judge Goldfobber who, despite his title, is a most successful defense lawyer for criminals rather than a judge, to steal for $10,000 some embarrassing letters that Jabez Tuesday, the automat restaurant mogul, had written to Miss Amelia Bodkin. Miss Bodkin, Tuesday's lonesome, longtime and aging fiancée who had lent him money to get his business going, regards herself as once pretty but now as "old and ugly" (ROB 15). Now that he is planning to ditch Miss Bodkin to marry Miss Valerie Scarwater of a "high-toned" family, the unscrupulous rascal Tuesday is afraid Miss Bodkin will sue him for "breach of promise." Knowing Runyon's concern for names and his infatuation with language, we might pause for a moment over the name Bodkin. While a bodkin is a dagger or a stiletto, an appropriate image for Tuesday's fear of Amelia's wrath, in Britain a bodkin is a person closely wedged between two others. Just as Tuesday is wedged between Amelia and Valerie, so Amelia is wedged between Tuesday and Valerie.

In "Breach of Promise" Runyon is cynically smiling at the ethics of lawyers. Judge Goldfobber straddles a fine line between advocate and participant. He spends much of his time mingling with potential clients in nightclubs and is not above seeking the narrator's advice about who would commit a crime on behalf of his client Tuesday. As with some Mafia lawyers today, the line between advocacy and participation in crimes is not always clear.

While preparing to steal the compromising letters, Harry inadvertently runs his car into the wall of Miss Bodkin's Tarrytown house. After Amelia cares for him during his convalescence, he shows an uncharacteristically soft heart and intervenes by having the love letters Tuesday wrote to her read to Tuesday's current blond "high-toned" girlfriend, the comically named Miss Valerie Scarwater, which has the effect of bringing Tuesday back to Amelia. To recall the title, Harry has breached his promise to Tuesday to steal the letters and bring them to Tuesday by sending Educated Edmund— whom Harry had enlisted "in case any reading becomes necessary, because Spanish John and Little Isadore do not read at all, and I read only large print"—to read them to Valerie and thus undermine Tuesday's plans to ditch Amelia (ROB 20). Harry extorts $10,000 from Tuesday for keeping quiet about his behavior. Having an oddly scrupulous honor code when it comes to self-interest, Harry wants to sue because he didn't get the silver he was promised. To Harry's credit, we remember from "The Snatching of Bookie Bob" that, within his code, Harry keeps his own promises.

THE BRAIN STORIES

The Brain is the nickname for Armand Rosenthal, a thin disguise for the gambler Arnold Rothstein, although in one story that we have discussed, "Baseball Hattie," a figure who has some resemblance to Rothstein and tries to fix a game is called Arnold Fibleman. We recall Runyon's fascination with criminals and with people who find ways to get an edge as well as his belief that businessmen trying to make a profit were no different.

In the second Broadway story Runyon published, "A Very Honorable Guy" (*Cosmopolitan,* August 1929), Feet Samuels, a very fat guy with huge feet and no money who is a minor hustler and gambler, promises to deliver his own dead body to Doc Bodeeker within thirty days in exchange for Bodeeker's giving him $400. We later learn that Doc Bodeeker—whose name resonates with "body seeker"—makes this deal because Feet is a rival for a showgirl named Hortense Hathaway. (Hortense, whose real name is Annie O'Brien, typifies Runyon's characters who change their names or are given nicknames or wear some sort of mask that disguises who they really are—or once were.) Because Feet has always paid off his loans and is "very honorable about his debts," The Brain vouches for Feet with Doc Bodeeker (ROB 416).

Among other things, The Brain is a loan shark who insists on having the interest and principal paid back on time. He presides over a world where violence is always lurking in the shadow. He always sits at a table facing the door, just in case those entering want to injure him. From the outset, the emphasis on violence in the story creates an ominous atmosphere in which the reader anticipates further mayhem.

When Feet suddenly begins to win at gambling beyond his wildest dreams, he reneges. After a farcical scene in which Doc Bodeeker chases him through the streets with a knife—not so much to get his body but to eliminate his rival—Feet and Hortense marry, have kids, and live off their bond investments and chickens under the protection of Hortense's father, a "very rough guy" whose reputation protects them (ROB 429). The Brain, proving that within his world he is "A Most Honorable Guy," makes good to the doctor for the $400 the latter gave Feet for his body, but The Brain publicly vows to avenge his loss and denounces Feet as "a dirty welsher for not turning in his body to you as per agreement" (ROB 429).

As we have seen, the magical transformation of marginal people from the demimonde into middle class respectability recurs in quite a few Runyon stories. No doubt metamorphosis into prosperity was one of the appealing features of these stories to a Depression audience who could identify with a situation such as Feet's economic plight. We see this appeal in the advertising of the various state lotteries, which seem to be most effective in seducing those to buy tickets who are in the lower economic echelons.

In his early stories of 1929 to 1931, as if Runyon knew he was developing an elaborate imagined world for a large group of stories, he defines the hyperbolic and cynical narrator, the moral geography, and introduces characters he will use again even as he invents the language—syntax, diction, prose rhythms—that will become the verbal coinage of this world.

In this, the second of the Broadway stories, money is the measure of all things: The Brain's stature; Hortense's affection for Feet, which develops after he can afford to give her diamond bracelets; and the motivation for the narrator's friendship for The Brain. Even bodies are measured in dollars. Quite typical of Runyon's stories, the narrator is a hanger-on who avoids anyone who does not have money, and who seeks his friends and acquaintances among those who have it.

While Runyon does not use Freudian terms, he is a keen observer of obsessive compulsive disorders and delusional behavior. For example, Doc Bodeeker is a borderline psychopath who hasn't practiced in years and is obsessed with finding a young wife in the

Broadway demimonde. Until he prospers, Feet compulsively wants to pay off all his debts by his death.

"The Brain Goes Home," another early story (*Cosmopolitan*, May 1931), is a grim noir tale about The Brain's demise and a lugubrious parable in which the hubristic Brain is refused four times by women he thinks love him but who really cynically take advantage of his generosity. The Brain is always watchful of enemies, but he is killed at the behest of someone who owes him money. About forty and known as the Love King, The Brain has been keeping four women in high style, and deludes himself into thinking these women, whom he has bought, love him (ROB 219).

After the first half of the story, in which The Brain's celebrated harem is introduced by the narrator in leisurely, albeit playful, fashion, the story takes a noir turn. When The Brain is slashed by a knife-wielding thug, none of his four women (his wife and three others—all of whom are narcissistically immersed in their own lives and sexual affairs) shows any interest in his plight. After the cab driver leaves the narrator and Big Nig at the home of the last lover, who is entertaining another man, the narrator and Big Nig carry The Brain down the street, "going very slow and hiding in dark doorways when we hear anybody coming" (ROB 229). It is as if he were already dead and this was his funeral cortège.

The Brain is left to die in a hovel after being carted from one home to another of his various lovers. The only person who takes care of him is a woman who sells apples; in fact, that very night he has told her to keep the change from $5 he paid for an apple. She used the money to buy medicine for her sick son. Recalling Kafka's "The Hunter Gracchus," where the deceased man cannot find a comfortable resting place, "The Brain Goes Home" recreates the noir atmosphere of Kafka's mysterious labyrinth in which anxious characters abortively search for a receptive friend. Befriended and cared for only by the destitute apple-seller, The Brain pays her by rewriting his will to make her his beneficiary. While the narrator avows in the final sentence that The Brain has no conscience, The Brain does a good deed—partly out of spite, but partly perhaps because he has, from the apple woman's nursing him alongside her son, learned the meaning of home. The Brain is given a splendid funeral with a plethora of flowers, and the women he has supported engage in paroxysms of weeping. But the narrator's recognition that the apple lady's flowers are the most meaningful homage returns us to the claustrophobic urban world in which The Brain is both perpetrator and victim: "These faded carnations represent the only true sincerity" (ROB 230).

The story reflects Runyon's fear of loneliness and rejection and is a parable of what happens to a cynical hustler who lacks conscience and who tries to buy affection from equally hard-boiled and unscrupulous women. It is also a rather misogynistic story that sees women as either whores or saints, and usually the former. Finally, it demonstrates Runyon's awareness that for all their charisma and apparent power, major players in the criminal world, like Rothstein himself, may die a premature and violent death.

GANGSTER CHIC

"Gangster chic" defines stories like "Tobias the Terrible"(*Collier's,* December 10, 1932), where respectable folk want to be part of the supposedly glamorous world of gangsters, or "Bloodhounds of Broadway" (*Collier's,* May 16, 1931), where the gangster or demimonde world is more admirable than the so-called respectable world and where crime is depicted as justifiable. We saw aspects of these attitudes in "Madame La Gimp," where the wealthy and apparently respectable Rodney B. Emerson hobnobbed with Dave the Dude and wanted to play the butler at a party hosted by gangsters.

In "Tobias the Terrible," a satiric story about what Winchell called the "underworld complex," Tobias Tweeny—note the enervated if not effeminate last name—loses his girlfriend Deborah Weems, to Joe Trivett, a local tough guy, because he does not retaliate when Trivett punches him. Tobias comes to Broadway in a search for tough guys and asks the narrator: "[D]o you know any desperate characters of the underworld?" (ROB 108). After hearing Tobias's tearful story over Hungarian goulash at Mindy's, the narrator takes him to Good Time Charley Bernstein's "little Gingham Shoppe over in Forty-Seventh Street" as a way of bringing a little business to his friend Charley (ROB 109). When they arrive, the narrator discovers that many major gangsters have stopped by after a meeting, and he introduces Tobias to them. At this point the police knock and want to search the men for weapons; they give all their guns to Tobias, who is discovered with twelve guns after he topples over due to the weight of the weapons. He is arrested and enjoys the notoriety that the police and newspapers confer on him: "[H]e is getting so much attention that it swells him all up" (ROB 113). But the comically named Judge Rascover—we think of a judge who covers up for rascals—lets him go, and, in the Runyonesque resolution of this farcical plot, Tobias marries Deborah because she thinks he is a great gunman.

In Runyon's world the incessant, almost obsessive listing of details (a kind of hyperealism) combines with the fantastic juxtapositions of surrealism to challenge—often to the point of absurdity—conventional patterns of reality. Tobias the Terrible plays on the name of a ruthless czar or king, but he is in fact a gentle, passive man goaded by his girlfriend to assume the mask of outlawry. Depicted as fools, as is often the case in Runyon's world, the police take Tobias for "a mighty bloodthirsty guy" (ROB 113). The newspapers, the major shapers of public opinion, label Tobias as a tough guy: "[T]he newspapers are plumb full of the capture of a guy they call Twelve-Gun Tweeney, and the papers say the police state that this is undoubtedly the toughest guy the world ever sees, because while they hear of two-gun guys, and even three-gun guys, they never hear of a guy going around rodded up with twelve guns" (ROB 112–13). To increase circulation, Runyon understood, newspapers rely on exaggeration, distortion, and other available tools of sensationalism.

To once again show the interchangeability of diverse worlds, Runyon has Tobias return to his small town, Erasmus, Pennsylvania, where he is elected constable, because "a guy with such a desperate reputation . . . is bound to make wrongdoers keep away from Erasmus if he is an officer of the law"; he chases his adversary Joe Trivett—who "bootlegs ginger extract to the boys in the back room and claims Al Capone once says 'Hello' to him"—out of town (ROB 116, 107). Indeed, he even arrests and fines a few of the New York gangsters for carrying concealed weapons—a charge not dissimilar to the Sullivan gun law charge on which he was arrested—when they are in his area "inspecting a brewery proposition" (ROB 113). Once he takes the side of respectability and becomes a constable, Tobias becomes terrible to the very gangsters and bullies whom he wanted to emulate. Runyon seems to have made up the geographic entity of Erasmus, Pennsylvania, and would have hoped that some of his readers recalled that Erasmus wrote *In Praise of Folly,* an appropriate subtitle for "Tobias the Terrible."

In "The Bloodhounds of Broadway," Runyon uses the high-spirited farcical technique of some of his early Western tales, but with many more turns of plot. When the narrator meets the illiterate Georgia rube John Wangle on Broadway, incongruously accompanied by man-hunting bloodhounds, and speaks of seeing "such animals chasing Eliza across the ice in Uncle Tom's Cabin when we are young squirts" (ROB 92), the reader realizes that Runyon is looking back to his own piece entitled "A Slight Hitch in Uncle Tom's Cabin" (RFAL 188–92).

A wealthy railroad heir who preys on showgirls, Marvin Clay is not only disgusting looking—with "a very ugly mugg, which is covered with blotches and pimples"—but "rough and abusive with young dolls such as work in night clubs" (ROB 91). Because Clay is a "very good customer," the narrator cynically observes that Clay is "very welcome indeed wherever he goes on Broadway" (ROB 91). Another ladies' man, the well-dressed and prosperous Regret, a horseplayer who makes his living from another unstated source, generously feeds John Wangle and his dogs. In fact, we learn at the end that the reason the dogs barge in on Maud Milligan—who has been seeing Regret while her boyfriend Big Nig is out of town—is that they are following Regret's scent. And suspicion falls on Regret because he had punched Clay in a dispute about Miss Lovey Lou. But Clay has apparently been shot dead by Lovey Lou because he had taken advantage of her sister—a dancer in Miss Missouri Martin's Three Hundred Club—as he had once taken advantage of Lovey Lou: "He has her in his apartment and when I find it out and go to get her, he says he will not let her go" (ROB 101). But after the apparent killer, Regret, is captured and the actual shooter, Miss Lovey Lou, has, with the narrator's intervention, been protected, it turns out that Clay is very much alive.

The bloodhounds are not only the dogs but also the narrator who unravels the mystery. As the unfolding plot characteristically turns against the respectable world, embodied by Clay, the narrator's intervention includes his carnivalesque word play of onomatopoeic words and nonsense sounds that undermine the pretension of the well-to-do, the police, and the newspapers; the bloodhounds bark a barely plausible "woofle-woofle" and an implausible "zoopie-zoopie" (ROB 99), the latter a comic version of sniffing and snooping. The narrator is a choreographer who sends Lovey Lou home and keeps silent while the process of exonerating Regret takes place over several weeks. He may feel that it is his responsibility to sort things out since he had suggested sending the bloodhounds after Clay's killer, even though "some think the [murderer] is entitled to a medal" (ROB 96). After hearing Lovey Lou's story, the narrator subscribes to this view.

Runyon resented the power of old money. He had a strong hostility to those who inherited wealth, such as Marvin Clay, and the privileges that it evoked. His sympathies are with the dancers and showgirls who are exploited by such men. In this story, he shows his characteristic sympathy for women as victims and for the powerless and poor such as John Wangle. He also shows cynicism about the police, who think a man is dead who is actually alive and will mindlessly arrest anyone when they need a culprit after a wealthy man is killed ("[T]he best way to do under the circumstances is to arrest everybody in sight and hold them as material witnesses for a month or so") and also apparently are on the take from crap games and speakeasies (ROB 96). Embarrassed in front of Inspector McNamara, who either is surprised or, more likely, feigns surprise to discover dice games, speakeasies, and hop joints, the police in McNamara's district are ironic versions of bloodhounds. The implication is that the local policeman are bribed, for one dishonest cop observes of the bloodhounds: "Why . . . these mutts are nothing but stool pigeons" (ROB 98). The narrator is very much part of the demimonde: "I do not care to associate with coppers, because it arouses criticism from other citizens" (ROB 95). Regarding the newspapers with bemused suspicion if not antagonism are both the police, who feel the brunt of their criticism and are at times on the take, and the gangsters (and most of the demimonde, including Runyon's narrators), who feel that the newspapers are violating the implicit code of tolerance by prying into their business and asking too many questions.

IVY LEAGUE: THE JUXTAPOSITION
OF THE HARVARD-YALE-PRINCETON
WORLD WITH BROADWAY'S DEMIMONDE

In Runyon's demimonde, characters are continually assuming roles, changing names, reinventing their pasts, and disguising themselves. Thus in "Undertaker Song" (*Collier's*, November 24, 1934), Runyon presents a world of distorting mirrors inhabited by fighters known as Pile Driver and Left Ledoux, Meyer Marmalade as an alias for "something like Marmalodowski," and Joey Perhaps, whose name stands not only for his dubious nature but for *perhaps not alive* (ROB 327). But the story also illustrates some resemblance between classes. Just as the wealthy fawn over Randolph and laugh at his remarks whether they are funny or not, so, too, does the narrator—a self-described hanger-on who hasn't had anything important to do "for the past ten years"—play up to Meyer Marmalade; the narrator is Meyer Marmalade's guest because Meyer "loathes and despises travelling alone" (ROB 327).

A story of predatory violence, "Undertaker Song" takes place in Boston and Cambridge at the time of the Yale-Harvard football game. The narrator disingenuoulsy opens by juxtaposing the world of wealthy college men with that of the underworld: "Now this story I am going to tell you is about the game of football, a very healthy pastime for the young, and a great character builder from all I hear . . ." (ROB 325).

But the story really has little to do with football and much to do with making an example of those who "holler copper," that is, betray fellow criminals. The story makes the distinction between college games such as football as sports events, and underworld games, where men die, gamblers lose on double crosses of supposedly fixed fights, and vengeance is deadly. Early in "Undertaker Song," Meyer Marmalade, a major gambler, speaks of meeting Ollie Ortega: "Ollie remarks that he understands Joey Perhaps is about due out, and that he will be pleased to see him some day" (ROB 328). We learn that Joey Perhaps is the man who, to reduce his own jail sentence, testified that his partner, Jack Ortega—Ollie's brother—was the hit man in a shakedown and was thus responsible for him going to the electric chair. Meyer sends for Ollie, who, as the victorious Yale crowd sing their "Undertaker Song," cuts Joey's throat, leaving him—in a dénouement of Runyonesque black humor—with "a big, broad crimson ribbon where he once wears his white silk muffler" as if he were a Harvard fan (ROB 338).

This story strongly focuses on moral cannibalism, where some men live at the expense of others. Before Ollie Ortega intervenes, Joey Perhaps is threatening to shakedown his former girlfriend, Doria Logan; Doria is now engaged to a wealthy Harvard man, the son of Phillip Randolph. The parasitic Joey Perhaps deprives Jack Ortega of his life and Doria of her self-respect; when he meets Randolph on the train from New York to Boston, he even spoils Randolph's good humor with his ostentatious rudeness.

Two other very similar stories revolving around Harvard-Yale sporting events and the clash between the Ivy League elite culture and Runyon's Broadway characters are "Hold 'Em, Yale!" (*Collier's*, November 4, 1931) and "A Nice Price " (*Colliers*, September 8, 1934). In "Hold 'Em Yale," an early example of an all's well that ends well story, the narrator, along with Benny South Street, Liverlips, Jew Louie, and Nubsy Taylor, is part of Sam the Gonoph's ticket-scalping crew for a Harvard-Yale football game. The crew meets an ingenuous if not frivolous upper-class young girl named Clarice who has run away from Miss Peevy's School to watch her brother, a substitute on the Yale team, and also to elope with a seemingly respectable man named Elliot, who turns out to be the Broadway character Gigolo George. After beginning as a common thief, Sam the Gonoph—the name Gonoph is based on the Yiddish word for thief (also spelled "ganef" or "ganof")—has become successful in speculating on sports tickets; he is angry at George for stealing money from him in a prior ticket-selling enterprise at the Harvard-Yale game. Harvard wins and tries to pull down Yale's goal posts, but at the behest of Clarice, whom they have befriended, the demimonde characters—Sam and his Broadway ticket salesmen—defend it with their street-fighting techniques until Elliot arrives and is revealed as Gigolo George to Clarice's father, the wealthy J. Hildreth Van Cleve.

Much of the story's fun depends on the juxtaposition of the blueblood Ivy League world and the Broadway world. When two Harvard men imitate the young girl's voice while she is rooting for Yale in the middle of the Harvard section of the stands, "all of a sudden these parties leave their seats and go away in great haste, their faces very pale, indeed, and I figure maybe they are both taken sick at the same moment, but afterwards I learn that Liverlips takes a big shiv out of his pocket and opens it and tells them very confidentially that he is going to carve their ears off" (ROB 151). And when she says she is chilly, two of Sam's assistants, Jew Louie and Nubsy Taylor, "slip around among the Harvards and come back with four steamer rugs, six mufflers, two pair of gloves, and a thermos bottle full of hot coffee for her, and Jew Louie says if she wishes a mink coat just say the word. But she already has a mink coat" (ROB 152). The Broadway guys defend the defeated Yale goal posts from Harvard's efforts to tear them down. Characteristically Runyon plays on his story's title with the Broadway guys "holding" off the Harvard men. To reinforce their fists, the Broadway guys put "the good old difference in their dukes" in the form of "a dollar's worth of nickels rolled up tight" (ROB 154).

In "A Nice Price," a story that owes much to the prior and more deftly plotted "Hold 'Em Yale," the focus is again on class distinctions between characters who are marginalized Jews trying make a buck any way they can and the WASP establishment. The ticket speculator Sam the Gonoph, Benny South Street, Liverlips, and the narrator are hustling tickets in New Haven for the annual boat race between Harvard and Yale. Sam and his guys take 3 to 1 odds—what in gamblers' lexicon turns out to be a "nice price"—from a wealthy Yale enthusiast, Mr. Hammond Campbell, and bet on Harvard. They befriend an ingenuous and fluffy young woman named (once again) Clarice, who turns out to be Campbell's daughter after the narrator returns a purse she has dropped; something of a rascal, he admits he returned Clarice's purse because "several parties who are standing around in the lobby see me" pick it up (ROB 192). Clarice's boyfriend goes to Harvard and very much wants his university to win.

Even for avid readers of Runyon, the idea that the outcome of the relationship between Clarice and her boyfriend Quentin depends on Harvard's winning the race is implausible—or at best an unsuccessful and undeveloped parody of Freudian father problems on the part of the young Harvard man. In another strand of this uncharacteristically loosely plotted story, Sam discovers Society Max, a gigolo who has stolen his girlfriend, aboard the boat from which he is watching the race and chases Max, who, thinking Sam might have his gun, jumps overboard. A Yale man breaks his oar on Max's head—although Max survives—and Harvard wins. In a final resonance of the title, Sam gets an extra $5,000 for saving Mr. Hammond Campbell's sister from Max's clutches.

Benny South Street, one of Sam the Gonoph's henchman, reminds us that marginal figures who don't have conventional jobs may harbor resentment. As a spokesman for a more egalitarian world, he anticipates the communism of Rupert Salsinger two years later in "Tight Shoes" (1936). Benny points out that many of the private yachts watching the race are examples of conspicuous consumption during the Depression.

In "Big Shoulders" (*Cosmopolitan,* December 1936), the last of the Ivy League stories, Zelma Bodinksi wants to marry Charley Flannagan, a Yale man and a substitute on the Yale team, on the basis of a four-hour meeting. She prefers Charley to the druggist (and from his name presumably Jewish) Jack Applebaum, to whom her father, Blooch Bodinski, owes $10,000. Blooch has lost his money in a bank failure, one of many in Runyon's stories that reminds us of the Depression and the economic instability of that time. Blooch now places bets that he takes with other bookmakers so as not to risk his own money, but most of Blooch's customers are now out of money, and he has few new customers.

Blooch has been reluctant to take bets on football, saying it is nothing but "big shoulders." After Zelma, following Charley's advice that he can scientifically handicap football games, bets and wins on Yale against the favorite Princeton, Charley and Zelma get married and Charley goes into business with Blooch as a major bookmaker. Runyon is amused that Charley's Ivy League education has not only taught him to compete successfully with the Broadway characters, but that he has become one of them, now making the biggest football book in the country. Or put another way, Charley becomes the "big shoulders" for Blooch's and Zelma's prosperity.

The story sustains its title motif by beginning with Zelma's crying on the narrator's shoulders in Mindy's about having to marry Jack Applebaum. Although sympathetic to Zelma, the narrator is, in his commentary to his audience, ironically patronizing to her in the mode of Runyon's misogynistic speakers who think of women in terms of their bodies; he remembers her mother as a showgirl who does "a hot wiggle": "[Zelma] is never much of a hand at thinking, just like her mama" (ROB 579, 583).

Runyon stories continually show that divisions between social classes are arbitrary. His plots often strip the mask from assumed identities and hidden motives. In a 1938 story entitled "Neat Strip" (*Collier's,* April 9), the apparently straitlaced mother of Daniel Frame, who supposedly "comes of the best people in New England," turns out to be a sensational former stripper (ROB 612). How often in Runyon do we see unlikely marriages—and pursuits of showgirls by the wealthy and socially prominent—as if they were intentionally invading, undermining, and overturning the class pretensions of the elite? The title, "Neat Strip," refers also to the stripping away of presumed identity to expose Laura as the person she once was, but she is not ashamed or embarrassed at all to claim her superiority to her son's stripper girlfriend, Rosa.

It is worth noting that, at a time when Jews were virtually excluded from the Ivy League, in all five of these Ivy League stories the principal Broadway guy is Jewish. Runyon's audience would have recognized that his describing Blooch as "coming up out of Essex Street" meant Blooch was from the Jewish Lower East Side (ROB 579). Certainly Runyon's stories helped establish the Lower East Side as the Jewish district in the popular imagination for those living beyond New York. Even in 1933, when in "Broadway Complex" Cecil Earl, who has a multiple personality disorder, wanders around the Lower East Side telling people he is Hitler, he would have caused severe discomfort. Sam the Gonoph not only has a Yiddish appellation but "comes from the Lower East Side" (ROB 147). While in "Undertaker Song," it is possible that Marmalodowski could be Polish, but not Jewish, his first name, Meyer, strongly suggests that he is Jewish. Nor are these stories without ethnic stereotyping; according to the narrator, "Blooch is a very careful character by nature, and about as loose as concrete with his money" (ROB 580). That, within this culture, the Jewish father thinks he has the prerogative to arrange his daughter's marriage recalls "Tight Shoes," where the abortive arrangement between Schultz to marry his daughter to Gus Schmelk, his fellow delicatessen owner and perhaps fellow German Jew on Tenth Avenue, falls through.

Even as he shows the Broadway and racetrack worlds to be melting pots, Runyon captures for his Jewish characters the conflict between traditional and modern ways, the inability to escape one's ethnicity, and something of the anguish of assimilation. Like Charley Bernstein, whose appellation comes from the stock phrase "a good-time Charlie"—a phrase not usually associated with Jews—because he provides good times during Prohibition, Runyon's Jewish characters often shed their names or take on other identities. We have seen how the narrator resents Good Time Charley Bernstein's celebration of Christmas in "The Three Wise Guys" because the narrator knows that Charley has his own holidays and his own Jewish New Year. In "Old Em's Kentucky Home" (1939), the Jewish racehorse owner, Itchky Ironhat, has been given a new name by his cohorts to substitute for a forgotten last name that needs twelve letters to spell. While other ethnics are given new names by Runyon, his Jews seem to have a proclivity for inventing assimilated identities; they also seem to be magnets for names invented by others, as if changing names were a requirement of acceptance.

Of course Runyon knew that in the 1920s and 1930s, transformation of last names with the purpose of taking on a new assimilated identity—cross-dressing as someone of different ethnicity—was especially identified with Jews. We may think of the irony of the great Jewish entertainer Al Jolson cross-dressing as a black man, which in 1923 was in the tradition, as Ted Gioia put it, of "the scalawag servant with his surface dullness and hidden cleverness . . . [and] the theatrical presentation of the slave as comic and a sly commentator on the world of masters and rulers."[3] Does not wearing a mask to disguise one's identity as "the scalawag servant with his surface dullness and hidden cleverness" also apply to the nameless narrator, who is a factotum to the more powerful men and women whom he often satirizes and ironizes?

RACETRACK STORIES

Runyon's enthusiasm for horseracing can be traced to his attending the 1922 Saratoga racing meeting (season) at the time when he was in the "doldrums."[4] He reveled in the colorful history of racing and the excitement of the races.

One of his most moving Saratoga stories is the 1937 parable "All Horse Players Die Broke" (*Cosmopolitan,* May 1937). The misogynist narrator tells of a bettor named Unser Fritz, who dedicates his life to a woman named Emma, called Emerald Em, who regards him with disdain. He puts all his winnings into diamonds and emeralds for her and is oblivious to her cheating on him or her disappearing nearly thirty years ago when he hit a losing streak in 1908. A denizen of what Runyon calls "dream street," Fritz has shaped his entire life around the delusions that he can pick winning horses consistently and that Emma loves him. Fritz is obsessed with Emma to the point of being a borderline psychotic. His losing streak continues until the current meeting when he parlays a $2 loan from the narrator into a huge stake of $101,000. But because he needs $100,100 to buy the expensive set of jewelry he thinks Emma will expect on her return, he loses a bet on a supposed sure thing—a 1 to 100 show bet on the ironically named Mia Cara ("my beloved"). Coincidentally, Emma returns to see her grandchildren on the very day that Fritz loses his bet. Knowing he has lost Emma forever, he shoots himself—one of Runyon's rare suicides.

A gambler himself, Runyon not only was fascinated with gambling addictions but needed to write about an obsession he shared. Just so he wouldn't be a loser, he adopted the irrational strategy of placing a small bet on every horse and a large one on the one he really favored. Thus he begins the article "All Horse Players Die Broke": "Horse players, like rumpots, swear off occasionally. Usually it is when they are broke and disgusted" (ST 164). Runyon understands how obsessive gamblers find excitement in losing money they desperately need. In "Friendliness Goes Out the Window," he wrote that gamblers were "the weakling type obsessed by a gambling passion" and therefore were not reliable friends (ST 185). He knew, too, of the gambler's wild swings between exhilaration and depression. Those who take such a person "over his head" are no more his friends than those who invite "a drunkard to have a drink knowing that one drink will poison him" ("Friendliness Goes Out the Window," ST 185).

Runyon understands how the gambling compulsion takes over the life of a horseplayer; after telling some anecdotes about the compulsion of a horseplayer known as "the Singing Kid," he concludes: "[H]e was a high player in that he would bet all he had which I contend makes a man a higher player than one to whom the losses mean nothing. . . . I am sure that his passing was in strict accordance with the immutable law of racing that all horse players must die broke" (ST 167). In Runyon's poem "The Old Horse Player," often circulated as "All Hawss Players Must Die Broke," the narrator concludes: "But they are all alike when they quit their scenes—/All hawss players *must* die broke!" (PFM 101).

"That Ever-Loving Wife of Hymie's" (*Cosmopolitan,* September 1931) is the first of the Florida racetrack stories. It sympathetically depicts a Jew name Weinstein, known as Hymie Banjo Eyes, as a continuing victim of a greedy and duplicitous wife, 'Lasses, a named derived from someone once saying "she is just as sweet as Molasses" (ROB 593). She is a former adagio dancer whom the narrator doesn't like: "[A]t the time I meet her she is sweet just the same as green grapefruit" (ROB 593). Like Unser Fritz, the untidy Hymie seems oblivious to his wife's two-timing him; "Ever-Loving" in the title ironically refers to her running around with a major bookmaker and handsome former boyfriend, Brick McClosky. Like Emma in the later "The Old Horse Player," she has convinced Hymie that she is very delicate and high strung and therefore that she needs to stay at expensive hotels.

The narrator himself is a sucker who lets Hymie euchre him out of $250 so that his wife can travel from New York in style, while he and Hymie sleep in a horse car with Hymie's one broken-down horse, Mahogany. Hymie enters Mahogany in a race where he is a long shot and bets his wife against Brick's $500 that Mahogany will win—and Mahogany does win. Unbeknownst to Hymie, his wife was rooting for the favorite against him. But after she hears Brick disparage Hymie's wife as worth only "two dollars and a half," she pretends that she was rooting for Hymie's horse and has loved him continuously (ROB 606). Posing as an all's well that ends well story, because Hymie gets his wife back, "That Ever-Loving Wife of Hymie's" is actually another misogynist noir story.

"A Story Goes with It" (*Cosmopolitan,* November 1931) is Runyon's second Florida racetrack story and the one that introduces Hot Horse Herbie, a racetrack hustler. The title takes its name from a story that a tout tells to hook his customer. Of course Runyon is smiling, because just as the narrator is hooked by Hot Horse Herbie, we as readers are hooked by his narrator who tells us the "first-class" story that arouses our human interest (DRO 235).

After he sees the narrator win $300 in a dice game, Herbie tries to convince the narrator to bet on a sure thing, Never Despair. Never Despair wins. But the narrator did not believe Herbie's story and bet on another horse, Loose Living. It turns out that Herbie, too, bets on another horse, Callipers, because he thinks that Never Despair's jockey, Scroon, is so incompetent he can't win a "boat"—or fixed—race (DRO 242). A calliper, Runyon would want us to recall, is an instrument for measuring the thickness of internal or external diameters, which here ironically applies to the thickness of Herbie's mind when deciding to bet against the horse he knows will win the race. The only person who wins on Never Despair is a man named Harter—Runyon plays on the word "heart"—who has been thrown over by his girlfriend and, following his own feelings when he sees a horse on the program with the name Never Despair, parleys his winnings into $6,000; he uses that money to convince the girl that "she really loves him more than somewhat" (DRO 242).

"Pick the Winner" (*Collier's,* February 11, 1933) focuses on the hard times of the Depression, even as it juxtaposes the racetrack world with the respectable world. The story is as much about economic desperation in 1933 as it is about racing. The tout Hot Horse Herbie—whom we know from "A Story Goes with It"—postpones his wedding with his very longtime fiancée, Miss Cutie Singleton, until he loses her to an Ivy League professor. Desperate for business, Hot Horse hustles an unlikely Princeton professor named Woodhead (another Runyon playful name), who is a lonely bachelor and has the very kind of home—"a little white house with green shutters"—of which Cutie, like so many of Runyon's women, dreams (ROB 320). The story mocks methods of intuiting horserace winners and the foibles, follies, and superstitions of gamblers.

Notwithstanding the narrator's cynical humor and an aversion to work typical of racetrack figures, the story reveals something about the humiliatingly straitened circumstances brought about by the Depression. A naive fool posing as a worldly member of the demimonde, the narrator is something of a double of Herbie's. Like Herbie, he is a perpetual loser, living a hand-to-mouth existence far different from that of the professor. At the outset, the narrator is as down on his luck as Herbie; he doesn't have an overcoat or "flogger" to protect him from the winter chill and is left "thinking what a cruel world it is" (ROB 311). (With a smiling recognition of how art displaces logic, we might note that no matter how bad things are, Runyon's narrators can always afford to eat at Mindy's.) Thus he agrees to join Herbie and Cutie in accepting from an undertaker the task of accompanying a body on a train to Miami. In Miami all three live in the same "fleabag"; lacking the means to pay his rent, the narrator is harassed by his landlord. According to the despairing speaker, in Miami the horseplayers are doing so badly that "many citizens are wondering if it will do any good to appeal to Congress for relief for the horse players" (ROB 315). While Cutie has the wiles and courage to pick a winner in the form of a life she desires, Herbie and the narrator, without skills or will to work, seem bereft of economic alternatives.

"Money from Home" (*Cosmopolitan,* October 1935) and "Ransom ... $1,000,000" are Runyon's only novella-length stories. "Money from Home" is about how Eddie Yokum, an innocent rube and a hater of horses, gets the socially prominent but not wealthy Miss Phyllis Richie. With far too many plot turns and amazing coincidences, the story's slapdash plot inadvertently makes us appreciate the efficiency, tautness, and forward thrust of Runyon's best stories. Reading "Money from Home," we wonder if Runyon was deliberately extending this story to exploit a set fee for each word or page. Adding to our dismay are the various unpalatable racist terms that the narrator or other characters uses to refer to Black men: "zugga-boo," "smoke," "coon," "Jig," "smudge rider," and "boogie."

With its various machinations revolving around self-interested behavior, the story could be subtitled "School for Scoundrels." While the so-called respectable world provides one completely unscrupulous scoundrel, Mr. Marshall Preston, the demimonde provides the other, Philly the Weeper. Philly, whose first name ironically echoes that of the story's heroine, is a whining weasel, "a little, dark-complected, slippery-looking guy" who is "always weeping about something" and is completely out for himself and so "downright dishonest" that even such members of the racetrack world such as The Seldom Seen Kid, Hot Horse Herbie, and Big Reds "do not associate with parties of this caliber" (DRO 168). Philly's fiancée, Lola Ledare, is the story's slut, making a play for different guys whenever she has a chance and finding her sexual amusement behind Philly's back if not right under his nose.

While hired to be a sandwich man for Barker's Dog Crullers—wouldn't Runyon have enjoyed that name?—and dressed up in a fox-hunting outfit, Eddie is mistaken for a heavy-drinking English steeplechase rider named Honorable Bertie Searles. Eddie will do anything to please Miss Phyllis Richie, with whom he falls in love at first sight. Her name suggests "filly" and "rich" as well as "filthy rich"; because she is a member of the respectable world, the name is always preceded by the appellation "Miss." Even though Eddie hates horses, he paints himself in blackface to ride her steeplechase horse, the ironically named Follow You—which describes how Eddie follows Phyllis—because the horse's black jockey, Roy Snakes, has disappeared and the horse will run only for black jockeys. The reason the jockey is not at the big race is due to the nefarious behavior of Eddie's chief rival, Mr. Marshall Preston, a member of Miss Richie's social set; Preston gets the other rascal, Philly the Weeper, to slug the jockey and to pay the other two black jockeys to go elsewhere.

The story contains a large cast of racetrack hangers-on and street characters. In a world where social relations are often based on who is hustling whom, the racetrack touts—The Seldom Seen Kid (who "is seldom seen after anything comes off that anybody may wish to see him about" [DRO 167]), Hot Horse Herbie (who lost his fiancée in "Pick the Winner"), and Big Reds—originally are not very interested in Eddie because he does not provide them with any way to make a score and "anyway there cannot be any percentage in talking to such a guy" (DRO 173). After Hot Horse Herbie collects reward money from returning some lost hunting dogs—money that he chisels from Eddie who himself could have returned the dogs—the others are not reluctant to take part of the money. But The Seldom Seen Kid proves to be one of Runyon's generous characters from the demimonde; to help give Eddie a hand in pleasing his beloved Phyllis Richie, he not only gives Eddie the pawn tickets for jewelry Philly stole from the Oriole Hunts Club the night when Eddie met Phyllis, but $1,000 to reclaim those items from hock.

The title "Money from Home" comes from an expression in the story for a sure thing; Big Reds says of Follow You when ridden by Roy Snakes, his Black jockey, "Any time they go to the post . . . they are just the same as money from home" (DRO 170). While the narrator is familiar with the members of the racetrack world, he takes a rather distanced and ironic stance in regard to the entire tale. In a deviation from Runyon's usual hyperrealism about sources—hyperrealism deriving undoubtedly from his reportorial background, where he learned to authenticate the facts by speaking to firsthand observers—this narrator does not explain how he knows the whole story and what the characters said.

Runyon's stories are often hilarious satires of a culture of materialism where wealth matters and where people adopt whatever names and identities suit them. In "It Comes Up Mud," a 1933 story that appeared in *Collier's* (June 10), he explores the relationship between commercial culture and entertainment culture. When Beulah Beauregard (who pretends to come from a wealthy Southern family, but who is dirt poor and whose real name is Benson) is given a very small engagement diamond by Little Alfie, she retires from displaying her shape to customers at the 900 Club. But no sooner does she meet a banker Paul D. Veere, whom the narrator regards from the first as "a stone-hearted guy," than she breaks her engagement with Little Alfie, who, like Hymie, smells from being around horses (ROB

534). Because Alfie has no money, he decides to ride Governor Hicks, one of his two racehorses, from Miami to Louisville, the site of the Kentucky Derby. Mounted on Governor Hicks, he leads the horse he plans to enter in that race, the ironically yet prophetically named Last Hope, a supposedly great horse for running in mud.

By amazing coincidence that typifies the serendipitous quality of Runyon's world, Little Alfie comes across Beulah, now living with her father in poverty on a small piece of land in Georgia. The story emphasizes the poverty of both Alfie and Beulah. It is one of Runyon's rare looks at the plight of rural America during the Depression. Beulah and her parents and brother live in a "ramshackly old house" and plough their ground with a single mule, while the brother does a little bootlegging with an alcoholic drink called "skimmin's" (ROB 539–40). As David M. Kennedy notes, "There was no denying the destitution and squalor that lay over much of the American countryside in the 1930s."[5] Veere has proven a scoundrel—the kind of wealthy womanizer in a business suit that Runyon detested—who is not only married with three children but tried to sexually assault Beulah before she ran away from his shooting lodge (which for plotting purposes is conveniently nearby).

Veere is another example of how the wealthy make their own rules. To avoid being arrested for a white collar crime, Veere had to return to New York suddenly to make a mysterious bank transaction. On his return, Veere "puts back in his bank whatever it is that it is advisable for him to put back, or takes out whatever it is that that seems best to take out" (ROB 547). By contrast, Alfie is banished from Hialeah (in Florida near Miami) because he took "a punch at a guy who has as many coconuts as Mr. Paul D. Veere" (ROB 535); the narrator ironically calls Veere "Mr.," an epithet used for no other male in the story.

Beulah's father restrains Alfie from going over to have words with Veere about his transgressions with Beulah because "the proud old Southern families in this vicinity are somewhat partial to the bankers and other rich guys from the North who have shooting-lodges. . . . [T]hese guys furnish a market to the local citizens for hunting guides, and corn liquor, and one thing and another" (ROB 541). Here Runyon, always skeptical of ideals and always cynically believing that economic self-interest drives almost all behavior, is laughing at how the South adheres to its myth of protecting its women. That Beulah, another of Runyon's gold-digging females, epitomizes a culture in which money matters, adds to the irony. Indeed, after Veere gives Alfie $50,000 to borrow Last Hope on a muddy day when Veere desperately needed to make a train to New York, Beaulah and Alfie leave the rat race in which both live and settle into domestic happiness.

Although self-interest and the pursuit of private pleasure and gain are the ruling passions in "It Comes Up Mud," there are surprising exceptions. Motivated by his love for Beulah, Little Alfie is generous to Veere. Alfie should hate Veere for getting him thrown out of Hialeah and for exploiting Beulah, but he enables Veere to extract himself from trouble; for Alfie the result is that "it comes up gold" rather than the mud of the title. That Little Alfie finds domestic happiness with his wife, Beulah Beauregard, and the twins who arrive after marriage illustrates—as the anthem of the Rolling Stones puts it—"You can't always get what you want, but if you try, sometimes, you just might find, you get what you need." Within Runyon's world the fulfillment of the desire for domestic happiness is a dénouement that usually banishes one from the Broadway scene—and the narrator's attention.

"The Lemon Drop Kid" (*Collier's*, February 3, 1934) is a poignant, dark story about an orphan who as a tout since he was fourteen has been "telling the tale"—with a pun on "tail"—and is doing none too well at twenty-four, when the story begins. One of Runyon's best stories, it is about a loner who finds a fulfilling life outside the track only to lose it. This story is an unusual paean to intimacy and rustication.

Of course, telling the tale is what the narrator does when he tries to convince his audience that his fantastic stories happened, and telling the tale is what Runyon does to us readers. Just as the tout must "discover citizens who are willing to listen to him tell the tale," so must the narrator and ultimately his creator (ROB 368). And, of course, just as the tout needs to find a reason to engage the audience's attention, so must the teller and author. At the racetrack even the wealthy listen "to the tale from guys who do not have as much as a seat in their pants, especially if the tale has any larceny in it, because it is only human nature to be deeply interested in larceny" (ROB 371). We realize that our subversive interest in larceny and other shortcuts to success that our respectable selves eschew is one reason we listen to Runyon's tales and watch *The Sopranos*—and why the tales were especially appealing during the economically frustrating Depression.

As a way of opening conversation The Lemon Drop Kid, pretending lemon drops will cure arthritis, gives one to a wealthy curmudgeon, Rarus Griggsby, who has been confined for three years to a wheelchair by arthritis. He then gives him a tip on the number two horse in the fifth race without knowing which horse that is. Once he learns that the number two horse has little chance of winning, he holds the $100 with the intent on keeping it rather than placing it with another bookmaker. After the number two horse wins, The Lemon Drop Kid can't pay off the $100 bet at 20 to 1 and Griggsby angrily gets out of his wheelchair and chases him. The Lemon Drop Kid keeps walking until he comes to a small town named Kibbesville, where he meets and soon falls in love with a beautiful woman named Alicia Derring. He leaves the racetrack world and marries her.

But this is another story of the toll taken by the Depression; because The Lemon Drop Kid doesn't have funds for proper medical care, his wife and child die in childbirth. In desperation, he robs the local hotel, is caught, and goes to prison for two years. After these four or five intervening years, The Lemon Drop Kid returns to the track world, and soon he meets Griggsby, who gives him $4,900 of the $5,000 he had promised to anyone who cured his arthritis. Griggsby doesn't care if the cure came from the lemon drop or from The Lemon Drop Kid's making him angry by cheating him of his winnings on the race.

Beginning this noir story with "I am going to take you back a matter of four or five years" to an August day at Saratoga, and ending it in the previous winter at Hialeah, the narrator concludes grimly as he leaves Griggsby and the kid together: "I look back only once, and I see The Lemon Drop Kid stop laughing long enough to take a lemon drop out of the side pocket of his coat and pop it into his mouth, and then he goes on laughing, ha-ha-ha-ha-ha" (ROB 366, 382). But The Lemon Drop Kid has no "laughter in [his] laugh" (ROB 382). The reader understands the bitter irony that he could do nothing for his beloved wife but cures Griggsby with a placebo and that now, too late, he has far more money than he desperately needed to save his wife and child.

After Runyon died, the 1951 film entitled *The Lemon Drop Kid* was a Bob Hope vehicle. Except for a few similarities such as the Kid liking lemon drops and being a horserace hustler at the beginning, and the presence of members of the Broadway demimonde—but with new names and characteristics who bear only slim resemblance to the originals—the film hardly reflects Runyon's story.

The last of the racetrack stories, "Old Em's Kentucky Home" (*Collier's*, June 17, 1939), is about a Jewish racehorse owner, Itchky Ironhat, who speaks with "a slightly Yiddish dialect" and whose "right name is something in twelve letters" (MGAD, 285). Itchky has a one horse stable consisting of a fourteen-year-old mare, Emaleen. No sooner does Itchky's wife Mousie ask him to choose between her or the horse than he chooses his horse, and she promptly packs and leaves. After being chased from the New York tracks for harassing an assistant starter for using a "twitch" to make Em stand quiet at the starting gate, Itchky decides to take his horse to Churchill Downs. He buys an old truck to take Em to Kentucky and he talks the narrator into joining him since the Kentucky Derby is approaching. After some high-spirited and humorous adventures driving the tiny truck that transports the horse, they arrive at Tucky farms, Em's original home. They discover that the owner has closed the farm and become something of a recluse after his barns burned down and his wife was killed trying to save her beloved horse, Love Always. But the return of Em, one of the horses he sent away after the fire, reinvigorates Salsbury and pulls him out of his depression. Deciding to restore the farm to its former glory, he buys Em from Itchky for $3,000 and gives him an award of $1,000 for caring for the horse. Itchky sends $1000 to Mousie. She returns only to be abusive because she hears him sending his love to Em after promising, as a condition of her return, "never as much as think of Old Em again" (MGAD 295). Recalling with black humor the beginning when Em was abused by the starter, the story ends with Itchky's "ever-loving wife, Mousie" throwing an ash tray at him.

While the story provides an emotional transfiguration for Salsbury and an economic one for Itchky, it is another story of aging and loss. However, it contains moments of Runyonesque playfulness, such as when the man who turns out to be Salsbury's doctor says to Itchky: "[K]eep away from [Tucky Farms] anything that looks like a horse. Although . . . I am not sure that the object you have on your truck answers such a description." When Itchky responds angrily: "You do not like my horse?" the doctor asks snidely: "Oh, it is a horse, then?" (MGAD 290).

BOXING STORIES

Runyon owned boxers' contracts as well as racehorses. An ardent and reckless bettor, his darker side was intrigued by the possibility of a sure thing, particularly the fixed fight or horse race or even baseball game, and he enjoyed being an insider to these kinds of manipulations. By occasionally putting favorable comments about gangsters in his columns, Runyon earned the trust of the underworld and may have earned access to sports fixes; he also understood that knowing is power.

Man-to-man combat captivated Runyon. Boxing was a major focus of his attention in the teens and 1920s, and he covered major fights. Runyon was fascinated with the primal energy of boxing, the aggressively masculine will to power and dominance in a contest for survival. He had been brought up in the West, where men fighting was a common occurrence. Even in the comparatively sedate world of the Turps, men settle differences with their fists far more than was probably customary in similar real-life neighborhoods. And does not the depiction of two men in combat have a homosocial aspect, as in Runyon's "Leopard's Spots" (*Collier's,* May 16, 1939), where the two matched fighters, one a contender, the other someone who throws fights to build up contenders, are fast friends?

We might think of the artist George Bellows, another Midwesterner fascinated with boxing. Stressing the muscularity and raw physical power of boxers, Bellows is notable for his realistic depictions of prizefights; his famous painting "Stag at Sharky's" (1909) was often reprinted and hung in speakeasies and bars, where Runyon would surely have seen it. Indeed, the fight in the painting took place on Broadway, across from the painter's studio. Such fights, which could result in fatalities, occurred when boxing—albeit banned—took place under "police" protection in private clubs.

The 1924 Bellows work "Dempsey and Firpo" is more about what Dan Morris calls "a spectacle of injury and pain," but it is also about legend and myth, because the audience knows that while Dempsey has been knocked out of the ring, he is the eventual winner.[6] In both the 1909 and 1924 paintings of fighters, Bellows depicts himself as a spectator. Runyon must have strongly identified with Bellows, almost as if Bellows as spectator were a surrogate for Runyon. Indeed, what Joyce Carol Oates writes in *On Boxing* about Bellows could also apply to Runyon: "What more visually compelling metaphor of man's aggression than the boxing ring? What more striking image, for a fiercely ambitious and competitive young artist from the Midwest, involved in his own struggle for recognition?"[7]

Because boxing drew a great deal of gambling money, the legitimacy of fights was often suspect, even in those matches between legendary figures. For example, Runyon speculated whether in a 1915 fight in Havana the black boxer, Jack Johnson, had thrown the fight in the twenty-sixth round to the white fighter, Jess Willard. Runyon's story of the fight began on the *Daily Mirror's* front page, and continued on the entire eighth page. Johnson was the subject of fascination and hatred from the white press and white fans because he had been convicted in 1913 in Chicago for violating the Mann Act by transporting a white minor across state lines. After he had escaped from prison, he married the girl, and moved to Europe with her. Runyon was a strong booster of Jack Dempsey's career, but he lost his money on a 100 to 1 bet in 1919 that Dempsey would knock Willard out in the first round. It took Dempsey until the third round to become champion.

Runyon had a fixation on owning—that is, controlling the professional career—of a championship heavyweight fighter, but his fighters were not particularly successful. Indeed, Runyon used his fighters as chauffeurs and bodyguards for his wife, Ellen, and their two children. Ironic explorations of Runyon's fantasy of being a successful boxing manager, the Spider McCoy stories—"Bred for Battle" (*Cosmopolitan,* May 1934), "The Big Umbrella" (*Collier's,* August 7, 1937) and "Leopard's Spots" (*Collier's,* May 1939)—are not only about boxing, but all point to the corruption of the sport. Indeed, nothing brings out Runyon's high-spirited cynicism like his stories about boxing. It is as if for him boxing—with its mask of respectable man-to-man combat and its underbelly of fraud—is a metaphor for competitive and often predatory capitalism.

"Bred for Battle" is a story of Spider McCoy's failed championship dream. He decides that the way to pick a great fighter is to follow his lineage as if he were a racehorse, and he finds a prospect whose father was a fighter and whose mother was a strong, tough woman. His heavyweight fighter, Thunderbolt Mulrooney, proves a flop; when he enters the ring for his first fight, he not only refuses to box but breaks down in tears. The narrator discovers that Thunderbolt's genetic heritage is not what it had seemed, for Mulrooney's mother had her son out of wedlock as a result of a prior affair.

Charging every expense to the fighter's account before taking their agreed-upon share of the fighter fee, many managers took advantage of their fighters and treated them like commodities. Runyon was aware that many boxing bouts were to be fixed in order to build the credentials of a contender. The narrator has a comic imagination when he speaks of how Spider chooses opponents for his heavyweights; these matches are under "his own professional supervision. . . . These matches are with sure-footed watermen [i.e., fighters who pretend to be knocked out] who plunge in swiftly and smoothly when Jonas waves at them, and . . . while everyone knows these are strictly tank jobs, nobody cares, especially the customers who almost break down the doors of the clubs where Jonas appears, trying to get in" ("The Big Umbrella," ROB 556). Runyon enjoys presenting comic versions of set scenes in which he not only draws upon his sportswriting background but uses the specific vocabulary from that aspect of his experience. We see this in particular in his boxing stories. In "The Big Umbrella"—the term for a boxer who folds the minute he is punched—Runyon plays with the way that boxing creates the public desire for a potential champ by building up his resume with fixed fights.

Runyon understands how the fighter becomes fetishized as a valuable commodity by not only establishing a complicit relationship between his supposed opponent—"Anybody will tell you that it helps build up a young fighter's confidence to let him see a few people take naps in front of him" ("The Big Umbrella," ROB 557)—but also between himself and a willingly gullible public. As Spider puts it, with the cynicism that marks legal and illegal businesses transactions in Runyon's Broadway stories, "what a sap I will be to throw him in with competition as long as the suckers will pay to see him as he is" (ROB 558).

"Leopard's Spots" is about financial machinations as much as about boxing. The Louisiana Leopard is a waiter named Caswell Fish—Runyon would have expected readers to know that a fish is a boxer who takes a dive; Fish is drafted into service as a "waterman" to fight a contender named Chester Nubbs in place of Pigsfoot Groody, who "is not only very sure-footed in these matters but moreover he appears with Chester Nubbs before in other spots under other names and they are very good friends and understand each other" (MGAD 60). But Groody has appendicitis and ends up in the hospital. Fish accepts the assignment because he needs the money to get married and open a diner in Pottsville, Pennsylvania: The narrator's cynicism extends to the customers who know the fight is a fiasco: "[A]ll the customers know very well that Chester is only fighting some parasol, for in Philadelphia, Pa., the customers are smartened up to the prize-fight game and they know they are not going to see a world war for three dollars tops. In fact, all they care about is seeing Chester Nubbs with his clothes off" (MGAD 68). Yet Caswell does not take his dive, for his fiancée has written Chester to avoid contact in the ring at all costs because Caswell—the Louisiana Leopard—has leprosy.

The humor in this story depends on hyperbole and upon words meaning whatever the narrator and the fight game cronies want them to mean. Within this corrupt boxing world, words are fluid in meaning and there is no compass to locate the truth. Leopard's spots refers to the iodine Spider uses to disguise Caswell as the Louisiana Leopard; the spots also refer not only to the shibboleth that a leopard can't change its spots, but also to the realization that small-town innocents like Caswell and his girlfriend Babs may have spots of ingenuity to match city-slickers. And in a final irony, Pigsfoot and Spider catch the measles from a hospital nurse.

Runyon regarded boxing as he regarded other criminal enterprises—with cynical bemusement, a sense of excitement, and a curiosity about how one might be able to find an edge. Indeed, at times when covering boxing—or, indeed, other criminal activities—he crossed over the line that divides collaborator from reporter. As Hoyt puts it, "He did not believe it was his responsibility to save the world or interfere in the affairs of others."[8] Yet he did write an editorial on the sports pages of the *American* attacking the New York boxing system for "the failure of its attempted reform of boxing" in the state.[9]

Given Runyon's cynical view of the differences between some legitimate businesses and criminal behavior, it is hardly surprising that boxing's violent man-to-man combat was a metaphor not only for aggressive capitalism but for criminal enterprises—except, in the latter case, combat might involve guns and knives. Like boxers, criminals connived to break the rules—sometimes with the active complicity of their adversaries, the police, and politicians—and were looking for ways to control the odds by means of violence, if necessary. Just as in the case of Prohibition, much of society was complicit in allowing boxing to remain crooked; in fact, the Philadelphia fans in "The Big Umbrella" went to fights knowing that they were fixed.

CONCLUSION

Runyon, to be sure, glorified the world of the gangsters and the demimonde, and also winkingly implied that wretched excess need not be always wretched. Yet, notwithstanding bursts of anger in such stories as "The Lily of St. Pierre," his popularity during the Depression and World War II owes something to a toughness that rarely gave way to bitterness, a humorous skepticism rather than a nihilistic cynicism, a shared laughter with his audience that helped them appreciate the small pleasures of life. In his attitudes to women, he sometimes has aggravatingly sexist views, but often his idealistic views of family, children, human worth, and generosity are quite compelling. At times, as Jean Wagner observes, "beside the cynic, there was also the tolerant, at bottom kind-hearted and often sentimental humorist whose warmth and sympathy went out instinctively to the underdogs, the downtrodden and the outcasts."[10] Frequently, Runyon is on the side of idealized small-town virtues: honesty, innocence, generosity, and respect for idiosyncrasies.

CHAPTER 7

THE GENRES OF RUNYON'S LATER FICTION

Nicely-Nicely, Political Satire, Ambrose Hammer, Miami Noir, and Wartime Stories

INTRODUCTION

While my organization is not strictly chronological, in this chapter my focus is on the later stories. Here I include only two written before 1936, and that is to keep together the stories of Runyon's fictional surrogate, Ambrose Hammer. On balance, the later stories are some of his darkest ones, particularly those that take place in the 1940s as illness, awareness of mortality, and loneliness dominate his perspective. Not only are they more likely to take place outside New York and to be more attentive to world politics, especially World War II, but often they have a more acute and bitter awareness of class difference. Compared to the earlier stories, we are less likely to see character transformation, and the tone is more cynical. Yet in most of these stories Runyon retains his characteristic hard-boiled sense of humor, his pleasure in human diversity, his sympathy with outsiders, his playful enjoyment in inventing new forms of Runyonese, and his love of talking for its own sake. In the Miami noir stories, Runyon builds on the icy noir of his earlier New York stories.

I should reiterate that I propose my categories as a way of organizing and understanding Runyon's achievement, but that other taxonomies are quite plausible.

NICELY-NICELY STORIES

In 1937 Runyon published two stories in *Collier's* about Quentin Jones, known as Nicely-Nicely. Both stories focus on eating as a metaphor for predatory behavior. The first, "Lonely Heart" (January 16, 1937), is a noir story about a widow who advertises for a prospective husband in *Matrimonial Tribune,* a magazine with personal ads. Recovering from pneumonia in a hospital in Newark and away from his Broadway world, Nicely-Nicely is especially lonely and answers the ad entitled "Lonely Heart." No sooner does he meet the author, Widow Crumb, than he gets married. Since few demands are made upon him in the form of work, at first he enjoys her excellent cooking and the simple life on a remote farm. But after she pays for an insurance policy on his life, he discovers that Widow Crumb has killed several husbands before him and collected on the life insurance policies of all but one of those who died. She has been assisted by her first husband, Harley, who still lives with her as a kind of hired hand; because he couldn't get insurance with his weak heart, they were divorced thirty years ago.

Harley and Widow Crumb's relationship is based on her complete dominance of a man willing to be her slave; had he been healthy, Harley implies, she would have killed him. The psychotic Widow Crumb is also a spiritualist who believes in the possible return of the dead and serves her best food to an absent former husband named Jake, whom she now regrets killing; his supposed return scares her into hysterically running out of the house and falling into a well whose cover she had Harley remove as a the trap meant to kill Nicely-Nicely.

The second, "A Piece of Pie" (*Collier's,* August 21, 1937), is a high-spirited tale focusing on an eating contest in 1937 between a Bostonian named Joe Duffle and a New Yorker named Miss Violette

Shumberger, a pleasant but enormous woman—with "a face the size of a town clock and enough chins for a fire escape" (ROB 682)—who is a stand-in for Nicely-Nicely Jones and emerges victorious. When Violette whispers to Nicely-Nicely that she can't go on, one of the judges asks whether she has broken the rules by seeking his advice. He responds untruthfully, "[A]ll she asks me is can I get her another piece of pie" (ROB 688–89). Violette's opponent falls for the ruse and retires from the competition.

In the midst of the Depression, Runyon emphasizes the distinction between gourmandizing and food deprivation. Nicely-Nicely is prevented from entering the contest by his girlfriend, Miss Hilda Slocum, a supposedly expert dietician who writes a column for *Let's Keep House* magazine and who has put him on a rigid and enervating diet that finally requires him to be hospitalized. The tale ends with Nicely-Nicely's eloping with Violette and opening a barbecue stand in Florida, while Hilda seems to be pairing off with her editor and boss.

During the 1930s there were a number of such gourmandizing contests, with gambling on the side. Apparently, Nicely-Nicely was modeled on an actual character named Carmine DeNoia, known also as Jardine, who had a gargantuan capacity for food and on whose appetite underworld figures took bets.[1] By quoting Professor D.—obliquely reminding his audience of his source figure, DeNoia—in "A Piece of Pie" on more primitive eating contests, Runyon calls attention to savage and cannibalistic antecedents (ROB 676). That the contestants eat with knife and fork—or at least knife—rather than with their hands emphasizes the incongruity between the surface amenities of so-called modern civilization and the decadence and sordidness of the contestants' behavior.

Like the "Lestrygonians" chapter of *Ulysses,* which presents the grim shibboleth "Eat or be eaten" as a basis of behavior that must be rejected in civilized life, the focus on excessive eating reminds us of kinds of moral cannibalism within the often predatory Broadway culture. In "Lonely Heart," Widow Crumb feasts on the remains—or crumbs—of her dead husbands in the form of insurance money; metaphorically she eats their very hearts to survive. Just as she discards the overflowing plate of food that Jake does not eat, she discards the husbands who do not support her. She is, as Joyce puts it in *Ulysses,* a "Chewer of corpses." The well on her own property—"Deep, and dark, and cold, and half full of water"—in which Widow Crumb falls is a suggestion of the bowels, as if she were grotesquely swallowed by a monstrous mouth by which she had planned to swallow Nicely-Nicely (ROB 497).

The grotesque banquet, as Mikhail Bakhtin reminds us, has ties to the traditional underworld, namely hell. Widow Crumb's belief that the dead return reinforces this connection with folk motifs, even if Runyon might not have believed in the return of the dead. Indeed, as Bakhtin suggests, "All these variations of the carnivalesque hell are ambivalent and include in one way or another the symbols of fear defeated by laughter.... The image of the netherworld in folk tradition becomes the symbol of the defeat of fear by laughter."[2] As does Joyce in his "Hades" section of *Ulysses,* Runyon organizes the underbelly of his urban hell to suggest site parallels to the traditional underworld. Like Joyce, he also creates a hell of interior demons that plague the modern psyche: loneliness, depression, the effects of poverty. The aforementioned demons all play a role in Nicely-Nicely's temporarily recusing himself by retiring to a rural world that turns out—including the widow's scheme to get insurance money—to mirror the urban world. Yet, like Joyce and Rabelais, Runyon uses laughter to overcome the grim reality of life in the city and its rural mirror. As Bakhtin reminds us, "Folk culture strove to defeat through laughter this extreme projection of gloomy seriousness and to transform it into a gay carnival monster."[3] Much of Runyon's laughter derives from the folk culture, which he knew well from his Colorado past as well as from the ethnic neighborhoods of New York.

With feasting carried to unimaginable extremes, "A Piece of Pie" contains the very essence of Bakhtinian carnival. The city is depicted as a giant body, its grotesque mouth represented by contestants ingesting food in a Rabelaisean fashion. Writing of Rabelais, Bakhtin speaks of the grotesque in terms appropriate to Runyon: "The grotesque concept of the body lived especially in the familiar and colloquial forms of language. The grotesque was the basis of all abuses, uncrownings, teasing, and impertinent gestures (as pointing at the nose or the buttocks, spitting and others)."[4] Like Rabelais, Runyon flouts and mocks traditional Christian ideas of temperance.

In both Nicely-Nicely stories, Runyon has his narrator inventory each course in material terms to emphasize exactly what is taken into the body. In "Lonely Heart," when Nicely-Nicely speaks to Jake, Widow Crumb's murdered former husband, he speaks of shared stomach problems that excessive eating causes. When Nicely-Nicely realizes he can save himself by playing on Widow Crumb's fear of the dead returning in the person of Jake, he performs a pantomime of lifting a person who has been felled by such excesses.

Read within the context of Runyon's collected stories, "A Piece of Pie" reminds us how often characters are devouring not just food but one another and how some people during the Depression years lived in parasitic relationships with their hosts. Nicely-Nicely, a kind of host at the contest, passes out from hunger while enormous quantities are consumed. Even though his hunger is induced by Miss Slocum's ridiculous diet, he has recognizable symptoms of malnutrition. With contestants consuming food sufficient to feed thirty or more adults and many more children, the contest reminds us how conspicuous waste and gourmandizing occurred even during the Depression and of the difference between the haves and have-nots in America.

POLITICAL SATIRE

In "Tight Shoes" (*Collier's,* April 18, 1936), Runyon's most scathing political story, he shows his deep disdain for Marxism, especially for personal pique disguised as political rhetoric, and indeed a deep skepticism about the political process. Within the Runyon canon, the story is a rare, and quite effective, sharp-edged political satire. After being fired by Bilby, the proprietor of a shoe business, for selling size 10½ EE shoes to Hymie Minsk, a horseplayer, who expected the wrong and more flattering 8½ D size, Rupert Salsinger joins forces with Calvin Colby, a spoiled rich drunk, to arouse the rabble to political action. Quite comically, political action takes the form of a march down Broadway that concludes with breaking into Bilby's shoe store and stealing his stock of shoes, a theft in which Rupert participates. That Bilby has always given Minsk the larger shoes while telling him they are the smaller size is an example of how so-called respectable businessmen rely as much on guile as the underworld does.

Runyon stresses that Rupert's political program derives from Colby's drunken and barely coherent speeches. The narrator makes clear his disdain for rabble-rousing and sloganeering Marxists posing as social activists in Manhattan's Columbus Circle. Indeed, Runyon makes clear that Rupert's sanctimonious political views are shaped not by deeply felt concern for injustices endured by the have-nots but by personal pique over his own inability to get a job. No sooner does Rupert announce the formation of the "American Amalgamation for Social Justice and his candidacy for Congress on the Social Justice ticket" than Tammany Hall also announces its support because the current congressman "often votes in a manner that is by no means to the interest of this splendid organization" (ROB 476).

The story has a nice noir touch when, wearing the tight shoes that he has stolen, the supposed people's friend Rupert kicks Hymie Minsk around out of pure malice and then, because the shoes are increasingly uncomfortable, he fails to get to his girlfriend, Minnie Schultz, in time to make his proposal—at which point he throws the shoes through the delicatessen window of his rival Gus Schmelk. Runyon includes in his political satire an anonymous Communist who makes off with Rupert's stolen shoes while Gus chases Rupert.

Among the culprits are the news media who glorify the stealing and marauding as a social justice movement and "a revolution of youth against the old order" (ROB 474). They interview Rupert and give him publicity as if he and Calvin really did have ideas and a program. A former Yale football player who is "generally figured as nothing but a lob as far as ever doing anything useful in this world is concerned," Colby has been in the newspapers often as a rascal who crashes automobiles and injures his female companions (ROB 468). But once he becomes involved with politics during his drunken spree, he is described in the papers "the well-known young multimillionaire thinker" (ROB 474). In other words, the credibility of the Amalgamation for Social Justice depends on money and publicity rather than the quality of ideas or the officers and candidates.

Rupert is a political charlatan; his speeches contain a hardly comprehensible mélange of extracts from a wide variety of contradictory figures such as Father Coughlin—a noted anti-Semite—Franklin Roosevelt, Patrick Henry, and Abraham Lincoln. Shrewdly knowing how to follow his self-interest, Rupert uses his wiles to succeed in the political line, as gangsters use theirs to succeed in their illegal endeavors. "[Seeing] that all this publicity may lead somewhere," Rupert wins the election and becomes Congressman Rupert Salsinger, a narcissist who wears the mask of public servant but who is concerned with his own well-being at every moment and, finally, marries a wealthy widow (ROB 476).

For Runyon words are not fixed, flat, and lifeless but malleable, dynamic, sometimes absurd, often full of contradictions; they are part of a continuing verbal game in which meaning is simultaneously reflected, refracted, obscured, and undermined. Runyon's story titles and the names he chooses for characters are particularly notable examples of how Runyon sustains his verbal game—a game also evident in dialogues where facial expressions and tiny gestures often undermine what is being said. What Ron Jenkins has written about the Italian Nobel Laureate satiric playwright Darlo Fo is applicable to Runyon: "Mr. Fo transforms language into an elusive living entity, teeming with paradox and absurdities that leap out at you unpredictably."[5]

Thus "Tight Shoes" refers to the discomfort of being in shoes that are too small but also to the slogan "If the shoe fits wear it," and the shoe that fits Rupert is that of a self-indulgent man who puts off marriage while for years making love to Minnie; he hides behind his Marxist rhetoric—he carries a copy of Marx in his back pocket—because he cannot keep a job. That his brief and unsuccessful career as shoe salesman is the only job he has had during the Depression is the reason that Minnie's father thinks he is a bum. Rupert neglects Minnie when he finds a way to get elected and achieve political success, only to lose her to the self-interested Calvin Colby. While supposedly representing Rupert's suit for Minnie, Calvin jumps into Rupert's shoes and woos Minnie successfully. He reinvents himself as a functioning capitalist and opens a chain of delicatessens with her father and integrates Gus's store into his chain. "Tight Shoes," the title, refers not only the stolen shoes but to stolen political ideas that Rupert and Colby wear uncomfortably.

THE AMBROSE HAMMER STORIES

The five Ambrose Hammer stories—"Broadway Complex" (*Collier's,* July 28, 1933), "What, No Butler?" (*Collier's,* August 5, 1934), "So You Won't Talk!" (*Cosmopolitan,* May 1937), "Broadway Incident" (*Cosmopolitan,* November 1941), and "The Melancholy Dane" (*Collier's,* March 18, 1944)—draw the character of an often mean-spirited drama critic who "loves to heave the old harpoon into actors if they do not act to suit him" (ROB 384). Besides those five stories, Hammer makes cameo appearances in "Princess O'Hara" (*Collier's,* March 3, 1934) and "Cleo" (*Collier's,* July 12, 1941). Hammer's quixotic and somewhat mysterious personality, which baffles his fellow denizens of Broadway, recalls his creator's. We see a strong resemblance between Runyon and Hammer's dandyish appearance, pessimism, cynical iconoclasm, fascination with crime, and strong attraction to younger and sexy women without great intellect. In fact, Hammer, whose ruling passion seems to be curiosity and who uses his knowledge of other people as a means of control, is something of a surrogate for Runyon. Ambrose Hammer's name has the same number of syllables as Runyon's, and both their first and last names begin with a stressed syllable—in other words, each name is a double trochee.

Like his creator who hangs out at night in various Broadway spots, most notably Lindy's, Hammer is a nighttime character: "[I]n all the years I know Ambrose, I never catch him out in the daylight more than two or three times, and then it is when we are both on our way home and happen to meet up" (ROB 383–84). In "What, No Butler?" Hammer is described as "a short, chubby guy with big round googly eyes, and a very innocent expression, and in fact it is this innocent expression that causes many guys to put Ambrose away as slightly dumb" (ROB 384). We have mentioned that there was an aspect of the wide-eyed innocent about Runyon, who was known to listen rather than talk and was also a man of slight stature who worried about his weight. According to Edwin P. Hoyt, in 1920

Runyon at forty "was short, slim, trim, precise, dudish and a little like an owl in his new spectacles."[6] Not unlike his creator, Hammer is a pessimist who "is seldom pleased with anything" (DRO 274).

A Harvard graduate who thinks he is smarter and more perceptive than anyone else, Hammer is constantly falling in love with very attractive showgirls who are often not very bright. He is not only a womanizer but also an amateur sleuth: "He often vexes cops quite some by poking his nose into their investigations and trying to figure out who does what" ("So You Won't Talk," MGAD 313–14). Hammer also has a great eye for details and "a good memory for names" (MGAD 314). An intellectual snob, he is intent on demonstrating not only in his columns on theater, but also in his conversation and his clever crime solving that he is smarter than everyone else.

Hammer is a sensualist who has never found a suitable wife. Extremely flirtatious, he takes great pride in his dancing ability. Finally, like his creator, he is a lonely man who often seems to find his only crumbs of real intimacy—as opposed to intermittent sexual pleasure—in homosocial relationships, especially with the anonymous narrator, to whom he is constantly demonstrating his acumen and sharing the problems he is having with women. Indeed, the Hammer stories revolve around an uneasy friendship with the narrator. On occasion Hammer takes the narrator to plays and dinner as a kind of companion. The ongoing relationship between Hammer and the narrator—both at times alter egos for Runyon—explains less awkwardly than many of the stories how the narrator knows what he knows.

In "Broadway Complex," the first of the Hammer stories, we learn he has been writing a play for years; in kind of a coda we learn that he gets it written. Writing a play was a fantasy of Runyon's that was not fulfilled until 1935, when he collaborated with Howard Lindsay on a Broadway play entitled *A Slight Case of Murder,* which was a modest success, running for sixty-nine performances and getting mixed reviews; the play was made into the 1937 film of the same title. Notwithstanding that the main character, Remy Marko, a former bootlegger and racketeer who has become a legal beer brewer after the end of Prohibition, finds dead bodies in a house he has rented for the Saratoga racing season, the play is a farcical comedy.

While some of the other gangsters in the play are often nostalgic for the simpler world of Prohibition, Marko believes that his daughter must marry into a respectable family. Characteristically the play puts Runyon on the side of the little guy and against exploitive big business and indifferent self-interested government. Thus it is something of a Depression play in which the fantasy of the outsider—the downtrodden, the immigrant—of making it into respectability if not prominence is central; as Marko puts it to the supposedly respectable Theodore Whitelaw: "I am an orphan and I'm starting a new family and I want my family to amount to something in this country for years to come."[7]

Marko's house is the center of the Saratoga social whirl; important political figures like Commissioner Mahoney—an intimate friend of the President of the United States—and bankers are happy to enjoy his hospitality and consort with his gangster friends. Yet Marko finds that the bankers Post and Ritter, who wish to foreclose on his brewery and take it for a fraction of its value, are tougher to do business with than his gangster associates in the Prohibition days; he calls the bankers "boys" as if they, too, were gangsters and their business extortion. Marko, who gives $25,000 a year to an orphanage, often shows more character than the respectable people. He makes a favorite Runyon point that all of the major American families first made their fortunes in dubious activities: "All of them started just the way I did, only they had real estate, and furs and railroads."[8]

Invoking his own snobbery and concept of family lineage, Marko has his own scruples and resists marrying his daughter into the ironically named Whitelaw family because that family is tainted by "police blood."[9] In keeping with Runyon's cynicism about the similarity between so-called respectable people and hoodlums, the aristocratic high strung elitist father of the prospective groom, Theodore Whitelaw, proves to be a thief. Marko changes his mind about Whitelaw as a future in-law when he learns that despite Whitelaw's humbug, the two men share the same morality: "I've got a lot of respect for you. You didn't get away with it, but I respect you for trying."[10]

The play has its funny moments, but it is not as tightly plotted as Runyon's stories. It has a flaccid structure, not the best thing for a farce, and much of the action takes place offstage and has to be explained in dialogue. According to Hoyt, "Damon's major contribution to his collaborators in preparation of movie and play scripts came from his sharp ear for dialogue and his genius at plot development. He had little to offer in the matter of dramatic structure."[11] But Lindsay, his collaborator, certainly did not organize the two acts tightly either, and often too many characters are on stage. The original cast called for twenty-eight roles with twenty-eight actors, plus twenty figures that are listed in the cast as "passers-by." As the authors themselves acknowledge in a "Playwrights' Note" accompanying the printed version, some of the principal characters are superfluous.

But let us return to "Broadway Complex," a story in which Runyon uses a characteristic double plot and a characteristic resolution in which the unraveling of one mystery unravels the other. The actor Fergus Appleton, whose performance in a play called *Never-Never* Hammer disdains, courts a beautiful woman named Miss Florentine Fayette without revealing that he is married to a woman who refuses to divorce him "because he knocks her downstairs a long time ago, and makes her a cripple for life" (DRO 277).

The subplot is the enmity between Hammer and Appleton, whom Hammer eventually exposes as an adulterer. Given Hammer's sense of importance, it is worth noting that, notwithstanding his bad review, the play is a hit. To free himself to marry Miss Fayette, Appleton befriends the mentally ill and probably schizoid Cecil Earl—who is, as Hammer explains with his usual arrogant verbosity, "very susceptible to suggestion from anything he reads, or is told"—for the sole purpose of manipulating him to murder Appleton's crippled wife (DRO 268). We see Cecil play several roles, from Jack Dempsey to Mussolini to Hitler—and he makes the mistake "of wandering down on the lower East Side and saying so" (DRO 270).

Wanting to foil Appleton's plans, Hammer suggests to Cecil that he be Don Juan to Ms. Fayette. In a typical over-the-top plot ending that mocks neat romance endings, Cecil successfully woos and elopes with her. They become a hit in the screen version of *Never-Never*. Hammer had compared Cecil to an actor playing parts, "only Cecil tries to live every part he plays" and assumes additional personalities (DRO 269). Of course we wonder how Cecil can sustain his relationship and his film career without curing his personality disorder.

Gradually we realize that even though Cecil Earl suffers from delusions that make him think he is someone else, Appleton the wife-beater is more of a social misfit. That we see Appleton from his first appearance as a bully, who hits Hammer with a cane and crushes his hat because he doesn't like his review, anticipates our learning later that he has crippled his wife. Until Appleton realizes he can make use of Cecil Earl, he takes the lead in making fun of Earl, who works at a nightclub as a master of ceremonies. The narrator's rendering of Appleton's appearance tells us a great deal about not only Appleton's need for attention but his bent for dominance. We are told twice that he wears "a slave bracelet"; he also wears large rings on both hands, smokes from a cigarette holder a foot long, has a phony monocle in one eye, and "is a very chesty guy . . . [who] likes to pose around in public places" (DRO 271).

The narrator in the Hammer stories wears a different mask from the one he wears when consorting in other stories with criminals and gamblers, and does not seem to be cut from the same cloth as that voice. In the Hammer stories he is more likely to think about who is smart and who is dumb, as if Hammer's Harvard degree was affecting his own standards; for example, the narrator stresses how Miss Fayette "never seems much interested in anything . . . [and] is slightly dumb" (DRO 271). The narrator is quite loyal to Hammer and promises that the next time Appleton shows up in a new derby, he will avenge Appleton's destroying Hammer's hat.

It is a mistake, as I have mentioned, to resolve the narrator of Runyon's stories into one figure. He is a chameleon-like figure modified by the tale he tells and the figures he describes. In "Broadway Complex," where the narrator's behavior and attitudes are usually civilized and generous, his only anti-social moment is when he empathizes with Appleton's desire to marry a beautiful, rich, if stupid, wife as if a woman were a commodity to own. Even if the standard Runyonese is much the same, the narrator's quality of perspicacity and the density of the prose vary; for example, the title "Broadway Complex" refers not only to both Cecil Earl's psychological problems and Fergus Appleton's enormous ego and bullying nature but also to a Broadway in a more *complex* mode than some of Runyon's other tales.

Hammer next makes a cameo appearance in "Princess O'Hara" (*Collier's,* March 3, 1934), an all's well that ends well tale—really a sentimental farce—that also has a slight noir aspect. The story not only includes a predatory older lover trying to take advantage of an eighteen-year-old girl, but the dénouement leaves an innocent truck driver as well as two gangsters dead. Often, even within a story with a strong slant toward a sentimental fairy tale, Runyon kills off supernumeraries about whom he doesn't much care.

After beginning with a demurral—"Now of course Princess O'Hara is by no means a regular princess, and in fact she is nothing but a little red-headed doll"—the narrator is in a hyperbolic mode befitting the fairy tale of how the poor daughter of a drunk, who supports herself by driving a victoria, is about to marry a prince (ROB 429). King O'Hara, the now deceased alcoholic victoria driver, "is always bragging that he has the royal blood of Ireland in his veins, so somebody starts calling him King . . . although probably what King O'Hara really has in his veins is about ninety-eight per cent alcohol" (ROB 431). After her father dies, Princess O'Hara—called that because of her father's nickname King O'Hara—is the only child old enough to work, and she takes over her father's business: "[A]ll he leaves in this world besides his widow and six kids" is the comically named horse Goldberg and the victoria (ROB 434).

Even though things are especially bad on Broadway and the Depression has not helped her father's trade, the demimonde Mindy crowd looks after Princess O'Hara. As in "Little Miss Marker," the Broadway guys take care of a young girl in distress, although it doesn't hurt that she has grown into quite a beauty. To be sure, because they find her attractive, the horseplayer Regret and especially the prosperous, although unscrupulous Last Card Louie also have ulterior motives in caring for her.

The demimonde makes its own rules. When Goldberg becomes ill, the Broadway crowd steals a replacement horse from the track— a horse that turns out to be a star racehorse named Gallant Godfrey. With Hammer as a passenger in the backseat and Georges, a French prince with whom Princess O'Hara is falling in love, a passenger in the front seat, she inadvertently witnesses, in the 66th Street transverse of Central Park, a beer truck hijacking and murder. Fats

O'Rourke, the perpetrator, who "does not wish to have spectators spying on him when he is giving it to somebody," tries to kill those who observe him (ROB 442). For, as Runyon stresses, one can know too much, and the city as spectacle can become dangerous if one shares a glimpse into secrets that are not meant to be shared. Gallant Godfrey's racehorse speed saves Princess O'Hara's life by allowing her to escape Fats's gunfire.

Runyon's gentle and idealistic side loves a sentimental ending. To assist Princess O'Hara's marriage to Georges, the horseplayer Regret generously gives her $1,000, although the money comes from swindling Last Card Louie by making Louie think that he has bought Gallant Godfrey rather than Goldberg from Princess O'Hara. Runyon points up the fairy tale aspect of the story by having Princess O'Hara remark to the narrator about her forthcoming marriage and Last Card Louie's supposed kindness in buying her horse: "[I]t is a beautiful world in every respect" (ROB 447). The story ends with the delicate Hammer in a hospital recovering from a "nervous breakdown"—brought on by thinking about what would have happened to him if Goldberg, not Gallant Godfrey, had been pulling the victoria the night of the hijacking—and characteristically flirting with "a nice-looking nurse" (ROB 447). His self-immersion contrasts with the generosity of the other Broadway characters.

The 1943 Abbott and Costello film *It Ain't Hay* is very loosely based on "Princess O'Hara," with the young girl driving a horse-drawn carriage around Central Park and the theft of a prize race-horse when her horse dies; containing some music, the film is really a vehicle for Abbott and Costello's brand of slapstick. Interestingly the name of the girl's horse is changed from Goldberg to Finnegan and the film is given an Irish context, with the Central Park West neighborhood turned into an Irish enclave. The film is wartime es-capist fare with a handsome male serviceman—who has little to do with the original Runyon story—trying to organize a variety show for other servicemen.

In both "What, No Butler?" and "So You Won't Talk!," Runyon sends up the crime stories of Hammett and Chandler, among others, with implausible plot reversals. Like Waldo Winchester, the other scribe who appears in Runyon's Broadway stories, Hammer is also something of a ladies' man. And in both stories Hammer seems to be the temporary lover of exotic dancers. In both stories, the drama critic Ambrose Hammer searches for the murderer of a wealthy man who has become entangled in the Broadway demimonde. In "What, No Butler?" the victim is a wealthy fifty-year-old named Justin Veezee, an "old stinker" who "is on the grab for young dolls" (ROB 385). Ambrose thinks that the murderer is an Arabian exotic dancer named Miss Cleghorn billed "as Illah-Illah, which is maybe her first name" (ROB 392). He knows she could break Veeze's neck because she has almost broken his own when he showed her his etchings—a clichéd euphemism for making love—which Hammer claims, with typical Ambrose Hammer vanity, are better than Veezee's. But it turns out that Mr. Riggsby, a former butler, killed Veezee when he came to rob him and found Miss Cleghorn struggling with Veezee's unwelcome sexual aggressiveness.

Although Hammer in "So You Won't Talk!" is "maybe thirty" (MGAD 258), he is already a prominent drama critic. While in "What, No Butler?" the narrator describes him as "a great hand for thinking," the stories often reveal Hammer as an ingenuous yet obsessive figure defined by episodes of tunnel vision (ROB 384). Thus in the implausible 1937 story "So You Won't Talk!" Ambrose's hobby is murder cases, and he mistakenly thinks he has solved the murder of an eccentric millionaire animal owner named Grafton Wilson. Thanks to a fortuitous comment made by a parrot that Hammer thinks has witnessed the crime, Hammer does find the real perpetrator, Polly Oligant.

Typical of Runyon's misogyny is the slight 1941 "Broadway Incident," a rather late cynical story in which predatory women dupe innocent men, lack any capacity for warmth and affection, and are interested only in money and play. While Hammer thinks the woman who calls herself Hilda Hiffenbrower will marry him when she gets a divorce, the narrator knows her as a cold, manipulative former waitress named Mame who marries for short periods to squeeze her husbands in divorce settlements. Runyon uses his characteristic double plot in which the resolution of one plot turns out, fantastically, to be the resolution of the other.

Written, like "A Light in France" and "The Lacework Kid," for *Collier's* in 1944 with a wartime audience in mind, "The Melancholy

Dane" is about both intense male sexual rivalry and the ravages of war. Hammer is in love with Miss Channelle Cooper, who is seeing an actor named Mansfield Sothern who is performing in *Hamlet*. Hammer, whose affections change almost as rapidly as do Samantha's in the HBO series *Sex and the City*—a contemporary comedy whose fast-talking hip women's brunches owe something to Runyon's verbally aggressive male camaraderie at his fictional Mindy's—gives Sothern's performance a terrible review, which leaves the actor in tears. The narrator of "The Melancholy Dane" recalls how actors and playwrights "feel that [Hammer] is nothing but a low criminal type because it seems that Ambrose practically murders one and all connected with any new play" (MGAD 333).

In the kind of amazing coincidence that is almost a send-up of conventional war story plotting, Sothern heroically saves Hammer's life when he gets in trouble in North Africa as a war correspondent, although not before Sothern enjoys watching him suffer. The serious points here are the toll of war on the civilian population and the way dramatic criticism is refracted through the lens of personal motive. War, Runyon reminds us, is violent, unpredictable, and a game played for high stakes without any rules. War is writ large on the story. As the narrator of "The Melancholy Dane" puts it with poignant irony to Hammer, when he returns after two years looking "no longer a roly-poly but quite thin" after being wounded in the North Africa campaign: "[W]e are so busy missing other personalities that we do not get around to missing you as yet" (MGAD 335).

The early days of the North African campaign in late 1942 were difficult for the Allies; as David M. Kennedy notes, "Eisenhower's rickety binational command structure and his unblooded, ill-prepared American troops at first proved no match for Rommel's seasoned staff and battle-hardened veterans."[12] When Runyon has Hammer complain, "[T]he enemy is always dropping hot apples all over the landscape out of planes, and sprinkling the roads with bullets or throwing big shells that make the most uncouth noises around very carelessly indeed," Runyon catches the violence and unpredictability of war (MGAD 337).

While they are hiding together from the Germans in North Africa, Sothern angrily recalls Hammer's dismissive view of his

Hamlet. They begin to quote lines from the gravediggers' scene, lines that are applicable to their current situation and their past rivalry. Hammer ironically takes on the role of Horatio, the loyal friend, to Sothern's Hamlet. When Sothern quotes Hamlet's speech in Act V, scene one, upon discovering Yorick: "Now, get you to my lady's chamber, and tell her, let her paint an inch thick, to this favour she must come," both are thinking of Miss Cooper, whom they have been discussing. And when Hammer and Sothern are liberated by the Americans the same day, the nurse in the hospital is none other than Miss Channelle Cooper, with whom Hammer falls in love once again. When she asks about Sothern, he tells her, "Forget him, Channelle. He is a cad as well as a bad Hamlet" (MGAD 342).

The lines that Sothern as Hamlet delivers to Hammer as Horatio stress human mortality and the ephemeral nature of life: "Alas, poor Yorick! I knew him well, Horatio; a fellow of infinite jest, of most excellent fancy; he hath borne me on his back a thousand times" (MGAD 339). But within the story, the speech is laden with irony. Hammer has been anything but a Horatio, and it is Sothern as Yorick who is carrying Hammer to safety as if Hammer were child Hamlet. As Hamlet, Sothern is also mocking Hammer as a jester as well reminding him that if it were not for his intervention, Hammer would be dead: "Where be your gibes now? your gambols? your songs? your flashes of merriment, that were wont to set the tables on a roar?" (MGAD 340). As a journalist in New York, Hammer was powerful and Sothern was reduced to tears by his words, but here in North Africa Hammer is reduced to a helpless invalid dependent on Sothern for his life.

Finally, before the German officer, who was in civilian times Professor Bierbauer, interrupts their private performance by attempting to capture them, Sothern recalls the lines about Alexander the Great's dissolution into dust. Those lines mock man's pretensions, including by implication Hammer's—but perhaps also Sothern's own and of course those of the aging and ill Runyon: "To what base uses may we return, Horatio! . . . Why may not imagination trace the noble dust of Alexander"—a line that Professor Bierbauer, emphasizing recognition of his mortal kinship with one of the enemy, finishes: "'Till he find it stopping a bunghole?" (MGAD 340).

"A Melancholy Dane" takes some of its meaning from the *Hamlet* parallel. We recall too how Hamlet lives in a Danish monarchy at war with its neighbors; his stature depends on his acting boldly, as Sothern does. Finally, Hammer does play the role of the supportive Horatio. In another parallel, in lines Sothern speaks to Hammer, Yorick has been recalled as "a fellow of infinite jest" who had borne Hamlet on his back. Originally an entertainer if not a jester as a musical comedy actor, Sothern had been—to echo Hamlet's words to Yorick—a man of songs and gambols before venturing into Shakespeare. In a sense, while they are in hiding, he ironically plays the loyal friend Horatio to Hammer's Hamlet; note the homophonic resemblance between the two names. We realize the title refers to the melancholy of both Sothern and Hammer, when each thinks the other is in the ascendance in Channelle Cooper's mind. It is also worth noting some playful ironies on the *Hamlet* parallel. Sothern gets his Ophelia (Channelle); the Hamletizing figure who cannot decide is quite comically Channelle; unlike the major characters in *Hamlet,* the rivals survive.

Back in New York, Hammer goes to another performance of Sothern as Hamlet only to find the actor unable to perform because of his thoughts about Hammer and Channelle Cooper making love in North Africa. In other words, like Hamlet he is immobilized by sexual jealousy and is paralytically self-conscious. He may not only be traumatized by his war experience but also intimidated by the memory of Hammer's earlier review. But Hammer tells Sothern that it is he, Sothern, whom Channelle loves and that she has rejected Hammer's proposal. The story closes with Hammer's glowing review of Mansfield Sothern's *Hamlet.*

One might argue that Runyon's depiction of the comically named Professor Bierbauer (in German: beer knave), formerly a famous drama coach in Heidelberg, but in North Africa eventually a wounded and captured German colonel, humanizes the Germans in ways that "The Lacework Kid" and "A Light in France" do not. Indeed, we are reminded by Bierbauer's knowledge of Hamlet of the incongruity between the Nazis' supposed interest in the arts and their boorish and inhumane behavior. Bierbauer had witnessed the scene in which Hammer plays the loyal Horatio to Sothern's Hamlet and had praised Sothern's dramatic performance to Channelle.

Runyon is aware of how war turns humans into agents of death and destruction. The Germans have reductively turned even their professors into instruments of violence; Professor Bierbauer offers no mercy to the fellow thespian whom he temporarily captures. Unlike boxing, the outcome of war is not prone to manipulation. Confusion often prevails, and newspaper notions about finding the front are belied by the actual turmoil: "I later learn from an old soldier that nobody ever finds the front because by the time they get to where it ought to be, the front is apt to be the rear or the middle" (MGAD 337). For the civilians who stay home, war is measured—and we see this in #62 of the Turps stories—by who comes back and whether the returning veterans come back in one piece.

Runyon was too old to repeat his stint as a war correspondent; he was sixty-one years old when the Americans entered World War II, but his stories reflect his emotional immersion in the conflict and his awareness of what the war meant. When presenting Hammer's role as war correspondent, Runyon is a bit sardonic but also rather nostalgic for the excitement of war—the violence, the confusion, the serendipitous sexual encounters, and the glamour. Yet one feels he wishes he were there as a war correspondent. Perhaps Hammer speaks to some extent as Runyon's fantasy surrogate: "It is by no means a soft touch to be a war correspondent who is supposed to find out how the soldiers live and how they talk and what they think about, and when I mention my difficulties to one of the officers, he says I may get closer to the boys if I enlist, but naturally I figure this will be carrying war corresponding too far" (MGAD 336).

In this quotation, Runyon at first has us sympathize with Hammer, but when Hammer begins to lower his idealistic mask beginning with the phrase "and when," we step away and begin to examine his lukewarm patriotism and enlightened self-interest a bit more closely. And this is a recurring pattern; beginning with Hammer's review of Sothern's acting performance, his streak of selfishness runs throughout the story. Until he graciously repays Sothern for saving his life in his second review, Hammer is a self-dramatizing and self-interested persona who, in his acts of talking to our narrator, barely disguises his whining and wheedling.

Runyon not only satirizes the objectivity of the drama critic but even makes fun of the tendency of war correspondents to turn their personal adventures into books and to exploit the profit potential. Hammer withholds most of "his terrible personal experiences" for his book; indeed he wishes to write three books but his publisher tells him, "one book per war correspondent is sufficient for the North African campaign" (MGAD 336).

"The Melancholy Dane" takes its place among another group of stories focusing on World War II and its implications. These include the 1944 stories "The Lacework Kid" and "A Light in France" and the somewhat earlier "Cleo" (1941). The war impacts the Broadway world just as it does in the Turps' world in Brooklyn. We recall how Ambrose Hammer is wounded in "A Melancholy Dane"; war affects the neighborhood youths and even Joe in #62 of the Turps series. In the case of Mindy's, as the narrator ironically remarks in "The Lacework Kid," "[I]t brings many strangers to the city who crowd Mindy's restaurant to the doors and often compel the old-time regular customers to stand in line waiting for tables, which is a great hardship, indeed" (MGAD 391). We learn from Runyon's late stories that these strangers are refugees from Europe, Americans on the way to Europe to fight or in New York as part of the war effort, and even an occasional sabateur.

MIAMI NOIR

The hard-edged cynical Miami noir stories date from the later 1930s and early 1940s, but in theme and technique are part and parcel of the Broadway stories. Runyon would have subscribed to the aphoristic lines from Joe Orton's farce *What the Butler Saw:* "All classes are criminal now. We live in an age of equality."[13] "Cemetery Bait" (*Collier's,* December 12, 1936) is a noir story in which a cuckolded husband mistakenly kills his wife rather than her lover; the story takes place at "a certain winter resort spot about as far below the Mason & Dixon's Line as you can get" (ROB 516).

The story shows Runyon's view of marriage as a material arrangement. Colonel Samuel B. Venus's much younger wife has apparently married him for his money and now seeks to get rid of him.

She and a man who calls himself Count Tomaso, whose real name is Carafelli, try to kill the colonel so that she will inherit his fortune. Tomaso is a gigolo who dupes wealthy women by putting them in compromising positions and then blackmailing them. As they all sail to New York on the same ship and a fire breaks out aboard, the colonel shoots at a person whom he thinks is the bogus count, but, because the count has forced the colonel's wife—at knife point and unbeknownst to the husband—to change clothes with him and thus cross-dress, the colonel mistakenly kills his wife, who ironically has been trying for years to kill him. Considering the duplicitous behavior of the ironically named Mrs. Venus, who gave her husband an overdose of sleeping pills in 1931 and planted a bomb in his car in 1933, we realize that Colonel Samuel B. Venus is an example of a man who lives within his own delusions: "[S]he is scarcely more than a child and does not know right from wrong" (ROB 526).

In a second plot, Gentleman George is a thief whose commodity of choice is jewelry and who is part of an elaborate scheme by which insurance companies buy back jewelry to save the full replacement cost. The narrator speaks about George and his thieving associates as if they were successful and admirable businessmen, and appropriates encomiums that would apply to admirable figures: "In the old days, Gentleman George is very prominent in the jewellery trade with Tommy Entrata and his associates, and anybody will tell you that Tommy and his crowd are the best in the country, because they pursue strictly business methods, and are very high principled. . . . To tell the truth, when Tommy Entrata and his associates go into a town, it is generally as well-organized from top to bottom as Standard Oil" (ROB 514–15). It as if the narrator were writing a short column in a business journal describing a particular kind of innovative enterprise.

At the end we learn that Gentleman George has killed Lou Adolia, a participant in the theft ring and subsequent insurance scam, because Lou had absconded with the money the insurance company had given to him as a reward for returning the jewelry. In "Cemetery Bait," every character except the colonel is motivated by compulsive greed. And it is worth noting how capitalists—insurance companies and bankers—are in some way dependent on criminals and perhaps actually involved in criminal activities.

Finally, the title refers not only to a cuckolding wife who is married to a jealous husband with a propensity to violence but also to someone who betrays—as Lou Adolia did Gentleman George—a fellow criminal. It also refers to the consequences for those who commit murder like George, as well as those who—like Mrs. Samuel Venus—trigger a cycle of violence by seeking to commit murder. Indeed, within the world of Runyon's imagination, the title may refer to all of us living amid self-interested predators.

George's tale to the narrator recalls speakers in Dante's *Inferno* confiding to Virgil and Dante on the assumption that they too are fellow denizens of hell. The story ends with a most effective noir exchange, one that reaches beyond the dialogue to include the audience of this tale of intrigue, mean-spiritedness, revenge, and moral turpitude. Desperately uncomfortable visiting prison hell and wanting to leave, the narrator closes with words that resonate with memories of the homicidal voyage from Miami to New York: "Well, George . . . *bon voyage*" (ROB 530). The story appeared during the Christmas season—December 12, 1936; "bon voyage" is a kind of grim replacement for the traditional Christmas Greeting, "Merry Christmas," which George's response—"The same to you . . . and many of them"—evokes.

"A Job for The Macarone" (*The Saturday Evening Post,* September 25, 1937) involves a semi-retired gangster named Chesty Charles who owns a bar near the docks on Biscayne Bay in Miami. While Charles and the narrator are playing rummy, two gangsters, The Macarone—which in Italian slang denotes a jerk or a dolt or even moron—and his henchman, Willie, try to rob Charles. Charles recognizes The Macarone and they begin drinking together; Charles offers him a proposition—$5,000 minus Charles's 25 percent finder's fee—to kill Cleeburn T. Box, who supposedly wants to die. But in fact Charles has set up The Macarone—fulfilling his slang nickname—and Willie to kill Box's nephew, Lionel Box, so that Cleeburn will be the heir to his brother's estate. While Cleeburn has a moustache and is bald, Chesty insidiously describes Cleeburn as "smooth-shaved," "with thick black hair," when it is in fact Lionel whose features he depicts (ROB 698).

After Mary Peering, a young waitress, saves The Macarone from drowning, both The Macarone and Willie take a strong liking to her. By killing Cleeburn, Lionel's uncle, Willie makes it possible for Mary to marry Lionel. Indeed, Willie's killing Cleeburn rather than Lionel and thus dashing Cleeburn's malevolent intentions is an example of how Runyon is able to give ruthless violence the guise of sentimentalism.

Yet in this darkest of tales, Runyon depicts a harsh world where moral cannibalism is the rule rather than the exception. When someone complains that Charles's Shark Fin Grill is no grill and thus that Charles is advertising under false pretenses, Charles hits him on the head with a beer mallet. Worse yet, when the cynical narrator, a nonswimmer, sees The Macarone drowning, he does not shout for help. Because the narrator presents his inability to swim as something of an afterthought, we cannot think of him as much less of a scoundrel than those he describes, including his friend Chesty.

"Little Pinks" (*Collier's*, January 27, 1940) is the quintessence of Runyon's noir stories. Told by a cynical, even bitter narrator, the tale is about an unfortunate woman, known as Your Highness because she only consorts with wealthy men. One night after the club in which she works closes, she refuses to accompany a big-spending bookmaker named Case Ables, and he retaliates for her rebuff by beating her so badly that she is crippled. With scathing irony, the narrator, who seems to be an observer of the original assault, suggests that Ables is "a little out of line" since he outweighs her by 180 pounds. When a busboy called Little Pinks, a tiny man of 90 pounds "who has a very large nose and short forehead" (MGAD 358), shows concern, not only Case but the club owner, Joe Gloze, and two of his captains beat him up: "[I]t is the consensus of opinion that a bus boy has no right to admire anybody" (MGAD 358). Runyon stresses how distinctions of wealth and position are observed even among the demimonde. Because Your Highness's spine is injured and she can never walk again, Case Ables "talks some of paying her hospital expenses, but Joe Gloze convinces him that it will be setting a bad precedent in these situations" because chorus girls will begin to deliberately fall down stairs (MGAD 359).

Little Pinks, who has been infatuated with Your Highness from a distance, now takes care of her as if she were his feudal queen and he her knight, although she treats him in a high-handed and even abusive manner. Because she always feels cold after her injury, Little

Pinks hitchhikes with her to Florida. The narrator and the reader understand that her body coldness mirrors her self-absorbed and narcissistic nature. But Little Pinks has myopia when it comes to seeing what Your Highness is about, and when she asks him to steal jewelry for her so as to make her more attractive, he does so. As the narrator learns from Little Pinks, whom he meets in Florida, Your Highness is physically deteriorating. She is no longer a commodity whose shape attracts men. After Your Highness dies, Little Pinks goes to prison for the jewel theft; upon his release, Little Pinks avenges himself on behalf of Your Highness by tying Ables up "at the point of a Betsy"—a gun—and hitting him with a baseball bat "until he permanently injures the poor guy's spine" (MGAD 367).

The telling of this dark story about repellent behavior takes place on four distinct occasions. The narrator begins with the original anecdote of Ables' abuse of Your Highness. Then he recounts meeting Little Pinks "some years" later on Broadway when Little Pinks is caring for Your Highness in New York (MGAD 359). The third occasion is when the narrator meets Little Pinks when the latter is working as a porter in Chesty Charles's grill in Miami; at this time he learns about Little Pink's three years in prison and the trip to Florida, the jewel theft, and Your Highness's death. A few weeks later the narrator learns how Little Pinks avenges himself on Ables. Runyon's surrogate narrator strongly disapproves of social codes that allow predatory behavior in which the strong sadistically prey on the weak and the haves on the have-nots. Nor does he approve of Little Pink's slavish and self-demeaning devotion to an unappreciative woman, notwithstanding his protestations of love.

Based on "Little Pinks," the well-received film *The Big Street* (1942) was produced by Runyon and was directed by Irving Reis; it included Henry Fonda as a big-nosed busboy and Lucille Ball as the shrewish showgirl. According to Edward H. Weiner, Runyon fastidiously supervised the production, watching the film over a hundred times before it was released.[14]

"Barbecue" (*Collier's,* August 1941) is a late story that again begins with the narrator in Chesty Charles's Sharkskin Grill, Runyon's Miami counterpart to Mindy's. While in "A Job for The Macarone," Charles's place was called the Shark Fin Grill, the Biscayne Boulevard location is the same in both stories. Indeed, Runyon often forgets minor details of his earlier fiction and does not bother to check them for consistency. The narrator is chatting with High-C Homer, who likes to sing in a high voice and claims to have had potential as a singer before someone threw a turnip at his throat while he was performing. Runyon often uses such exaggerated, unpredictable, and improbable incidents to stress the role of chance in human affairs.

While "Barbecue" has a kind of a shaggy-dog, implausible plot, rather than the taut structure that holds together Runyon's best stories, the story does have moments of slapstick hilarity and verbal play. Homer has a reputation as a swindler; when $50,000 is swindled, the police erroneously suspect him and invite him to leave town. The tale then becomes something of a road story. At an out of the way barbecue shack, run by Homer's ex-wife, Sadie, who is called Barbecue, Homer and the narrator discover not only the real swindlers—Dandy Jock McQueen and Johnny Acquitania—but, in a fine Runyonesque touch, an older man named Greebins stuffed in a bull fiddle case by his young wife, Dimples, and a younger musician named Juilano. While the couple believe Greebins is dead and think they are taking his dead body into a swamp, Homer and the narrator replace the living Greebins (which resonates with "gray" bin or even "Grey beard") in the bull fiddle case with one of Barbecue's pigs.

At this point a storm blows the barbecue shack's roof away, and McQueen and Acquitania are killed, while Juliano and Dimples quickly depart. Homer takes the money, claiming that since it has been stolen, turning it over to the heirs of the deceased will only cause "legal complications" (MGAD 354). When upon returning to Miami, Homer learns that Greebins was the one who changed the course of Homer's life by throwing the turnip that ruined his singing prospects, he swings the case containing the stolen money at Greebins. When the money falls out, the police are convinced that Homer—whose name "High C," we realize, ironically stands not only for the notes he sings but for packages of money ("C-notes") he reputedly steals—is the actual swindler.

Runyon expects the reader to enjoy the title's black humor. Because in her rage, Barbecue has reported the theft of a lost pig, she is responsible for "barbecuing" her former husband, Homer—as Dimples and Juliano would have "barbecued" Greebins, and as the storm at her bar "barbecued" the two swindlers. Finally the Miami authorities, whose morality is no better than that of the demimonde, "barbecue" tourists by withholding reports of a major storm and calling it a "slight squall" (MGAD 355).

OTHER WARTIME STORIES

Wartime stories constitute a major category of the late stories. They are informed by Runyon's personal illness and tribulations combined with his knowledge of the harsh reality of war. In the later stories, whether or not the subject is war, we see some new metonyms: "lawbooks" for lawyer, a "pretty" or a "beautiful" or "this marvelous" for an attractive woman, and a "sawsky" for a sawbuck or ten dollars.

"Cleo" (*Collier's,* July 12, 1941) has a preposterous plot even by Runyon standards. A prosperous horseplayer—a rarity in Runyon—known as Fat-Fat "because he is not only fat but he is double fat" has been called by his draft board, only to be rejected for being "too corpulent" (MGAD 380, 384). While traveling with the narrator—a fellow horseplayer—from Maryland to New York to answer with patriotic enthusiasm the call of his draft board, Fat-Fat buys a calf, which he names after his fiancée Cleo, because he thinks the calf's eyes resemble hers. (Runyon, the former Westerner, enjoys Fat-Fat's thinking a calf is a dwarf cow.) Fat-Fat thinks his Cleo is a conscientiously hard-working innocent, but she is running around with Henri, a one-eyed man who claims to be a nobleman and a refugee—although, as the restauranter Mindy remarks, "Everybody is a nobleman refugee these days" (MGAD 383).

Hammer makes a cameo appearance in "Cleo." Apparently in addition to his play reviewing, Hammer has a regular column, and like Runyon in real life, he has become a powerful figure. Not surprisingly, when Hammer writes about Fat-Fat and his calf Cleo in his column the next day, Fat-Fat's girlfriend Cleo takes umbrage at Fat-Fat's suggesting to Hammer a resemblance between her eyes and a cow's. Part of the joke is that Runyon's readers know this sharing of gossipy human interest anecdotes is exactly what Runyon does in his columns when he discovers something unusual in his nighttime excursions.

Henri turns out to be a spy and saboteur named Muller. When Cleo is in danger of "being arrested as an accomplice to a saboteur," Fat-Fat intervenes on her behalf (MGAD 388). In response she calls him by his given name, "Irving," and declares her love; in one of Runyon's sentimental and also patriotic endings, Fat-Fat is not only going to marry Cleo and buy a little farm "and raise a lot of Cleos on both sides"—that is, children and cows—but he is also going to, as he puts it, "serve my country after all" (MGAD 390). As reward for what is a purely accidental role in catching Muller, Fat-Fat is not only going into the service but to a special school for undercover guys "to run down other secret agents and saboteurs and such" (MGAD 390). (Although we are never told by the narrator, we assume that Muller is a German.)

Runyon, who became a bit jowly in his later years, seems rather repelled by fatness and sees Fat-Fat's obesity as a serious infirmity. In the 1938 "Palm Beach Santa Claus," the obese Fatso was hilariously but poignantly caught in a door while Mrs. Mimm kicked him for switching gifts.

War is an extension of the tendency in males to dominate and control. The Germans in "The Lacework Kid" and "A Light in France" are bullies, and Runyon's caricatures play on anti-German sentiment in the United States in 1944. Like Schultz in "The Lacework Kid" and Vasserkopf in "A Light from France," at times the Germans are also former criminals. We also see that con men and underworld characters can exploit wartime situations to their own advantage. In both stories, we see that private motives are more important than political loyalties.

In "A Light in France" (*Collier's*, January 15, 1944), one of Runyon's darker stories, the Germans take over a French harbor village in the summer of 1940 and begin to construct a submarine base. Vasserkopf, a "real high-muck-muck" in the Gestapo but "a former underworld figure," is motivated by his desire to seduce a young French innkeeper, Marie, and is willing to take bribes to provide refuge for an assortment of American criminals. These include Blond Maurice, who in 1943 tells the story to a frame narrator who relays it to his imagined audience; Thaddeus T. Blackman, an older man of means involved in an oil scandal; and Mike the Mugger, who has committed a homicide in Boston while plying his trade.

Although his real name is Klauber, Vasserkopf—which translates as "waterhead"—has his odd nickname "because he has an extra large sconce piece that is practically a deformity" (MGAD 275). Maurice threatens to expose Vasserkopf as a former drug runner if the German arrests him. As Maurice puts it to Vasserkopf, "I hear your Fuehrer is a strait-laced gee, and what will he say if he hears one of his big coppers peddles junk and maybe uses it?" (MGAD 276).

In the summer of 1940, Americans are regarded as neutrals even though their strong sympathies are with the British, whom they are supplying. The Germans are constructing a submarine base in the harbor because, as Blond Maurice tells the narrator, "it is a very handy spot for the subs to sneak out of and knock off the British ships" (MGAD 274). As Kennedy reminds us, "German attacks were sinking British ships at nearly five times the rate that new construction could replace them. . . . The deadliest marine weapon, responsible for over half the lost tonnage, was the U-boat (from the German word for submarine, *Unterseeboot*). . . . From their pens on the Nazi-occupied Atlantic Coast of France, Donitz's U-boats now swarmed into the midocean 'gap' south of Greenland where British air reconnaissance was thinnest and little or no escort was available."[15]

Rarely has Runyon written such a grim and cynical tale with so little humor as the ironically titled "A Light in France." Devoid of sentiment, the story combines the senseless violence of war with the perfidious behavior of every figure except the innocent Marie. After forestalling an attempted rape by Vasserkopf, Marie is a fatal victim of the successful effort to direct the British bombers to the French village. The story contains not only one of Runyon's rare sexual assaults but also the introduction of hard drugs. It is not, as is customary in Runyon, liquor that Vasserkopf smuggled, but "morphine, heroin, opium, and similar commodities" (MGAD 275).

The story depends on multiple double crosses. Since it looks as if the Germans are going to put them in a detention camp, Vasserkopf sells Thaddeus and Mike a boat and some gas, ostensibly for the three Americans to escape. It turns out that Vasserkopf has arranged to have the Americans shot while they are escaping, but Vasserkopf inadvertently tips Maurice off because the latter smells the freshly dug gravesite Vasserkopf has prepared. Claiming that the gas is watered, as if to mock Vasserkopf's name, Mike and Thaddeus spill the gasoline on Vasserkopf and set fire to him as a way to gain the attention of the British bombers and fulfill Marie's desire to shine a light for the British. By setting fire to Vasserkopf—perhaps at Marie's behest—Thaddeus and Mike help the British bombers to destroy the German position and submarine base, even though they are both shot by the Germans. A 1944 audience would have considered them to have died heroically for the Allied cause.

Runyon gave this noir story a patriotic reversal appropriate for a wartime story in an American popular magazine. Marie is the bold and proud resistance figure who will not submit to German occupation: "Oh, if we can only show a light here to let them know this is a place to strike—this nest of snakes" (MGAD 277). She is the one ethical light in morally dark conquered France, the patriotic woman who gives up her life for the Allied cause rather than become sexually and politically enslaved. With "a big beam across her chest," her dying last word is "Thanks" (MGAD 282). Maurice knows it is for Thaddeus and Mike and the light rather than for him, since Maurice eschewed heroism and deserves the narrator's opening description: "a scamp and of no great credit to the community" (MGAD 270). Maurice, master of self-preservation and hardly concerned with geopolitics, demurs: "[W]e are Americans and very neutral. Let us not even think of showing a light" (MGAD 277).

The wartime story contrasts Maurice's cynical amorality with Marie's patriotism. The narrator seems conversant with mob activities, personalities, and machinations and pushes the reader to see parallels between international intrigue and criminal hugger-mugger. The narrator had thought that Maurice had been killed in a mob war because in 1938 Maurice's shoes and odds and ends had been found in a lime pit in Sullivan County. In 1943, he learns from Maurice in Mindy's that Maurice had managed to kill the man who was sent to kill him and put him in a freshly dug grave filled with quick lime. And that "odor of freshly turned earth" makes him suspect that

Vasserkopf will double cross him and his friends on the night they are supposed to escape (MGAD 283).

Another of the late stories is "The Lacework Kid" (*Collier's*, February 12, 1944), a story my father loved to retell, about a card shark known on Broadway as The Lacework Kid who, while imprisoned in a World War II German prisoner-of-war camp, won freedom for himself and his fellow prisoners by beating the camp commandant at gin rummy. Serving as "the waist gunner" for a Flying Fortress, The Lacework Kid is shot down over Germany and captured. The story ironically domesticates the war into a gin rummy game between The Lacework Kid and Captain Kunz, the German prison camp commandant who had learned the game while an attaché of the German embassy in Washington. By dropping a single card under the table and knowing what that card is, The Lacework Kid—the son of an Irishman whose given name is Sergeant Fortescue Melville Michael O'Shay—always has the advantage.

In "The Lacework Kid" war is an extension of male aggressive behavior. Once again Runyon shows how the underworld community's survival skills and lack of scruples are invaluable assets in wartime. Indeed, wartime reduces humankind to the daily struggle to keep afloat without recourse to legal niceties, a struggle that defines the life of the underworld. If the war strips the title character of his Broadway name and returns him to the world of his Irish parents in Providence, Rhode Island, it does not deprive him of his legerdemain.

Before the war, one of the camp personnel named Schultz had connived with The Kid to find card victims on a German ocean liner. He now arranges to back The Lacework Kid in a game of gin with the camp commandant. Although a card shark, The Lacework Kid is somewhat disdainful of the element of luck in gin and resorts to cheating to help the odds. By surreptitiously dropping one card and thus having a great advantage, a trick taught him by Kidneyfoot, a waiter in Mindy's who taught him gin rummy, The Kid wins so handsomely that Kunz begins to borrow funds from Schultz. After Schultz kills Kunz, he draws upon his earlier criminal experience to make the homicide seem like a suicide.

Runyon wrote this story with his American mass magazine wartime audience in mind. It includes some anti-Nazi rhetoric and some nefarious conduct on the part of Germans. Typical of American wartime writing for a general audience, the closest Runyon comes to mentioning the Holocaust in any these stories is when The Lacework Kid tells the narrator, whom he meets in Mindy's, that Captain Kunz "is sometimes called The Butcher because it seems that in the early days of the war he is in command of an outfit in Poland and thinks nothing of killing people right and left for no other reason whatever except he enjoys seeing them die" (MGAD 394).

The narrator sets up his story by reminding us that it is wartime. He introduces his title subject as a soldier sitting in Mindy's across from him, "who is this soldier but a guy by the name of The Lacework Kid who is eating as if Hitler is coming up Broadway" (MGAD 390). The allusion to Hitler is an apt introduction to a tale about World War II, and a reminder that the draft and enlistment homogenizes everyone into soldiers—or almost everyone—for the narrator's only "hardship" seems to be that Mindy's has become more crowded. This may be Runyon's way of reminding those who are not in the army to stop complaining about petty inconveniences.

For Schultz, for whom self-preservation and self-interest are what matter, the war is between himself and Kunz, the camp commandant. Schultz shoots and kills Kunz because the latter had threatened to make trouble for Schultz "over certain matters that transpire[d] in Poland"—presumably Schultz's participation in massacres that have earned Kunz his nickname, The Butcher—if he doesn't give him money (MGAD 400). Moreover, Schultz is afraid Kunz will discover the nine of diamonds—the card The Lacework Kid dropped on the last night they played and forgot to retrieve.

To be sure, each of the three major figures—The Kid, Kunz, and Schultz—are motivated by self-interest, and national alliances are less important than personal arrangements. But the American Lacework Kid uses the 25 percent of his winnings that he is allowed to keep "to bribe Schultz and the rest of the German soldiers to leave the doors and gates unlocked that night and to be looking the other way when we depart" (MGAD 401). In other words, he is a good soldier who not only is indirectly responsible for the killing of a Nazi nicknamed The Butcher, but also—thanks to giving up his winnings—responsible for the escape of his fellow American and many of the British prisoners.

The wartime stories anticipate the final two stories where Runyon—especially in "Blonde Mink"—seems to be preoccupied with violence and bloodshed. The gory scene in which he emphasizes Kunz's blood dripping "down off the table and splatter[ing] over the nine of diamonds"—which, according to Schultz, fortune tellers consider a "very unlucky card" and "sign of death"—anticipates the denouement of "Blonde Mink," where Julie the Starker's blood dyes the fur red (MGAD 401).

Runyon's self-consciousness about aging and mortality in 1944 is reflected in his commenting in "The Lacework Kid" on the importance of youth—particularly in one who uses "mechanics" (i.e., cheating) to improve his chances—in a card-player: "Age is a drawback in everything in this wicked old world" (MGAD 392). The Lacework Kid's successful machinations are a metaphor for Runyon's own ongoing contest with death and his fantasy that he or his doctors might, by some wily means, outwit cancer by legerdemain.

FINAL STORIES

Runyon became sour in his final years. In 1941, claiming that sex was what sold in Broadway theaters, books, and magazines, he wrote: "What the public wants is all of those things about which we were once so prim. It wants pruriency. It wants smut. It wants indecency. It wants suggestiveness and nastiness."[16] This from a man whose stories contained a good deal of teasing sexuality about showgirls. Moreover, he became even more cynical than he had been about government and the "old men" who "give all the orders."[17] As Hoyt notes, "He wrote against war profiteering and in favor of special treatment for servicemen."[18]

But Runyon had always been an independent man who thought for himself and snubbed his nose at the establishment even while feasting on its sumptuous buffets. Even after January 1945, as his life narrowed to his losing battle with illness and to a few close friends, in his last months he wrote some of his finest columns. His trachea had been removed, he could not talk, and required a tube in his throat to eat and drink. He reconciled with his son, Damon Jr.

In August 1945, when Runyon was obsessed with illness and death, "Blonde Mink," his last noir story, was published in *Collier's*. It is a story of how a cynical and materialistic showgirl named Miss Beatrice Gee—note the play on the word Gee ($1,000) and the ironic link with the spiritualized Dantean Beatrice—betrays the last wishes of her lover, a gambler and bookie named Slats Slavin who gave her his last $230,000 for a blond mink, provided that she saves $2,600 for his gravestone. On his deathbed, Slats tells Beatrice: "I am always a restless soul and long have a fear I may not lie quietly in my last resting place but may wish to roam around unless there is a sort of lid over me such as this stone. And besides, . . . it will keep the snow off me. I loathe and despise the snow" (MGAD 78). Disregarding Slats's wishes, Beatrice spends all her money on the mink and is now wooing a wealthy man less than twenty-one years old. What makes Beatrice's betrayal all the worse is that Slats seems to have had a heart attack after a quarrel about her getting the coat, while she goes off partying.

"Blonde Mink" is a story with homoerotic overtones. Except when Slats is with Beatrice, he and Julie the Starker—*Shtarker* in Yiddish means strong—are together, and it is Julie who lovingly cherishes his friend's memory. In the one story that includes a specter experience, Julie visits Slats's gravestone and thinks that he sees him walking restlessly; he thinks he hears the dead Slats speaking to him about the missing stone with characteristic generosity about Beatrice's motives: "I am sure Beatrice will wish something sentimental on it like Sleep well my beloved" (MGAD 79). In an effective coda Runyon reprises Johnny Brannigan, the often cynical cop who at times consorts with hoods and at other times is on their tail; he kills Julie in a shoot-out at Slats's gravesite after the police find Beatrice's body and all her possessions except the blond mink.

Runyon brilliantly uses color to highlight the visual aspects of this finely crafted, spare noir story. After shooting Julie in the snow, Brannigan asks where "this nice red fox comes from?" and we know the grim answer even before the narrator explains: "[T]he red is only Julie's blood and that the coat is really blonde mink," which Julie has brought to Slats's grave (MGAD 84). To add to the black humor of the tale, the narrator's main concern when he hears that Slats's ghost is walking about is that Julie get from him some tips on horses. Given the resemblance between Runyon's rendering of moral paralysis in

New York and Joyce's in his 1914 collection *Dubliners,* one wonders if the equation of snow and death owes something to Joyce's "The Dead." To be sure, the equation of winter and cold with death has a long heritage. Emotionally dead, Beatrice has eyes like "ice cubes," and her body temperature supposedly freezes the mercury of a doctor's thermometer (MGAD 80, 76).

Runyon's cynicism is unqualified in this story. The revenge of Slats's close friend Julie the Starker—a rough, grim (or stark) guy who is a former fighter with a Sing Sing background—who kills Beatrice Gee and takes the mink to Slats's grave to keep him warm may be Runyon's dark fantasy of getting even with those who demean his memory after his death. Deserted by Patrice, his second wife, and relying on his male friends—and particularly one loyal one, Walter Winchell, for companionship—Runyon uses "Blonde Mink" to express his concern with how he will be treated by those who survive him. Perhaps Runyon is consciously or unconsciously threatening those who misuse his legacy or memory that they will be watched by those loyal to him.

As in "Blonde Mink," Runyon often dramatizes a small group of characters making their way through private mazes even while abortively seeking connections with others. Dialogue is often less a two-way street than a juxtaposition of speakers trying unsuccessfully to be heard. In the final years Runyon became more and more of a misogynist; he concludes, as we have noted, "Passing the Word Along," a piece on communicating with a pad and pencil now that he has lost his voice, with an attempt at ironic overstatement that thinly disguises his rage at his deteriorating physical condition and Patrice's abandoning him: "I do not pull the pad and pencil on the dames. I just shake hands and grin idiotically. Most women are near-sighted since infancy and too vain to wear cheaters and why should I embarrass them. Besides not all of them can read" (ST 384).

In Runyon's final story, "Big Boy Blues" (*Collier's,* September 29, 1945), an anonymous narrator meets West Side Willie, a Broadway ticket speculator who is now in the army and who has organized an all-soldier musical presentation, *Gee Eyes,* that has now reached Broadway. The show features Little Boy Blues, the ballet-dancing, cross-dressing son of a ruffian known as Big Boy Blues. Big Boy

Blues is a bully who, after climbing "on the seat of a stray truck and driv[ing] it off," transforms himself from bouncer to successful trucker (MGAD 88). To call "Big Boy Blues" a "war story," as Runyon's biographer Edwin P. Hoyt does, is to perhaps miss the major point.[19] The story reflects Runyon's penchant for secrets, his fear of betrayal, and his sense that we all live in our own worlds. Big Boy Blues is obsessively suspicious that his son is small, "and [he] goes around peering into the faces of various Broadway personalities who infest the Golden Slipper" (MGAD 88). Certainly there is a strong hint that Miss Rosie Flynn's son Little Boy Blues may have had another father even if "it is generally conceded she is pure" (MGAD 88). And there is a strong hint that Little Boy Blues may be gay; while displaying his considerable talent, he dances dressed as a woman. Perhaps the name "blues" plays on the past tense of "blow"—as in the slang for oral sex performed on a man—underlines the suggestion of Little Boy Blues's homosexuality. (We also recall the nursery rhyme where little boy blue blows his horn.) Failing to understand his wife's feelings, Big Boy Blues—loutish and perhaps scared of the truth—wrong-headedly thinks Rosie will be disappointed to learn that her son is a dancer.

Perhaps it is not a stretch to think that the police captain, Caswell, is Little Boy Blues's father. There is no other explanation for Big Boy Blues's clobbering of Caswell some years earlier and not being arrested for it. Nor, despite Caswell's claim that he thinks Big Boy Blues will disrupt Little Boy Blues's performance, is there a compelling explanation for Caswell's clobbering Big Boy Blues.

CONCLUSION

Runyon was a complex man, and his Broadway stories often reveal his insatiable curiosity, his bemused response to diverse human behavior, and his peculiar code of morality. He takes pleasure in recounting not only the oddities of life among gamblers, criminals, and hangers-on but the everyday life of Broadway and Miami: their sights, scenes, objects, and rhythms. The speaker is absorbed in his world, often oblivious to our presence, even as he speaks to us in confidence about a world that he knows will be strange to his audience.

His assumed audience (or narratee)—the person the narrator imagines himself addressing within the imagined world—may be an insider, but we, his actual audience, are outsiders. By stressing by his choice of present tense that the now matters, Runyon suggests how we insulate ourselves in the now, oblivious to past and future. He also suggests the possibility that anyone can, as he did, overcome the disadvantage of not belonging to the upper social strata, the members of which derive their place from *past* accomplishments. That is, we can set aside the past and—with talent, recognition, and, later, the rewards of money—remake our world in the present. Rather than think about an idealized past or future, Runyon uses the present tense to encompass past and future, for it is the present that we can affect and that matters. Such a view had a political urgency to his Depression readers. In his final years, the present tense also enabled him to recuse himself from the disease that deprived him of his speech and would soon deprive him of his life.

CHAPTER 8

THE TURPS

Domesticity in Brooklyn

If I wake up some morning and say someone else can do a better job, I'll tell Sue, "Let's go to Italy or maybe back to Brooklyn." Either one of those two countries is good enough for me.

> —Joe Paterno, in Joe Lapointe,
> "Paterno is Looking Ahead."
> *The New York Times Sports Section,*
> August 9, 2001, D1

INTRODUCING THE TURPS

In the Turp stories, written originally as columns, Runyon demonstrates his understanding that New York reached beyond Manhattan and that he had given the customs and conventions of Greater New York, and in particular Brooklyn, scant attention. As Edwin G. Burrows and Mike Wallace note, "[T]he nation's first- and fourth-largest cities [Manhattan and Brooklyn] would merge into a supercity—Greater New York—that would encompass not only Manhattan and Brooklyn, but Queens, Staten Island, and the Bronx as well. . . . A colossus had been born. Over three million strong, over three hundred square miles huge, larger than Paris, gaining on London, New York was ready to face the twentieth century.... A great merger movement from 1897 to 1904 would forge the modern American capitalist economy, of which New York City would be the headquarters, its ever taller skyscrapers affording the new order both shelter and symbolic expression."[1]

The Turps letters—imaginary letters that Joe Turp writes to an editor about his working and married life—show us Runyon's less cynical and more idealistic side. Were these letters republished in a volume, as they deserve to be, they would show readers a less materialistic and acerbic figure. Runyon was more of a divided self than has been recognized. One part of his psyche envied the conventional middle class marriage where the working male lived on a daytime schedule.

According to Tom Clark, in 1972 the sportswriter Jimmy Cannon told an interviewer, "I didn't think [Runyon] thought very much of the human race," but the Ethel and Joe Turp epistolary anecdotes often reveal the gentle and tender side of Runyon.[2] These anecdotes testify to his empathy and sympathy with the small joys and problems of characters who typify the prewar American couple, quite in love and attracted to one another, with a working husband trying to get by and a wife who stays at home, keeps house, and awaits his return to put the finishing touches on dinner. Joe counts on knowing what he will eat every night and is quite put out when he expects corned beef and cabbage and it is not there for him. These stories all reveal the role that homemaking women are expected to play in a one-career marriage. Indeed, at times part of the fun of these stories is the disproportion between the Turps's emotions and the small things that generate those emotions.

The Turps are the kind of people for whom Runyon wrote, the people he imagines reading his columns. He often extols the simple lives they lead and stresses their separation from the cultural elite. In these letters he shows an awareness of social mobility and social stratification within America. Living in Brooklyn, the Turps are recused from the Broadway world and some of the razzle-dazzle of Manhattan. Runyon neither condescends to the Turps nor steps back and moralizes. While he does not completely restrain his characteristic cynicism, the dominant tone is a boundless American optimism that, no matter what happens this time, next time everything will work out. Runyon was fascinated by what he called "little people" of modest means, semi-educated people who were trying to make their dreams come true and enjoyed the pleasures of decent meals, new clothes, movies, and companionship. Ethel's father was a track walker on the subway; Joe's Uncle Tim was a twice convicted Brooklyn bookmaker, and Ethel's father was one of his customers.

As in the Broadway stories, Runyon recreates through the persona—in this case Joe Turp—the ebb and flow of informal conversational rhythms without formal punctuation. Here he uses Joe's first person narration and his reporting of his and his wife Ethel's dialogue to give his readers a feel for the small details of domestic life in the late 1930s and the first half of the 1940s. He enjoyed imagining how the Turps would respond to the world of celebrities and films.

The Turps was published originally in Great Britain by Constable in 1951 and didn't appear in the United States until six years later under the title *Joe and Ethel Turp* (King Features). It is worth noting that, like other Runyon stories, this volume was a success in Britain, which derived some of its stereotypes about America, and specifically New York, from Runyon.

Although lacking the best known Turp story, the 1937 "A Call on the President" (*The Saturday Evening Post,* August 13), the Publisher's Note to the 1951 British edition eroneously claims that it contains all seventy-two of Runyon's columns on Ethel and Joe Turp arranged roughly in the order in which they were printed. The Note states that the volume not only includes the forty-four letters that were collected in the late 30s—with lively cartoon drawings by "Josef"—in the volume *My Wife Ethel* (Philadelphia: David McKay Company, 1940), but also an introductory story, and seventeen more letters that appeared in *Short Takes* in 1947. Moreover, according to the Note, the last ten Turp letters in *The Turps* (reflecting in subject matter the birth of twins and a greater stress on the traditional American nuclear family) were "never before printed in book form," and were written "on [Runyon's] death-bed when he doggedly tapped them out on a portable typewriter" (*The Turps* 6). Added to the original illustrations by Josef were wonderful ones by Lieutenant-Colonel Frank Wilson for the Turp stories #1 and #46 through #72.

In fact, careful examination reveals that quite a number of stories that appear in *My Wife Ethel,* including such important ones as "Do You Love Me?," "God's Country," "One Seconder Kiss," "Hefty Hogan and a Black Eye," "A Good Cry," "What Is Oomph?," "Ethel's Experiments," "Fashionable Manners," "Gentlemen Stand," "Some Good Advice," and "Ethel Entertains a Celebrity," do not appear in *The Turps.* Thus the Publisher's Note's claim that *The Turps* contains all the Turp stories is untrue. All the above but "Do You Love Me?" lack one of Josef's illustrations, and the illustration from "Do You Love Me?" is transposed to "Ethel's Dream House" (#22), which is not in *My Wife Ethel.* (Since he was still alive, Runyon in all probability selected the order of *My Wife Ethel.*) Nor is the order or titles of *My Wife Ethel* strictly observed; the fourteenth anecdote in *My Wife Ethel,* entitled "Do It With Etiquette," becomes #56 "Etiquette" in *The Turps;* "Liver and Onions," the eighth anecdote in *My Wife Ethel,* becomes #40 in *The Turps.* The very last story in the 1951 volume *The Turps,* #72, entitled "Is Uncle Dan a Cracky?," was #44 entitled "Are You a Cracky?" in *My Wife Ethel,* and some of the other titles have been changed, too. We can only speculate why the Publisher's Note is so disingenuous, but it seems to have fooled many critics and scholars writing on Runyon. In any case a complete edition of the wonderful Turps anecdotes would be welcome.

The first story in *The Turps,* "Nothing Happens in Brooklyn" (*Collier's,* April 30, 1938), introduces the Turps and is the length—approximately 5,000 words—of his Broadway stories. Therafter Runyon turns to the epistolary mode, using fictional letters of about 1,000 words. By beginning all but the first Turp story with the salutation "Dear Sir" and signing them "Yours truly, Joe Turp," the 1951 volume *The Turps* (and the selections in *Short Takes*) make clear that these are fictional letters. By contrast, the earlier *My Wife Ethel* lacks the epistolary format that was in the original columns.

Joe reveals his life to the public through letters to the editor. The conceit of the letters assumes Joe Turp would share intimate feelings with an anonymous editor. What is odd about the Turps stories is how Joe discusses virtually all the intimate details of his private life other than blatantly sexual details. But the self-dramatizing letter writer, a stereotypical male who feels more committed to stereotypical male attitudes than to introspection, would hardly in real life be likely to write intimate letters to someone he barely knows and whom he addresses as "Sir." Nor would his wife have allowed him, without her making vociferous objections, to continue to write letters that made her look foolish to a large audience of readers. After all, Joe seems responsive to her views about when he can write to his nameless editor-correspondent; she forbids him to write about the forthcoming twins, even though he has already informed his correspondent that they are having a baby.

The ongoing series of columns covers almost every aspect of Joe's life, but mostly they are focused on his relationship to his wife Ethel. The Turps stories recall Ring Lardner's epitolary baseball tales collected in *You Know Me, Al.* Runyon used the Turps to explore the intricacies of domestic life and explore social and political issues. In Runyon's work almost all politics, except perhaps the world wars, are finally one to one local politics. While most of the stories are slight anecdotes in themselves, collectively they are a mirror of life in the late 1930s and first half of the 1940s, and cumulatively they have the power of an urban novel. Readers' concern for the Turps was whetted by their having read Runyon's prior Turps columns. Although the stories can be read like a postmodernist hypertext rather than chronologically, our engagement in the Turps' lives is intensified by reading the columns consecutively, as we do when they are in book form.

That these self-described little people have a name that resonates with "Twerp" may be part of Runyon's humor since in other series of columns he had written about the time he himself was a "Young Squirt." Perhaps he is mocking some Manhattanites who might arrogantly patronize them. But since the couple is a bit provincial and xenophobic, the term "Turp" also plays on "turf," as in the idiom "on one's turf" or "protecting one's turf." And since the Turps are concerned with the competitive economic race and keeping up with their neighbors, Runyon is playfully evoking the turf over which horseraces are run. "Turp" may also play on turpentine, which is used as a paint cleanser or, more precisely, as a solvent and thinner—a role Runyon knew that these stories play in relation to his own darker self that dominates his Broadway stories.

The Turps have a strong sense that they belong to Brooklyn, not New York. It is worth remembering that until January 1, 1898, Brooklyn was a separate city from Manhattan, and that Runyon arrived in New York in 1910, only twelve years later. William Randolph Hearst—whose papers provided the major part of the circulation system for the combined city as a new political body—produced and paid for most of the Festival of Connection. But although most political leaders understood the need for consolidation, there had been considerable resistance from families that had lived in Brooklyn for a few generations or more and had a strong sense of Brooklyn as a community of its own. Indeed, Ethel and Joe had grown up in Brooklyn with their families, and so had Ethel's mother. As Joe says on the very first page of the volume *The Turps,* "my family the Turps have lived around here all my life and so has yours" (*The Turps* 11).

The Turps are in some awe of their government and take great pride in their neighborhood. In the sketch "Brooklyn Is All Right," Ethel remarks to Joe, "[D]o you know there are places in the world where if I went out walking like I do here in Brooklyn somebody would drop a bomb on me and blow me to little pieces? . . . Pops always thinks Brooklyn is all right. He ses Brooklyn is allrighter than any other place in this whole world and so does my Moms because she does not know about any other place" (*The Turps* 33–34). Nor, we realize as we appreciate Runyon's irony, does Ethel.

As a portraitist, Runyon is often more interested in types than he is in psychological scrutiny, more interested in life lived within a community context than in the inner emotional life of his characters. And this is especially true of his depiction of the Turps, who are a representative family. Even the eccentrics who populate the Turps' world are characterized by behavioral idiosyncrasies that are unexplained by psychology. Thus Uncle Dan's bizarre propensity in "Uncle Dan and the Fan Dancer" to spit little lead shots at near-naked fan dancers does not deserve speculation by the Turps on his motives or psyche.

The well-read Runyon would have known that, beginning with Samuel Richardson's eighteenth century novels *Pamela* and *Clarissa,* exhibitionism is a convention of the epistolary novel. When we realize that radio, films, and newspapers shape the Turps' lives, we understand that their validation would come from seeing themselves as subjects of others' interest. Ethel is taken with how the actress Carole Lombard orchestrates her arrivals, asking Joe: "dont you ever look at the pictures in the papers of important people like movie stars when they go travelling and arrive in places?" ("Arriving Places," *The Turps* 122). By the turn of the century, newspapers began to print stories with pictures; as the century progressed, news with pictures increasingly emphasized the sensationalism that most readers sought.

Ethel and Joe's imaginations are filled with images of Bette Davis, Hedy Lamar, Greta Garbo, and Paulette Goddard. Moreover, when Ethel and Joe drive to Miami, Ethel's expectations are shaped by what she has seen in the movies. Thus her southern accent is derived from Bette Davis's accent "in those southern pictures" ("The Sunny South," *The Turps* 126). Although we look in vain for advocacy of black rights in Runyon, he does expect us to see the humor of Ethel's expectations that black people, whom she calls "darky people," will be playing banjoes: "In the movies all darky persons are always twanging on their banjos and singing sad songs especially when old massa dies" (The Sunny South," *The Turps* 127).

By holding a mirror up to the Turps' own lives, Joe's letters to the editor make the couple into the very kind of public celebrities whom they envy. Their lives are exposed as surely as mannequins in a window; they become a spectacle against which members of Runyon's reading audience measure themselves to see how they are doing. Assuming his editor does not excise anything, their emotional lives are exposed in whatever rawness Joe allows his audience to see. (Had Joe been edited, he certainly would have mentioned it in some fashion in conversation with Ethel or perhaps in the opening of the letter.) If newspapers created a fictional mask for movie stars or perpetuated the masks that celebrities chose to wear, Runyon by contrast created a mask of down-to-earth reality for his fictional characters. When the Turps, his fictional creations, can almost walk off the page and out of their Brooklyn world and visit President Franklin Roosevelt at the White House, has not Runyon created a hyper-realistic world where the lines between fiction and reality blur?

The Turps' first-person revelations owe a good deal to the personal revelations of 1930 radio, especially the *Burns and Allen Show* and a show called *Easy Aces,* and anticipate the more graphic revelations of intimate domestic details not only in *All in the Family,* where the Bunkers recall the Turps, but more recently in the work of photographers Cindy Sherman and Sally Mann as well as in Woody Allen's films, HBO's *Sex and the City,* and certain Internet sites, where one can peek in and see the private lives of supposedly ordinary people. Knowing that a voraciously voyeuristic audience sought data about movie stars from the newspapers, Runyon assumed that this same audience would also want to know the details of how fictional lower middle class people conducted their domestic lives. Perhaps he understood that Americans needed to recuse themselves from endless stories of Depression and international turmoil and that reading of the Turps' travails would provide a kind of pleasant sabbatical from the uncertainties of their own lives.

The paradox of the Turps stories is that the newspapers are not only their major source of information beyond their immediate family and the agency of shaping their desires and anxieties, but also, through Joe's letters, the means by which their lives become public and shape the desires and anxieties of others. Reading about and seeing a picture of Roosevelt's dream house makes Ethel think of her own dream house in Bay Ridge or Flushing with two bedrooms and a little breakfast room off the kitchen. The more she imagines her dream house, the bigger and fancier it becomes; the house expands to two stories, gets a third bedroom and a powder room downstairs. But Ethel's reality principle intrudes when she awakens that night crying and tells Joe, "We cannot afford my dream house now any more than the man in the moon" ("Ethel's Dream House," *The Turps* 103). When he responds with his characteristic American optimism, "Ethel baby some day I will buy you a whole town of dream houses," she accepts the reality of who they are economically and socially (103). Using evidence from a 1939 poll, David M. Kennedy reminds us that "workers realistically appraised their economic circumstances but also clung to their faith in an inclusive, egalitarian democracy and to the hope for social mobility. Even in the midst of the country's greatest depression, for millions of working-class citizens the American dream had survived."[3] Reading of the slightly upwardly mobile Turps gave hope and stability to the dreams of struggling Americans.

To be sure, in some of the Turp stories we do see ingredients of Runyon's Broadway stories. In "At the Races," we see the characteristic surprise ending when Ethel takes the advice of a tout whom Joe disdains and wins, while Joe loses after getting the inside word from a "fellow from Brooklyn I know who works for Tim Mara the bookmaker" ("At the Races," *The Turps* 74). In this story we see more of Runyon's tough-minded cynicism than is present in the more sentimental and gentle Turp anecdotes. After Joe tells Ethel that her believing the tale of a racetrack tout is throwing away money, "she ses O Joe you think there is something wrong with everybody and I ses well there generally is" ("At the Races," *The Turps* 73). At such times, not only Joe's monologue but also his and Ethel's dialogue strongly recall the present-tense male discourse of the Broadway stories. Thus, speaking of a play for which he has been given free tickets and to which he plans to take Ethel, he writes: "I ses my boss ses in fact it must be a little better than all right" ("Bad Language," *The Turps* 155).

THE TURPS' MARRIAGE AND VALUES

Joe Turp's tone is far different from that of the narrator of the Broadway stories. It is almost as if Runyon created the stories to explore a different side of himself. At times it seems as if Runyon were drawn to the domestic working class and middle class world—the world of upwardly striving "muggs"—that he missed in his own flamboyant life. The fictional letters make clear that he likes and admires the Turps and perhaps envies their ability to make simple moral decisions, live within modest means, and belong to a community that gives them stability and definition. Writing about them and imagining their relatively ordered lives—revolving around Joe's 9-to-5 job, breakfasts and evenings and weekends together—perhaps provided a refuge from his own frenzied life and expressed the fantasy of a more conventional life than the increasingly uneasy one he lived with Patrice.

Joe Turp's letters to the imaginary editor not only express a fundamental decency, ingenuousness, and optimism but also a realization that America is a good place to live. Implicit in the Turp stories is the view that life is manageable if one works hard, knows one's place while having modest ambitions, loves one's family, and remains good-humored and good-natured.

These anecdotal columns about a young Brooklyn couple with modest aspirations present a more domestic and human side of Runyon. The Turp anecdotes use narrative techniques quite different from the Runyonese of the Broadway stories (a term I use to include all the 1929 to 1945 stories narrated by a member of the demimonde). He invents a different prose style—run-on sentences, absence of contractions, terms of endearment, brief dialogues in which the Turps sometimes speak at oblique angles to one another—to capture their speech patterns. Runyon has Joe Turp use the present tense to render the urgency, circumlocutiousness, and rapidity of urban conversation. Yet, within the customary present tense, Joe occasionally jumps back into the past tense—a tense switch that is a rarity in the Broadway stories.

Runyon uses the Turps to show us how a representative middle class family in the outer boroughs reacted to the Depression and to World War II, in which Joe serves. We see how they live their lives, how they organize their leisure time, how and why they dine out, how they respond to films and plays, how they go to prizefights—including the second Louis-Schmeling fight (#13)—and Brooklyn Dodger ball games. They own an older car and take trips to Saratoga, Washington, D.C., and Florida, although the latter is underwritten by Joe's boss as a business trip because the company's traveling salesman is ill.

Even though the personal and national economic needs caused by World War II dramatically changed women's roles, leaving many women playing important roles in the job market after the war, do we not recognize something of the Turp world in the films and family television situation comedies of the 1950s? Runyon's columns not only shaped how America saw itself in terms of domestic relations, but even gave Europe—and certainly England—its views of life in the borough of Brooklyn. Joe and his wife are the consummate urban people; looking for the first time at orange trees in Florida, where Joe has taken Ethel on an automobile business trip, Ethel remarks: "O Joe look at the beautiful yellow light bulbs on those trees. I wish we could stay and see them turn on" ("The Sunny South," *The Turps* 129). In these columns Runyon tries to create a Brooklyn dialect to suggest how ordinary outerborough New Yorkers speak to one another and what their concerns are.

At times Joe is puzzled by his wife, who seems stereotypically circumlocutious, inconsistent, vain, illogical, manipulative, and a tad ditsy, and whose characterization may owe something to Gracie Allen. More precisely, Ethel begins as a Gracie Allen figure, but becomes more savvy and less quirky as the stories progress. Although she had—or so Joe thinks—many competing suitors, Joe has wooed and proudly won Ethel, whom he finds dazzlingly attractive. In the final ten anecdotes the Turps have twins—Cornelius and Constance, named after Ethel's parents—and evolve into a paradigmatic middle class family. Joe patronizes Ethel less, in part because she casts off her Gracie Allen mask and is far less idiosyncratic.

Throughout the Turp stories, Joe enjoys Ethel's otherness as woman. She knows how to humor and wheedle him to get from him what she wants—as when she gets him to buy her a red fox jacket in the anecdote of that name. Of her demand that he tell her that he loves her twice a day, he concludes with a rhetorical question, "Dont you think women are very unusual?" ("Do You Love Me?" in *My Wife Ethel* 32). At times, as in "A Call on the President," her energy and idealism motivate Joe. In terms of dress and manners Ethel is somewhat upwardly mobile; she copies designer clothing, likes the nicest clothing that she and her husband can afford, and is fascinated by Emily Post etiquette even if she is skeptical of its formality ("Etiquette," *The Turps*).

Joe and Ethel Turp were married April 2, 1936. They live in a two-family house—we assume it is a rental property—and share the front steps with the residents of the other floor. The Turps are conscious of the proximity of their neighbors and are aware that their neighbors hear them just as they hear their neighbors. When Ethel sings at night, Joe "ses please Ethel you will wake all the neighbors with that noise" ("Ethel Sings Husky Musky Dusky," *The Turps* 95). As we would expect, the house lacks air conditioning. Owning a car, even though it is old, young Joe is probably a step up on the socio-economic ladder from some of his neighbors, although, following Ford's lead, cars were made that middle-class families could afford. Surprisingly perhaps to us, Joe has a tuxedo, but so did my father, who, although college educated, was of approximately similar age and economic circumstances.

The Turps are not educated; their speech is a common vernacular and often ungrammatical, but without the slang and demimonde argot of Runyon's Broadway stories. The Turps are extremely family oriented. Ethel is close to her parents, who live in the same neighborhood. After they have twins toward the end of the series, Ethel asks her mother to baby-sit. While the Turps see themselves as little people, they both take the initiative to protest social customs and political policies that affect them or their neighborhood.

Contemporary readers may find off-putting Runyon's conventionally sexist concept of marriage in his depiction of the Turps. To get what she wants, the woman has to make a case as if she were a child asking for an allowance. But the wife also has sex appeal, and knows how to use it as an asset to fulfill her husband's desire to show her off. This is a world of presumptive male privilege, one in which the man patronizes the woman because he is the breadwinner and is therefore entitled to decide how money is spent. The man needs to feel he is smarter and wiser, and his wife—perhaps in part to get what she wants—reinforces that image. We might recall an old and tired joke—a favorite of my father's—where the man says he has his way in big things, like foreign and domestic policy, and the woman takes care of small things, like where the family lives, what they want to buy, and what goes on in the home.

Ethel stays home and takes care of her husband and later her children. But Ethel is quite assertive about her needs and desires, something she has learned from her mother. While Ethel's father spoke about his political opinions at some lengths, her mother seemed to make the rules within the house; she "did not allow anybody to talk about the weather in our house" ("Weathering It," *The Turps* 199).

Notwithstanding his general cynicism about full communication in relationships, Runyon believed in the power of words, and it is the verbal rapport of the Turps that makes their marriage work. With each other, Joe and Ethel are alternately tender and aggressive. Their repartee is the stuff of standup vaudeville comedy, which probably was one of Runyon's sources; an example is when Joe complains, "I ses why you always try to tell me what I mean when I may mean something else?" ("A Tough Audience for Underwear," *The Turps* 178). That they are both prone to exaggeration links these stories to the Broadway stories.

Ethel is a feisty, sometimes naive, and sometimes disingenuous woman who is protective of her prerogatives. She objects loudly that men do not give up their subway seats to women. In "Gentlemen Stand," she announces on the subway to her husband that a man is "so fat" that he takes "up two seats instead of one"; not only is her voice loud enough for the fat man to hear, but she repeats the insult to the fat man's face ("Gentlemen Stand," *My Wife Ethel* 196). To those outside New York, her boisterous objections to having to stand would have seemed not merely aggressive and belligerent behavior, but social barbarism. Yet, while she succeeds in embarrassing the man on the subway into giving up his seat, she defers to other ladies (98).

The Turps are reasonably informed about politics, thanks to radio and newspapers—indeed, much of their information and desire for consumer goods come from the newspapers. They frequently go to films and occasionally to Broadway shows, but they are more likely to attend shows when someone gives them tickets. Joe is most pleased to be married to Ethel and thinks he is the envy of a great many men in Brooklyn. Although Ethel enjoys showing off her figure in a bathing suit, the Turps are quite conservative and even a bit prudish about some things—far more so than their fictional counterparts in the Broadway stories. Joe is proud that Ethel has a great body, but embarrassed and jealous when she displays it in skimpy clothing; taking her lead from movie stars and mannequins, she is something of an exhibitionist: "I ses well if that is a bathing suit I wish you would hurry up and hide yourself in the water before somebody else sees you and she ses why Joe I want somebody else to see me" ("Ethel's Bathing Suit," *The Turps* 130). The irony is that while Joe is objecting to her displaying herself, he displays both their lives every time the editor prints his letters.

In "A Tough Audience for Underwear," Ethel asserts: "I would like to see a picture where nobodys pants or skirts got torn off to show them in their underwear. . . . [N]o underwear ever made me laugh much" (*The Turps* 178). Indeed, when she speaks for family values, she is representing Runyon's conservative side, which objected to sex in books and films. Perhaps in response to the gathering storms of war and the lingering Depression, Ethel wants to recuse herself from turmoil and ugliness and find refuge in light fare. But the irony is that after listing all her stipulations—little drinking, only good manners, everyone acting like ladies and gentleman—there is hardly anything of which she approves as subject matter for plot or humor—except perhaps (and this may be part of Runyon's joke) making a film of the Turps anecdotes.

While like their creator, the Turps like movies and are familiar with the major actors—they seem to go several times a week—they are indifferent to the kind of modernist revolution in American art that began with the 1913 Armory show. When the Turps go to a play praised by drama critics, Ethel objects to the "bad language," which makes her physically uncomfortable ("Bad Language," *The Turps* 157). Moreover, she assumes that drama critics used bad language. Indeed, Ethel even objects to films that lack "nice people" and provocatively wonders if it is because filmmakers don't know nice people. She objects to the supposed humor of rude "smart cracks" between husband and wife, to drunkenness, to seeing underwear, and to people hitting one another.

The epistolary Turps anecdotes rarely have much of a plot but are more slice of life windows into outerborough culture than stories. The Turps' concept of America derives from their own lives in a Brooklyn neighborhood. For the Turps so much comes down to personal relationships. Their little-people perspective is pragmatic and concerned with getting from Monday to Tuesday. To be sure, a macho code prevails and males frequently exchange insults. Rather than gang wars or gunplay, there are occasional punches in the nose when men disagree or feel their wives are insulted. Joe is an aggressive New Yorker who is quick to take offense. At one point, after a man named Moriarity punches Joe in the nose while the Turps are celebrating their wedding anniversary, Joe, with characteristic New York hyperbole, rather proudly remarks to Ethel: "I have had five hundred fights with fellows who liked you and have been sore at me ever since we got married" ("Wedding Anniversary," *The Turps* 171).

Prior to World War II, politics is to the Turps what happens in the district rather than in the world beyond. Joe lives in a world where Sweeney, the district leader, is powerful and where the middle class looks up at cafe society and the world of the wealthy from a frog's perspective. Perceiving himself and Ethel as "little" people, Joe is very conscious of the power of Sweeney and Sweeney's district captain, Johnny Wolf, whom he dislikes but with whom he talks because Wolf "stands all right with Sweeney" and for that reason Wolf "can do me plenty of good if he wants to" ("Two Face," *The Turps* 148).

"NOTHING HAPPENS IN BROOKLYN"

"Nothing Happens in Brooklyn" (*Collier's*, April 9, 1938) is a wonderful opening to the collection entitled *The Turps*. The story defines the combination of wiliness and naiveté that is the essence of Ethel's character, while giving us a view of Brooklyn as a suburban retreat and adjunct of the city. Like Runyon's Broadway stories, this story humanizes criminals. To Ethel, the bank robber and murderer is only Clem Chambers, a guy she grew up with and whose family lives next door. Clem once loved Myrt McGuire, the same woman as Petey Angelo, a former friend of his who became a cop and who is now wooing her. Ethel says, "Clem is not a tough guy. He is just full of pep," to which Joe responds: "I ses look Ethel robbing a mail truck is a little different from tying your pigtails to a desk and it is something more than just pep too" (*The Turps* 17).

Clem presents himself as a fellow who eschews routines and chooses a different business. To Ethel, Clem and Petey are neighborhood kids who grew in different directions, and she relates to both of them as friends. Indeed, Clem had saved Pete from drowning when they were boys and, when he got hurt trying to capture Clem by falling through a skylight window, Clem bandaged him up. To Ethel, Clem is something of a gentleman who has confided his own love for Myrt but has told no one else. Indeed, there is a Runyonesque subtext hinting that Myrt agrees to marry Pete, climaxing a six-year courtship, only after Clem is sent to Sing Sing.

For Ethel, only the immediate family situation is what matters, not the larger implications of Clem's sociopathic behavior. Given that the Chambers are neighbors, her concern is that Clem's dying mother see her son. When Ethel wants to deliver a message to Clem that his mother is dying after he is cornered by cops, Joe's mention of Sweeney, the district leader, is effective in getting the police captain's cooperation, for in this world the political infrastructure reaches everyday life.

In Runyon's world, as we know from the stories, the cops are motivated by self-interest as often as by their commitment to public good. Indeed, they are often bullies. To a threat by the captain that he will lock Joe and his wife up and think about a reason later, Joe responds: "I ses look Captain you are big people and we are only little people but do not be talking about locking somebody up unless they have done something" ("Nothing Happens in Brooklyn," *The Turps* 21). (Runyon enjoys the irony of Clem's shooting a man named Coolidge, whose presidency Runyon regarded with some disdain.)

"A CALL ON THE PRESIDENT" AND DEPRESSION POLITICS

"A Call on the President," published in *The Saturday Evening Post* on August 21, 1937, is a Turps story that did not appear in any collection of the Turps columns but does appear, along with the 1938 "Nothing Happens in Brooklyn," in *More Guys and Dolls* (Garden City Books, 1951). In neither story does Runyon use the convention of writing to an editor that he uses in all the other shorter Turps pieces. Showing The Turps' ingenuous but well-founded faith in democracy, "A Call on the President" is in some ways a paean to Franklin D. Roosevelt. The story is told in Joe's usual digressive manner, one that is taken further off track by his wife's even more digressive comments; the narrative decision to include those comments results from Joe's respect for—and even awe of—his wife.

The Turps protest what they feel is the unfair firing of their mailman, Jim, and drive down to Washington to straighten things out. When Joe arrives, he speaks for everyone who is a citizen and has the right to speak up when he says to the man in striped pants in front of the White House: "I am a citizen of the United States of America and know my rights. . . . I ses Mister, what is so tough about seeing the President of the United States? When he was after this job he was glad to see anybody. I ses is he like those politicians in Brooklyn or what?" (MGAD 247–48). Joe is an innocent expecting the Bill of Rights and the Constitution to work for him. Perhaps as a vestige from his wilder Western days, perhaps from his intimacy with criminals in his newspaper career, Runyon has Joe express his creator's suspicion of, if not outright disdain for, the police.

In keeping with *The Saturday Evening Post* view of the ideal marriage, in this story the Turps are especially gentle and loving toward one another, and their private dialogue lacks any of the edge we see in some of the Turps stories. That Ethel comes from a modest but strong two-parent family, where the working class mother supports and nurtures the father, is evident when she explains to the president why she gave Jim lard to rub on his sore feet: "My mother used to rub my pops with lard when he came home with them aching. My pops was a track walker in the subways she ses" (MGAD 249). Joe addresses Ethel as "sweets," "honey," and "sugar plum" (MGAD 246–47). She has complete faith that her husband, with her input, can fix any injustice. Indeed, she is the one who proposes the visit to the president.

On occasion Runyon tempers with some subversive irony his admiration of the aggressive chutzpah of New Yorkers. When the first cop they encounter is rude, Ethel responds: "We are from Brooklyn and we do not like to have hick cops get fresh with us" (MGAD 247). While Runyon is laughing at the insouciant arrogance and rudeness of New Yorkers, doesn't such dialogue in *The Saturday Evening Post,* a story not about gangsters but about a middle class couple, contribute to the image of New Yorkers—irrepressible, inveterate, loquacious, tactless, and direct to a fault—that most of Middle America stills hold?

Joe characteristically thinks of himself as one of the "little" people and contends that the government is run by "big people" (MGAD 247). But Ethel convinces Joe to share her belief in fair play within America and her faith that once the president learns the facts, democracy will work. As Kennedy puts it, "A heightened sense of class consciousness did indeed emerge in the United States in the Depression years, but it was of a stubbornly characteristic American type. It did not frontally challenge existing institutions but asked—demanded—a larger measure of participation in them."[4]

The Turps and Ethel's family are Roosevelt fans, and her Pops "will not stand for anybody knocking Mr. Roosevelt" ("Ethel's Pops and the Mustard Plaster," *The Turps* 91). In "A Call on the President," the Turps meet the president—who is not identified by name as Roosevelt, but is Runyon's version of a president who cares about the average American or "little fellow." The president sees the Turps at once. We are outsiders in awe of the meeting and beholding the spectacle, but we are also in the Turps' shoes as engaged citizens imploring the president. Although Joe presents himself as one of those who is controlled by—rather than controlling—events, he exemplifies the very spirit of democracy in his belief that he can change the course of events. Resonating with the Rockwellian spirit that readers of *The Saturday Evening Post* would have recognized, Joe says to the president: "I ses it is only fair to tell you if you do anything to help Jim the mailman we cannot do anything for you in return because we are just very little people and all we can do is say much obliged and God bless you and that is what everyone in our neighborhood would say" (MGAD 246). To the Turps, the president is simply the district leader's district leader, someone in the larger neighborhood of the United States who can fix an injustice.

The president responds to the Turps as a fellow citizen who temporarily occupies the presidency because we elect him rather than in his role as an authority figure. While at first they seem to talk a different language—the president does not know what Joe means by a "broad" (MGAD 250)—they find a common language. Soon the president and Joe are talking as one man to another. The president responds to Joe's complaint about the Brooklyn Dodgers' pitching with a remark that goes beyond speaking about the baseball team, the

Washington Senators: "The Dodgers are doing better but they need more pitching, I ses. How are things in Washington? He says not so good. He says I guess we need more pitching here too" (MGAD, 248). The president is referring self-ironically to his Washington team—his advisors and cabinet—which is struggling with the Depression.

Joe tells the president the sad tale about Jim, the sixty year old mailman whose shoulders are bent from carrying the mail and who has wrongfully lost his job. For the past ten years, to protect the feelings of Mrs. Crusper, the only woman he had ever loved, Jim the mailman had been writing and delivering to her bogus letters from her reprobate son, Johnny; these letters tell her how much her son loves her and how well he is doing. Johnny had to leave town with money Jim borrowed against his paycheck from a loan shark. When a real letter arrives announcing the son has been killed while escaping prison, Jim burns it to spare the now dying woman further pain.

The president not only invites them to lunch after hearing their story on behalf of Jim, but also responds to them positively and gets Jim reinstated. The president personifies a government that is caring and paternal, and to whom little people like the Turps can look for recourse. What he represents is security in the face of the vicissitudes of life; he is able to set things right when they go wrong for the little people. In the story he is a metaphor for interventional government that prevents arbitrary decisions made in the interests of predatory capitalism. Runyon depicts the federal government as the ultimate refuge for citizens from the travail brought on by the Depression, an economic disaster that hit New York City harder than most places.

Public employment in the form of the Postal Service as well as elaborate Public Works projects, along with such New Deal programs as Social Security and Unemployment Insurance, turned the U.S. Government from an indifferent distant relative into a paternal figure personified by Roosevelt in his fireside chats, the very kind of figure portrayed in "A Call on the President." That Roosevelt was a former governor of New York and had taken a hand in the removal of the corrupt mayor Jimmy Walker accentuated the link between New York City residents and the president.

Runyon's characterizations and cityscapes are themselves cartoons and thus provide wonderful material for his illustrators. The illustrations of the Turps stories in the book—by Frank Wilson and the man who called himself simply Josef—give them a visual dimension with which Americans can identify as fellow members of the aspiring middle class in difficult times. In "A Call on the President," the images—drawn by E. F. Ward in the Norman Rockwell manner familiar to readers of *The Saturday Evening Post*—often complement and reinforce the implications of the texts. Thus the president, visualized by Ward at an angle from the back, has a striking resemblance to Roosevelt. At other times, images oddly free themselves from the text; for example, in the same story Ward's image of Jim the old mailman is far more sprightly than we would imagine from Runyon's words.

The Turps' visit to the president is based on the very principle of specificity that makes Runyon's stories and best columns work. Runyon convinces us that the details of the world are what matter. He flouts those intellectuals who conceive the world in terms of ideals and abstractions. The Turps have a kind of indigenous naive New York aggressiveness and believe that they can solve any problem. In their way they perform small acts of kindness without turning into larger than life heroic figures or pretending to be superhuman.

Runyon is showing *The Saturday Evening Post* readers that democracy works and, at least under Roosevelt, without bribes or special favors. Perhaps one reason that Roosevelt is not identified is because Runyon knew the *Post* would not want to offend Republicans. Runyon supported Roosevelt for a third term. When the president died in early 1945, at a time when Runyon himself was close to death, Runyon wrote an eloquent column consisting of an imaginary dialogue between a well-dressed man who had hated Roosevelt and had spoken ill and snidely of him and his teenage son watching the funeral cortège. The man observes to his son: "He only did the best he could. No man could do more. . . . I used to say I hated him when he was alive but now it is difficult for me to pick out any reason why. How could I hate a kind man?"[5]

Runyon in "A Call on the President" enacts the democratic fantasy that we are all equal, and perhaps owes something to Walt Whitman, the patron saint of the common man and of New York—and especially Brooklyn—as the quintessential city in which all men share a common bond, regardless of class. In the Turps stories, Runyon's values are conservative and traditional and closely resemble those of his *Saturday Evening Post* counterpart, Norman Rockwell. Runyon's "A Call on the President" shows the Turps as caring about others, effective, working as a marital team, believing in the promise of democracy and the ideal of free speech. This is the America of Rockwell's 1942 series of paintings, "Four Freedoms"—inspired by Roosevelt's January 6, 1941, speech to Congress—especially "Freedom of Speech," where a lone dissenter, a working class man, presumably at a New England town meeting, is given a chance to speak. In "Freedom of Speech," our surrogate beholders are the tolerant men in suits and ties framing him.

Runyon was aware of the economic downturn of 1937 and the pain it caused. As Kennedy writes, "In May 1937, the economic recovery building since 1933 had crested, well short of 1929 levels of employment. By August the economy was once again sliding measurably downward; in September rapidly downward. . . . By the end of the winter of 1937–38, more than two million workers had received layoff notices. . . . [I]t was a depression within a depression."[6] It is worth noting that when, in the anecdote "Ethel's Pops Knocks the Government," Ethel's father is displeased about how the government has treated an individual, he does nothing; his daughter's generation is more aggressive, as when she and Joe call on the president. In "Ethel's Pops Knocks the Government," her father is outraged that when the country is in a drastic downturn, the government is peremptorily foreclosing on a friend's mortgage. Graphically bringing home the Depression to Brooklyn, Runyon has Joe rather angrily assert: "I ses a lot of people borrowed money off the government on their houses and could not pay back and lost their houses" (*The Turps* 98).

Runyon understood that for those having tough times, socioeconomic abstractions are irrelevant garble. In "Ethel's Pops and Danged Hard Times," Joe explains the difference between a recession that they are having now and the Depression when "business is bad and nobody had much money and a lot of people got out of work"; but Ethel responds that "My Pops says they are just fancy names for danged hard times" (*The Turps* 183–84). Joe takes umbrage at her father's exploding his distinctions. We are not sure if her father's recollections of even harder times in the past refer to the early 1930s or if they predate the Depression. But her father refers to a worse time when people in the neighborhood were "danged near starving to death because nobody had any money or any jobs and the danged banks were busting everywhere and it was danged cold besides" (*The Turps* 184). Apparently her father has some antagonism to both capitalists "who will do any danged thing they can think of to hurt Mister Roosevelt" and to Communists (*The Turps* 184).

LIVING IN AN INFORMATION AGE

Orson Welles's elaborate radio hoax in 1938 about the invasion from Mars, "War of the Worlds," took the mediathon to another level, involving as it did millions of listeners. Indeed, as Kennedy notes, Welles's show not only "led millions of Americans to believe than Martians had invaded the country" but gave Hitler fuel for patronizing the supposed low intelligence of American citizenry.[7] Ethel describes Welles's media coup as the broadcast "about some fellows coming down from Mars and landing in New Jersey and killing people right and left" ("The End of the World," *The Turps* 108). Interestingly, with characteristic optimism, Ethel quotes her mother's homespun worldly wisdom—wisdom that recalls some of the sentiments of My Old Man: "My Moms ses that if the world did not come to an end after all the wickedness and meanness she has seen in her life there is no reason for it to come to an end now when it is getting better" (*The Turps* 110). It is worth noting the absence of religion in the Turps anecdotes, even though religion was a staple of life in this period. The Turps do not go to church even though they seem to have imbibed the values of ordinary Protestantism minus God. Indeed, there is an ostentatious absence of God as subject in these stories as in most of Runyon's work.

The Turps are the products of mass media, particularly newspapers. Reading the Turps stories, one can see how they live in the midst of the information age where the media affected the shape of lives. Interestingly, the Turps learn about the Welles broadcast from the newspapers, because they were at the movies. After Ethel reads about the Dionne quintuplets in the papers, she and Joe discuss how they would manage if such a thing happened, and how the babies would be delivered ("Quins," *The Turps*). Comically, Joe gets the concept of "oomph"—the seductive appeal of female film stars—from reading the newspaper ("What is Oomph," *My Wife Ethel*).

Window shopping is an important activity, even if sometimes it takes the form of reading newspaper advertising. Thus Ethel learns about fancy Parisian gowns from the papers and manipulates Joe into agreeing—on condition that she stop talking about smuggling dresses in from Paris—to give her $16 for "a lovely dress just like I would buy in Paris" ("Ethel's Pops and Joe's Uncle Tim," *The Turps* 30). The window display—often with dressed mannequins wearing fashionable clothes for sale—occupies a halfway zone between private commercial space and the pubic street, and its purpose is to seduce the eye of the person walking by in the street and transport him or her into the commercial zone. Thus Joe begins "Larcenous Ladies" (*The Turps*) with an anecdote about how Ethel sees a dress she admires in a Fifth Avenue shop window. But, not having the means to buy a designer dress, she disrupts the intent of commodity fetishism when she makes a sketch of the dress so she can make it herself. The female half of another couple walking by not only copies hats, but makes a sketch—to Ethel's dismay—of the hat Ethel herself designs. Like his Broadway characters, Runyon's middle class characters also do the best they can. They are aware that they live in a capitalistic environment during a time when the Depression has reduced upwardly mobile expectations.

Reading "Larcenous Ladies," we might think of an earlier chronicler and onlooker of the evolution of New York, Everett Shinn, whose paintings rendered the essence of New York from its narrow rundown streets with physical conflicts between men to its Broadway theater to its social glamour and commercial magic. In Shinn's "The Shop Window" (1903), we see a woman stopped in her tracks before a brilliantly lighted scenic shop window in the early 1900s. Containing not an entire mannequin but just its stockinged legs, the shop seduces the onlooker to purchase and emulate the displayed legs, but also reminds us how imaginative marketing will separate the organic body of the city into component parts or neighborhoods to highlight their individuality.[8] Like Runyon, Shinn was an acute observer who breathed life into separate individuals within the seeming hurly-burly of the city.

Newspapers help create the Turps' appetite for goods and pleasure. In "Red Fox Jacket," a characteristic Runyon opening immediately engages the reader with a puzzling anecdote when Joe describes how he turns to the continuation of a story in the Sunday paper only to find holes in his paper. Ethel has cut out the fur ads, which have fed her desire to have a fur coat. After telling him of mink and ermine furs that cost $3,500, she focuses on her real target, a red fox jacket reduced to $98. Her words to Joe comically repeat those of the ad. We realize how the newspaper has become an extension of the shop window and how advertising has become the life-blood of the economy circulating through the newspapers. Ironically, what fur advertisements imply is that especially deserving (read: those who can afford) human bodies should be clothed in the skins of *wild animals*.

When Joe imagines and even commodifies Ethel as a glamorous lady wearing the jacket, and allows her to purchase the jacket on time for $5 down and $2 a week, does Joe not become the surrogate of the store that is advertising? This is an example not only of how advertising seduces its customers but of how people of modest means are hooked into buying on installment. It will be next summer before Ethel owns the jacket—and with interest adding to the price, perhaps the following fall. How foxy is either Ethel or Joe really in this transaction? And, since fur adds rather than subtracts inches from a figure, we see the incongruity of a fur jacket with the advertised "slenderizing" qualities ("Red Fox Jacket, *The Turps* 79).

Living in Brooklyn, the Turps are urban tourists when they come to Manhattan. They have learned about what goes on in Manhattan from newspapers. When Joe makes a little extra money or when the couple celebrates a special occasion or holiday, he takes Ethel to a show on Broadway and a fancy nightclub. Their lives are influenced by the plethora of Hollywood films they see; in the 1930s and early 1940s, Hollywood began to compete with New York, as it still does, for the leadership of commercial culture. But the Turps also have a reservoir of down home sense that resists bogus claims; when they celebrate at a nightclub, where the entertainment is a society debutante pretending unsuccessfully to be a singer, Ethel lets the nightclub owner know her sounds are strange noises unpleasant to the ear ("The Deb Sings Wuh Wuh Wuh," *The Turps*).

By implying that the Turps are people of influence rather than "little people," Ethel wheedles her way out of a traffic ticket for running a red light; specifically, she intimidates the cop who stops her by suggesting she has powerful relatives: "[I]f you are smart you will just stick that pencil back in your pocket and go on about your business. If you want to give me a ticket go ahead and give it to me but remember I tried to warn you" ("The Cop Says Turp Turp Turp," *The Turps* 87). Has she not learned to present herself as a person of influence by watching films?

THE TURPS IN WARTIME

The Turps understand political news in terms of their own lives and those of their neighbors. Runyon's ability to show how political events have local consequences is one of his strengths.

Ethel's father is described as a track walker for the subway in the 1937 "A Call on the President." But in one of the very late anecdotes, we learn that he seems to have prospered a bit, although we don't know how. According to Ethel's mother, when she and Ethel's father married, presumably in the second decade of the 1900s, "we was very poor"; but later Ethel's mother not only speaks of her father's doing "very well" but recalls suggesting to him that they hire some domestic help ("Moms on Strike," *The Turps* 271). Ethel's parents are representative of a family that has worked its way out of the Depression into the middle class. For many, the preparations for war—the need to manufacture and transport materials for the war effort—provided the catalyst for well-paying jobs.

Hovering over the end of the 1930s was the specter of American involvement in the gathering international storms of war. The anticipated results of the Great War as the "War to End All Wars" had vanished. There is a strong implication that Uncle Dan's eccentricity and inability to hold a job derives from the horrors of his World War I service in France. In 1938, with the international situation deteriorating and with a strong isolationist bent in the United States, Runyon uses the Turps to explore the fear and anxiety pervading the nation. At first, in the starkly titled "Ethel's Uncle Dan and War," Joe is skeptical about Uncle Dan's prediction of war involving the United States. In that piece, Runyon movingly links a human whose life has been shaped by war with the grim abstraction War. Ethel reports how Uncle Dan "ses a fellow is a sap to go to war. He told me how he suffered when he was in France. Joe do you know soldiers do not have mattresses to sleep on" (*The Turps* 82). Dan says if he had known what suffering was in store for him, he would have shot a finger off his hand to avoid service. But Joe ambivalently rejects that alternative as "cowardly and besides I would not have the nerve" (82); he seems fatalistically to accept that if there were a war, he would have to go: "[I]f there was a war I would not have anything to say about whether I would go or not because they could make me go" (82).

Joe vacillates between, on one hand, his characteristic optimism and desire to assuage Ethel's anxiety and, on the other hand, his realism and acceptance of the responsibility of being an American. When Joe says he will be too old to go by the time there is another war—which we subsequently learn is not the case—Ethel quotes Uncle Dan, who would have known about the Spanish Civil War and Hitler's and Mussolini's territorial ambitions: "[Uncle Dan] says look at all the wars every place right now. He ses everybody in Europe will be in a war pretty soon and then the United States will have to get in because they will sink our ships and drown our citizens" (84).

According to Kennedy, by 1930 the typical American "soon concluded that the whole business of sending American troops to Europe was a useless, colossal blunder and an inexcusable departure from the venerable American doctrine of isolation."[9] In "Ethel's Uncle Dan and War," the eccentric Dan is a kind of Tiresias figure with whose gloomy views Runyon has some sympathy, although Runyon was not an isolationist. But Runyon knew the cost of war and what it was like for the soldiers. During the war, as Edwin P. Hoyt reminds us, Runyon "wrote against war profiteering and in favor of special treatment for servicemen."[10]

The poignantly titled "If It Works the Way They Hope It Will" was written in 1946, when Runyon couldn't speak and knew he was in his last weeks. We learn from Ethel that Joe has been in the Second World War: "[I]t is war that you still go around limping a little when you used to walk so quick and proud and it is war that Tommy Katz has only one leg left and Rickie Smith is out of his mind from his nerves and so many boys from this neighborhood are hurt and sick" (*The Turps* 244). Due to medical advances such as whole blood transfusions and penicillin, many wounded American servicemen survived, who in earlier times would have died. The Turps are aware, too, that while for most Americans war caused inconvenience if not hardship, and some families suffered devastating losses, others like Tom Davey in "Tom Is a Little Snug" profited handsomely (*The Turps*). More than anything else, it was World War II that lifted the country out of the Depression, but it also gave profiteers an opportunity to exploit the situation.

Within a thousand-word Turp column, Runyon in "If It Works the Way They Hope It Will" eloquently presents what war might mean to the Turps and people like them. The epistolary column begins with a probing question by Ethel: "[O]ut of a clear sky last night my wife Ethel ses Joe do you think they have fixed it so there will never be another war?" (*The Turps* 244). The use of "they" in the title typifies how the wartime government is an impersonal other remote from the Turps' lives and reminds us that the idealized paternal figure in "A Call on the President" has been replaced by a remote, dying president who gave way on April 12, 1945, to his successor Harry Truman. The Turps view the war as not so much an international conflagration but as a local event that wreaks havoc among their friends and acquaintances in their neighborhood. Put another way, war tears the organs from the neighborhood body and amputates its limbs. In "If It Works the Way They Hope It Will," Runyon locates within the local community the pain of World War II, focusing on the inclusiveness of ethnic variety (Katz and Levine are Jewish names) and the effects of war on particular families whom the Turps know. By extension, Runyon invites his readers to identify with the losses in their own communities.

After visiting the grieving Mrs. Tyler—whose name is both "Tyler" and "Tylers" in the occasionally sloppy 1951 Constable edition—Ethel returns home and looks at her son: "I got to thinking what a terrible thing it was that Willie [Tyler] had to go all the way from this little corner of Brooklyn to the Philippines to get killed and Jakey Levine to Sicily and Freddy Williams to Germany. Joe it made me sick at heart.... [T]he same thing could happen to [our son] Cornelius if there should be another war when he is as old as Willie was and I would have nothing left of him but his memory and a picture" ("If It Works the Way They Hope It Will," *The Turps* 244–45). True, there is a naiveté in Ethel's remarks, but it is a naiveté unpolluted by cynicism and driven by her characteristic belief that the world should be organized on humane and decent principles— indeed, should mirror the microcosm of the ideal family and neighborhood. Characteristically Joe tries to comfort her concerns. With the United Nations in place, Joe can hope that his son will not be called to war: "[T]hey have got a new set-up now that ought to prevent another war if it works the way they hope it will" (*The Turps* 245). Of course, we know that, as Kennedy puts it, "[T]he end of World War II almost instantly introduced a new era of conflict with a martial name of its own, the Cold War."[11]

As Kennedy reminds us, "For millions of men born during and just after the Great War of 1914–18, their experience as GIs defined their generational identity as nothing else could, not even their long boyhood agony during the Great Depression. World War II took them away from home, taught them lessons both dreadful and useful, formed their friendships, and, if it did not end them, shaped the arc of their lives ever after."[12] That Joe is patriotic we know from his wish—which Ethel vetoes—to name the male of his twins "Eisenhower MacArthur Turp" ("A Rose by any Other Name," *The Turps* 238). Yet what the Turps never mention—for example, the rise of Hitler and the suppression of Jewish life in Europe—is as interesting or more so than what they do talk about. Jewish names in the neighborhood remind the reader that the war was fought in part to halt the Nazi epidemic sweeping Europe, although these names also remind us how little resistance the world put up when Hitler began his war against the Jews. Like most Americans of that period, the Turps had their heads in the sand about the Holocaust.

FURTHER POLITICAL AND HISTORICAL CONTEXTS

However, at times the later anecdotes do reveal quite a political and historical awareness. When Ethel complains in "Ethel's Legs Are

Tired" about standing in line waiting for a table at their favorite local restaurant, now that times have improved since the Depression, Runyon expects us to understand how much better off we, like the Turps, are and how naive she and an old guy who agrees with her are: "Ethel says I wish another depression would come along tomorrow Joe. I am just sick and tired of standing in line waiting waiting waiting" (*The Turps* 251). Joe, who seems now to have his own business and to be taking part somewhat in the rising tide of postwar prosperity, has little patience for Ethel's complaint. Kennedy reminds us of the effects of World War II: "It was a war that so richly delivered on all the promises of the wartime advertisers and politicians that it nearly banished the memory of the Depression. . . . [It] had opened apparently infinite vistas to the future."[13]

In "Ethel's Legs Are Tired" Runyon insists on revisiting that memory lest Americans forget how far they have come. Joe starkly reminds Ethel and the reader what the Depression was like. It turns out, too, in a Runyonesque irony, that the old curmudgeon who has whined that "the people have too much money and they are spending it on their stomachs and their entertainment" has his money salted away and is concerned only with his own convenience and comfort (*The Turps* 251–52). As Kennedy observes: "If the New Deal had stabilized America, the war energized the country in ways inconceivable just years earlier. The goal of the New Deal had been to achieve a measure of security for all Americans in a presumably static economy. The goal, even the obsession, of Americans in the postwar years would be the pursuit of individual prosperity in the midst of apparently endless economic growth."[14]

Runyon is skeptical about the selfish motives of union organizers and labor protesters. In "Uncle Dan, Union Organizer," Ethel's extremely odd Uncle Dan is a braggart about his role in winning World War I, even while claiming to have lost his health in that war. He is a notorious sponger, borrowing money in $2 installments, which he never repays. But he also may be something of a "cracky"—another term for someone who was called "cracked" but what we now call "emotionally disturbed." At one point Dan is organizing a union for Santa Clauses as a scheme to make money for himself.

In "Uncle Dan and the Spies," Runyon shows how Dan's anger at Kroffy the tailor for scorching a hole in his pants becomes delusional paranoia when Dan convinces himself that the tailor is a spy. In a prescient anticipation of McCarthyism, Runyon is responding not only to the obsession with rooting out spies that began in the late 1930s,when American involvement in World War II began to look quite likely, but also to the notion during the buildup to American participation and during the war that some Americans were more loyal to their country of origin than to the United States. Indeed, isolationism and paranoia about foreign intrigue goes back past the Red Scare of the 1920s to the Civil War. Of course, the real spy is Uncle Dan, the man who maliciously spies on his neighbor and who is willing to lie to get a personal enemy in trouble.

Runyon continues his mockery of wartime political paranoia in "Belittling Dan," where Uncle Dan falls in love with Maude, a large blond woman, after he had first suspected her of being a spy. When he follows Maude home so he can send her address to "Mister Hoover," the FBI director, Maude assumes he is a pervert, a "dirty masher," and slugs him (*The Turps* 203).

In the early Turp stories, Runyon addressed the difference between democracy and dictatorship. In "Laughter at the Movies," Runyon has Ethel discover in the newspapers that Mussolini has forbidden Italians to enjoy the Ritz Brothers, the Marx Brothers, and Charlie Chaplin, and Joe and Ethel think about what it would be like if Roosevelt forbade Joe to laugh at W. C. Fields. Runyon would have endorsed the insight of Primo Levi, the Italian Jewish writer who lived under Mussolini's fascism: "Dissension, diversity. . . . Fascism does not want them, forbids them. . . . [I]t wants everyone to be the same."[15] If some in America were praising Mussolini, or even being tolerant of dictatorial rule, Runyon wants to remind us of what was at stake if Roosevelt could decide what we could laugh at.

But within the anecdote is a second anecdote of a theater manager telling Joe that he is laughing too loudly and later telling Ethel that for that reason Joe is not welcome at the theater. Here Runyon reminds us that even within a democracy there are subtleties of local power, and we are not totally free to behave as we wish. But the important distinction is that within the United States authorities don't impose nearly as many arbitrary rules as a totalitarian regime, and they allow us more freedom in our idiosyncrasies and tastes as long as we do not become abusive to others.

In this story Runyon is also alert to how members of ethnic groups feel conflict between pride in their country of origin and their adopted country. The next door neighbors, the Angelos, who run the Italian grocery store, seem to take Mussolini seriously; as Joe says, "I bet Mussy never even heard of Missus Angelo or old Johnny either although John is always boosting him to me" (*The Turps* 104). But, as we see in "Nothing Happens in Brooklyn," the next generation is more assimilated; the Angelos' son, Pete—once a kid other kids bullied—is a policeman.

CONCLUSION

The Turps stories are a mirror of America in the late 1930s and 1940s and show how the Turps cope not only with day-to-day life but how they respond to major historical events, such as the Depression and World War II, that shape their lives. These stories are a heartfelt paean to the class with which Runyon identified even in his wealth and fame, realizing that were it not for good fortune, he—hardly born to privilege and without formal education—would have been one of them. The goodhearted, generous urban couple—self-described "little people" who think that their Brooklyn neighborhood is the center of the world—are the antithesis to the wise guys of the Broadway stories. The Turps love one another, often laugh together, enjoy movies and dinners together, appreciate the routines of their home life, and especially take great pride and pleasure in their twins. Within the Runyon oeuvre, the Turps, living together effectively, provide a domestic juxtaposition to the dysfunctional relationships and economic instability depicted in the Broadway stories and the cynical columns about My Old Man and Our Town.

For the most part, Runyon depicts the Turps in a gentle, loving relationship—particularly after the twins' birth—that is not only refreshingly innocent but close to idyllic. The more we read of the Turps, the more we realize that Ethel is less eccentric and more a supportive wife as well as neighborhood conscience. Notwithstanding a somewhat combative nature, occasionally focused on protecting her own prerogatives, she is often employed in the service of others, such as Jim the mailman in "A Call on the President" and the reprobate Clem and his mother in "Nothing Happens in Brooklyn." And she is often the catalyst if not the source of Joe's pride and confidence. When Joe tries to dissuade Ethel from complaining directly to the president about Jim's firing because "I do not think he would have time to see us even if we went there" ("A Call on the President," MGAD 246), she responds: "there you go rooting against yourself like you always do" (MGAD 246). She has boundless American optimism. Not only Joe but Runyon himself is often in awe of Ethel's energy, emotional range, and manipulative powers. She is the kind of wife that Runyon always sought and perhaps found for a while in Patrice.

Conclusion

B y examining Runyon's work within the contexts of social and intellectual history and popular culture, I have argued that he not only is a significant figure in American culture between 1910 and his death on December 10, 1946, but that his legacy continues. Like Norman Rockwell, whose work was featured in *The Saturday Evening Post,* where a few of Runyon's stories appeared—including the idealistic view of the American presidency embodied in "A Call on the President"—Runyon was despised by elitist critics who disdained popular culture. Yet like Charlie Chaplin, another relentless and often cynical comedian and at times relentlessly idealistic satirist, who also posed as a lowbrow, Runyon makes serious artistic claims.

While Runyon spent some time in Miami and Hollywood, it was to New York that he returned, for he was drawn to the city that represented the distillation of American opportunity, ambition, and energy. Runyon thrilled to the beauty and variety of New York, even while recognizing the challenge and difficulty of living there. Despite his cynicism, he understood that it was his job to reveal that city to outsiders, to show them the seamy side but also to hold out the hope that their dreams, like his, might be fulfilled. He understood that for some, New York was not merely a place but an illusion. In the Turps stories especially but not exclusively, he may have realized at some level that, as Herbert Muschamp put it, "It's our job to pass on an even more open and energetic [New York] than the one that took us in."[1]

Like e.e. cummings (1894–1962), Runyon appreciates the anonymity of those who are simple folk, those who exist and love and are spontaneous and childlike. Like cummings, he embraces the specific and nominalistic; celebrates the idiosyncratic individual; enjoys the irrational, the spontaneous, the playful and even the nonsensical; and is wary of abstractions. Like cummings, Runyon writes from a set of simple values and without philosophic pretensions. Yet also like cummings, Runyon could write of universal experience; his focus, too, was on those anonymous people, each of whom, as cummings wrote in "anyone lived in a pretty how town," "sang his didn't . . . danced his did."[2] Just as cummings with his odd punctuation and his allowing letters to spill over into the next line without concern for syllables, so did Runyon with his slang challenge conventional typography and orthography. Neither Runyon nor cummings had much use for those who belonged to the political and social elite. But while the often iconoclastic cummings did not like the crowded hustle of the modern city or people who had to struggle to eke out a living as salesmen, Runyon was fascinated by both groups. Runyon embraced the seamy side of bars and the ambiguities of human behavior. Yet that one side of Runyon yearned for simple middle class values is illustrated by the Turps epistolary anecdotes that differ markedly in tone from much of his work.

Runyon's importance depends on his major contribution to the image of New York that most Americans and Europeans have today. His trial reporting contributed to the spectator culture by which we regard such celebrity events as the Lewinsky-Clinton scandal, the Simpson trial, and Woody Allen's private life today. With its focus on the act of observing, the spectator culture is a counterpart to the emphasis in modern art and literature on looking and being looked at. The emphasis in part has its origins in such paintings as Édouard Manet's "Déjeuner sur l'herbe" (1863) and "Olympia" (1865) and continues in such diverse texts as Henry James's *The Turn of the Screw* (1898), Thomas Mann's *Death in Venice* (1912), and Joseph Conrad's "The Secret Sharer" (1911). In this respect popular media culture has much in common with high or elitist culture to which Runyon often had a disdainful attitude.

Taking his cue in part from photography, Manet was an observer of city life who did for Paris in the second half of the nineteenth century what Joyce was to do for Dublin and Runyon for New York. Beneath the glitter and glamour of Baron Haussmann's Paris, Manet demonstrates, were workers who lived in slums and eked out a day-to-day existence. His oeuvre displays his exuberant response to the variety of the city, its range of classes, its stories of seemingly insignificant people, and its energy and complexity. Like Manet, Runyon sees the spontaneous human actions—including the foolishness, sensuality, and greed—of city inhabitants, and he understands the need for individual survival skills in an indifferent urban environment. Also taking his cue from the visual arts, including photography, Runyon believed modern urban life required chroniclers, and news reporters and columnists (which for Runyon were a form of reporters) were the ones for this task. It is worth remembering that George Luks, John Sloan, and Everett Shinn, whose paintings have an easy realism and seemingly casual sense of observation, began as newspaper reporters. Runyon owed something to their keen observation—and that of their Ash Can school colleagues—of the sights and sounds of urban life.

Runyon's short stories contributed to our interest in the sleazy side of theater, the underbelly of sports, including gambling, and the complicit relationship between criminals and police. His focus was on the long artery that cuts through Manhattan known as Broadway, or the Stem, and more particularly the area beginning in the financial district, peaking for him in the streets of the thirties and forties, and ending at 59th Street. He explored the world of those who live by deception on New York's mean streets. He dissected the sham beneath the glitter and the glitter beneath the sham. In his Broadway short stories, Runyon seems to enjoy—in the personae of his narrators—cross-dressing as a marginal figure, living on the borderland between criminality and respectability, and transgressively consorting with hardened gangsters as if being a member of the underworld were a fantasy of his. The voyeuristic narrator is our Virgil taking us through the inferno of the criminal world and teaching us its customs. Indeed, Runyon paved the way for our interest in the criminal life, the life that constitutes the underground of our relatively politically stable society. He presents his fascination with what we might call the sensuality of violence. In "Ransom . . . $1,000,000," the kidnappers and kidnapped form what we now might call a Patty Hearst bond.

Runyon invented his own language. Like that of Mondrian's "Broadway Boogie Woogie" (1942–43), Runyon's style is dynamic, colorful, and exuberant. For his locutions, he borrows and combines terms from vaudeville, jazz, headlines, gangster argot, sports, and diverse ethnic discourses, especially Yiddish and Italian. His sentences teem with life, move in several directions at once, and overflow with intensity. His prose has the circumlocutiousness of the New York culture that loves talk for its own sake without sacrificing the manic comic energy that he borrowed from vaudeville. Like a jazz musician, the speaker relentlessly plays on a central theme, but moves into solo flights or riffs that are oblique variations of that theme.

Runyon's Broadway stories anticipated the noir films of Humphrey Bogart, especially *High Sierra* (1941), which provocatively questioned standard views of public morality and was ambivalent about violent criminals. Runyon influenced the director Jules Dassin, especially in films like the noir 1955 black and white *Rififi*, in which the French gangsters seem like New York figures transported to Paris. Rififi means "rough and tumble," and the characters in *Rififi* virtually step out of Runyon's stories and films. Dassin, like Runyon, engages his audience on the side of the gangsters. The gangsters live by their own code and the informer is killed by the lead gangster, a Runyonesque down and out figure in ill health who has been recently released from prison. Runyon, like Ernest Hemingway, lauded the rugged individual and believed in codes of trust and honor, even among criminals. Thus one always pays one's markers. Runyon also sympathized with the dispossessed and admired those who excelled—even if it was in sports gambling and manipulation—like Arnold Rothstein and Al Capone.

Runyon stylized both the language and the behavior of gangsters, and depicted them as another part of the socio-economic system, providing liquor, speakeasies, gambling opportunities, showgirls, and sought-after sports tickets. We see this interest continuing in the popularity of Mario Puzo's novels, Francis Ford Coppola's *Godfather* films, Martin Scorsese's *Goodfellas,* Barry Levinson's *Bugsy,* and, more recently, the HBO series *The Sopranos.*

Indeed, *The Sopranos* owes a great deal to Runyon. Runyon humanized criminals as people, not abstractions. In stories like "Situation Wanted" and "The Brain Goes Home," Runyon took the lead in examining criminals' behavior outside a cops and robbers setting. In a version of underworld chic, the suburban world in *The Sopranos* is fascinated with Tony Soprano's mob ties; his neighbors invite him to social events and to play golf with them at an exclusive club not only so that they can ask him questions but because they can feel that they are taking a walk on the wild side. As in Runyon, the respectable world in *The Sopranos*, with its insider trading tips and offshore banking, often mirrors the criminal world (episode 10, 1999). Moreover, the respectable world enjoys thinking about skeletons in the family closet, as when a Jewish psychoanalyst brags about a relative who was a "wheelman" for the Jewish gangster, Lepke.

When we think of *Seinfeld, Sex in the City,* and Woody Allen's films, we realize how Runyon's flamboyant characterizations and his aggressive one-line retorts that flout social convention helped define what we call the New York style. Indeed, Allen's *Broadway Danny Rose* (1984), with its flamboyant hangers-on and street characters, pays specific homage to Runyon's world.

Runyon's characters yearn for simple solutions and control but understand how difficult solutions are in the contemporary urban labyrinth. His major characters are often inscrutable to their companions and surprise with their words and behavior. They are often idiosyncratic, even misfits, who are—like The Brain in "The Brain Goes Home"—driven by their ruling passion to obsessive and self-destructive behavior. Above all, they need to be alert to whatever menaces arise. Do we not identify with mobsters such as Tony Soprano or Don Corleone because they fulfill our fantasies of settling issues without ambiguity? Or because of their seemingly neat autocratic family structure, or at least its facade? Why do we secretly and not so secretly sympathize with socially marginalized figures, often identified in Runyon as belonging to one or another ethnic group with its own tribal customs? Is it because so few of us belong to a dominant ethnic group or social caste?

Modernism in painting and writing depends on a cult of difficulty and the need for interpretive critics to explain the tribal practices of that cult. As someone who has written books on James Joyce, Wallace Stevens, and Joseph Conrad, and parts of books on Virginia

Woolf, D. H. Lawrence, Pablo Picasso, and Henri Matisse, I am a card carrying member of the interpretive tribe that mediates between text and audience. Runyon, like Rockwell, communicates effectively without us. Nearly a half-century after his death, our role is to show how he mastered sophisticated literary techniques to make this communication work, to understand why he was read by millions, to recapture his contexts, and to reintroduce him to a contemporary audience. For Damon Runyon not only reflected but created our images of New York City, urban culture, and ourselves.

Notes

INTRODUCTION

1. See William R. Taylor, "Broadway: The Place that Words Built," *Inventing Times Square: Commerce and Culture at the Crossroads of the World,* ed. William R. Taylor (New York: Russell Sage Foundation, 1991), 228.
2. Jimmy Breslin, *Damon Runyon* (New York: Ticknor and Fields, 1991), 4.
3. Jonathan Mandell, "Admiring Itself in a Thousand Mirrors," *New York Times; Arts and Leisure,* December 10, 2001, 38.
4. Ralph Waldo Emerson, *The Portable Emerson,* ed. Carl Bode with Malcolm Cowley (New York: Viking Penguin 1981), 620.
5. See Neal Gabler, *Winchell: Gossip, Power and the Culture of Celebrity* (New York: Alfred A. Knopf, 1994), 89.
6. See William Kennedy, *Guys and Dolls: The Stories of Damon Runyon* (New York: Penguin, 1992), xi.
7. Vicki Goldberg, "You Don't Need a Weatherman: Just Point Your Camera and Shoot, Man," *New York Times,* December 22, 2000, E46.
8. Mandell, 38.
9. Mandell, 38.
10. Damon Runyon, in Ira Berkow, "Putting the Best Through Qualifying," *New York Times Sunday Sports,* 27 August 2000, 15.
11. Roger Lowenstein, "Alone at the Top," *New York Times Magazine,* 27 August 2000, 34.
12. David M. Kennedy, *Freedom From Fear: The American People in Depression and War, 1929–1945* (New York: Oxford University Press, 1999), 42.
13. Edwin P. Hoyt, *The Gentleman of Broadway* (Boston: Little, Brown and Company, 1964), 169.
14. Taylor, 228.
15. Taylor, 229.
16. Gabler, 189.
17. Hoyt, 170.

18. Runyon, in Ann Douglas, *Terrible Honesty: Mongrel Manhattan in the 1920s* (New York: Farrar, Straus and Giroux, 1996), 56.
19. Gabler, 349.
20. Runyon, in Gabler, 350.
21. Runyon, in Gabler, 350.
22. F. Scott Fitzgerald, "Hollywood Etc." in "Notes," *The Last Tycoon, an Unfinished Novel* (New York: Charles Scribner's Sons, 1941), 163.
23. Michiko Kakutani, "As American as Second Acts and Apple Pie," *New York Times, Week in Review,* February 3, 2001, 3
24. See Jedediah Purdy, *For Common Things: Irony, Trust, and Commitment in America Today* (New York: Alfred A. Knopf, 1999).
25. Allen Barra, "The Sports Story That Changed America," *New York Times, Week in Review,* October 17, 1999, 2.
26. Ira Berkow, "For Jackson, Déjà Vu of Sorts," *New York Times,* February 26, 2001, 1.
27. Jim Squires, "Can do!" review of *Seabiscuit: An American Legend,* by Laura Hillenbrands, *New York Times, Sunday Book Review,* March 11, 2001, 12.
28. Squires, 12.
29. See also Michiko Kakutani, "No Beauty, but They Had the Horse Right There," review of *Seabiscuit: An American Legend,* by Laura Hillenbrands, *New York Times,* March 6, 2001, 7. (The title of Kakutani's article is an allusion to the opening song from "Guys and Dolls" beginning "I Have the Horse Right Here").
30. Runyon, in Hoyt, 98.
31. Runyon, in Hoyt, 99.
32. Hoyt, 99.
33. Runyon, in Hoyt, 105.
34. Runyon, in Hoyt 159.
35. Taylor, 230.
36. Hoyt, 169.
37. Runyon, in Gabler, 173.
38. Hoyt, 204.
39. Runyon, in Hoyt, 203.
40. Douglas, 12.

CHAPTER 1

1. Dell Upton, in Michael Kimmelman, "Knickerbocker's Knicknacks," *New York Times,* September 22, 2000, E30.
2. Edwin G. Burrows and Mike Wallace, *Gotham: A History of New York City to the 1890s* (New York: Oxford University Press, 1999), 1066.
3. Burrows and Wallace, 1151.
4. Burrows and Wallace, 1137–38.
5. Lampard, Eric, "Introductory Essay," in *Inventing Times Square: Commerce and Culture at the Crossroads of the World,* ed. William Taylor (New York: Russell Sage Foundation, 1991), 16.

6. See Taylor, 179.
7. Burrows and Wallace, 1153.
8. Neal Gabler, *Winchell: Gossip, Power and the Culture of Celebrity* (New York: Alfred A. Knopf, 1994), 73.
9. Lampard, 27.
10. See Lampard, 28.
11. Neil Harris, "Urban Tourism and the Commercial City," in *Inventing Times Square,* ed. Taylor, 74.
12. Ann Douglas, *Terrible Honesty* (New York: Farrar, Straus and Giroux, 1995), 20.
13. Ann Douglas, 26.
14. Herbert Muschamp, "The Passages of Paris and of Benjamin's Mind," *New York Times, Arts and Leisure,* January 16, 2000, 1, 20.
15. Muschamp, 20.
16. Muschamp, 20.
17. Taylor, xiii.
18. Taylor, xiv.
19. Lewis Erenberg, "Impresarios of Broadway Nightlife," in *Inventing Times Square,* ed Taylor, 164–65.
20. Burrows and Wallace, 1001.
21. Muschamp, "A Message from a Poet of Public and Private Memory," *New York Times, Arts and Leisure,* April 1, 2001, 40.
22. Martin Arnold, "The City's Glory, Seen by Writers," *New York Times,* September 27, 2001, E3.
23. Taylor, xvi.
24. Taylor, xvii.
25. William R. Taylor's collection *Inventing Times Square: Commerce and Culture at the Crossroads of the World* is excellent for the geography. See his chapter "Broadway: The Place that Words Built."
26. Erenberg, in Taylor, 166.
27. Erenberg, *Steppin' Out: New York Night Life and the Transformation of American Culture: 1890–1930* (Chicago: University of Chicago Press, 1981), 235.
28. Laurence Senelick, "Private Parts in Public Places," in *Inventing Times Square,* ed. Taylor, 332.
29. Erenberg, *Steppin' Out,* 216.
30. Erenberg, in Taylor, 164.
31. Senelick, 332, 334.
32. Erenberg, *Steppin' Out,* 218–9.
33. Gregory F. Gilmartin, "Joseph Urban" in *Inventing Times Square,* ed. Taylor, 282.
34. Erenberg, *Steppin' Out,* 234.
35. Erenberg, in Taylor, 166, 169.
36. Margo Jefferson, "A City Impinges, Through a Lens, Not Always Darkly," *New York Times,* October 18, 1999, E2.
37. Stephen Kinzer, "Far from New York, Images of the City at Its Liveliest," *New York Times,* March 8, 2001, 2.

38. Georgia O'Keeffe, in Kinzer, 2.
39. Kinzer, 2.
40. Ann Douglas, 59.
41. Muschamp, "For Now, Restricted Access. But What of the Future?" *New York Times, Arts and Leisure,* October 7, 2001, 35.
42. Max Weber, *The City* (New York: Free Press, 1958), 10.
43. John Mosedale, *The Men Who Invented Broadway* (New York: Richard Marek Publishers, 1981), 188.
44. Bonnie Menes Kahn, *Cosmopolitan Culture* (New York: Atheneum, 1987), 3.
45. Joseph Rykwert, *The Seduction of Place* (New York: Pantheon, 2000), 7.
46. Anthony Vidler, "A City Transformed: Designing 'Defensible Space,'" *New York Times, Week in Review,* September 23, 2001, 6.
47. Philip Lopate, *Writing New York: A Literary Anthology* (New York: Library of America, 1998); in Martin Arnold, "Making Books," *New York Times,* September 27, 2001, E3.
48. Kahn, 11.
49. Sam Hunter, *Modern American Painting and Sculpture* (New York: Dell, 1959) and Barbara Rose, *American Painting: The Twentieth Century* (New York: Rizzoli, 1969).
50. Rose, 15.
51. Hunter, 36.
52. Hunter, 7.
53. William T. Henning Jr. *A Catalogue of the American Collection* (Chattanooga, Tenn.: Hunter Museum of Art, 1985), 166.
54. Stuart Davis, in Hunter, 129.
55. Taylor, xi, xxv.
56. Douglas, 356.
57. Douglas, 358.
58. Vidler, 6.
59. Kahn, 15.
60. Taylor, 230.
61. Douglas, 101.
62. Photograph is in the New York City Historical Society Collection. 170 Central Park West, New York.
63. Taylor, 228
64. Quoted in Paul Berman, "Tell Me What Street Compares to Mott Street," *New York Times Book Review,* November 12, 2000, 18–19, see 19.
65. Gabler, 90–91.
66. Stephen Holden, "Not for Just an Hour, Not for Just a Day . . . but Always," *New York Times,* October 31, 2001, E10.
67. Erenberg, *Steppin' Out,* 252.
68. Russell Banks, "A Novelist's Vivid Memory Spins Fictions of its Own," *New York Times,* December 6, 1999, E1-E2.

CHAPTER 2

1. Terry A. Cooney, *The Rise of the New York Intellectuals:* Partisan Review *and its Circle, 1934–45* (Madison: University of Wisconsin Press, 1986), 7.
2. Cooney, 18.
3. Norman Podhoretz, *Making It,* 32–33, in Cooney, 15.
4. Lewis Mumford, *The Culture of Cities* (New York: Harcourt, Brace, and Company, 1938), 480
5. Walter Benjamin, in *Manet 1832–1883* (New York: Metropolitan Museum of Art, 1983), 481.
6. Aleksander Shevchenko, in Michael Kimmelman, "Sisters, for a Time, in Revolution," *New York Times,* September 8, 2000, E5.
7. See E. P. Thompson, "Time, Work-discipline, and Industrial Capitalism," *Past and Present,* 38 [1967], cited in Frederic Jameson, *PostModernism or, The Cultural Logic of Late Capitalism* (Durham, NC: Duke University Press, 1993), 75.
8. Stephen Kern, *The Culture of Time and Space, 1880–1919* (Cambridge, Mass.: Harvard University Press, 1983), 208.
9. Peter Fritzsche, *Reading Berlin 1900* (Cambridge, Mass.: Harvard University Press, 1996), 1.
10. Fritzsche, 9.
11. Fritzsche, 10.
12. David M. Kennedy, *Freedom from Fear: America in Depression and War, 1929–1945* (New York: Oxford University Press, 1999), 22–23.
13. Fritzsche, 61.
14. Fritzsche, 94.
15. Fritzsche, 210.
16. Fritzsche, 209.
17. Michael Kimmelman, "Knickerbocker's Knicknacks," *New York Times,* September 22, 2000, E30.
18. Edgar G. Burrows and Mike Wallace, *Gotham: A History of New York City to the 1890s* (New York: Oxford University Press, 997).
19. Burrows and Wallace, 997.
20. John Mosedale, *The Men Who Invented Broadway* (New York: Richard Marek Publishers, 1981), 122.
21. Runyon, in Mosedale, 165.
22. Runyon, in Mosedale, 165.
23. David M. Kennedy, 321.
24. Patricia Ward D'Itri, *Damon Runyon* (Boston: Twayne, 1982), 47–48.
25. Taylor, 3.
26. Murray Schumach, in Edwin P. Hoyt, *A Gentleman of Broadway* (Boston: Little Brown and Company, 1964), 303.
27. See Hoyt, 313.
28. Clark Kinnaird, in preface of Damon Runyon's *Poems for Men* (New York: Duell, Sloan and Pearce, 1947), xii.

29. Runyon, *Poems for Men,* 107.
30. D'Itri, 80.
31. Runyon, "A Jew," *Cosmopolitan,* November 1922, 11.
32. Runyon, "A Jew," 11.
33. Runyon, "A Jew," 11.
34. Peter Schjeldahl, "Fanfares for the Common Man: Norman Rockwell Reconsidered," *The New Yorker,* November 22, 1999, 190.
35. Normal Rockwell, in Judy L. Larson and Maureen Hart Hennessey, "Norman Rockwell: A New Viewpoint," *in Norman Rockwell: Pictures for the American People,* ed. Maureen Hart Hennessey and Anne Knutson (Atlanta: High Museum, 1999), 35.
36. Deborah Solomon, "Once Again, Patriotic Themes Ring True as Art," *New York Times Week in Review,* October 26, 2001, 14.
37. Anne Knutson, "The Saturday Evening Post," in *Norman Rockwell,* ed. Hennessey and Knutson, 152.
38. See Knutson, 144.
39. Knutson, 144.
40. See Knutson, 144. Her source is Jan Cohn, *Creating America: George Horace Lorimer and the Saturday Evening Post* (Pittsburgh: University of Pittsburgh Press, 1989).
41. Rockwell, in Knutson, 14.
42. Dave Hickey, "The Kids Are All Right: After the Prom," in *Norman Rockwell,* ed. Hennessey and Knutson (Atlanta: High Museum, 1999), 119.
43. Neil Harris, "The View from the City," in *Norman Rockwell,* ed. Hennessey and Knutson, 139.
44. Larson and Hennessey, 52–3.
45. Solomon, 14.

CHAPTER 3

1. Stephen Kern, *The Culture of Time and Space, 1880–1919* (Cambridge, Mass.: Harvard University Press, 1983), 115.
2. Kern, 115.
3. Henry Adams, *The Education of Henry Adams,* 409, in Kern, 126; William Dean Howells, *Through the Eye of the Needle* (New York: Harper and Brothers 1907), 10–11.
4. Kern, 117.
5. Irwin Panofsky, in Kern, 118 (from Irwin Panofsky, "Style and Medium in Motion Pictures," *Critique* [January-February 1947]; reprinted in *Film: An Anthology,* ed. Daniel Talbot [Berkeley, 1969], 16).
6. John Lofton, *Justice and the Press* (Boston: Beacon Press, 1966), 99.
7. See C. E. Bechhoger Roberts, *The New World of Crime: Famous American Trials* (London: Eyre and Spottiswoode, 1933), 230–41.
8. See Lofton, 99.
9. Lofton, 99.
10. Roberts, 240.

11. Roberts, 235.
12. Runyon, *New York American,* March 14, 1921, in Edwin P. Hoyt, *A Gentleman of Broadway* (Boston: Little Brown and Company, 1964), 170.
13. Hoyt, 171.
14. John Mosedale, *The Men Who Invented Broadway* (New York: Richard Marek Publishers, 1981), 24.
15. David M. Kennedy, *Freedom from Fear: The American People in Depression and War* (New York: Oxford, 1999), 228–29.
16. David M. Kennedy, 229.
17. David M. Kennedy, 245.
18. David M. Kennedy, 245.
19. Susan Douglas, *Listening In* (New York: Random House, 1999), 55.
20. Susan Douglas, 65.
21. Susan Douglas, 65, 72.
22. For the history of radio, see Kenneth Jackson, *New York Encyclopedia* (New Haven: Yale University Press, 1995), 972–73.
23. William R. Taylor, *Inventing Times Square: Commerce and Culture at the Crossroads of the World* (Baltimore: Johns Hopkins University Press, 1996), eds. xi.
24. Susan Douglas, 176.
25. Susan Douglas, 174.
26. Mosedale, 238.
27. See Mosedale, 234.
28. Susan Douglas, 171.
29. Susan Douglas, 175.
30. Mosedale, 162.
31. Runyon, in Mosedale, 163.
32. Mencken, in Ludovic Kennedy, *The Airman and the Carpenter* (New York: Viking Penguin Inc, 1985), 255
33. Ludovic Kennedy, 257.
34. Albert Friendly and Ronald L. Goldfarb, *Crime and Publicity: The Impact of News on the Administration of Justice* (New York: The Twentieth Century Fund, 1967) 10.
35. William Randolph Hearst, in Frank Rich, "The Age of the Mediathon," *New York Times Sunday Magazine,* October 29, 2000, 94.
36. Rich, 60.
37. Susan Douglas, 162.
38. Susan Douglas, 166.
39. See Noel Behn, *Lindbergh: The Crime* (New York: The Atlantic Monthly Press, 1994), 242.
40. Ludovic Kennedy, 256.
41. See Noel Behn, *Lindbergh: The Crime* (New York: The Atlantic Monthly Press, 1994), chapter 21, 246–67.
42. Ludovic Kennedy, 340.
43. Runyon, in Ludovic Kennedy, 340–41.
44. Runyon, "6 Men 4 Women Jurors Picked on 1st Day of Hauptman Trial," *The New York American,* January 3, 1935, 1.

45. Runyon, *The New York American,* 1.
46. Runyon, *The New York American,* 2.
47. Ludovic Kennedy, *The Airman and the Carpenter* (New York: Viking Penguin Inc., 1985,) 256.
48. Ludovic Kennedy, 261. See also Runyon, *The New York American,* 2, where he remarks with bemusement on this procedure.
49. Winchell, in Behn, 206.
50. Behn, 242.
51. Susan Douglas, 170.
52. Friendly and Goldfarb, 10
53. Runyon, *The New York American,* 1.
54. Dr. Edward Spencer Cowles, "A Colossal Egotist: Psychiatrist's View of Hauptmann," *New York American,* 3 January 1935, 5.
55. Neal Gabler, *Winchell: Gossip, Power and the Culture of Celebrity* (New York: Alfred A. Knopf, 1994), 212–3.
56. Lofton, xii.
57. Lofton, 124.
58. Runyon, in Hoyt, 24.

CHAPTER 4

1. H. L. Mencken, in William R. Taylor ed. *Inventing Times Square: Commerce and Culture at the Crossroads of the World* (Boston: Johns Hopkins University Press, 1991), 218.
2. Taylor, 222.
3. Edward Rothstein, "Why American Pop Culture Spreads," *New York Times,* June 3, 2001, B11.
4. Rothstein, B11.
5. Rothstein, B11.
6. Taylor, 227.
7. Edward Rothstein, "Shelf Life," review of *The Seduction of Place: The City in the 21st Century,* by Joseph Rykwert, *New York Times,* January 27, 2001, B11.
8. Rothstein, "Shelf Life," B11.
9. See Tom Clark, *The World of Damon Runyon* (New York: Harper & Row, 1978), 180ff.
10. See Robert Boynton, "Memories in Transit, On the Nostalgia Train," *New York Times,* June 29, 2001, E39.
11. Ann Douglas, *Terrible Honesty* (New York: Farrar, Straus and Giroux, 1995), 367.
12. Mikhail Bakhtin, *Rabelais and His World,* trans. Helene Iswolsky (Cambridge, Mass.: MIT Press, 1965), 10.
13. Ann Douglas, 70.
14. Ann Douglas, 72.
15. Ann Douglas, 36.
16. Groucho Marx, in Ann Douglas, 420.

17. Ann Douglas, 361.
18. Ted Gioia, "A Megastar Long Buried Under a Layer of Blackface," *New York Times: Sunday Times Art and Leisure,* October 22, 2000, 34.
19. See Douglas, 360.
20. Gary Giddens, "Bing Crosby, the Unsung King of Popular Song," *New York Times, Sunday Art and Leisure,* January 28, 2001, 37.
21. Debra Bernhardt and Rachel Bernstein. *Ordinary People, Extraordinary Lives: A Pictorial History of Working People in New York City* (New York: New York University Press, 2000).
22. Fredric Jameson, *Post Modernism or, the Cultural Logic of Late Capitalism* (Durham, NC: Duke University Press, 1993), 15–16.
23. Taylor, 11.
24. Edward Rothstein, "Modern and Postmodern, The Bickering Twin," *New York Times,* October 21, 2000, B1.

CHAPTER 5

1. Jean Wagner, *Runyonese: The Mind and Craft of Damon Runyon* (Paris and New York: Stechert-Hafner, Inc, 1965), 24.
2. Wagner, 42.
3. David M. Kennedy, *Freedom from Fear: The American People in Depression and War, 1929–1945* (New York: Oxford University Press, 1999), 14–15.
4. David M. Kennedy, 399.
5. David M. Kennedy 399.
6. David M. Kennedy, 162–3.
7. Edwin G. Burrows and Mike Wallace, *Gotham: A History of New York City in the 1890s* (New York: Oxford University Press, 1998), 1117.
8. Burrows and Wallace, 1158.
9. Burrows and Wallace, 1158.
10. *The Gideon Holy Bible* (Philadelphia: The National Bible Press, 1954), 727–28.
11. *The Gideon Holy Bible,* 728.
12. *The Gideon Holy Bible,* 960.
13. *The Gideon Holy Bible,* 727.
14. Bruno Bettelheim, in Richard Bernstein, "The Reality of the Fantasy in the Harry Potter Stories," *New York Times,* November 30, 1999, E2.
15. William Taylor, *In Pursuit of Gotham* (New York: Oxford University Press, 1992), 179.
16. Wagner, 45.

CHAPTER 6

1. Stephen Fox, *Blood and Power* (New York: William Morrow and Company, Inc., 1989), 116.
2. Fox, 117.

3.   Ted Gioia, "A Megastar Long Buried Under a Layer of Blackface," *Sunday New York Times, Arts and Leisure,* October 22, 2000, 34.

4.   See Edwin P. Hoyt, *A Gentleman of Broadway* (Boston: Little, Brown and Company, 1964), 175.

5.   David M. Kennedy, *Freedom From Fear: The American People in Depression and War, 1929–1945* (New York: Oxford University Press, 1999),201.

6.   Daniel Morris, "'Figuring and Disfiguring': Joyce Carol Oates on Boxing and the Paintings of George Bellows," *Mosaic* 31:4 [December 1998] 135–50, see 149.

7.   Joyce Carol Oates, in Morris, see 144.

8.   Hoyt, 150.

9.   Hoyt, 169.

10. Jean Wagner, *Runyonese: The Mind and Craft of Damon Runyon* (Paris and New York: Stechart-Hafner, Inc. 1965), 79.

CHAPTER 7

1.   See Ralph Blumenthal, "Some Retired Runyon Guys Are Still Handing Out Dolls," *New York Times,* December 17, 2000, B1-B2.

2.   Mikhail Bakhtin, *Rabelais and His World,* trans. Helene Iswolfsky (Cambridge, Mass.: MIT Press, 965), 394–95.

3.   Bakhtin, 395.

4.   Bakhtin, 341.

5.   Ron Jenkins, "Comedy That Starts in the Muscle," *New York Times, Arts and Leisure,* September 16, 2001, see pp. 5, 21.

6.   Edwin P. Hoyt, *A Gentleman of Broadway* (Boston: Little, Brown and Company, 169.

7.   Runyon, "A Slight Case of Murder," in *Strictly Dishonorable and Other Lost American Plays,* selected and edited by Richard Nelson (New York: Theatre Communications Group, 1986), 187.

8.   Runyon, in Nelson, 186.

9.   Runyon, in Nelson, 187.

10. Runyon, in Nelson, 204.

11. Hoyt, 269–70.

12. David M. Kennedy, *Freedom from Fear: The American People in Depression and War, 1929–1945.* (New York: Oxford University Press, 1999), 583.

13. Joe Orton, in Margo Jefferson. "A City Impinges, Through a Lens, Not Always Darkly," *The New York Times,* October 18, 1999, E2.

14. Edward H. Weiner, *The Damon Runyon Story* (London: Longmans, Green and Co., 1964), 217.

15. Kennedy, 488–89.

16. Runyon, *New York Mirror,* January 6, 1941, in Hoyt, 282.

17. Hoyt, 284.

18. Hoyt, 284.

19. Hoyt, 294.

CHAPTER 8

1. Edwin G. Burrows and Mike Wallace, *Gotham: A History of New York City to the 1890s* (New York: Oxford University Press, 1999), 1219, 1235.
2. Jimmy Cannon, in Tom Clark, *The World of Damon Runyon* (New York: Harper and Row, 1978), 117.
3. David M. Kennedy, *Freedom from Fear: The American People in Depression and War, 1929–45* (New York: Oxford University Press, 1999), 322.
4. Kennedy, 322.
5. Runyon, in Edwin P. Hoyt, *A Gentleman of Broadway* (Boston: Little, Brown and Company, 1964), 288–89.
6. Kennedy, 350.
7. Kennedy, 392–3.
8. See John Russell, "The Sympathetic Eye on a Metropolitan Beat," *New York Times,* December 15, 2000, E42.
9. Kennedy, 42.
10. Hoyt, 284.
11. Kennedy, 854.
12. Kennedy, 712.
13. Kennedy, 857.
14. Kennedy, 786.
15. Primo Levi, *The Periodic Table* (trans. Raymond Rosenthal, New York: Schocken, 1984), 34.

CONCLUSION

1. Herbert Muschamp, "A Gift of Vienna that Skips the Schlag," *New York Times,* April 19, 2002, E33, 38; see E38.
2. e. e. cummings, *Selected Poems 1923–58* (London: Faber and Faber, 1960), 44.

Works Cited and Discussed

Arnold, Martin. "The City's Glory, Seen by Writers." *The New York Times,* September 27, 2001, E3.

———. "Making Books." *The New York Times,* September 27, 2001, E3.

Bakhtin, Mikhail. *Rabelais and His World.* Trans. Helene Iswolsky. Cambridge, MA.: MIT Press, 1965.

Banks, Russell. "A Novelist's Vivid Memory Spins Fictions of Its Own." *The New York Times,* December 6, 1999, E1-E2.

Barra, Allen. "The Sports Story That Changed America." *The New York Times, Week in Review,* October 17, 1999, 2.

Behn, Noel. *Lindbergh: The Crime.* New York: The Atlantic Monthly Press, 1994.

Bender, Thomas. *New York Intellect: A History of Intellectual Life in New York City, from 1750 to the Beginnings of Our Own Time.* New York: Alfred A. Knopf, 1987.

Berkow, Ira. "Putting the Best Through Qualifying." *The New York Times, Sunday Sports,* August 27, 2000, 15.

———. "For Jackson, Déjà Vu of Sorts." *The New York Times,* February 26, 2001.

Berman, Paul. "Tell Me What Street Compares to Mott Street." *The New York Times Book Review,* November 12, 2000, 18–19.

Bernhardt, Debra E. and Rachel Bernstein. *Ordinary People, Extraordinary Lives: An assessment of archival sources documenting 20th century New York City social history.* New York: Robert F. Wagner Labor Archives, New York University, 1994.

Bernhardt, Debra E. and Rachel Bernstein. *Ordinary People, Extraordinary Lives: A Pictorial History of Working People in New York City.* New York: New York University Press, 2000.

Bernstein, Richard. "The Reality of the Fantasy in the Harry Potter Stories." *The New York Times,* November 30, 1999, E1-E2.

Blumenthal, Ralph. "Some Retired Runyon Guys Are Still Handing Out Dolls." *The New York Times,* December 17, 2000, B1-B2.

Boynton, Robert, "Memories in Transit, on the Nostalgia Train," *New York Times,* June 29, 2001, E31, E39.

Breslin, Jimmy. *Damon Runyon.* New York: Ticknor and Fields, 1991.

Burrows, Edwin G. and Mike Wallace. *Gotham: A History of New York City to the 1890s.* New York: Oxford University Press, 1999.

Clark, Tom. *The World of Damon Runyon.* New York: Harper & Row, 1978.

Cooney, Terry A. *The Rise of the New York Intellectuals: Partisan Review and Its Circle, 1934–45.* Madison: University of Wisconsin Press, 1986.

Cowles, Edward Spencer. "A Colossal Egotist: Psychiatrist's View of Hauptmann." *New York American,* January 3, 1935, 5.

cummings, e. e. *Selected Poems 1923- 1958.* London: Faber and Faber, 1960.

D'itri, Patricia Ward. *Damon Runyon.* New York: Twayne, 1982.

Douglas, Ann. *Terrible Honesty: Mongrel Manhattan in the 1920s.* New York: Farrar, Straus and Giroux, 1996.

Douglas, Susan. *Listening In.* New York: Random House, 1999.

Emerson, Ralph Waldo. *The Portable Emerson.* Edited by Carl Bode in collaboration with Malcolm Cowley. New York: Viking Penguin, 1981.

Erenberg, Lewis. *Steppin' Out: New York Night Life and the Transformation of American Culture, 1890–1930.* Chicago: University of Chicago Press, 1981, 158–177.

———. "Impresarios of Broadway Nightlife," in *Inventing Times Square: Commerce and Culture at the Crossroads of the World,* ed. William R. Taylor. New York: Russell Sage Foundation, 1991.

Fitzgerald, F. Scott. *The Great Gatsby.* New York: Scribners, 1925.

———. "HOLLYWOOD, ETC.," in "Notes." *The Last Tycoon, An Unfinished Novel.* New York: Charles Scribner's Sons, 1941.

Fox, Stephen. *Blood and Power.* New York: William Morrow and Company, Inc., 1989.

Friendly, Albert, and Ronald L. Goldfarb, eds. *Crime and Publicity: The Impact of News on the Administration of Justice.* New York: The Twentieth Century Fund, 1967.

Fritzsche, Peter. *Reading Berlin 1900,* Cambridge, MA: Harvard University Press, 1996.

Gabler, Neal. *Winchell: Gossip, Power and the Culture of Celebrity.* New York: Alfred A. Knopf, 1994.

Giddens, Gary. "Bing Crosby, the Unsung King of Popular Song." *The Sunday New York Times, Arts and Leisure,* January 28, 2001, 1, 37.

Gideon Holy Bible. Philadelphia: National Bible Press, 1954.

Gilmartin, Gregory F. "Joseph Urban." In *Inventing Times Square: Commerce and Culture at the Crossroads of the World,* ed. William R. Taylor. New York: Russell Sage Foundation, 1991, 271–283.

Gioia, Ted. "A Megastar Long Buried Under a Layer of Blackface." *The Sunday New York Times, Arts and Leisure,* October 22, 2000, 1, 34.

Goldberg, Vicki. "You Don't Need a Weatherman: Just Point Your Camera and Shoot, Man." *The New York Times,* December 22, 2000, E46.

Harris, Neil. "Urban Tourism and the Commercial City." In *Inventing Times Square: Commerce and Culture at the Crossroads of the World.* ed. William R. Taylor. New York: Russell Sage Foundation, 1991, 66–82.

——. "The View from the City." In *Norman Rockwell: Pictures for the American People.* eds. Hennessy, Maureen Hart and Judy L. Larson. Atlanta: High Museum, 1999, 131–41.

Hennessey, Maureen Hart, and Judy L. Larson, eds. *Norman Rockwell: Pictures for the American People.* Atlanta: High Museum, 1999.

Henning, William T. Jr., ed. *Hunter Museum of Art: A Catalogue of the American Collection.* Chattanooga, TN: Hunter Museum, 1985.

Hickey, Dave. "The Kids Are All Right: After the Prom." In *Norman Rockwell: Pictures for the American People.* Atlanta: High Museum, 1999, eds. Hennessy, Maureen Hart and Judy L. Larson. 115–29.

Holden, Stephen. "Not for Just an Hour, Not for Just a Day . . . but Always." *The New York Times, Books of the Times,* October 31, 2001, E10.

Holquist, Michael, ed. *Speech Genres and Other Late Essays.* Trans. Vern McGee. Austin: University of Texas Press, 1986.

Howells, William Dean. *Through the Eye of the Needle* (New York: Harper & Brothers 1907)

Hoyt, Edwin P. *A Gentleman of Broadway.* Boston: Little, Brown and Company, 1964.

Hunter, Sam. *Modern American Painting and Sculpture.* New York: Dell, 1959.

Jackson, Kenneth. *New York Encyclopedia.* New Haven, CT: Yale University Press, 1995.

Jameson, Fredric. *Postmodernism or, The Cultural Logic of Late Capitalism.* Durham, NC: Duke University Press, 1993.

Jefferson, Margo. "A City Impinges, Through a Lens, Not Always Darkly." *The New York Times,* October18, 1999; E2

Jenkins, Rob. "Comedy That Starts in the Muscle." *The New York Times, Arts and Leisure,* September 16, 2001, 5, 21.

Joyce, James. *Ulysses.* New York: Vintage Books, 1986; original edition, 1922.

Kahn, Bonnie Menes. *Cosmopolitan Culture.* New York: Atheneum, 1987.

Kakutani, Michiko. "As American as Second Acts and Apple Pie." *The New York Times, Week in Review,* February 3, 2001, 3.

——. "No Beauty, but They Had the Horse Right There." *The New York Times,* March 6, 2000, E1

Kennedy, David M. *Freedom from Fear: The American People in Depression and War 1929–1945.* New York: Oxford University Press, 1999.

Kennedy, Ludovic. *The Airman and the Carpenter.* New York: Viking Penguin Inc., 1985.

Kennedy, William. *Guys and Dolls: The Stories of Damon Runyon.* New York: Penguin, 1992.

Kern, Stephen. *The Culture of Time and Space, 1880–1919.* Cambridge, MA: Harvard University Press, 1983.

Kimmelman, Michael. "Sisters, for a Time, in Revolution." *The New York Times,* September 8, 2000, E5.

——. "Knickerbocker's Knicknacks." *The New York Times,* September 22, 2000, E29–30.

Kinnaird, Clark. Preface. *Poems for Men.* New York: Duell, Sloan and Pearce, 1947.

Kinzer, Stephen. "Far from New York, Images of the City at Its Liveliest." *The New York Times,* March 8, 2001, E2.

Knutson, Anne. "*The Saturday Evening Post.*" In *Norman Rockwell: Pictures for the American People,* eds., Hennessy, Maureen Hart and Judy L. Larson. Atlanta: High Museum, 1999, 143–53.

Lampard, Eric. "Introductory Essay." In *Inventing Times Square: Commerce and Culture at the Crossroads of the World,* ed. William R. Taylor. New York: Russell Sage Foundation, 1991, 16–35.

Lapointe, Joe, "Paterno is Looking Ahead." *The New York Times Sports Section,* August 9, 2001, D1.

Larsen, Judy L. and Maureen Hart Hennesy, "Norman Rockwell: A New Viewpoint, in Hennessy, Maureen Hart and Judy L. Larson, eds. *Norman Rockwell: Pictures for the American People.* Atlanta: High Museum, 1999.

Levi, Primo, *The Periodic Table* (trans. Raymond Rosenthal, New York: Schocken, 1984), 34.

Lofton, John. *Justice and the Press.* Boston: Beacon Press, 1966.

Lopate, Philip, *Writing New York: A Literary Anthology* (New York: Library of America, 1998).

Lowenstein, Roger. "Alone at the Top." *The New York Times Magazine,* August 27, 2000, 34.

Mandell, Jonathan. "Admiring Itself in a Thousand Mirrors." *The New York Times, Arts and Leisure,* December 10, 2000, 38.

Manet 1832–1883. New York: Metropolitan Museum of Art, 1983.

Melville, Herman. "Bartleby, the Scrivener." In *The Great Short Works of Herman Melville.* New York: Harper & Row, 1969.

Morris, Daniel, "'Figuring and Disfiguring': Joyce Carol Oates on Boxing and the Paintings of George Bellows," *Mosaic* 31:4 [December 1998] 135–50.

Mosedale, John. *The Men Who Invented Broadway.* New York: Richard Marek Publishers, 1981.

Mumford, Lewis. *The Culture of Cities.* New York: Harcourt, Brace, and Company, 1938.

Muschamp, Herbert, "The Passages of Paris and of Benjamin's Mind." *The New York Times,* January 16, 2000, 1, 20.

———. "A Message from a Poet of Public and Private Memory." *The New York Times, Arts and Leisure,* April 1, 2001, 40.

———. "For Now, Restricted Access. But What of the Future?" *The New York Times, Arts and Leisure,* October 7, 2001, 35.

———. "A Gift of Vienna That Skips the Schlag," The *New York Times,* April 19, 2002, E33, 38.

Nelson, Richard, ed. *Strictly Dishonorable and Other Lost American Plays.* New York: Theatre Communications Group, 1986.

Purdy, Jedediah. *For Common Things: Irony, Trust, and Commitment in America Today.* New York: Alfred A. Knopf, 1999.

Rich, Frank. "The Age of the Mediathon." *The Sunday New York Times Magazine,* October 29, 2000, 58–94.

Roberts, C. E. Bechhofer. *The New World of Crime: Famous American Trials.* London: Eyre and Spottiswoode, 1933.

Rose, Barbara. *American Painting: The Twentieth Century.* New York: Rizzoli, 1969.

Rothstein, Edward. "Modern and Postmodern, the Bickering Twins." *The New York Times,* October 21, 2000, B11.

———. "Shelf Life." *The New York Times,* January 27, 2001, B11.

———. "Why American Pop Culture Spreads." *The New York Times,* June 3, 2001, B11.

Runyon, Damon. "A Jew." *Cosmopolitan,* November 1922, 11.

———. "For a Pal." *Collier's,* January 9, 1932.

———. "The Twilight of the Gangster: An Interview with Police Commissioner Mulrooney." *Cosmopolitan,* June 1932, 178–180.

———. "Six Men and Four Women Picked on First Day of Hauptmann Trial." *The New York American,* January 3, 1935.

———. "Why They'll Never Forget the Trial of the Century." *Cosmopolitan,* May 1935, 36.

———. "Horse and Buggy Governor." *Cosmopolitan,* November 1935, 30–31, 172 74.

———. *My Old Man.* New York: Stackpole Sons, 1939.

———. *My Wife Ethel.* Philadelphia: David McKay Company, 1940.

———. *Damon Runyon Omnibus.* Garden City, NY: Sun Dial Press, 1944; reprinted, Jackson Heights, NY: the American Reprint Company, 1976.

———. *In Our Town.* New York: Creative Age Press, 1946.

———. *Short Takes.* New York: Somerset Books, Inc., 1946.

———. *Poems for Men.* New York: Duell, Sloan and Pearce, 1947.

———. *Trials and Other Tribulations.* Philadelphia: J. B. Lippincott Company, 1947.

———. *Runyon from First to Last.* forward by Clark Kinnaird, Philadelphia, 1949.

———. *More Guys and Dolls.* Garden City, NY: Garden City Books, 1951.

———. *Runyon on Broadway.* London: Constable, 1951.

———. *The Turps.* London: Constable, 1951.

———. *Runyon from First to Last.* London: Constable, 1964.

Russell, John. "The Sympathetic Eye on a Metropolitan Beat." *The New York Times,* December 15, 2000, E42.

Rykwert, Joseph. *The Seduction of Place.* New York: Pantheon, 2000, 7.

Schjeldahl, Peter. "Fanfares for the Common Man: Norman Rockwell Reconsidered." *The New Yorker,* November 22, 1999, 190.

Senelick, Laurence. In "Private Parts in Public Places." *Inventing Times Square: Commerce and Culture at the Crossroads of the World,* ed. William R. Taylor. New York: Russell Sage Foundation, 1991, 329–53.

Solomon, Deborah. "Once Again, Patriotic Themes Ring True as Art." *The New York Sunday Times, Week in Review,* October 26, 2001, 14.

Sopranos: The Complete First Season. Directed by David Chase. With James Gandolfini. HBO, 1999.

Squires, Jim. "Can Do!" *The New York Times Book Review,* March 11, 2001, 12.

Taylor, William R. " Broadway: The Place that Words Built." In *Inventing Times Square: Commerce and Culture at the Crossroads of the World,* ed. William R. Taylor. New York: Russell Sage Foundation, 1991, 212–231.

———. *In Pursuit of Gotham.* (New York: Oxford University Press, 1992.

Vidler, Anthony. "A City Transformed: Designing 'Defensible Space.'" *The New York Times Week in Review,* September 23, 2001, 6.

Wagner, Jean. *Runyonese: The Mind and Craft of Damon Runyon.* Paris New York: Stechert Hafner, Inc., 1965.

Weber, Max. *The City.* New York: Free Press, 1958.

Weiner, Edward H. *The Damon Runyon Story.* London: Longmans, Green and Co. 1964.

Wickberg, Daniel. *The Senses of Humor: Self and Laughter in Modern America.* Ithaca, NY: Cornell University Press, 1998.

Wilford, John Noble. "In Maya Ruins, Scholars See Evidence of Urban Sprawl." *The New York Times,* December 19, 2000, F1, F5.

Index